HISTORY OF WOMEN IN THE UNITED STATES

HISTORY OF WOMEN IN THE UNITED STATES
Historical Articles on Women's Lives and Activities

Edited by Nancy F. Cott

Series ISBN 3-598-41454-4

1. Theory and Method in Women's History
   ISBN 3-598-41455-2 Part 1
   ISBN 3-598-41477-3 Part 2

2. Household Constitution and Family Relationships
   ISBN 3-598-41456-0

3. Domestic Relations and Law
   ISBN 3-598-41457-9

4. Domestic Ideology and Domestic Work
   ISBN 3-598-41458-7 Part 1
   ISBN 3-598-41475-7 Part 2

5. The Intersection of Work and Family Life
   ISBN 3-598-41459-5 Part 1
   ISBN 3-598-41476-5 Part 2

6. Working on the Land
   ISBN 3-598-41460-9

7. Industrial Wage Work
   ISBN 3-598-41461-7 Part 1
   ISBN 3-598-41693-8 Part 2

8. Professional and White-Collar Employments
   ISBN 3-598-41462-5 Part 1
   ISBN 3-598-41694-6 Part 2

9. Prostitution
   ISBN 3-598-41463-3

10. Sexuality and Sexual Behavior
    ISBN 3-598-41464-1

11. Women's Bodies: Health and Childbirth
    ISBN 3-598-41465-X

12. Education
    ISBN 3-598-41466-8

13. Religion
    ISBN 3-598-41467-6

14. Intercultural and Interracial Relations
    ISBN 3-598-41468-4

15. Women and War
    ISBN 3-598-41469-2

16. Women Together: Organizational Life
    ISBN 3-598-41470-6

17. Social and Moral Reform
    ISBN 3-598-41471-4 Part 1
    ISBN 3-598-41695-4 Part 2

18. Women and Politics
    ISBN 3-598-41472-2 Part 1
    ISBN 3-598-41697-0 Part 2

19. Woman Suffrage
    ISBN 3-598-41473-0 Part 1
    ISBN 3-598-41696-2 Part 2

20. Feminist Struggles for Sex Equality
    ISBN 3-598-41474-9

HISTORY OF WOMEN IN THE UNITED STATES

Historical Articles on Women's Lives and Activities

1. Theory and Method in Women's History PART 1

Edited with an Introduction by

Nancy F. Cott
Yale University

K · G · Saur
Munich · London · New York · Paris 1992

Publisher's Note

The articles and chapters which comprise this collection originally appeared in a wide variety of publications and are reproduced here in facsimile from the highest quality offprints and photocopies available. The reader will notice some occasional marginal shading and text-curl common to photocopying from tightly bound volumes. Every attempt has been made to correct or minimize this effect.

Copyright information for articles reproduced in this collection appears at the end of this volume.

Library of Congress Cataloging-in-Publication Data

History of women in the United States : historical articles on women's lives and activities / edited with an introduction by Nancy F. Cott.

p. cm.

Includes bibliographical references and indexes.

Contents: 1. Theory and method in women's history -- 2. Household constitution and family relationships -- 3. Domestic relations and law -- 4. Domestic ideology and domestic work -- 5. The intersection of work and family life -- 6. Working on the land -- 7. Industrial wage work -- 8. Professional and white-collar employments -- 9. Prostitution -- 10. Sexuality and sexual behavior -- 11. Women's bodies -- 12. Education -- 13. Religion -- 14. Intercultural and interracial relations -- 15. Women and war -- 16. Women together -- 17. Social and moral reform -- 18. Women and politics -- 19. Women suffrage -- 20. Feminist struggles for sex equality.

ISBN 3-598-41454-4 (set)

1. Women--United States--History. 2. Women--United States--Social conditions. I. Cott, Nancy F.

HQ1410.H57 1992

305.4'0973--dc20 92-16765

CIP

Die Deutsche Bibliothek - CIP - Einheitsaufnahme

History of women in the United States: historical articles on women's lives and activities / ed. with an introd. by Nancy F. Cott. - Munich ; London ; New York ; Paris : Saur.

ISBN 3-598-41454-4

NE: Cott, Nancy F. (Hrsg.)

Vol. 1. Theory and method in women's history.

Pt. 1. - (1992)

ISBN 3-598-41455-2

Printed on acid-free paper/Gedruckt auf säurefreiem Papier

K.G.Saur Verlag GmbH & Co. KG, Munich 1992

A Reed Reference Publishing Company

Printed in the United States of America

Printed/Bound by Edwards Brothers Incorporated, Ann Arbor

ISBN 3-598-41455-2 (vol. 1/part 1)

ISBN 3-598-41454-4 (series)

Contents

Series Preface

In the space of one generation, women's history has become the fastest-growing area of scholarship in U.S. history. Since the resurgence of feminism in the late 1960s and 1970s, insistent questions about the historical meanings of "woman's place" have sowed and reaped a garden of scholarship. Where scholarly works used to be bare of mention of women, academic enterprise has now produced a vigorous growth of books and articles, bringing to light diverse women of every region, race, class and age. This research is marked by a renovating intent that refuses to accept as "human" history a history of men. Interest is lively and debate is stimulating and sought after: attendance at the Berkshire Conference on the History of Women rivals the size of the annual convention of the American Historical Association.

While books in women's history are daily increasing in numbers and strength, as in any fast-developing field the scholarly literature in the form of articles is most expansive and up-to-the-minute. All the history journals now publish articles on women's work, domestic settings, family relations, household matters, female politics and organizations and so forth, and new journals have sprung into being to concentrate on such topics. Women's historians publish in numerous regional and thematic history journals as well as in feminist outlets and in journals of other social science disciplines. This series brings together a collection of outstanding articles from the field, almost all written in the past twenty years and more than half published during the 1980s. It brings together, in volumes organized by topic, essays otherwise widely dispersed. These volumes reprint only articles that originally appeared in journals, not chapters of books; review articles are not included. Articles have been chosen for overall quality and for range. Each one was chosen for one or more of the following reasons: because it is the standard authority on its subject matter; represents an important statement on a topic by a recognized scholar; presages an important book to come; provides a first look at new evidence or new methods; or opens an untapped area or new controversy. Older articles have been reprinted if their data or interpretation have not been surpassed or if they marked an important stage in the historiography, even if since superseded.

The historical coverage of the series extends from the Revolutionary era to the 1960s. The articles themselves are dated from the 1940s through 1988. Volumes are organized by topic rather than time period. Within each volume, the articles are ordered chronologically (with respect to substance), so that the whole can be read as an historical overview. The only exception to this ordering principle is volume 1, on Theory and Method, in which the contents are arranged in order of publication. Within each volume there is an attempt to include articles on as diverse kinds of women as possible. None of the volume topics is regionally or racially defined; rather, all volumes are topically designed so as to afford views of women's work, family lives, and public activities which cut across races and regions. Any volume in the series stands on its own, supplying as full a treatment of a designated subject matter as the scholarly literature will provide. Several groupings of volumes also make sense; that is, volumes 2 through 5 all center around domestic and family matters; volumes 5 through 9 consider other varieties of women's work; volumes 9 through 11 concern uses and abuses of women's bodies; volumes 12 through 14 look at major aspects of socialization; and volumes 15 through 20 include organizational and political efforts of many sorts.

As a whole, the series displays in all its range the vitality of the field of women's history. Aside from imbuing U.S. history with new vision, scholarship in this area has informed, and should continue to inform, current public debate on issues from parental leave to the nuclear freeze. By bringing historical articles together under topical headings, these volumes both represent accurately the shape of historical controversy (or consensus) on given issues and make historians' findings most conveniently available for current reference.

Introduction

Over the past twenty years there has been an evolving discussion of theory and method in women's history, which the articles in this volume represent. The articles span from the first articulation of a framework to be designated "women's history," to very recent discussion of the concept of gender in history. Also included are critiques of standard American history texts from the perspective of women's history, controversies among women's historians concerning the definition of the field, and assessments of its distinctiveness as compared to family and social history. Since books on theory and method in women's history are rare, this collection of articles gives an unsurpassed overview of historians' thinking about their field.

As in women's studies more generally, the first self-named practitioners in women's history, starting in the late 1960s and early 1970s, saw before them three tasks: a task of critique, a task of research, and a task of theorizing. That is, first it appeared necessary to point out omissions and distortions in existing historical scholarship regarding the historical experiences of women. Both the findings (or lack of findings) and the theory behind traditional historical scholarship appeared to exclude or minimize women's parts as historical actors and to wholly neglect questions about the relations between the sexes on any but a superficial level. Second, it appeared equally necessary to devise new kinds of research, to rescue women of the past from their relative obscurity or invisibility by producing new evidence, by finding documentary or other sources which would reveal women's lives. Third, it also appeared necessary to think anew about what was important in history, to question the assumptions of traditional historical scholarship regarding the historical actors and eras worth defining, to bring to light new questions, new models of inquiry in which women's lives and roles would be more obviously central than had been the case with traditional historical questions about nation-states.

In these tasks historians of women also shared a great deal with others busy defining a "new social history" which would concern ordinary people more than affairs of state, and would focus on continuous processes of social experience more than discrete political events. Spurred by social reform and political protest in the 1960s, these scholars wanted to look at history "from the bottom up" rather than from the point of view of ruling elites. To do so, social historians looked beyond the famous treatises, diplomatic correspondences, or records of state which had supplied historians for generations, and sought first-person sources of the nonfamous population (such as folktales, oral histories, diaries, religious narratives), and also sources which would yield quantifiable data about masses of people, such as registers of births and deaths, factory rolls, records of prisons and hospitals. With the latter data, some social historians began to stress social science methods: explicit conceptualization and hypothesis-testing, systematic comparison and analysis of long-term social trends, in preference to the narrative chronicle or the description of unique or extraordinary events.

Historians of women fostered and participated in these same trends, but not simply or entirely. Sometimes, rather than search for new kinds of documents, women's historians had only to look anew at commonly-used sources to find that material on or by women there had been overlooked because of historians' foregoing lack of attention to questions about women. Often, rather than using social science methods, women's historians employed traditional narrative forms or biographical treatments--some of the oldest arms in the historian's arsenal--but used these to the revelation of female experience. By and large, feminist aims distinguished women's historians from other social historians. If the overall intent of new social historians was to reveal the lives of the "anonymous," the overall intent of women's historians was to show the unlooked-for possibility--as an important art museum exhibit titled it--that "Anonymous' Was a Woman."

The gathering force of investigations into women's history in the early 1970s propelled basic rethinking of periodization and conceptualization in history, once women were seen as part and makers of it. Some of the most striking early scholarship questioned whether the standard periodization of Western civilization "worked" from women's point of view: "Did Women Have a Renaissance?" asked Joan Kelly, in an important essay. Arguing that developments in state formation, advancement of capitalism, and extension of learning to men in Italy in the 14th and 15th century brought a contraction rather than expansion of women's liberties, she concluded that the answer must be "no."[1] Historians of women highlighted the significance of their endeavor by showing that eras typically characterized as ones of progress or democratization--e.g., the Jacksonian "era of the common man" in the United States--might have opposite meaning for women.[2] Conversely, historians' investigation of women as historical actors revealed phenomena thought to be well-known in entirely new light: with attention to women's participation (in the factory and at home), the "industrial revolution," for example, now appeared as a transformational stage in the sexual and familial division of labor as well as a matter of technological or narrowly economic change.

At the same time, historians had to consider how to conceptualize women as a social group. Were women always the subordinate sex? What were the constraints or choices that shaped women's place? Did women's situation vis-a-vis men resemble, or could it be understood as analogous to, the proletariat's relation to the bourgeoisie in Marxist theory; or the inferior caste's relation to the superior in traditional Hindu society; or blacks's relation to whites in the United States? Like feminists in many other walks of life, historians of women debated these analogies and emerged with consensus that none was suitable: the relation between the sexes was foundational and unique, and deserved analysis in its own terms. "We [historians of women] have made of sex a category as fundamental to our analysis of the social order as other classifications, such as class and race," Joan Kelly asserted in 1976.[3] Theoretical questions stemming from this premise have animated the field of women's history since then. The implications of making sex a fundamental category have remained to be argued. Questions of women's consciousness of themselves as a gender group--formulated on Marxist, feminist, and other sociological grounds--have been central to many historical investigations. Whether to evaluate women's experiences from a point of view inside women's culture, or also from men's vantage point, has been a matter of some contention. Equally important has been the effort to clarify how to conceptualize and treat historically the relations between the sexes. Since Natalie Zemon Davis sounded this theme in 1975--"we should not be working only on the subjected sex any more than an historian of class can focus exclusively on peasants. Our goal is to understand the significance of the *sexes*, of gender groups in the historical past"--it has echoed in and out of women's history.[4] Recent scholarship can be described as being both about women and about gender--the symbology and social organization of the sexes. While the awesomely large work of uncovering women's lives has often taken precedence, practitioners in women's history have embraced the double aim, especially more recently. Both efforts have been needed, and they are complimentary. Without historical investigation of women's lives, the functions and meanings of sex in the social order remain inexplicable. Without examination of the power relations and inclusive aspects of interrelations between the sexes, women's situation cannot be understood.

Notes

1. Joan Kelly, "Did Women Have a Renaissance?" in *Becoming Visible: Women in European History*, ed. Renate Bridenthal and Claudia Koonz, (Boston, Houghton Mifflin, 1977), 137-164.

2. E.g., Gerda Lerner, "The Lady and the Mill Girl: Changes in the Status of Women in the Age of Jackson," *Mid-Continent American Studies Journal*, 10:1 (Spring 1969), 6 [in vol. 5].

3. Joan Kelly, "The Social Relations of the Sexes: Methodological Implications of Women's History," *Signs: A Journal of Women in Culture and Society*, 1 (Summer 1976), 816.

4. Natalie Zemon Davis, "Women's History in Transition: The European Case," *Feminist Studies* 3 (Winter 1975-76), 90.

Theory and Method in Women's History

GERDA LERNER

NEW APPROACHES TO THE STUDY OF WOMEN IN AMERICAN HISTORY

The striking fact about the historiography of women is the general neglect of the subject by historians. As long as historians held to the traditional view that only the transmission and exercise of power were worthy of their interest, women were of necessity ignored. There was little room in political, diplomatic, and military history for American women, who were, longer than any other single group in the population, outside the power structure. At best their relationship to power was implicit and peripheral and could easily be passed over as insignificant. With the rise of social history and increasing concern with groups out of power, women received some attention, but interest was focused mainly on their position in the family and on their social status.[1] The number of women featured in textbooks of American history remains astonishingly small to this day, as does the number of biographies and monographs by professional historians.

The literature concerning the role of women in American history is topically narrow, predominantly descriptive, and generally devoid of interpretation. Except for the feminist viewpoint, there seems to be no underlying conceptual framework.

Feminist writers, not trained historians, were the first to undertake a systematic attempt to approach the problem of women's role in American life and history. This took the forms of feminist tracts, theoretical approaches, and compilations of woman's "contributions."[2] The early compilers attacked the subject with a mis-

GERDA LERNER, a historian, is a member of the faculty of Sarah Lawrence College.

[1] Cf. Arthur Schlesinger, Sr., *New Viewpoints in American History* (New York, 1922), chap. 6. For a contemporary historian's viewpoint, see David M. Potter, "American Women and the American Character," in *American History and Social Sciences*, ed. Edward N. Saveth (New York, 1964), pp. 427-428.

[2] The most important feminist tracts before the launching of the woman's rights movement are: Charles Brockden Brown, *Alcuin: A Dialogue* (Boston,

sionary zeal designed, above all, to right wrong. Their tendency was to praise anything women had done as a "contribution" and to include any women who had gained the slightest public attention in their numerous lists.[3] Still, much positive work was done in simply recounting the history of the woman's rights movement and some of its forerunners and in discussing some of the women whose pioneering struggles opened opportunities to others. Feminist writers were hampered by a two-fold bias. First, they shared the middle-class, nativist, moralistic approach of the Progressives and tended to censure out of existence anyone who did not fit into this pattern. Thus we find that women like Frances Wright and Ernestine Rose received little attention because they were considered too radical. "Premature feminists" such as the Grimké sisters, Maria Weston Chapman, and Lydia Maria Child are barely mentioned. The second bias of the feminists lies in their belief that the history of women is important only as respresenting the history of an oppressed group and its struggle against its oppressors.

This latter concept underlies the somewhat heroic, collectively authored *History of Woman Suffrage*. This work, probably because it represents an easily available though disorganized collection of primary sources, has had a pervasive influence on later historians. Following the lead and interpretation of the feminists, professional historians have been preoccupied with the woman's rights movement in its legal and political aspects. Modern historians, too, think that what is important to know about women is how they got the ballot.[4]

The only serious challenge to this conceptual framework was offered by Mary Beard in the form of a vigorous though often

---

1798); Sarah M. Grimke, *Letters on the Equality of the Sexes and the Condition of Woman* (Boston, 1838); and Margaret Fuller, *Woman in the Nineteenth Century* (Boston, 1844). The publications of the feminist movement are too numerous to list here; a representative collection is incorporated in Elizabeth C. Stanton, Susan B. Anthony, and Matilda J. Gage, *History of Woman Suffrage* (6 vols.; New York, 1881-1922).

[3] Typical of the "compilers" are: Lydia M. Child, *History of the Condition of Women* (2 vols.; New York, 1835); Sarah J. Hale, *Woman's Record. . . .* (New York, 1853); Phebe A. Hanaford, *Daughters of America, or Women of the Century* (Augusta, Me., n.d.); and Frances E. Willard and Mary A. Livermore, *American Women* (New York, 1897).

[4] Cf. Eleanor Flexner, *Century of Struggle: The Woman's Rights Movement in the United States* (Cambridge, Mass. 1959); Aileen S. Kraditor, *The Ideas of the Woman Suffrage Movement* (New York, 1965).

fuzzy polemic against the feminists.[5] What is important about women, said Mary Beard, is not that they were an oppressed group—she denied that they ever were—but that they have made a continuous and impressive contribution to society throughout all of history. It is a contribution, however, which does not fit into the value system generally accepted by historians when they make decisions as to who is or is not important to history. Mary Beard undertook in several of her books to trace the positive achievements of women, their social role, and their contributions to community life. Her concepts are most successfully reflected in *The Rise of American Civilization,* which she coauthored with her husband Charles Beard. In it the position of women is treated throughout in an integrated way with great attention to the economic contributions made by women.[6] But the Beards's approach to the subject of women had little influence on the historical profession. Perhaps this was due to the fact that in the 1930's and 1940's both the general public and historians became somewhat disenchanted with the woman's rights movement.

The winning of suffrage had made only a slight change in the actual status of women, and other factors—technological and economic changes, access to higher education, changing sexual mores—now loomed a great deal larger. The impact of Freudianism and psychology had made reformers in general somewhat suspect. Feminism was not infrequently treated with the same humorous condescension as that other successful failure: temperance.

Women have received serious attention from economic historians. There is a good deal of excellent literature dealing with the problem of women workers. Women as contributors to the economy from colonial times on, the laws affecting them, their wages and working conditions, and their struggle for protective legislation have been fully described.[7] Although female labor

---

[5] *Woman as Force in History* (New York, 1946).

[6] Mary R. Beard, *America Through Women's Eyes* (New York, 1934), *On Understanding Women* (New York, 1931), and *Women's Work in Municipalities* (New York, 1915); Charles R. and Mary R. Beard, *The Rise of American Civilization* (New York, 1927).

[7] For the economic life of colonial women see: Elisabeth A. Dexter, *Colonial Women of Affairs: Women in Business and Professions in America before 1776* (Boston, 1931), and *Career Women of America: 1776 1840* (Francestown, N.H., 1950); Richard B. Morris, *Government and Labor in Early America* (New York, 1946); and Julia C. Spruill, *Women's Life and Work in the Southern Colonies*

leaders have not generally been given much attention, their activities are on record. Excellent collections of material pertaining to women at Radcliffe and Smith College are available but remain insufficiently explored.

Modern historians of the reform movements have done much to restore a sane balance to female achievement in reform; yet one still finds excluded from notice certain women who would have been included as a matter of course had they been men. Sophie Loeb, Grace Dodge, and Mary Anderson could be cited as examples.[8]

The historical literature on the family in America is quite scanty, but there seems to be a revival of interest in the subject. Several interesting monographs have begun to deal with the family role of women in its various aspects. This approach is promising and will hopefully be pursued by other historians.[9]

A new conceptual framework for dealing with the subject of women in American history is needed. The feminist frame of reference has become archaic and fairly useless. The twentieth-century revolution in technology, morality, education, and employment patterns has brought enormous changes in the status and role of American women; these changes demand a historical perspective and understanding. The emergence of a recent "new feminism" is a social phenomenon requiring interpretation. Most importantly, women themselves are as entitled as minority group members are to having "their" history fully recorded.

Yet the subject is complex. It is difficult to conceptualize women as a group, since they are dispersed throughout the popu-

(Chapel Hill, 1938). For women's economic role in nineteenth- and twentieth-century America, see: Edith Abbott, *Women in Industry* (New York, 1918); J. B. Andrews and W. D. P. Bliss, *Report on Condition of Woman and Child Wage-Earners in the United States* (19 vols.; Doc. No. 645, 61st Congress, 2nd Session; Washington, 1910); and Elizabeth Baker, *Technology and Women's Work* (New York, 1964).

8 For women in reform movements, see: Robert Bremmer, *American Philanthropy* (Chicago, 1960); Clarke E. Chambers, *Seedtime of Reform: American Social Service and Social Action, 1918-1933* (Ann Arbor, 1963); Christopher Lasch, *The New Radicalism in America: 1889-1963* (New York, 1965); and Daniel Levine, *Varieties of Reform Thought* (Madison, Wis., 1964).

9 For a history of the family, see Arthur W. Calhoun, *A Social History of the American Family* (3 vols.; Cleveland, 1918); Sidney Ditzion, *Marriage, Morals, and Sex in America* (New York, 1953); Paul H. Jacobson, *American Marriage and Divorce* (New York, 1959); and William O'Neill, *Divorce in the Progressive Era* (New Haven, 1967).

lation. Except for special interest organizations, they do not combine together. The subject is full of paradoxes which elude precise definitions and defy synthesis.

Women at various times and places were a majority of the population, yet their status was that of an oppressed minority, deprived of the rights men enjoyed. Women have for centuries been excluded from positions of power, both political and economic, yet as members of families, as daughters and wives, they often were closer to actual power than many a man. If women were among the most exploited of workers, they were also among the exploiters. If some women were dissatisfied with their limited opportunities, most women were adjusted to their position in society and resisted efforts at changing it. Women generally played a conservative role as individuals and in their communities, the role of conserving tradition, law, order, and the status quo. Yet women in their organizations were frequently allied with the most radical and even revolutionary causes and entered alliances with the very groups threatening the status quo.

If women themselves acted paradoxically, so did society in formulating its values for women. The rationale for women's peculiar position in society has always been that their function as mothers is essential to the survival of the group and that the home is the essential nucleus of society as we know it. Yet the milllions of housewives and homemakers have throughout our history been deprived of the one tangible reward our society ranks highest: an income of their own. Neither custom, law, nor changes of technology, education, or politics have touched this sacred tradition. The unpaid housewife-and-mother has affected attitudes toward the women who perform homemaking services for strangers. Traditionally women in the service trades have been the lowest paid among all workers. Nor has this pattern been restricted to the unskilled groups. When women have entered an occupation in large numbers, this occupation has come to be regarded as low status and has been rewarded by low pay. Examples for this are readily found in the teaching and nursing fields. Even intellectual work has been treated with the same double standard. Creative fields in which women excel—poetry, the short story—have been those carrying the lowest rewards in money and esteem. Only in the performing arts has individual female talent had the same opportunity as male talent. Yet a cursory glance at the composition of any major symphony orchestra even today will reveal that in this field, too, opportunities for women have been restricted.

In dealing with the subject of women, studies frequently use other distinctive groups in our society as models for comparison. Women's position has variously been likened to that of the slaves, oppressed ethnic or racial minorities, or economically deprived groups. But these comparisons quickly prove inadequate. The slave comparison obviously was a rhetorical device rather than a factual statement even at the time when Harriet Martineau first made it.[10] While the law denied women equal citizenship and for certain purposes classed them with "Indians and imbeciles," it never denied them physical freedom nor did it regard them as "chattel personnel." In fact, even within the slavery system, women were oppressed differently from men. The "minority group model" is also unsatisfactory. All members of a minority group which suffers discrimination share, with a very few exceptions, in the low-status position of the entire group. But women may be the wives of Cabinet members, the daughters of Congressmen, the sisters of business leaders, and yet, seen simply as persons, they may be disfranchised and suffer from economic and educational discrimination. On the other hand, a lower class woman may advance to a position of economic or social power simply by marriage, a route which is generally not open to members of racial minority groups. In one particular respect the minority group comparison is illuminating: like Negroes, women suffer from "high visibility"; they remain more readily identifiable for their group characteristics than for their personal attainments.[11]

Modern psychology, which has offered various conflicting theories about the role and place of women, has further complicated the task of the historian. If a social historian wishes to study a particular ethnic or religious minority, he can study its location and economy, its culture, leadership, adjustment to American society, and contributions. The question of psychology would only arise in dealing with personal biographies. But the historian of women is at once faced with the necessity of making psychological

---

[10] *Society in America* (New York, 1837), I, 158.

[11] Helen Hacker, "Women as a Minority Group," *Social Forces*, XXX (1951-52), 60-69.

judgments. Is it not a basic fact that the psychology as well as the physiology of women is different from that of men? Therefore they must of necessity have different expectations, needs, demands, and roles. If so, is the difference in "rights" not simply natural, a reflection of reality? The problems become more vexing when dealing with individual women. The biographer feels obliged first of all to concern himself with his subject's sexual role. Was she married? A mother? If she was not, this indicates that whatever she achieved was the result of sexual frustration. If she was married, one is under an obligation to explain that she did not neglect her children or perhaps that she did. And always there is the crucial question: "What was her relationship to her father?" This is not intended to disparage the efforts of those biographers who wish to enlist the aid of modern psychology for their work. But it should be pointed out that a great deal of excellent history about men has been written without the author's feeling compelled to discuss his subject's sex life or relationship to his mother in explaining his historical significance. In dealing with women, biographers are impeded by the necessity of dealing first with sex, then with the person. This is an approach which must be examined in each case for its applicability: where it is useful, it should be retained; where it is not, it should be discarded without apology.

In order to broaden the study of women in American history, it is not really necessary to suggest new sources. Primary research material is readily available, not only in the several manuscript collections devoted to the subject, but in the usual primary sources for social historians: local historical records, letters, diaries, the organizational records of women's clubs, religious and charitable organizations, labor unions in fields employing women workers. There are numerous magazines, especially written for women, which provide good source material. Archives of Congress and of state governments contain petitions and statements made at hearings which can yield valuable information about the activities and interests of women. Many of these readily available sources remain neglected.

A fresh approach to known material and to available sources could provide valuable new insights. The following suggestion might make a useful beginning:

First, the subject "Women" is too vast and diffuse to serve as a valid point of departure. Women are members of families, citizens of different regions, economic producers, just as men are, but their emphasis on these various roles is different. The economic role of men predominates in their lives, but women shift readily from one role to another at different periods in their lives. It is in this that their function is different from men and it is this which must form the basis for any conceptual framework. In modern society the only statement about women in general which can be made with validity concerns their political status. Therefore the subject should be subsumed under several categories and any inquiry, description, and generalization should be limited to a narrower field. It is useful to deal with the *status* of women at any given time—to distinguish among their economic status, family status, and political-legal status. There must also be a consideration of class position, as has been usefully proven in recent studies of the feminist movement.[12]

Second, we should look at different aspects of women's role in American history. We must certainly be concerned with the woman's rights movement, but only as part of the total story. Historians must painstakingly restore the actual record of women's contributions at any given period in history. It is interesting that the history of women before the advent of the feminist movement has been more fully recorded and in a more balanced way than it has afterward, so that the story of colonial women can be quite fully traced through secondary literature.[13] But when we deal with the period after 1800, it often proves difficult to establish even descriptive facts. During the early national period, women organized elaborate welfare and relief systems which they staffed and administered. This story should be part of the history of the period; it is not now. Women were the teachers in most of the nation's public schools during the nineteenth century; this is worth recording and exploring. Women made a significant contribution to the growth and development of frontier communities. These are but a few of the many areas in which more research and uncovering of factual information are needed.

Third, we might well discard the "oppressed group model" when

12 See Kraditor and Lasch.

13 A full bibliography of colonial women is to be found in Eugenie A. Leonard, Sophie H. Drinker, and Miriam Y. Holden, *The American Woman in Colonial and Revolutionary Times: 1565-1800* (Philadelphia, 1962).

discussing women's role in the political life of the nation. Instead, we might start with the fact that one generalization about women which holds up is that they were, longer than any other group in the nation, deprived of political and economic power. Did this mean they actually wielded no power or did they wield power in different forms? My research has led me to believe that they wielded considerable power and in the middle of the nineteenth century even political power. They found a way to make their power felt through organizations, through pressure tactics, through petitioning, and various other means; these later became models for other mass movements for reform.

Fourth, another important fact is that women are a group who for a considerable period of history were deprived of equal access to education. While they were not illiterate, their education was limited, usually to below the high school level. This was true of the majority of women until the end of the nineteenth century. It might be very useful to investigate what impact this had on female behavior and more specifically, women's performance as a group in terms of outstanding achievement. To put it another way, how many generations of educated women are necessary to produce a significant number of outstanding women academicians? How many generations of college-trained women are necessary before women in sizable numbers make contributions in the sciences? When do women begin to move from the small-scale, home-centered creative forms, the fiction, poetry, and article-writing, to the larger-scale work within the framework of cultural institutions? Is the proverbial dearth of female philosophers really a result of some innate distinctiveness of female mental function or rather the product of centuries of environmental and institutional deprivation? This type of inquiry lends itself to a comparative cross-cultural approach. A comparison between the educational deprivation of women and that suffered by certain minority groups might lead us to a demonstrable correlation between educational deprivation and a gap of several generations before adequate and competitive performance is possible. This could explain a great deal about some of our problems with minority groups, public schooling, and academic achievement.

Fifth, it would be most worthwhile to distinguish the ideas society held at any given moment in regard to woman's proper "place" from what was actually woman's status at that time. The two do not necessarily overlap. On the contrary, there seems to be a considerable gap between the popular myth and reality. Social historians might legitimately be concerned with the significance of this gap, how to account for it, and whether it fits any distinguishable pattern. It would also be important to understand the function of ideas about women in the general ordering of society. Was the fact that colonial women were idealized as thrifty housewives and able helpmeets cause or effect of the labor shortage in the colonies? Are the idealized suburban housewife, the fashion-conscious teenager, the sex-symbol model, causes or effects of our consumer-oriented society? And what effect does the socially held concept of woman's role have on the development of female talent, on woman's contribution to the society?

Finally, we come back to the initial problem of how to judge the contribution of women. Are women noteworthy when their achievement falls exactly in a category of achievement set up for men? Obviously not for this is how they have been kept out of the history books up to now. Are women noteworthy then, as the feminists tended to think, if they do anything at all? Not likely. The fact remains that women are different from men and that their role in society and history is different from that of men. Different, but equal in importance. Obviously their achievements must also be measured on a different scale. To define and devise such a scale is difficult until the gaps in our historical knowledge about the actual contributions of women have been filled. This work remains to be done.

But we already know enough about the subject to conclude that the role women played at different times in our history has been changing. The patterns and significance of these changes, the continuities and discontinuities, the expectations and strivings of the pioneers, and the realities of the social scene—all these await study and new interpretations. One would hope at once for a wider framework and a narrower focus—a discarding of old categories and a painstaking search of known sources for unknown meanings. It is an endeavor that should enlist the best talents of the profession and, hopefully and at long last, not primarily female talent.

WOMEN IN AMERICAN SOCIETY

An Historical Contribution

Ann D. Gordon
Mari Jo Buhle
Nancy E. Schrom

PART I

The rise and fall of concern for women's history has followed the intensity of organized women's movements. Not since 1920, when the suffrage movement ended, has there been the interest evident today. As women were forced back into individual lives, understood through the personal lens of psychological adjustment (a process examined in the last part of this article), history as a study of their collective experience over the centuries no longer seemed to explain their condition. Historians, always more interested in writing about the powerful, studied a history without women. Only social scientists documented the changing presence of women at fixed times in a variety of situations, but their fragmented analyses did not provide a way to understand the totality of daily life for women. Neither did these evaluations describe the overall changes in society. But today, women with renewed caste-consciousness are returning to historical questions in a search for their collective identity and for an analysis of their condition.

Within the last decade, blacks have shown the role history plays in defining a social movement. The search to understand the collective conditions and the relation of the race to the dominant society has enabled black people in America to locate their strengths, their social importance, and the sources of their oppression. Further, this process has provided the analytical framework for recognizing their unity through their experiences, rather than simply through their racial difference from the ruling caste. Similarly, feminists of the Nineteenth Cebtury looked to the past to describe their common bond as women and to explain their current situation. That inquiry supported their theoretical development.

Nineteenth Century feminist writers enlarged the perspective of their analysis by making explicit the connections between the lives of individuals and the social movement for their emancipation, thus offering women definitions of the changes necessary to alter their lives. They studied women who overstepped the boundaries of prescribed roles and made important contributions to society or to a re-definition of female possibilities; and they created the chronology and analysis of women's historical subjection to men. But this search through women's history basically described the limits on their lives without a sense of the changes which had occurred in their "sphere". They isolated a few women or the relations of women to men from the total history of civilization. These women were not aware, for example, that the current family structure was of recent historical origin. They ignored the history of what was closest to them and placed their hopes for change outside their own lives in the industrial revolution or in the inevitable progress of democracy.

This feminist definition of women's historical role was challenged by Mary Beard in her book Woman as Force in History (1). Principally she addressed herself to the emphasis on an endless history of subjection. That stress, she argued, led to a misunderstanding by women of their own strength in the past. Women had internalized the "myth" of their secondary status and enshrined it in their analysis. By emphasizing only the obstacles to their fulfillment, women were prevented from understanding the power they had held historically in other avenues of social activity.

Mary Beard went on to propose an outline of a rewritten world history capable of describing the contributions women made to world civilization. At the base of her work and the source of her concern was her acceptance of the notion that women, in 1946, were about to cast off their chains and emerge as leaders in the advance of civilization. Because she accepted the inevitability of democratic progress, she conceptualized the reconstruction of women's history as limited to their role as a civilizing force. Without accepting her faith, we believe it is important to recognize and respond to her realization that women must come to a history which does not negate their activities in the past. Mary Beard believed that the real history of women's lives was more important than society's limitations of their activities.

Faced again with the task of defining women's history in relation to the re-emergence of women as a collective force, we find it essential to define what we understand to be our past. Through a historical critique we can begin to transcend the imposition of contemporary institutions and values on our lives. Without such a critique our view of daily life remains at the level of individual reaction to what strikes us as intolerable. Our analyses tend to document our feelings of subjection rather than the underlying historical conditions of the subjection of all women.

The forms of history familiar to the women's movement in the United States have re-appeared with the addition of histories of that earlier movement. They expand our knowledge, but their limitations also must be examined. Documentation and analysis of the women's rights movement offers a tradition of struggle: We see that women in the past not only were aware of their oppression as a sex, but also organized themselves and devoted their lives to changing the conditions they saw between themselves and freedom for their sex. The history of women who ignored social conventions and sexual restrictions serves both to probe the proscriptive roles imposed on them and to offer a sense of the possible to all women. But our advantage of hindsight over the earlier feminist assault and our overall perspective on the development of American capitalism necessitate a larger definition of our past. Our vision must mediate between the objective historical conditions and the changes in daily life. We cannot afford to locate the logic of our movement in apparently anonymous forces, such as technology, lying outside the lives of women, and measure our transcendence by our ability to respond masterfully to that external development. By doing so, we would accept the dominant ideology that the inner logic of "women's sphere" is too slight to examine and too slight to have a significant effect on the course of society.

That women have not had access to the means of social definition and have not lived and worked in the spheres of reward and recognition is obvious. They have lived in what Simone de Beauvoir has described as the historical anomaly of "the Other". The problem remains: As objects, do we have a history, properly speaking? As long as historical enquiry is constrained by equating initiative and mastery with life, the lives of women are, at best, a "situation", as Juliet Mitchell has noted. (2) The seeming timelessness of women's lives may describe one source of the lack of female consciousness through long periods; the processes affecting their lives are frequently slow and without immediate impact on their awareness. But to assume that their lives were, as a result, without time and without change, ignores the role that the subjection of women has played in world development. Historians' chronic blindness to that fact prevents them from probing the fullest meaning of history. If we can succeed in defining the "specificity of their oppression" (3), we will as well have moved closer to realizing the dynamics of all historical development — a necessary prerequisite for changing it.

Margaret George, in her recent biography of Mary Wollstonecraft, One Woman's Situation, suggested that we are examining women's pre-history. Within that pre-history is a variety of experiences and responses, some of them initiated by women, most of them not. The experiences of women, she noted, have a time and space dimension that is subject to inquiry and capable of enlarging our understanding of the historical conditions of all women. (4) The world women have inhabited has its own history, intimately related on one hand to the changes in their lives, and on the other to the progress of world history, encompassing the lives of all people. The organization of society around age, the privatization of the family, and the emergence of a culture of motherhood around the biological function are instances of women's sphere being subject to historical analysis. As Philippe Aries demonstrated in *Centuries of Childhood*, the history of that intimiate world is at the root of the changes in all modern social relations (5). The disintegration of pre-industrial family relations both symbolized and mediated the transformation of *all* personal relations, based on changes of the means of production and the new stratification of social classes.

Historians and feminists alike have assumed that "woman" is a transhistorical creature who for purposes of discussion can be isolated from social development. Recently, some writers for the Women's Liberation Movement have appropriated this concept, designating all other class, race, and historical conditions of women as secondary and derivative. For these writers, sex becomes the primary contradiction of life, and the male/female antagonism or dichotomy is therefore transformed into the theoretical principle underlying their view of the world and history. Women's history is consequently divorced from its content and reconstructed around the peculiar bond women share. The conditions imposed by gender relegate women to a caste, that is, a group located outside itself by its visible (sexual) characteristics, applicable to all present and past forms of social organization. "Caste" in this usage is an idea imposed on women, a definition derived from their subordinate position in male-dominated culture. Caste, then, defines the *negativity* of women's relationships within the larger society. Within the historical and social experience in which power is denied to their sex, the caste situation contains — in this view — the inherent seed for liberation through the collective identity of women's peculiar situation. The oppressive isolation from male culture, which defines caste, is then transformed into the positive metaphor of shared consciousness.

The major dilemma of any collective recognition of woman's peculiar situation revolves around the simple functionalism that the caste notion implies as being both the condition of woman's oppression and the source of her as yet unrecognized strength. First of all, an essentially static concept of oppression does not account for the changing degree to which women have been conscious of sharing a collective identity. Thus, Simone de Beauvoir, who made a decisive contribution in defining the usefulness of what women have shared, specifically rejected the idea that women have been a caste, because they have not reached a required consciousness of self. (6) Our history in fact must record the movement of women toward that consciousness and not assume that caste relationships necessarily define its inevitability. For example, in describing the bond between women in any particular period or across centuries, caste fails because it ignores the forms that oppression took at different times for different women. Women have been kept apart in their oppression, separated from one another; yet the notion of caste tends to presuppose a greater recognition of shared history than women have ever actually exhibited. To assert centuries of sisterhood will not explain —or help overcome —the historic reality of antagonisms and conflicting experience. It is precisely the interrelationship between women's oppression and the "rest" of history that enables us to understand why, for example, black and white women in the ante-bellum South could not unite around their "common" oppression.

An example from American colonial history illustrates the relatively recent development of women's self-identification as a caste. Some women recognized their sexual identity but did not differentiate themselves from men according to any common female experience, and therefore did not express their discontent in sexual terms. Anne Bradstreet, one of the few to articulate a sense of women's subjection, reflected on the harships of motherhood in her poetry, yet accepted these burdens as natural to woman's condition on earth. The passing of an English culture which had respected the mental capacities of women under Queen Elizabeth symbolized for her the secondary status of her sex. While she wrote her poetry in the Massachusetts Bay Colony, other women such as Anne Hutchinson and Mary Dyer gained notoriety for their pursuit of religious diversity in a male theological world. Anne Bradstreet's caste sense, if it may be called that, had distinct limitations, and her resentments against male culture were defined primarily in terms of its denial of women's reason and did not extend to include the disagreements of the mind which other women were having with men. (7)

Nineteenth Century women, for the first time in history, recognized a collective experience for members of their sex and defined that as a position of subjugation. Their belief in an eternal, special condition of women helped provide power for their movement, for it gave them collective identification as a caste (although they did not specifically use the term) and a separate location for their history. Yet those perceptions were marred by identifying the sense of oppression they felt in their lives with the specific forms that sexual subjection had taken over the centuries. Their particular historical situation was obscured. The· caste feeling blurred the reality that their own consciousness had been made possible by their class position based on the new roles of woman as producer and reproducer introduced by Nineteenth Century industrialization.

A paradoxical view of woman's proper role in society has developed out of the caste idea of women's historical condition. On the one hand, women were said to have been denied the feeling of strength and the possession of real power which defined men's control over the world. On the other hand, by virtue of powerlessness women were assumed to have retained a kind of moral superiority over aggressive, warlike men. A major argument for the introduction of women's suffrage was the public necessity for an expression of moral values that had been saved in the isolation of women's sphere, the defense of the family, and the uplifting of all humanity. Today, as Branka Magas has noted in a recent New Left Review essay, some feminists have returned to the essence of this argument by contending that women will make the Revolution. (8) Women, according to this view, will mend the world because their hands are clean from the blood, profit, and power with which men have ruled the world. Thus distance from decision-making in society is translated from a description of oppression into a virtue of transforming proportion. This argument not only accepts a view of the past in which women were outside of history, but also asserts that now, and in the future, that condition which has separated them from men will be the basis for their entrance into history.

The bond women have had and currently share is, in the caste argument, the nature of their oppression. That women have suffered oppression is not to be denied. Sexual exploitation, ego damage, the double standard, stereotyping, and discrimination are past as well as present realities. But oppression has meant different things at different times to different groups and classes of women. A historical perspective on the realization that sexual exploitation forms a core of female oppression clarifies some of the weakness in leveling historical differences. Today women explain sexual exploitation partially in terms of the repressive nature of monogamy that binds a woman to one man, depriving her of the gratification of her capacity for multiple orgasms. While men utilize women for their own gratification, they deny women the right to sexual fulfillment by specifying the forms of sexual activity. Many of the special complaints center on the denial to women of equal pleasure. For Nineteenth Century feminists, sexual exploitation was also focused on the unnatural marriage relationship: the form which gave the husband command over his wife's body. But they accepted much of the Victorian double standard and denied feminine sexuality, expressing their grievance at the necessity of vile sex to satisfy their vulgar, sensual husbands. Liberation in practice meant chastity rather than free love. The forceful reaction of feminists to Victoria Woodhull's association with their movement reflected this tension.

Within one period of time, the conceptual confusion created by the unvarying and undifferentiated term "oppression" can be illustrated by the debate over the validity of using the same word to describe the condition of the white plantation mistress and the black slave woman. For the slave woman, oppression meant physical cruelty and sexual exploitation. For the leisured, financially comfortable plantation mistress — feminist — oppression, consciously realized or not, was not physical hardship but social and legal constriction and repressive sexuality. The limitations of focusing entirely on this one factor of their lives, this bond they shared by their sexual characters, underscore the essentially static nature of the caste/oppression framework. The concept of oppression does little to explain the dynamic of either woman's life or the historical conditions underlying it. In addition, to ignore the important differences which distinguish the lives of the two women is to do violence to the lives of black men and women under slavery.

The middle-class base of Nineteenth Century feminism is frequently noted, lamented, and rejected as a model for today's movement. To transcend that limitation we must know as much about what kept women apart as we know about what brought them together. The Women's Liberation Movement has reached sufficient consciousness of its own class background to endorse the need to include working-class and colonized women in the movement. But the expansion of view from the generality of our Nineteenth Century sisters is apparently forgotten when historical conditions are analyzed. Working-class women in the last century felt their oppression in class terms and organized around their work. Women in ethnic communities recognized the alienation and subjection they shared with men of the same nationalities more than they identified common bondage with upper-class or WASP sisters.

The rejection of class in the modern liberation movement is often based on the observation that a woman received her class (or race or nationality) through a man — father, brother, or husband — and not through her own productive relations. The historical relevance of such an assertion in a period when women increasingly enter the work force is immediately suspect. But more important, the insight explicit in that assertion, which is related to the concept of subjection, must not become a simple conceptual negation of the differences in class experience in America. Economic well-being, social relations, life expectancy, ranges of personal choice are dependent on the changing relations among classes, and those conditions of daily life have been as real for women as for men.

The very real powerlessness felt and frequently expressed by women of the last two centuries becomes, ironically, a source of misunderstanding about the complexity of women's role throughout the history of humanity. Generalizations from specific forms of subjugation may serve only to mystify the real sources of women's strength in their historical evaluation and the specific form of their dependency

ART SUPPLEMENT MILWAUKEE FREE PRESS

DESIGN FOR A BACHELOR'S WALL PAPER

on the predominantly male world. Out of a caste analysis, women, as the subject of study, are projected into a static role rather than one which allows for change. In essence, history becomes an external process, a force which presses against women's lives without a reciprocal interaction. Women become in the truest sense the objects of history, bound by their peculiar situation as victims of oppression.

Without denying what we share as women we must develop categories to fit women into history that transcend feelings of oppression. Our subjection as a philosophical description mobilizes us by articulating the alienation we feel. It can be concretized within any particular period. As an element in the history of civilization it must be clearly recognized and overcome. But that still makes oppression a truth which stands above all other historical or philosophical observations.

The contours of women's history have been determined in large part by the questions historical writers have been interested in exploring, the assumptions researchers have brought to their work, and the sources available for examining the lives women led in previous centuries. What quickly becomes apparent to someone interested in learning about the historical development of women's status and consciousness in the United States is the limited scope of the work which fall into the category of women's history. Most historical studies fall into one of three categories: institutional histories of women's organizations and movements; biographies of important suffragists and "token" women—First Ladies, isolated Nineteenth Century professional women, reformers, and eccentrics of one sort or another; and "prescriptive history"—that is, discussions of class or societal ideals rather than actual cultural practices. Such studies analyze articles on Nineteenth Century childrearing practices, for example, in order to gain insights into how parents actually may have raised their children.

The majority of historical studies fall into the first category: institutional history. Often, institutional studies are not women's history, but feminist history. Hence the history of women has often been conceptualized as women in organizations—women's rights, suffrage movements, and unions. These organizational studies are limited further by the fact that many historians have tended to concentrate almost exclusively on the suffrage campaign within the larger women's movement. One is led to assume through such studies as Eleanor Flexner's Century of Struggle and Mildred Adams's The Right to Be People that American feminism—or even women's history in general—is virtually synonymous with the fight for the vote. (9)

Because so much of what is called "women's history" has concentrated on the women's rights movement and the suffrage campaign, it is important to ask why historians and other writers have attributed so much importance to organized feminism to the neglect of the historical experience of women outside an organized movement. Part of the reason for such a heavy emphasis on institutional history lies in the nature of available source materials with which to work. There is a wealth of material dealing with the women's rights movement. Historians have at their disposal not only the standard memoirs and autobiographies of the leading suffragists, such as Stanton and Gage's mammoth compendium The History of the Women's Suffrage Movement and Carrie Chapman Catt's Woman Suffrage and Politics, but also the enormous quantity of correspondence, newspapers, magazines, and pamphlets that accumulated throughout the Nineteenth and early Twentieth Centuries. The early histories of the suffrage movement, written by participants, are sources in themselves, rich in personal insight and reminiscences. (10)

The abundance of sources available on the women's rights movement does not completely explain why so many historical studies of women have concentrated exclusively on organized feminism. This fact is readily attested to by the lack of historical studies dealing with women in the years after the passage of the Nineteenth Amendment, despite an overwhelming variety and abundance of materials: economic studies, census returns, Women's Bureau bulletins, and personal papers. Even studies which are not confined to a narrow organizational framework, such as Andrew Sinclair's The Better Half, do not deal with the years after 1920 in any depth. Institutional studies such as Flexner's Century of Struggle often conclude with a short impressionistic sketch of women's history since 1920, making reference to women's gains in education, employment, and legal status. Too often, then, women's history has been defined solely as the history of an organized movement. As such, the history of women begins in 1848 with the Seneca Falls Convention, and ends abruptly in 1920. The subjects for institutional women's history are women who were articulate, conscious, and members of organizations.

The questions which individuals concerned with women's history have brought to their research also have played a key role in determining the way in which their subject is defined. Part of the reason for the lack of interest in women's history since 1920 is the fact that there was no organized and vital feminist movement during these years. Just as the recent interest in black history was reawakened in response to the black movement, the recent resurgence of interest in women's history is due in good measure to the Women's Liberation Movement. Because interest is generated by an organized movement, it is understandable that many of the questions writers have asked of their material revolve around organizations and institutions. This was particularly true of the early historians of the suffrage movement, who, as participants in the suffrage struggle themselves, sympathetically chronicled their sisters' activities.

In addition, underlying assumptions and conceptions of women, American society, and the nature of social change have been important influences on historical writing dealing with women. The general lack of attention accorded to women outside the women's rights movement reflects the implicit assumption that it is only when women are behaving in ways usually attributed to men — that is, politically — that they deserve mention. In all other matters, these writers seem to assume, women's experience is either unimportant (that is, dismissed as women's work and therefore not the proper sphere of history, which has traditionally dealt with power relations and institutions) or identical to that of men.

Then too, underlying the emphasis on organizations is the implicit assumption that an organization in and of itself initiates social change. Although some historians have made passing bows to the forces of industrialization, urbanization, and socio-economic changes, often these are not meaningfully integrated into the institutional narratives or seriously analyzed. Both the early suffrage studies and their recent counterparts seem unaware of the changes that the Nineteenth Century brought to women's lives. (11)

Finally, the writers who have dealt extensively with the women's right and suffrage movements have tended to share a view of American society and institutions and have held in common certain assumptions about the nature of historical change which make institutional history a natural focus for their investigations. All share a faith in American political democracy and social institutions, and a belief in the linear progression of history. For most of them, women's history is set in an evolutionary framework depicting the development of Western civilization as the unfolding progress of mankind toward democracy. In this conception, the women's movement is interpreted as "another chapter in the struggle for liberty". (12) Although recent studies have been more sophisticated in writing and research, they share the optimistic Progressive notion of historical development and change. Mildred Adams, for example, writes: "It was a remarkably selfless campaign. The women who spent their lives in it were working not for themselves, but for the common good. They were working for the better status of women in a democracy and for the better conduct of that democracy. They honestly believed that women... should have the vote because they were citizens and as a tool with which to improve not only their own legal status, but also the laws and government of the nation." (13) This Progressive approach, largely unconscious in the early writers who wrote of their own movement in terms of optimism and sincerity, obscures many important facets of the women's rights movement and of the condition of women in general throughout history. Women enlisted in the suffrage cause for a variety of reasons and motivations. A women's club member generally had far different reasons for becoming a suffragist, came from a very different background, and worked for different goals than a young factory worker, for example. This Progressive approach also obscures the fact that the altruistic concern for the common good was the dominant ideological theme of the suffrage movement only in its last years, when the Progressive reform impulse had largely overtaken the original feminist concerns of the movement. The racist aspects of the early suffrage movement, its limited middle-class concerns, and the lack of feminist ideology are neglected in institutional studies.

Aileen Kraditor's The Ideas of the Woman Suffrage Movement and William O'Neill's Everyone Was Brave serve in some ways as correctives to the older institutional studies. (14) Kraditor traces the development of the suffragists' ideology from the natural rights arguments of the Nineteenth Century to the reform arguments of the early Twentieth Century. Her work, with its exegesis of the movement's ideological underpinnings, sheds much-needed light on the class base of the suffragists. She emphasizes the middle-class nature of the movement and its basic failure to overcome the boundaries of class interest and outlook. William O'Neill, in Everyone Was Brave and in "Feminism as a Radical Ideology", also emphasizes the middle-class base of the suffrage movement and the suffragists' failure to formulate a radical critique of the existing social structure. He documents the heterogeneity of the movement in which feminism as an ideology disappeared in favor of broad-based political reform to be enacted by women. Both Kraditor and O'Neill, however, despite their greater sophistication in analyzing the women's movement and its ideological limitations, still are confined by the traditional emphasis on institutions and organizations. Both authors define the history of women through an organizational perspective and are primarily concerned with the thought and activities of women who participated in the movement.

Even the best of institutional studies, then, are inherently limited in the scope of their inquiry. Because the history of women is defined in these studies as the history of organizations, little opportunity is available for exploring the insights and issues raised by recent psychological, sociological, and biological findings and theories dealing with the family, childrearing practices, individual differences, and sexuality.

History of the feminist movement can and should be important, and, despite a plethora of studies already published on the early movement, many questions remain unanswered. New questions need to be asked, drawn from our experience in the present movement: Why did the first feminist movement ultimately lose sight of feminist goals? What can we learn from the suffrage movement in the way of tactics? How did the tactics of the first movement relate to its ideology? How and why did the early feminists fail to transcend class boundaries? In addition, the movement has much to tell us about the nature and development of feminist consciousness? By studying the early movement, we will hopefully learn more about when and why women began to think of themselves as women, with a distinct status and distinct problems. Future investigators should be bound less by organizational framework and should try to relate the movement to a larger social context. Although questions dealing with familial and social relationships and the effects of industrialization generally lie outside of an institutional orientation, they are central to understanding the movement itself.

Biographical history, the second major form in which women's history has been written, manifests many of the same difficulties, assumptions, and weaknesses as institutional studies. Narrative biographies of women have served as the only way to reconstruct the lives women led, for the historical sources which exist for writing about the world of men — electoral politics, institutional organization, industry, and war — have not existed for the majority of women during most periods of history. The work of reconstructing the history of the inarticulate has just begun, and women make up the largest and probably the most silent of society's inarticulate groups. Anyone who has tried genealogical and demographic research knows that even basic facts about birth, death, and parenthood of a woman, particularly in the colonial period of American history or in any undeveloped region, are difficult to obtain.

Only a small number of women have left diaries, letters, and other sources with which to assess their role and their experience, and often these written sources prove sadly inadequate to reconstruct their history. Efforts to learn about women on the frontier, for example, are fraught with such difficulties. Although the lives of such atypical women as Cattle Kate and the San Francisco madams are well documented, finding out about the typical woman — or even defining what "typical" means — is far more difficult. The lack of feminist consciousness characteristic of a pre-industrial, organic society made it highly unusual for a woman to write of herself in letters or diaries in a self-conscious, detailed way, distinguishing her experience from that of her husband or children. For the same reasons, then, that historians have concentrated on the women's movement, biographers have concentrated on a small number of atypical women: those on whom sources are available.

Like the organizational studies, biographies are inherently limited. They tell us very little about the life style and status of the overwhelming majority of women who went to medical, law, or divinity school before the Twentieth Century, and were not members of a small elite social class, married to wealthy or famous men. The very existence of written materials on a woman tells us that she was atypical: She had the leisure and ability to write; she had the opportunity to experience something other than basic production for her household; and she lived in a family conscious enough of its heritage to preserve family records. Often the existence of sources indicates nothing in particular about the woman except the fact that she was married to a famous man. Alice Desmond's biography, Alexander Hamilton's Wife (1954) is a good case in point.

Biographies are usually narrative and anecdotal; thus characteristics singled out as quaint or eccentric are often emphasized at the expense of trying to see how the subject fit into her social environment. In essence, the woman is removed from history: The uniqueness of her life is exaggerated, because the biographer does not know the options and the expectations his subject had, or have a historical perspective on the time, place, and conditions in which the woman lived and worked. The history of women then, when confined to a biographical approach, is defined in ahistorical terms.

Biography can be a useful tool in understanding the exceptional woman who stands out in history, such as Anne Hutchinson, the Grimke Sisters, Margaret Sanger, and Emma Goldman. Perhaps sympathetic and analytical studies which attempted to come to terms with both the inner motivational factors and the external social environment could tell us a great deal about women's consciousness. Margaret George's biography of Mary Wollstonecraft is a good example of a study which attempts to delineate its subject in a social as well as a personal context. (15)

Often, however, exceptional women have been ignored, written off as quaint (such as the much-misunderstood Amelia Bloomer), or written about not as women but as professionals or reformers. Jane Addams has been the subject of a number of special studies, but generally the focus of the works has been Jane Addams as a social reformer, and not Jane Addams as a woman interested in women's special problems. When she is written about as a woman, it is for the purpose of exploring the psychological alienation of middle-class individuals, and not really about herself. (16) At the opposite pole, as Aileen Kraditor notes, is the effort to re-introduce these "abnormal" women into the mainstream of American womanhood. Hence many suffragists and reformers have been placed in the context of their homes and families and portrayed primarily as wives and mothers in an effort to lessen the taint of deviance which surrounded a woman who did not fit the prescribed role. Elizabeth Cady Stanton, for example, is the subject of numerous biographies which stress her role as wife and mother as well as her activities in the suffrage movement. Forgotten are her elaborate theories on marriage, divorce, and religion.

The psychological assumptions about women which historical writers have brought to bear on their subjects has also been an important factor in the writing of women's history and biography. In general, it is safe to say that American historians have assumed that a woman is a passive creature. While much of their conceptualization has previously been based on Freudian constructs, the recent discussions of the validity of psychoanalytic theories have made historians more reticent in making broad generalizations. Nevertheless, comprehension and use of Freud's ideas continue at a popular level, providing norms for judging deviance, and particularly for assessing women. The frequently appearing statement that Mary Wollstonecraft (or any other feminist) refused her passive social role because of an extreme case of penis envy is the most obvious example of such usage. Further, the assumption of innate feminine passivity has led historians to explain all feminist outbreaks as a result of immensely disruptive social forces — such as industrialization, war, or atheism — which threatened the sound bases of all earlier social relations (female deference included). Initiation in her own behalf would be out of feminine character, or at best a rationalization of some individual problem.

Recently, historians have dismissed the trend of using psychoanalytic assessments as mere conjecture. However this rejection of orthodox Freudian schemas is often replaced by an unsystematized form of personality theory — that is, a common-sense reasoning used to explain the peculiarities of outstanding individuals. The historian, therefore, imagined his task as determining what unique factors forced outstanding women to step outside their "natural" role. Needless to say, this process decidedly detracts from the historical validity of distinct contributions made by exceptional women. For example Robert Reigel, in <u>American Feminists</u>, criticized historians for misjudging the complexities of feminists' personalities. Too often, he asserted, these women were portrayed as old maids or as simple humanitarians devoted to an essentially maternal concept of social reform. In contrast Reigel intended to assess the peculiar personality make-up of individual feminists, concluding that most shared characteristics of good health, physical vigor, good education, et cetera. Substituting this framework, Riegel arranged a series of biographical vignettes, centered on the personal lives of his subjects. While correcting some of the unfair stereotypes, Riegel's concentration on life-style detail detracted from the accomplishments of these women, and almost completely ignored the conditions under which they fought. (17)

The third form in which women's history has been written — what we have called "prescriptive history" — also has failed to tell us much about women's experience in American history. Prescriptive studies ask important and broad-based questions about the nature of social institutions such as the family and marriage. They attempt to chart changes and developments in childrearing practices, marriage and divorce customs, and sexual mores, and to relate these developments to a larger ideological framework. For example Edmund Morgan, in The Puritan Family, used sermons and Puritan writings to relate Seventeenth Century New England childrearing practices to Puritan theology. Bernard Wishy, in The Child and the Republic, attempted to put changes in attitudes toward childrearing within a context of changing intellectual conceptions of the importance of environment in shaping a child's character. (18)

Although prescriptive studies ask important questions, they are weak in the evidence they employ. From reading such studies, we are left with hazy and often inaccurate ideas about the nature of actual cultural behavior. We cannot assume, when trying to learn about women's historical experience, that the models of behavior and attitudes found in sermons, books, or magazines accurately reflected how people acted. Was a Puritan minister describing how his congregation behaved when he wrote about childrearing or woman's role, or was he describing ideals for behavior and attitudes which he held up for his congregation to emulate? Did articles in Godey's Ladies' Book and other women's magazines describe how middle-class and upper-class parents treated their children, or were the articles largely unrelated to daily life? Hence prescriptive studies assume a relationship between ideology and attitudes and actual practice which may very well not exist. In addition, such writers seem to be talking about all families or all women without differentiating clearly between time periods and class lines. Finally, such studies presuppose a causal relationship between intellectual trends and a group's behavior. Too little attention is given to socio-economic factors in determining changes in behavior.

In conclusion, a woman today trying to understand herself in historical perspective has, despite myriad studies, precious little knowledge to rely on. Because institutional studies have defined women's history narrowly in terms of organizations, a woman today cannot get a sense of historical continuity or development outside the realm of the feminist movement. Changes in women's experiences and the nature of women's societal role during the years of the women's rights movement are left largely unexamined in the standard accounts, and questions about the patterns of familial and social relationships and the effects of industrialization on woman's role and on family structure are often left unasked. Finally, we still know very little about how women lived; how they interacted with their children, husbands, and parents; and how they began to develop a consciousness of their distinct role in society. Perhaps now, with a renewed feminist consciousness and with better, more sophisticated tools of historical analysis, we can begin to ask new questions about the actual historical experience of women, about the social and economic forces which shaped and changed women's lives, and about the nature of and factors involved in shaping feminist consciousness.

Underlying the analysis presented in this article is our belief that when history describes the totality of the female experience, it provides the essential identification for women to recognize their collective fate and to build a force that can move forward. The raw materials of the article are the books and studies which historians — mostly male — have written about the lives of women in the American colonies and the United States. At present, despite their limitations, they are the only tools we have to comprehend the historical experience of American women. We have tried to place the information contained in these works within a framework that American women can utilize to come to terms with their past. Through that history we can make personal connections previously unavailable to us. Our discomfort appears in terms of historical development rather than in terms of our personal failure or our unique perception. Our situation appears to us as a moment in history rather than as a condition of history.

PART II

The changes which took place in the lives of women during the colonial period — a span of almost two centuries — provide a valuable framework for an understanding of the relationship between greater economic and social complexity and the emergence of a distinct, and limiting, notion of femininity. At one end of the period there was the Virginia House of Burgesses describing why they granted land to wives as well as to husbands in 1619: "... in a new plantation it is not knowen (sic) whether man or woman be the most necessary." (19) At the other there was Mercy Otis Warren (1728-1814), a writer and historian, writing to a young woman that learning was useless to a lady (as useless as virtue to a gentleman). (20)

In this discussion we can point out some of the general outlines of colonial growth and some of the signs that transformations were occurring in daily life. At a minimum, the suggestions here should provide background for the more familiar tale of the Nineteenth Century, when the proscriptions on women and the definitions of their limited sphere were fully developed.

Colonial history was in part a beginning again. Each new coastal settlement and each move westward entailed a return to the simplest social organization: A family or a single man produced enough for survival and used virtually all available time for essential work. There were numerous sequences of development in different locations, and while one city may have resembled an English city, farms on the frontier were no doubt more similar to the earliest settlements. Still no one moved for long beyond the influence of colonial governments, and in most areas churches were established as rapidly as settlers moved in.

Colonial forms of increasing complexity, models for institutions and for social relations, came out of the European (primarily English) experience of the settlers. The majority of colonists, for example, accepted the logic of monogamous marriage, built single family houses, and assumed their right to own property. (21) They became members of churches with British or European counterparts, adopted elements of English common law, and organized their production and marketing along familiar lines. By the middle of the Eighteenth Century, when commerce, or reliance on commerce, created not only greater involvement with the mother country but greater similarities with it as well, colonists increasingly sought to duplicate the forms of English social life. (22)

Women throughout the period were tied to the fate of the family. Towns in New England assumed and legislated a family basis for social life, and single women were urged to live within a family household. (23) In some of the Southern colonies where settlement was initially conducted as an adventure by English investors, men were sent alone to begin productive work. It was found that little incentive for producing a surplus existed without families, so women were imported and sold to men for the cost of their passages. (24) That brief period may express as much about the importance of women in colonial development as any time when they were more conspicuous by their presence. Throughout the colonies the sex ratio between men and women favored women — a development unique to American society. As a result a woman's chance of marrying, her economic support, were very high, and the age at which she married was significantly lower than in England. It may have been true, as well, that the scarcity of women resulted in greater social mobility for women; they were in such demand that they could afford to choose. (25)

The simplicity of economic and social organization concentrated a variety of essential activities in the family. In family production each member contributed work of equal importance to the group's survival. Two aspects of this were no doubt important in providing women with useful roles: the independence of each family's work and the immediate necessity of it. The division of work was mostly along sex lines, but within that basic division of labor there were different patterns, depending on the relative wealth of the family, the degree of participation in a cash economy, the organization of the husband's work, and the size of the household — relatives, servants or slaves, numbers of children, et cetera. Most families were farming, producing

Purchase brides for the Adventurers in Virginia, about 1621. (From the Collections of the Library of Congress)

their own food, some surplus for trade, and their own clothing, soap, candles, and fuel. In this setting a large family was an asset, and thus the reproductive role of the mother, as well as her productive work, was valued. (26)

Education for the majority of colonists was something that took place in the family and consisted of teaching skills and morals. Boys and girls learned those from the work and daily life of their families. Where families were concentrated and homogeneous, as in New England towns or religious settlements, children occasionally attended schools or were traded into another family to learn skills or manners. (27) Mrs. Anna Grant, resident in New York before the Revolution, recorded in her Memoirs that among the Dutch in Albany, mothers took primary responsibility for educating children, especially for religious teaching. Janet Schaw, an Eighteenth Century traveler in North Carolina, noted that the sharp contrast in civility between men and women was a result of daughters being raised in the cultured environment of their homes while sons learned the rough and fighting ways of the woods from their fathers. Whatever its particular form, this responsibility to society, resting with the family, defined a major part of the work of both mothers and fathers. Not until education was more clearly defined as something that changed the relationship between parents and children by introducing new values into a society, and until the family unit was no longer concentrated with the work of both men and women, did learning require new structures and distinct duties of each parent. (28)

The accompanying rhetoric about marriage described a partnership between man and woman. The institution existed to produce offspring and, at least in Puritan thought, to control the natural sexual appetites by providing an outlet for their monogamous expression. In New England grounds for divorce applied equally to each sex: adultery, impotency, refusal of sexual favors, and desertion. However the Puritans, so often chided for their repressive attitudes toward sex, delimited only two major forms of deviation: Sexuality must never interfere with the ultimate relationship, that between human and God; and it must never take place outside of marriage. In practice, those restrictions may in fact have loosened during the Eighteenth Century, as records of children born to couples after less than nine months of marriage indicate. Other colonies appear to have accepted a double standard of sexual behavior somewhat earlier, at least in the application of the law. The partnership had economic reality when the family worked the land or in a craft and so long as the wealth provided for children derived from that common work. (29)

Throughout most of the Seventeenth Century, colonial society was relatively unfragmented, either by sex or by age. (30) Individual women occasionally stepped outside the limits set for them (Anne Hutchinson's doctrinal challenge to Massachusetts leaders, Quaker missionaries asserting the necessity of religious tolerance, a Southern woman refusing to utter the word "obey" in her marriage vow); but in general, neither men nor women seemed concerned with defining what women were or what their unique contribution to society should be. (31) Similarly, studies of children's toys, books, and care reveal very little special attention to children's particularity in the society. (32) The cultural expressions of the time indicate lack of consciousness about the possible differences which later came to characterize all discussion of women and children.

The emphasis on the social necessity of women in a wilderness environment and the consequent respect given to their labor must not be mistaken for a society without discriminations against women. Distinctions were made in laws, in education, in theology and church affairs, and in political and property rights. No one asserted equality. But there was flexibility in drawing the lines around women's work and men's work. Abstract theories about the proper role of women did not stand in the way of meeting familial and social needs. There is considerable evidence that women were engaged in numerous business and professional activities in the colonial period. Their work was not simply in those jobs extending their traditional domestic work out into more complex organization, such as production of foodstuffs and clothing. Women published and printed newspapers, managed tanneries, kept taverns, and engaged in just about every occupation existing in the colonies. Many of these women, who had learned the skills of the trade while sharing the work of their husbands, were working as widows to support their families. (33)

This "unique" presence of women is frequently taken to be a sign of the liberating effect of frontier conditions on traditional roles; but this view ignores the work experience of English women. In England, women had been members of craft guilds, had worked in their husbands' jobs as widows, and had been accepted in such professional capacities as midwives and attorneys in lieu of their husbands. But by the end of the Seventeenth Century women had lost those positions. Comparison with the more carefully documented English events throws new light on the origins of the colonial freedom so often located. Nothing in English culture or production militated against utilizing the talents of men and women in a variety of occupations as long as the economy needed their strength and numbers. When that need ended, and when women found their access to jobs limited by law or by their inability to gain the prerequisites, their presence sharply declined. However, a series of transformations in the organization of work protected the opportunities for male work (in the dying craft guilds, for example) and at the same time excluded women by edict or default. Two activities in the colonies underwent this limiting process: midwifery and the informal exercise of power of attorney. (34)

Midwifery was not only open to women; their monopoly was protected. In 1675 officials of York County, Maine presented "Captain Francis Raine for presuming to act the part of a midwife", and fined him fifty shillings. (35) But less than a century later formal learning began to replace practical experience for the job. Doctor William Shippen Junior — a leader in medical education in Philadelphia — announced a series of lectures on midwifery in 1765. He did not exclude women from training, but offered his expertise to women with "virtue enough to own their ignorance". Not only was there a serious problem about mortality rates in childbirth, but the situation was aggravated "by the unskillful old women...." (36) A similar process in the granting of powers of attorney has been documented in Maryland. Law became a career with prerequisites denied to women, and gradually the practical flexibility which had allowed women to appear in court in their own behalf if single or in behalf of their husband in his absence was abandoned. (37)

Similarly, by the middle of the Eighteenth Century the manifestations of a distinct world for upper-class women with its own standards of success and necessities were clearly emerging in the colonies. The culture was in part imported from England, but rapidly developed parallel but indigenous forms. A frequently cited instance is the interest in women's education. Special schools were opened in the major coastal towns of Boston, Newport, New York, Philadelphia, and Charleston. After the Revolution, female seminaries extended further inland. (38) These schools were designed to prepare women for their roles as wives and mothers. Some academic subjects such as appeared in the schools for boys were selected as suitable, but primarily the schools concentrated on styles of ladylike qualities and skills. Some theorists of this new education particularly aimed at providing what Abigail Adams called the "groundwork...of more durable colors"; they wanted to teach women to respect the serious literature of philosophy and morality, to read history and thus to be better prepared to talk intelligently with their husbands and to introduce their children to the great works of civilization. Others were more concerned with needlework and table manners, with dancing and carriage. To attract a suitable husband, to be a credit to his success, and to keep a good house after marriage seemed the primary goal for educated girls. Education as a means to expand expérience and to enlarge the opportunities of an individual was not considered for this particular field of learning and teaching.

Benjamin Rush, the alleged truly American theorist of female education, brought home in his writing the new needs that the society had to meet. (39) In an agressive and competitive economic system some stability was needed next to each man to protect the wealth of the family; thus women needed training as stewards and guardians of their husbands' money. Without a docile servant class, American women needed special skills to manage their domestic work force. Fathers were no longer at home all the time, and the burdens of raising children fell particularly on women who had to recognize their new duty toward children and receive some training to perform the work. Education according to Rush and the other theorists would condition women to their limited sphere in the home.

Prior to the middle of the century the primary source of ideas to "define" woman in an objective way was in theology, where her secondary status was clearly established, but not without granting her equal access to the final and more important rewards in the hereafter. The change came first through imported and reprinted English essays, novels, and prescriptive books. Later educated colonial men (and, even later, colonial women) wrote their own contributions presenting their views on fashions, on what and how women thought, on the manners of courting these odd creatures and the doom of marrying one. Such manner of writing had developed earlier in England, particularly addressed to men, as the idea grew that gentility or whatever qualities were valued in society were not inherited but could be acquired. Men delighted in describing their ideal woman, an ideal which women were then expected to emulate. The Lady — stylish, learned within limits, inconspicuously managerial with her servants, and tolerant of masculine foibles — existed, in this literature, for a gentleman's pleasure and display. Everything about the feminine life turned around her ability to please her husband by standards that he established. Although it is unlikely that women lived out or up to this ideal, their self-conscious attention to an earthy, domestic ideal was assumed. The life of Nancy Shippen, an upper-class Philadelphia belle unhappily married by her father's wishes, reveals some of the practical pain of living through the literary images of female life. (40)

In the literary record the progress of femininity was not altogether smooth. Despite a few native articles, some individual reactions to the published descriptions of women and the tyrannical practice of men, and widespread knowledge of the ideas of Mary Wollstonecraft in her Vindication of the Rights of Women, no framework was established to integrate the individual responses. Women might use their learning for more than their domestic success and teach school or try to support themselves by writing, but those changes did not serve as a basis for challenging the essential limitations of women's lives. (41)

British "sentimental" novels were more widely read than vindications and feminist dialogues. They were tales of seduction and of battles for female virtue against lustful male tempters, in which sensibility and domestic love triumphed over the temptations of flesh and passion. (42) Samuel Richardson's Pamela won readers' hearts by her heroic struggles against her employer who was, as Pamela saw it, intent on seducing her. In a later American counterpart, The Coquette, the heroine tried to rebel against decorum but died ignominiously for her efforts. In each of these stories the essential human struggle was transferred from one with abstract evil to one between the sexes. And the first victim in that transformation was healthy sex.

The morality of sentimentalism, however, defined a series of almost religious tests faced only by women and met by successfully avoiding participation in a masculine world of physical and degrading passion. Not only was the course charted highly repressive of both men and women, but it also set the central conflict of life between the sexes. The success of this formula for the upper class continued well into the Nineteenth Century, but its rules and some of its best best-sellers made their appearance before the Revolution in the colonies.

By the end of the Eighteenth Century, the development of a market economy had begun to disrupt and transform the social relations of the family. Pre-industrial labor, as Marx noted, was based on a spontaneous or natural division of work within the family, depending on tradition and differences in age and sex to determine productive roles. The labor power of each individual member was only a "definite portion of the labor power of the family" expressed in products — whether crops, livestock, or clothing. By the first decades of the Nineteenth Century, the growth of manufacturing in home industries had already challenged the basis of these relations by widening the division of labor within the family, and by widening class divisions between families. The development of a true factory system was slow during this period: As late as 1810 two-thirds of the clothing and household textiles of persons living outside the cities was produced by family manufacture. Yet for women this shift was significant. As products formerly produced at home came to be accessible on the common market, whether textiles, (several) food products, or household supplies like soap and wax, the prestige of women's labor inevitably declined. Moreover, the increasing expression of products as commodities, defined not primarily by their use value but rather by their exchange value on the market, dichotomized those produced under market conditions by socially-organized labor (that is, almost entirely by men) and those produced privately for direct use (that is, substantially by women and children in the home). The consequent mystification of the exchange process within society was called by Marx commodity fetishism, for it apparently replaced the pre-industrial, direct relationship between producers with "material relationships between persons and social relationships between things." (43) In a society of commodities, the subordinate and secondary value of women's work and of women themselves was necessarily degraded. To replace the spontaneous and relatively egalitarian division of labor in pre-industrial society had come a mode of organization which far more than before thrust women into the role of caring for the home, while men engaged in activities to reshape the world. Furthermore women's participation in the market economy was mediated through their husbands, thus relegating their own class, status, or privilege to a social function of their husbands' work.

CUPID, AUCTIONEER.

Similarly, the development of industrial capitalism transformed the roles of the family. While previously the family structure had encompassed a variety of forms and functions, the Nineteenth Century family tended to contract into an increasingly privatized set of relations. The compartmentalization of work and home activities was accompanied by a re-evaluation of women (and especially leisured women) as the guardians of traditional moral values. Within rapid industrialization men were necessarily an increasing part of social changes while women were ironically sacrificed for the preservation of a home which had lost its functional role in the economy. The home became "woman's sphere", fixed in terms of an Ideal rather than a realistic evaluation of women's potential roles. The older traditions of feminine usefulness, strength, and duty were cast aside for moral and decorative functions, and subjugation to domesticity became the most revered feminine virtue. Men, on the other hand, commonly were expected to show the inevitable effects of materialistic and base associations of a business life: aggression, vulgarity, hardness, and rationality. (44)

From these new definitions of men and women flowed the reappraisal of the Lady. Earlier, certain colonial imitations of British writings on manners and morals prescribed the gentility, style, limited education, and tolerance that could be expected from women of fashion; and in the South, this Imperial practice was greatly emulated. But not until the late Eighteenth Century did the Lady become the paragon for all American women. Colonial women generally, by contrast, had been respected because of the strength and sensuality of their characters, attributes which complemented their participation in the rugged family arrangement of an agricultural and frontier economy. As late as 1890, nearly half of all American women lived and worked in this immediate social environment of a farm family, providing many necessities for the home through daily hard work. Yet the farm wife lost her cultural standing to a new sector of women: the wives and daughters of the rising entrepreneurs and merchant capitalists of the urban Northeast. This new sector remained a numerical minority, while its ethos became central to the American Woman's self-definition. Because of their class position, these women gained a hegemony over female cultural patterns never attained by the Eighteenth Century elites. Taste, customs, religious and political principles, and above all morality were reshaped in the Nineteenth Century through the cultural equivalent of the economic power that capitalists themselves wielded. Thus for all women in the society, this new ideal of femininity became the model, however unrealizable it might be in their own lives. (45)

The Nineteenth Century replacement for woman's earlier role in the family was in fact idleness, expressed positively as gentility. The cultural manifestation of this ideal has been aptly called "The Cult of True Womanhood", for the rigid standards held by society amounted to religious-like rites. The True Woman symbolized and actualized stability, expressed in her own cardinal virtues of piety, purity, submissiveness, and domesticity. Religious literature and feminine novels continued and broadened a chaste idealization begun in the Eighteenth Century, and the newer women's journals emphasized the superficial and fashionable glamor of woman's new image. The functional character of household life was in effect replaced with an ornamental attraction of the Fair Lady. Since industrial ethics defined work as masculine, labor of almost any kind was deemed unsuitable for this Lady. Even gardening, a family necessity and appropriate pastime for colonial women, was perceived as a violation of the dainty image. While some contemporary journalists approved of flower cultivation (itself an apparent reflection of Victorian femininity), the usual editorial position unqualifiedly condemned the sight of a virtuous women tending an onion patch. Thus woman was in a sense transformed from a human being into a living object of art, existing for the pleasure and pride of her husband. She was a creature of solely decorative worth, possessing a beauty which rested on her frailty, delicacy, purity, and even asexuality. Woman's aesthetic contribution was herself, with her sensuality sublimated in the same sense in which Freud suggested that all Art was sublimated sexuality. Feminine culture was a highly romanticized shell, containing an apparently barren interior. (46)

The new demands on woman were expressed in a subtle but significant language of repression, reflecting and reshaping the very conceptions of its users. During this period, for instance, the substitution of "limb" for leg or arm first appeared, to the point of ruthless false consciousness where a breast of chicken was renamed "light meat". Correct table manners forbade offering a lady the chicken's leg; rather, she always received the "bosom", a common euphemism for this part. In polite company women were referred to as "ladies" or "females", in deference to the risque connotations of the womb in the more familiar generic label. In the areas of children and family, linguistic repression demanded a sheer absence of some vital discussions. Woman's newer interest in child rearing and infant care was paralleled by an accompanying secrecy involving pregnancy. Despite the rich detail in women's magazines on children's clothing, stories, and habits, pregnancy itself was proscribed even in the intimate relations of mother and daughter. Gestation was hidden as long as possible and then obscured by the retiring of the prospective mother into confinement. At last, even the term "pregnant" was replaced with the more delicate indirect suggestions like "with child" or "woman's condition". Such conditions viewed as mysterious and wonderful beyond contemplation involved a new level of Victorian myth making, such as the strange appearance of the stork. (47)

New cultural restrictions in Victorian fashion dictated the spread of sexual repressiveness to all aspects of social life. Feminine passivity was ensured by clothing which, through the sheer weight and number of garments, literally enclosed women from the outside world and severely limited their physical mobility. The home was transformed from functionalism to the atmosphere of the showplace, an apt surrounding for the Victorian woman. Similarly, cleanliness standards of domestic life matched the purity associated with such a feminine setting. More subtle circumscriptions were easily noticed by European travelers such as Harriet Martineau, who, in her accounts of American society, frequently remarked on the relative severity of woman's domestic subjugation. Martineau implied that the discrepancy between the self-proclaimed democratic ideals of the Republic and the actual condition of American life was best exemplified in the treatment of

THE SPAHI

Spring wrap, made of very rich black silk, and trimmed with a deep twisted chenille fringe. The bonnet is composed of black Neapolitan and white silk figured with chenille.

women. Her books, which pointed to romantic chivalry as sheer substitution for real freedom were not considered proper reading materials for American ladies. With Mary Wollstonecraft and other rebels, she was vilified as a half-woman or mental hermaphrodite. (48)

Nineteenth Century repressive sexuality was in fact only one manifestation of the total work ethic that required suppression of all social values previously associated with leisure and enjoyment. While the appearance of new wealth nominally provided new free time, the ascending capitalist norms demanded an individual sacrifice to work, especially among male members of the rising entrepreneurial classes. The accompanying social relationships altered the fundamental conditions of life for man and woman, based substantially on a sexual polarity established through the industrial revolution. This polarity took various forms of expression. While sex came to be considered dirty, base, and vile, gratification became part of masculine culture, based on the materialistic functions of male social life. Woman's superior nature depended on the absence of painful and humiliating sexual participation, save for the satisfaction of her husband and the propagation of the race. Since the relationship between husband and wife was considered based on property, the male could easily acquire added property without seriously affecting his current holdings. Consequently, promiscuity was allowed only for men, who thereby participated in the rise of prostitution. (49)

Evidence of the effectiveness of female repression may be ascertained in the decline of the birth rate from 1820 to the end of the century. For a society lacking in knowledge of contraceptive measures, such decline could only signify the moderation of sexual relations for the prescribed bearers of society's children. Simultaneously the increasing urbanization and privatization of life had enhanced the importance of family individual members. The new status within the family tended to derive from individual worth rather than from group function. Thus while the existence of many children imposed a financial hardship upon the father's income, the single child became more precious and idealized. Childhood was extended to nearly marriageable age, since the presence of few children lowered the burden of dependency. Repression thereby was provided with a new outlet, if not a resolution, through the intensified relationship of mother and child. (50)

The double standard ironically intensified the sexual connotations of all social roles. Critics of Victorian society complained of an "over sexed" concern for life, referring not to the presence of uncontrollable urges but rather to the overly obsessive consciousness of the gender

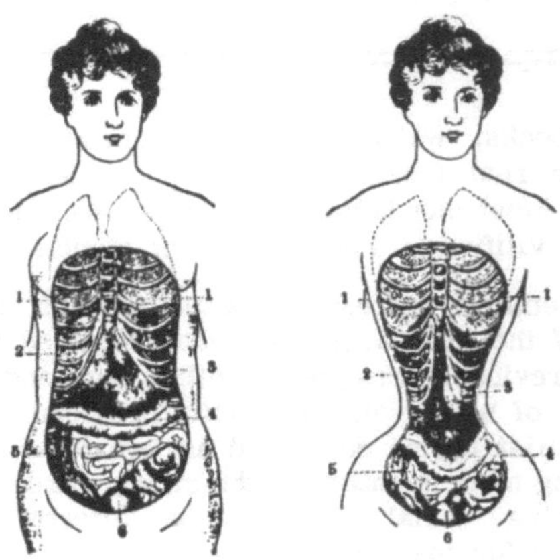

Above: Effects of lacing on the female body. (1-lungs, 2-liver, 3-stomach, 4-great-gut, 5-small intestine, 6-bladder).

of the individual. European travelers often noted the inhibiting effects of the separation of men and women in all public affairs and attributed the low level of American intellectual culture to the stifling effect of women's segregation. Yet isolation both allowed and forced an advanced sector to search out a special identity, to comprehend and finally act on it. The very nature of Victorian society encouraged women to regard themselves as a special group, as womanhood. (51)

◇

The assertion of woman's moral superiority had some important implications. For the first time, women as a group had been attributed an independent power of moral guardianship that, however intellectually degrading, contained the potential of a hidden challenge to woman's traditional political and social passivity. In community reforms, such as sewing and literary circles, middle-class women recognized the advantages in their forced isolation. Through closer contact with each other, these women gained a new sense of sorority for their common plight and their common aspirations. (52)

These early organizational forms provided models for the later women's rights movement. Political consciousness was added through women's participation in the major reform movements of the times, most of all Temperance and Abolitionism. Women gained organizational skills and a recognition that leadership was not an exclusively male capacity. By the end of the 1840s, many activists realized that they would not be satisfied with shaping the world indirectly through their moral influence, and demanded the right to personal liberty and control of their own property. The debates on slavery attended by women especially sharpened their awareness, since many of the issues posed concerning basic human rights carried implied analogies to women's deprivation and its basis in their material possession by white men. (53)

Most American women in the relatively leisured middle classes rejected the Feminist implications in the moral-guardian theory which would extend their traditional domain to social controversy. While these women shared with the feminists an uneasiness with the ideals of gentility and idleness, they responded to a new functionalism of woman's domestic role. The growth of "domestic science" for the home, the spread of women's teachers' schools, and the rationalization of new modes of child-rearing all provided reassertions in new forms of woman's distinct contribution to society. However the attempt to shore up family life and wifeliness through further training inevitably undercut the very aim of domestication, for a few women exposed to outside influences were bound to create, as did Jane Addams and other reformers, still newer patterns for women's social guardianship.

In a popular tract written in 1885, Mrs. A. J. Graves expressed a warning against the danger inherent in over-refinement. Luxurious habits were sapping the strength of the female character, drawing women out of their true sphere. "Home is our palladium" she explained, "our post of honor and of duty, and here we must begin the work of reform." Thus practicality became the counterpart of moral greatness.

But in order for women to accept this responsibility, other sources of activity had to be provided within the home. The new standards focused on women as supervisor of a renewed domestic life, responsible for quality of consumption and expanded childcare. Similarly, new standards of cleanliness arose in the Nineteenth Century, complemented by mechanical developments making housework less burdensome but not less time-consuming for the devoted housewife. Catherine Beecher, Emma Willard, and others publicized new forms of domestic science, stressing the demands of the newer business and scientific methods on woman's responsibilities. Meanwhile the influential Godey's Lady's Book mixed colorful fashions with detailed advice on domesticity. And various writers warned women against the "foreign influences" represented by the emerging servant class of Irish rather than native born women, resolving on the necessity of able women to manage without such help. (54)

In the early years of the Nineteenth Century literature addressed to women had come increasingly to focus on their motherhood, encouraging them to raise good, Christian citizens. This literature glorified the contributions mothers made to society by careful attention to the environment and potential of each child, thereby providing a career-like responsibility to the job. Theology slowly discovered children and offered a religious experience for young people different from that of their parents: Descriptions of their experience and the expectations set for them became less strict, and the Calvinist stress on their original sin was replaced by notions of childhood innocence. The psychology of John Locke and the pedagogues following him was transferred into popular writings about children, popularizing the impressionability of the human at birth and the need to implant the best hopes for each child and to discover the individual potential for each. These ideas were sharpened and their consequences for women deepened by the growing dichotomy established between men and women. Between passion and sensibility, mind and heart, the abstract and absent father and the leisured and confined mother, the gaps grew enormously. Women came to be viewed as peculiarly suited by nature and training to care for infants and their needs in the home. Culture was considered a feminine province in the world at large, but within each family respect for culture and communication of values was directly manifested by the relations between mother and child. The biological function of motherhood became elevated into a sophisticated and future-oriented definition of woman's social impact. The growing set of ideas with a wide range of detail about home, food, health, toys, clothing, and religious training was disseminated almost universally in sermons, women's magazines, books, and newspapers. (55)

Meanwhile, special schools had been established, such as Mount Holyoke in 1837, for the purposes of domestic science and the care and teaching of children. The very existence of these schools helped to legitimatize women's education, and led to the establishment of the first true women's colleges, such as Vassar in 1867. Women who graduated from the colleges or the transformed special schools became the first professionals and many of the leading feminists of the late Nineteenth Century. Thus, the concern for rationalizing women's domestic role had at last been transformed, in part at least, to its opposite. Woman's moral guardianship was re-interpreted by such reformers as Florence Kelley and Vida Scudder to be responsibility for influencing the organic evolution of society. (56)

By mid-century, women's roles in the modern class structure of America were becoming clear. The needs of the increasingly complex society called into existence a new middle class of doctors, lawyers, and other professionals. In the main, women attained this status vicariously through marriage; but in part, women too shared in the increase of opportunities for direct upward mobility through a variety of experiences and institutions including women's colleges. At the same time, a proletarianization process began on a wide scale for formerly rural populations, urban dwellers, and new immigrants. Here too women were for the most part wives, but with increasing frequency industrial workers for at least a portior of their lives.

At the beginning of industrial capitalism in America, women constituted a basic industrial work-force. As early as 1775, women had been employed during the first widespread use of spinning jennies. Government officials and entrepreneurs alike assumed women were the best candidates for service in this promising sector, in part because work in the developing textile industry involved no encroachment on traditional male-dominated trades or crafts. Women were similarly encouraged to enter early factories because their presence as a surplus labor force allowed men and boys to labor in agricultural production or in the exploration of the West. The first women workers were typically recruited from the town poor-roles, and for several decades thereafter orphans, widows, and unmarried women formed the ranks of the unskilled industrial laborers. (57)

New England textile mills provided the first opportunity for large numbers of women to work outside their immediate families in non-domestic labor. By the 1820s and 1830s, thousands of young women were attracted by the lure of the factory as an alternative to patriarchical farm life, and they traveled to the company towns of Massachusetts and Rhode Island searching employment. On the other hand, due to the migration of young men to the West, Eastern women between the ages of fifteen and thirty greatly outnumbered their male counterparts and were forced to provide their own living as single working girls. Thus the choice for factory labor was, for many, more apparent than real, especially when faced with the alternative of servitude in a brother's family. Moreover, the prevailing secondary value attached to woman's work restricted women from receiving an education or training to enable them to compete in professional or skilled occupations. Nevertheless, their preference for self-sufficiency obscured this discrepancy, and women competed with one another to gain entry into these new occupations. (58)

The early mills commonly operated under the Waltham system, a form of paternalism which provided the women with boarding houses and a strict code of moral conduct. Despite the lack of individual freedom, the mill environment offered a chance to live in a community of women, to accumulate a small savings from earnings, and to set a pattern for independent living. Although the hours were long, the work was not essentially hard, involving comparatively much free time and allowing the operative a chance for conversation and companionship. The first factories had not yet systematized the work process, and therefore production — although often experimental, sporadic, and irregular — had not yet been integrated into a rational routine of labor. Consequently the discipline of the wage-earner was far from complete. The early strikes were usually spontaneous outbursts against announcements (or even rumors) of changed policies: wage-cuts, speed ups, or lengthening of hours. Most important, this semi-agricultural factory population could respond to intolerable changes in working conditions and periods of unemployment by returning to the family farm. (59)

These first mills attracted attention for their superficially idyllic conditions. European visitors who were familiar with the grim plight characteristic of British textile industries marveled over the quaint towns operated by the mill owners and over the gentility and beauty of the young operatives. They were equally fascinated with the Lowell Offering, a journal devoted to the poetry written by the mill girls. However, these European promoters often missed the subtle fact that the Offering was published and funded by the employers to advertise their enterprise rather than to popularize the cultural achievements of their operatives. Conditions in the mills were tolerable, and wages were high enough to enable these early industrial workers to set aside a small savings. After four or five years of service, most women left the industry permanently: Some moved West where women (especially teachers) were in demand; some secured an education to set themselves on a brighter path; and others retreated to a life of alleged marital bliss.

By the 1830s, industrialism was developing rapidly, introducing new social and mechanical changes that would fundamentally alter the work situation. Technological improvements in machinery allowed greater efficiency and established the contest for speeding up the work process. The new ethos of discipline destroyed the aura of gentility of earlier days, making the mill girl's position less appealing for a rising middle class of women. The depressions of the 1830s and Western competition destroyed a large number of New England family farms, forcing many daughters into a permanent factory population. Similarly, the Irish immigration beginning in the mid-1830s introduced a new class of women into the mills. Thus, while factory conditions deteriorated (more looms to tend, speeding up, more noise, dust, longer hours, et cetera) the women who entered the textile industries represented a transformed working population and took these jobs for their lives' work. Labor in the mill became a permanent experience and was no longer the first step toward a broader range of opportunities.

By mid-century, the growing work-force of women had developed an internal hierarchy. While the unskilled, industrial workers showed life styles and attitudes characteristic of the proletariat, women in the growing professions such as teaching and nursing set themselves apart from their sisters. Moreover, the dichotomy between women who worked and those who remained at home was accentuated by the culturally-defined "proper sphere" of women. Thus, while a working woman of colonial American had been considered on her own merits, by 1850-1860 her counterpart was no longer perceived as an individual attempting to earn a living; rather, she was likely to be judged as a woman who had stepped out of her place and who had thereby invited negative evaluation from her society. (60)

Middle-class women who had gained their new leisure in part from the sweat of their working-class sisters customarily returned the favor with deprecation. Although the realization of True Womanhood was possible only as an aspiration for most women, its acceptance by the influential and educated groups in society furthered the degradation of lower-class women beyond their physical exploitation. A middle-class or upper-class woman who was privileged to work in the privacy of her own home was spared from the spectacle of her indelicacy, while her laboring counterpart was easily identifiable by appearance, dress, manner, and attitude toward life.

Working-class women were inevitably marked by their participation in activities considered masculine. They shared with men a life in the world of business, a material existence which seemed inherently lacking in virtue and purity. In a Victorian culture, class stratification was culturally broadened to divide women into The Good and The Bad. Because the American ideal of femininity was so widely held, even minor deviations from the image such as dress, carriage, speech, and manners placed lower-class girls outside the pale of respectability. For their part, working women had only one advantage: They alone retained a right to sexual fulfillment. But without birth control and general sexual freedom, this right constituted a negative differentiation. Lower-class white and black women became recognized as ideal objects of sexual exploitation, thus preserving the most precious virtue of the Fair Lady. Most lower-class women who entered prostitution did so because the way of life appealed to them, particularly as an alternative to the tedious and restrictive patterns of factory work. Meanwhile, middle-class reformers organized into social purity associations designed to "save" women from a life of degradation. Reformers were usually careful to attribute the rise of the Social Evil to the new industrial and urban order rather than to the individual wickedness of the prostitutes, but in general ascetic sexual standards were considered the apprropriate alternative. Interest in prostitutes was usually limited to charity orphanages and female reform schools designed to educate lower-class children into the ethics of self-control and repressive sexuality. For the individual prostitute, "rehabilitation" was thought unlikely, for Victorian morality was based on a standard which considered the woman who had lost her virginity as "ruined".(61)

With their own particular needs and desires, working women discerned only slight significance in the demands of organized middle class women. The ballot, legal rights, and other social reform issues seemed irrelevant or secondary compared to the more pressing problems of daily life. As they expressed to social workers later, they wished the "secret" of preventing contraception, and when told it was abstinence, scoffed at such a solution as unreal. They envied the

leisure of women who complained of boredom in their Victorian houses. And they viewed from afar the women's educational movement, designed for those of a privileged class.

Working women shared with their men the opportunities for earning money and participating in social production. Consequently, their first expression of feminist consciousness was determined by their status as a worker. By and large, they tended to join men in the ranks of organized labor and experienced their own sense of strength and power in trade unions. During the late 1830s, factory girls became involved in the first genuine trade-union protests against the fundamental technological changes in the industrialization process. The formation of a Factory Girls Association which soon attracted a membership of 2500 marked an organizational stage which transcended the spontaneous forms of earlier protests and strikes against employers. By the late 1840s, the Lowell Female Reform Association was strong enough to buy out the Voice of Industry, a paper which had long benefitted from female participation. The Voice projected a profound critique of True Womanhood, urging its female readers to attend the meetings of the New England Workingmen's Association "without false delicacy". Thus, in 1848, while their middle-class sisters met at Seneca Falls to discuss property rights and voting discrimination, advanced factory operatives such as Sarah Bagley and Huldah Stone directed their attention to subjects of wages and hours. They realized their wages were three to four times lower than those of men working in comparable jobs due to the inferiority ascribed to their position as workers. As working women, they pronounced a total rejection of the ideal woman which prevented their full participation and remuneration in industry. They rejected notions of feminine frailty, of weakness, of social purity and moral superiority, and of passivity. (62)

Nineteenth Century industrialization and urbanization had led to a fragmentation of social relations between classes and between men and women, transforming the form and content of women's roles. From the natural association of the family within pre-industrial farm life, American women passed to newer and more specialized relationships with each other through the situation of factory labor and the growth of political and social organizations. Gentility had become a widespread ideal, but even where realizable in middle-class and upper-class homes, it was undermined by the activist re-definition of moral guardianship. Working-class women, a marginal force in the early decades of the century, were by its end beginning to discover their existence as a class and their own special problems. In the Twentieth Century these changes in women's conditions were to become fully developed, intensifying for a period those class and generational differences which separated women from each other.

Several major themes emerge in Twentieth Century women's history. First, because of the breakdown of the organic family unit in which men, women, and children shared productive economic functions, women (particularly middle-class women) became society's primary

consumers. At the same time, structural changes in the economy and two world wars brought ever-increasing numbers of women into the labor force. Work for women, including married middle-class women, became respectable and desirable in the Twentieth Century. Despite dramatic changes in the social and economic conditions affecting women and altering their role in society, however, the ideological gestalt of assumptions and stereotypes concerning the nature of woman and the role she was to play in society — the Cult of True Womanhood — proved remarkably adaptable to Twentieth Century conditions. Ideas about woman's sexuality have changed strikingly in the last seventy years, but the basic traditional values associated with woman as the protector of moral values and guardian of the home which developed in the ambiance of Nineteenth Century industrialism persisted into the Twentieth Century. This traditional conception of woman's role is integrally linked to women's economic function of consumption. The mature corporate economy has depended on the consumption patterns of married middle-class women buying for their homes. The "feminine mystique" was not the creation of post-World War II advertisers, social scientists, and educators, but rather was the updated version of the Cult of True Womanhood which was in evidence throughout the Twentieth Century. Finally, most of the Twentieth Century has been marked by the lack of both a feminist movement and a strong feminist consciousness. Much has been written about the nature of women and about their fulfillment, but almost invariably it has been phrased in individualistic terms. After the decline of organized feminism with the passage of the Nineteenth Amendment in 1920, women have generally had little sense of their common difficulties and their collective power, and thus have attempted individual solutions to problems of identity, sexuality, work, and self-fulfillment.

The fact that middle-class women became America's primary consumers in the first decades of the Twentieth Century is enormously important in understanding women's recent history. The same industrial developments which broke up the organic family unit by sending men into factory employment also affected women's traditional duties in the home. What women had once produced in their own homes they now bought. By 1900 most of the items which women had customarily "put up" could be purchased as canned goods. By 1910, for example, the mass consumption economy had fully developed and technological changes greatly increased American industry's production capacity. An even greater number of products were designed for use in the home. Appliances such as washing machines and electric refrigerators came into wide use in the early years of the Twenties; electric and gas stoves followed a few years later. (63)

These structural and economic changes did not, in and of themselves, transform women's historical experience. Rather, these economic developments further altered and fragmented the relationships between men and women and between middle-class women and working-class sisters. Men and working-class women, unlike middle-class women, worked outside the home in what society deemed productive occupations. As Margaret Bengston has stated, a capitalistic society honors the production of exchange value, but regards the production of use value as non-productive because it does not receive financial remuneration. Hence, because women have not been paid for the work they have done in the home, society has judged such work to be devoid of productive value. The middle-class housewife's work has been separated further from the "productive" work of men because it is essentially unspecialized and unregimented. Whereas industrial production became increasingly specialized and routinized in the late Nineteenth and Twentieth Centuries, the work women did in the home underwent little structural transformation. In addition, unlike the "real" and important world of industrial production, woman's work has been geared not to clock time, but to task orientation. This fact has made housework even more of an anomaly in a society with norms based on industrial production methods. (64)

Middle-class women have been separated from their working-class sisters also in that modern technology gave middle-class women an abundance of leisure. The maturation of the corporate economy was accompanied by a growing recognition of the fact that housework no longer needed to be a full-time occupation. Many social commentators in the first decades of the Twentieth Century described the middle-class woman's "restlessness". In the early 1920s, psychotherapists and sociologists increasingly wrote about the "nervous housewife" faced with an overabundance of spare time and feelings of inadequacy,

boredom, and uselessness. Alice Beal Parsons's 1924 study Woman's Dilemma delineated the frustrations and tensions of the middle-class housewife who had nothing to do. Her analysis was strikingly similar to works of the 1950s and 1960s. Other social theorists and feminists in the early part of the century decried the middle-class woman's lack of a productive economic function. Simon Patten stated that "once the household industries gave to the staying-home woman a fair share of the labor, but today they are few and the 'homemaker' suffers under enforced idleness, ungratified longing, and non-productive time killing ...." (65) Feminists such as Olive Schreiner and Lorinne Pruette argued that middle-class women were social parasites, doomed to a symbiotic existence dependent on the more productive members of society. (66)

The middle-class woman's unused energy and tensions found outlets in the feminist movement, in social reform and volunteer activities, in psychoanalysis, and in employment outside the home. Increasingly, she defined personal liberation in terms of productive and meaningful work in the world of men. World War I marked the large-scale movement of middle-class women, including married women, into the labor force. By the mid-1960s, over a third of all married women were employed. In part, this shift was due to the role of the world wars in forcing acceptance of married women workers and making work outside the home a respectable avenue for self-fulfillment. War work, however, was generally industrial in nature and was usually regarded as a temporary patriotic duty rather than as a permanent career. This was one of the factors involved in the temporary shrinkage of the number of middle-class women in the labor force after both wars. More important than the wars in changing the nature of middle-class women's employment outside the home were the structural changes in the economy which resulted in the increasing emphasis on service industries employing large numbers of "white-collar" workers. The number of telephone operators, secretaries, typists, clerks, and stenographers rose phenomenally in the 1920s, thus shaping the contours for the majority of middle-class women's employment patterns since that decade. Other well-educated middle-class women trained for careers in professions traditionally filled by men. It is interesting, however, that proportionately fewer women trained for professional careers after the Twenties than in the two decades before the First World War. In the early decades of the Twentieth Century, to train for a professional career usually involved a conscious choice to forsake marriage. In the 1920s, younger women, alienated by the older feminists' denial of sexuality, were more attracted to occupations they felt could be easily combined with marriage and children. (67)

Although an abundant amount of literature was devoted to problems facing women who wanted to combine marriage with a job, very few collective solutions were proposed. The responsibility for being able to manage what amounted to two jobs at once fell on the individual woman alone. This reliance on individual solutions to solve problems working women faced in managing a home and a job was evident even during the world wars, when the media and the state encouraged married women to work outside the home. During World War II, for instance, a propaganda tract urging women to work as a patriotic duty offered only individual solutions for the problems involved in combining two jobs. Women were told to budget their time better, move to smaller homes, and buy prepared food. (68)

Despite the fact that many middle-class women entered the labor force during the Twentieth Century, their experience differed in many respects from that of working-class women. Whether a middle-class woman worked as a file clerk or studied to be a physician, work was a consciously-made choice and an effort to find self-fulfillment and independence, not an economic necessity. Exactly the reverse has been true of the Twentieth Century working-class woman, who has entered the industrial work force because it was the only choice open to her. With the shift from industrial home work to factory machine production in the late Nineteenth and early Twentieth Centuries, an ever-increasing number of women moved into industrial employment. Such factory jobs were hardly liberating: The hours were long (often well over sixty a week in the years before protective legislation), the working conditions poor, and sexist discrimination widespread. Women generally earned about half of men's wages for the same work. In addition, women, like blacks, were often assigned tasks which were considered too degrading for white men to accept, such as scrubbing the factory floor. (69) Working women's conditions were exacerbated by the scant attention paid them by the organized labor movement. Although the American

Federation of Labor passed annual resolutions calling for organization of women workers, no action was taken until well into the century. Women workers in a number of industries formed their own unions, with the help of organizations like the Women's Trade Union League, but these unions affected only a small minority. Unions considered women poor risks. Despite the efforts of groups like the Working Girls' Societies and the Women's Trade Union League to show otherwise the traditional belief that women were invariably temporary workers and the notion that a woman must only be working for "pin money" or out of selfish disregard for her familial responsibilities remained strong for many years in the Twentieth Century. Most men union organizers considered unions incompatible with "femininity". "Do they not tend to unsex them and make them masculine?" an AFL official asked Agnes Nestor, president of the women glove makers' union. (70) Thus working-class women, despite the fact that they were living contradictions to the "Cult of True Womanhood" ideal of frail, passive, and delicate femininity, suffered from the imposition of the same stereotype. (71)

Not surprisingly, working-class women who have worked out of necessity throughout the Twentieth Century have generally regarded marriage as liberation from the tedium and exhaustion of industrial employment. In addition, because working-class women have viewed work as an economic necessity and not as a kind of luxury, they have been more interested in collectively organizing to change the conditions under which they have worked rather than relying totally on individual solutions. By contrast, middle-class white-collar employees are only beginning to organize around common demands and in resistance to common forms of exploitation.

The differences in economic roles and personal expectations between working-class women and middle-class women were also reflected in the feminist movement in the early part of the century. Working-class women were generally apathetic to the goals of the organized feminist movement. They did not see the movement as furthering their collective aims of better working conditions and unionism. The National American Women's Suffrage Association, for example, was at best indifferent to the unionization of women workers, and some important suffragists were openly hostile toward organized labor. Then too, working women generally did not regard obtaining the vote as a tangible improvement in their condition, while middle-class suffragists often saw the vote as the only important goal of the movement. For them, suffrage was an end in itself. (72)

Women in the organized feminist movement accepted the economic transformation of middle-class women from co-producer to consumer and incorporated it into their thinking about their own lives and about their place in society. Some hailed woman's new role and the technological forces that had created it as the final prerequisite for the liberation of women from household drudgery. Charlotte Perkins Gilman, for example, urged that technological developments and labor saving devices be employed to liberate women from the unspecialized and inefficient ways housework was organized: Community kitchens and technological innovations would revolutionize the organization of the home and leave women free for other pursuits. Early Twentieth Century feminists combined this acceptance of consumerism with an acceptance of the Nineteenth Century ideal of woman as imbued with fixed and unchanging moral and biological characteristics and responsibilities to care for children and the home.

No longer advancing the individualistic political and legal arguments of Nineteenth Century feminism, early Twentieth Century feminists argued that women were different, morally and socially. For precisely these reasons should women be allowed to vote; the political system needed women's influence. Spokesmen in the movement constantly stressed that the home and the community were interrelated and interdependent, and that to women as buyers fell the responsibility for insuring that the work they used to perform inside the home was now performed efficiently, safely, and equitably outside it. Accordingly, women campaigned for pure food legislation and for other consumer oriented reforms. (73)

The arguments employed by organized feminism early in the Twentieth Century were not only ahistorical; they also disregarded many of the contemporary trends involving women—particularly the increasing participation of working-class women in the industrial labor force. Although some organizations within the feminist movement attempted to bridge the gap between working-class women and their middle-class counterparts, and although there was a great deal of talk about "sisterhood" within the movement, early Twentieth Century feminism remained tied to its middle-class moorings. Generally, attempts at cross-class co-operation were based on urging middle-class women to use their buying power as a way to help their working-class sisters. The consumer league movement, the union label organizations, and the women's labor groups like the Women's Trade Union League stressed that women controlled their communities' purchasing power, and thus should be knowledgeable about labor conditions. For example, middle class women were urged to insist on the waistmaker's union label when buying shirtwaists: "Now is the time for the women of New York, Philadelphia, and in fact everywhere where American shirtwaists are worn, to rise in their might and demonstrate that with them bargain hunting can be subordinated to principle and that they have said goodby to the products of the sweatshop....Friends, let us stop talking about sisterhood and MAKE SISTERHOOD A FACT." (74) But despite some earnest efforts, serious cross-class co-operation within the feminist movement failed.

The feminist movement's emphasis on the middle-class woman's consumer role, its acceptance of the basic Nineteenth Century ideal of women as morally superior to men, and its single-minded emphasis on winning the vote help to explain not only the movement's failure to reach working-class women, but also its increasing inability to move beyond its immediate goal of the franchise. By the time the Nineteeenth Amendment was enacted into law, the vote was no longer a means to an end, it was the only end most suffragists envisioned. Most of the women who had been involved in the movement turned to non-feminist political activity in organizations such as the League of Women Voters, a group which prided itself on its lack of "feminist consciousness".

In the years after 1920 feminism as a movement and as consciousness became increasingly isolated. The fortunes of the National Woman's Party in the 1920s tell us a great deal about why feminist consciousness and a strong, organized movement declined so radically in the years after the suffrage amendment. Early in the 1920s, the NWP began to campaign for an equal-rights amendment to the Constitution, arguing that legislation was the only way to achieve equality for women. Legislation had been successful in getting women the vote; when it was apparent that the vote was not enough, what was obviously necessary was more legislation. In this sense, the NWP was a victim of functional fixedness: It saw the solution to women's role in society solely in political terms.

The NWP's single-minded emphasis on the proposed equal-rights amendment alienated working-class women and labor organizations, who viewed the proposed amendment as destructive of their efforts for protective labor legislation. (75) In addition, the NWP and feminists such as Charlotte Perkins Gilman and Carrie Chapman Catt, who lived and wrote in the 1920s, were unable to appeal to young women. The Students' Council of the Woman's Party, for example, organized in 1924, had fifteen charter members. It quickly faded away. (76) Much of the reason for the lack of appeal that the feminist tradition had for young women lay in changing attitudes toward feminine sexuality. In this respect feminists accepted the "Cult of True Womanhood" stereotype of woman as devoid of sexual needs, and thus somehow more pure. Liberation for Nineteeenth Century feminists, then, included the right to abstain from sexual relations. By 1920, ideas about sexuality had changed and feminine sexuality was openly discussed. What was really "new" about the "New Woman" early in the century was not so much her desire for meaningful work outside the home as her affirmation of sexuality and her search for sexual fulfillment. In contrast, National Woman's Party members and other feminists decried the New Morality. Not surprisingly, the young women of the Twentieth Century did not respond to the traditional feminist ideology which stressed sexual repression and denial. (77)

The new ideas and attitudes about sex did not emerge suddenly. By the turn of the century, changing ideas about women's sexuality were evident in the novels of writers such as Kate Chopin, Robert Herrick, and Theodore Dreiser. The life styles of women such as Mabel Dodge Luhan and Edna Saint Vincent Millay, although their number was very small before the First World War, were indicative of social change. Freudian psychology was one of the factors which contributed to changing notions about feminine sexuality, particularly because of Freud's emphasis on the centrality of sex in human motivation. Other factors were important as well. New attitudes toward feminine sexuality emerged in a larger social context of the dramatic transformation of marriage and the family. The contours of family relations have been changing rapidly throughout the Twentieth Century. In an industrial, urbanized society, a large number of children was no longer an economic asset. This fact may account for the relatively rapid acceptance which middle-class families gave to the birth-control movement. Although Margaret Sanger's early efforts in the years before World War I met with public indignation, by the 1920s young middle-class women approved of contraceptive use. (78)

The changes in ideas and norms surrounding feminine sexuality have generally been regarded by women and by students of women's history as totally liberating, For most of the Twentieth Century women have not had to endure the sexual repression that marked Nineteenth Century Victorian ideas. On the other hand, the new definition of woman's sexuality has divided women from each other throughout the Twentieth Century. With the reaffirmation of feminine sexuality, the traditional notion of sisterhood broke down. In the Nineteenth Century, many women, because they accepted the societal view of themselves as more moral, pure, and pious than men, often found emotional fulfillment in friendships with other women. Women in the Twentieth Century learned that they were expected to have emotional attachments only to men. In this way, because women competed on an individual basis for men's attention, the possibilities for women coming together to develop feminist consciousness and realize their own power lessened.

In addition, the new definition of feminine sexuality further divided middle-class and working-class women. In the Nineteenth Century, women had been divided in similar fashion, but with some important variations. The working-class woman in the previous century was not affected by many of the repressive aspects of Victorian sexuality. Working-class women were expected to enjoy sexual relations. In the Twentieth Century, however, working-class women generally have not shared the personally liberating aspects of the New Morality. They were not affected by the tenets of Freudian psychology and the open discussion of sexual matters that the popularization of Freud's theories engendered. Often, because of religious sanctions or lack of knowledge, they have not had access to new, effective methods of birth control. Studies such as Mirra Komarovsky's Blue Collar Marriage document views on sexuality marked by fear of unwanted pregnancies, ignorance of contraceptive techniques, and often unfulfilling sexual relations. (79)

One is faced with an apparent paradox when studying Twentieth Century women's history. On one hand, ever increasing numbers of women, particularly married women, worked outside the home. In addition, for the middle-class woman at least, sexuality and the biological aspects of motherhood were no longer unspeakable topics. On the other hand, throughout the Twentieth Century, social theorists, psychologists, educators, advertising executives, and clergymen have told women that their "natural" place is in the home and that their "real" job is motherhood. In other words, the Twentieth Century has had its own updated version of the "Cult of True Womanhood".

The reason for perpetuating this traditional ideal in spite of its increasing incongruity with historical reality has been a simple one: As consumers, middle-class women have filled a vital and indispensable role in an economy based on mass consumption. In order to carry out this prescribed role, women had to be educated to accept their economic function.

The set of stereotypes and assumptions which has characterized most of Twentieth Century thinking on woman's nature and role might best be defined by Betty Friedan's term "the feminine mystique" to distinguish it from the Nineteenth Century "Cult of True Womanhood" ideal. (80) Twentieth Century thinking about women has differed from the previous century in several important respects. Although women were still taught that their place was primarily in the home, a new rationale had to be formulated to replace the obsolete reasons and theories behind the Nineteenth Century "Cult of True Womanhood". In addition, because historical changes had taken away any productive economic and social reasons why women should stay in the home, women needed to be invested with a contemporary sense of importance and productivity.

The Nineteenth Century ideal of woman was based in large part on biological arguments: Women were inferior biologically to men — they were weak, frail, incapable of strenuous mental and physical exertion. This biological "anatomy is destiny" argument was carried into the Twentieth Century in the writings of such theorists as Havelock Ellis. Ellis, in Man and Woman, expressed the view that biological differences were fundamental in determining the different social roles of men and women. He stressed that women's capacities did not "limit" her, but rather especially ordained her for certain functions. Ellis bolstered his thesis with an evolutionary biological schema based on painstaking anatomical measurements. He concluded that women were infantile types and, hence, better fitted by nature to take care of children. Ellis also theorized that women's "functional periodicity" made them vulnerable to dramatic and dangerous mood changes because they always lived on the "upward or downward slope of a curve". (81) Early in the century, Alice Beal Parsons and Leta Hollingsworth made impressive refutations of Ellis's theories. Parsons pointed out that Ellis's measurements had no statistical validity. Hollingsworth, a social psychologist, brought forth experimental evidence which revealed that women did not have a period of maximum efficiency or an emotional cycle. These new theorists stressed the importance of individual differences and concluded that women varied, just as men varied, from individual to individual. Hence one could not draw conclusions about woman's pre-ordained role from biological evidence. (82)

Strictly biological arguments could no longer be used convincingly to bolster the "Cult of True Womanhood". In their place rose a new internal, psychological rationale for explaining woman's nature and justifying her traditional role in society. The Twentieth Century affirmation of feminine sexuality was essential to the psychological rationale behind the "feminine mystique". Whereas in the Nineteenth Century women were defined — and defined themselves — by careful avoidance of sexuality, in the present century women have often been defined with reference to their sexuality alone. Sexuality has been elevated above any other factor in explaining woman's nature. In one sense, this recognition of feminine sexuality has made women more similar to men: They both have been recognized as sexual beings. But because sexuality has been isolated as the only major factor necessary to explain women's motivations and behavior, women have been further separated from male-oriented society. The popular psychological construct of women as innately passive, narcissistic, and masochistic parallels the Nineteenth Century biological argument that women were innately weak and frail. Both construct a picture of woman which is fixed and eternal and bears no relation to cultural factors. Many Twentieth Century psychologists have stressed that women find fulfillment only through marriage and motherhood, and that deviation from these norms indicates psychological maladjustment. Hence, to be a feminist has meant being "maladjusted" sexually. This emphasis on individual sexual and psychological adjustment has been another important factor in the decline of feminist consciousness which has characterized the years from 1920 to the very recent present. (83)

Two societal institutions which have had a major influence on the lives of women in the Twentieth Century — advertising and education — have done much to instill the view that woman's psychological fulfillment and "adjustment" depended on her natural role in the home. In addition, both advertising and educational institutions have attempted to stress the importance of the middle-class woman's roles as mother, housewife, and consumer in an effort to invest women with a sense of productivity. Much of the advertising directed to women in the Twentieth Century, for example, has attempted semantically to turn consumption into production. The housewife managing her home has been compared to the businessman running his firm. "Through her dealings as business manager of the home," one advertisement in the 1920s read, "the modern woman brings sound commercial sense to bear on her judgment of a Ford closed car." "Retail buying is a productive act," wrote one praiser of the new economic order. (84)

Feminists such as Charlotte Perkins Gilman had welcomed the appearance of new appliances and technological improvements as a way to help solve the dilemma of the married woman who wanted a career. Advertisements and women's colleges emphasized that women now had time to "put motherhood first", not embark on a professional career outside the home. In the Twentieth Century homemaking and motherhood became specialized professions for the first time. At the same time that technological developments made it possible for women to spend less time at housework, cultural values demanded that they spend more time perfecting household arts.

Education for women changed in the early Twentieth Century to stress the professional aspects of woman's role in the home. Educators began to emphasize that woman's economic role was different from man's and that she should be educated accordingly. (85) Home economics and child-study courses were introduced into college curricula. It was unfortunate, thought many educators and social critics, that women's education gave the impression that homemaking required no special preparation. Preparation for homemaking as a profession was conceived to give the position dignity. Women should know how to buy and prepare food, sew, and manage a well-run, attractive home. Such thinking represented a complete shift in the original rationale for education of women, which was to give women the same education that men could obtain. Some institutions continued to emphasize educating women to break away from their traditional role, but increasingly more common in the 1920s was the philosophy that women should be educated for their traditional status rather than encouraged to change it. (86)

Hence, despite economic, technological, and social changes, the ideological assumptions affecting women have remained strikingly familiar. Throughout the Twentieth Century, society has defined women in terms of distinct and limiting stereotypes, despite those stereotypes' increasing irrelevance to changing economic and social realities. For the most part, American women in the Twentieth Century have accepted and internalized the "feminine mystique", or have reacted to it as individuals. Because women have been divided from one another on class lines, because the Twentieth Century definition of sexuality has discouraged the concept of collective sisterhood, and because in the years since the early part of the century, women, like men, have been educated to act and think in a framework of individualism, feminism has been in decline throughout most of the century. Only in very recent years has feminist consciousness re-emerged. Like the women's rights movement of the late Nineteenth Century and early Twentieth Century, contemporary feminism arose out of a larger social and political movement. Unlike the first movement, however, the present movement is attempting not only to understand and change the facts of middle class women's condition, but also to understand and surmount effects of class division and social fragmentation.

"Woman's awareness of herself," Simone de Beauvoir has noted, "is not exclusively defined by her sexuality; it reflects a situation that depends on the economic organization." In the course of three and a half centuries, that awareness was reflected through the prisms of a new and labor-scarce colonial society, a transitional Victorian industrializing society, and a commodity-rich but labor-alienated modern Capitalist society. There has been no single definition of woman, but rather a succession of definitions in which self-conscious feminism has been provoked, transformed or suppressed, and provoked again. At the epochally Last Moment of the current order, the self-consciousness has gained new heights and promises to reach still further. Yet, for this to happen, women must comprehend the interior and exterior worlds of that growth, both the heightened perceptions of self and the heightened contradictions of a society whose most basic problems remain unresolved (and, to that degree, endanger all of women's progress). It is hoped that this essay will have made some small positive contribution to that comprehension.

◆◆◆ Footnotes

1. Mary Beard: Woman as Force in History (New York, 1946).

2. Juliet Mitchell: Review of The Petticoat Rebellion, in New Statesman (August 4, 1867), as cited in Margaret George: One Woman's Situation: A Study of Mary Wollstonecraft (Urbana, Illinois, 1970).

3. Branka Magas: "Sex Politics: Class Politics", New Left Review, Number 66 (March-April, 1971), Page 89.

4. Margaret George's discussion of this point is primarily in her preface, but her conclusions underly the whole book. We have found this discussion very useful. We are indebted as well to Branka Magas: "Sex Politics: Class Politics", previously cited, and Gerda Lerner for their critiques of the oppression model as a framework for historical methodology. See especially Gerda Lerner: "New Approaches to the Study of Women in American History", Journal of Social History III (Fall 1969), Pages 53-62.

5. Philippe Aries: Centuries of Childhood: A Social History of Family Life, translated by Robert Baldick (New York, 1962).

6. Simone de Beauvoir: The Second Sex (Modern Library Edition, New York, 1969), Page 129.

7. Jeannine Hensley (editor): Works of Anne Bradstreet (Cambridge, 1967).

8. Branka Magas: "Sex Politics: Class Politics", previously cited, Pages 90-91.

9. Eleanor Flexner: Century of Struggle: The Woman's Rights Movement in the United States (New York, 1968), and Mildred Adams: The Right to Be People (1967). Other studies which concentrate chiefly on the suffrage movement are Abbie Graham: Ladies in Revolt (New York, 1934), Emily Taft Douglas: Remember the Ladies (1966), and Olivia E. Coolidge: Women's Rights: The Suffrage Movement in America, 1848-1920 (1966). Over one half of Eleanor Flexner's Century of Struggle, probably the best known and most widely read general study of American women, is devoted to the suffrage campaign, and the last quarter of the book is devoted to the twelve years before the vote was won. Flexner's work is a detailed and valuable narrative study of the women's rights movement from its beginnings in the abolitionist movement through the passing of the Nineteenth Amendment. Flexner recognizes the importance of events and developments outside the scope of the movement, but, generally speaking, these aspects of women's history gain significance in her book only through their relation to the suffrage movement. The chapter on working women, for example, deals with working women's participation in the struggle for the franchise. Mildred Adams: The Right to Be People also is a narrative account of the women's rights movement, but with an even heavier emphasis on the suffrage campaign. Like Flexner, Adams gives a detailed account of factional struggles within the suffrage movement and a year-by-year account of the fight for the vote.

10. See, for example, Carrie Chapman Catt: Woman Suffrage and Politics: The Inner Story of the Suffrage Movement (New York, 1923), Harriet Robinson: Massachusetts in the Woman Suffrage Movement, 1774-1881 (1883), Molly Seawell: The Ladies' Battle (1911), and Belle Squire: The Woman Movement in America (1911).

11. There are some notable exceptions to this generalization. Carl Degler's essay on women, "Revolution Without Ideology: The Changing Place of Women in America", in Robert Jay Lifton (editor): The Woman in America (Boston, 1964), deals with women's history in a dynamic social context. There have also been a number of studies of the changes in women's employment patterns which have attempted to relate women's history to the changes in the economy. See Robert Smuts: Women and Work in America (New York, 1959), and Elizabeth Baker: Technology and Woman's Work (New York, 1964).

12. Belle Squire: The Woman Movement in America, previously cited, Page 285.

13. Mildred Adams: The Right to Be People, previously cited, Page 3.

14. Aileen Kraditor: The Ideas of the Woman Suffrage Movement (New York, 1965), William O'Neill: Everyone Was Brave: The Rise and Fall of Feminism in America (Chicago, 1969), and William O'Neill: "Feminism as a Radical Ideology", in Alfred Young (editor): Dissent (De Kalb, Illinois, 1968).

15. Margaret George: One Woman's Situation, previously cited.

16. See, for example, Christopher Lasch: The New Radicalism in America (New York, 1965).

17. Robert Reigel: American Feminists (Lawrence, Kansas, 1963).

18. Edmund Morgan: The Puritan Family (New Haven, 1948), and Bernard Wishy: The Child and the Republic (Philadelphia, 1967).

19. Cited in Eugenie A. Leonard: The Dear-Bought Heritage (Philadelphia, 1965), Page 33.

20. Cited in Thomas Woody: A History of Women's Education in the United States (New York, 1929, 1966), Volume 1, Page 135.

21. An excellent study exists of an exception to this statement at the Moravian Brethren's settlement in Bethlehem, Pennsylvania. Gillian Lindt Gollin: Moravians in Two Worlds: A Study of Changing Communities (New York, 1967) describes the institutional development of the colonial community in comparison with its German counterpart. In a separate article, Gollin wrote a good study of the attempt to get rid of the family structure in the community: "Family Surrogates in Colonial America: The Moravian Experiment", Journal of Marriage and the Family XXXI (1969), Pages 650-658. This essay deals only with white women in the American colonies. Black women were rare, since most slaves imported during the period were male. And most important, they left few records which the historian may utilize. At present, no worthwhile secondary sources exist in this area.

22. Until recent years, historians concerned with long-range developments in colonial history were little concerned with social history, and those who dealt with the smaller world of women and children were oblivious to broader questions about society. Thus,

throughout the books and articles available there is no integration between the home and change, between the society and individual lives. The most efficient way to begin gathering information about the period is through an extensive bibliography, The American Woman in Colonial and Revolutionary Times, 1565-1800 (Philadelphia, 1962), by Eugenie A. Leonard, Sophie H. Drinker, and Miriam Y. Holden. The breakdown of topics follows quite traditional and static lines: European background, heroic and patriotic activities, status and rights, role in religious life, education, and domain in the home, in productive life, in arts, and in charity. This arrangement is very helpful for gaining basic information but does not provide a sense of the historical dynamic during the period. Bernard Bailyn: Education in the Forming of American Society: Needs and Opportunities for Study (1960) provides a good bibliography on education in relation to the colonial family. His essay needs substantial updating in terms of research that has followed his suggestions. A more recent and similar bibliography is in Lawrence A. Cremin: American Education: The Colonial Experience (New York, 1970). Cremin lists the latest studies on English and colonial households which are useful for analyzing the forces affecting family growth in the New World. Unfortunately all of these studies are remarkably unimaginative when it comes to piecing together the changes for women; important family changes apparently are only between fathers and sons.

23. Edmund S. Morgan: The Puritan Family: Religion and Domestic Relations in Seventeenth Century New England (revised edition, 1966) deals primarily with the idea of, rather than the practice of, New England families, but is valuable for understanding the ideological and religious role that family played in Puritan communities.

24. Julia C. Spruill: Women's Life and Work in the Southern Colonies (Chapel Hill, 1938) is the most thorough documentation of the world of women for any geographical area. Her work does not pay adequate attention to the changes within the colonial period, but is a goldmine of information. Chapter 1 of her book describes the "womanless" years in the South and efforts to import women. A supplement is Walter Hart Blumenthal: Brides from Bridewell: Female Felons Sent to Colonial America (Rutland, Vermont, 1962).

25. The major study of the colonial sex ratio is Herbert Moller: "Sex Composition and Correlated Culture Patterns of Colonial America", William and Mary Quarterly, Third Series II (1945), Pages 113-153. His statistics are helpful, but the suggestions he offers about the cultural effects are so riddled with bad psychology and with elementary sexist assumptions (such as that only frustrated single women were interested in religious revivals) that they are useless. Some changes in marriage age during the Seventeenth Century can be found in John Demos: "Notes on Life in Plymouth Colony", William and Mary Quarterly, Third Series XXII (1965), Pages 264-286, and Philip J. Greven, Junior: Four Generations: Population, Land, and Family in Colonial Andover, Massachusetts (Ithaca, 1970).

26. Alice Norse Earle: Home Life in Colonial Days (New York, 1899) still affords a concise treatment of household production (particularly its tools and processes) in the period. Further suggestions appear in

the bibliography by Leonard, Drinker, and Holden: The American Woman in Colonial and Revolutionary Times.

27. Edmund S. Morgan: The Puritan Family..., previously cited, discusses the child-trading phenomenon in New England extensively, although his conclusions about parental fear of intimacy need revision since the work of Philippe Aries: Centuries of Childhood.

28. Anne Grant: Memoirs of an American Lady, With Sketches of Manners and Scenery in America (New York, 1808, 1846), and E. W. Andrews and C. M. Andrews (editors): Journal of a Lady of Quality, Being the Narrative of a Journey From Scotland to the West Indies, North Carolina, and Portugal in the Years 1774 to 1776 (New Haven, 1923). Most of Mrs. Grant's observations are more telling about the early Nineteenth Century than about the Eighteenth. Her frequent digressions on the glories of home and mother do not ring true to the pre-Revolutionary time.

29. Spruill: Women's Life and Work in the Southern Colonies, previously cited; Morgan: The Puritan Family..., previously cited; and Morgan: Virginians at Home: Family Life in the Eighteenth Century (Williamsburg, 1952) are useful here. Puritan attitudes toward sex and the evidence of freer practice in the late Eighteenth Century are in: Charles F. Adams: "Some Phases of Sexual Morality and Church Discipline in New England", Massachusetts Historical Society Proceedings, Series 2 VI (1891), Pages 477-516; Edmund S. Morgan: "Puritans and Sex", New England Quarterly XV (1942), Pages 591-607; and John Demos: "Families in Colonial Bristol, Rhode Island: An Exercise in Historical Demography", William and Mary Quarterly, Third Series XXV (1968), Pages 40-57.

30. Ironically, the social solidarity of pre-industrial American society is illustrated by the Salem witch trials. Nearly everyone in Salem was involved in the trials. While most of the accused witches were women, there were also men; while most were white, there was also a West Indian slave. Some of the accused were destitute, but others were respected and landed members of the village. The initial accusers were young girls (many of whom lived outside their own families), but their testimony was received by the authorities and their charges were echoed by adult men and women. Witchcraft was a problem for every resident of the village, and its extirpation a collective responsibility. Within that framework, the community mobilized young and old, men and women, poor and well-to-do. Marion L. Starkey: The Devil in Massachusetts: A Modern Enquiry into the Salem Witch Trials (1961) and David Levin (editor): What Happened in Salem? are standard beginnings. Starkey tells a story of adolescent energy to explain the trials. Not only do I disagree with her imposition of Twentieth Century psychology on the Seventeenth Century community, but I have tried to change the focus of the event.

31. The "outstanding" women of this period have received their share of biographies, most of them terrible, but some of them providing at least the outlines of the possible differences for women of the time. Emery Battis: Saints and Sectaries: Anne Hutchinson and the Antinomian Controversy in the Massachusetts Bay Colony (Chapel Hill, 1962) needs

an article of its own to describe the psychological assumptions about women which permeate the book; Battis is simply unwilling to take seriously the possibility that Anne was dealing intelligently with a religious challenge. Mary Agnes Best: Rebel Saints (New York, 1925) is a collection of biographies of heroic Quakers, including those women who martyred themselves in Massachusetts. Sarah Harrison was the unsung heroine who refused to swear obedience. See Edmund S. Morgan: Virginians at Home..., Page 47.

32. Most writers on colonial children are agreed on this point. Alice Morse Earle: Child-Life in Colonial Days (New York, 1899, 1929), Sandford Fleming: Children and Puritanism: The Place of Children in the Life and Thought of the New England Churches, 1620-1847 (New Haven, 1933), and Monica M. Kiefer: American Children Through Their Books, 1700-1835 (Philadelphia, 1948). None of these examine practice, but all make their judgments on the basis of the artifacts.

33. Elisabeth Anthony Dexter: Colonial Women of Affairs, Women in Business and the Professions in America Before 1776 (second edition revised, Boston, 1931). Dexter's examples, without her concluding discussion about reasons for the decline of female careers, have been picked up by most colonial historians. Her work remains one of the only histories which tries to deal with the transition into the Nineteenth Century. Her hypotheses — male codification of the law, middle-class defensiveness against immigrants, the "lady" as luxury for males with increasing wealth, and the inability of women to gain education — were suggested but not examined in relation to anything broader than the individual examples she found.

34. This discussion is based on Alice Clark's excellent study: Working Life of Women in the Seventeenth Century (London, 1919, New York, 1968). Unfortunately her insights and methods have been ignored by American historians.

35. Cited in Leonard: The Dear-Bought Heritage, Page 222.

36. From an advertisement in the Pennsylvania Gazette, cited in Woody: A History of Women's Education..., Volume 1, Pages 227-228. The triumph of this move is discussed by Gerda Lerner: "The Lady and the Mill Girl", Midcontinent American Studies Journal X (1969), Pages 5-15. Although a number of histories of midwifery in Europe exist, virtually every one is a history of mail contributions to the field. A good but brief account of midwives resisting control by doctors in England is in Thomas Rogers Forbes: The Midwife and the Witch (New Haven, 1969).

37. Sophie H. Drinker: "Women Attorneys of Colonial Times", Maryland Historical Magazine LVI (1961), Pages 335-351.

38. Thomas Woody: A History of Women's Education... is the most complete collection of information on women's education. However histories of education are undergoing great changes through re-defining learning to include what occurs outside of schools and analyzing what changes are going on in the relations between members of families and social classes that induce people to formalize learning in schools. Unfortunately, very little of this rethinking has been directed toward

women. Cremin, cited above, for example, ignores the problem.

39. Rush's essay is difficult to obtain; it apparently has not been reprinted since the Eighteenth Century. It is available on the microprint cards of the American Antiquarian Society and in Rush's collected essays published in 1792. Lengthy discussions of these ideas are in Woody and in Jean S. Straub: "Benjamin Rush's Views on Women's Education", Pennsylvania History XXXIV (1967), Pages 147-157. Neither of these, however, discusses his ideas in relation to social history.

40. Ethel Armes (editor): Nancy Shippen: Her Journal Book ... With Letters to Her and About Her (Philadelphia, 1935). This fascinating story includes her educational experience, her marriage, her divorce, and her Philadelphia social life. For a lengthy commentary by a young girl on the images and choices of women in the same period, see Elizabeth Southgate Bowne: A Girl's Life Eighty Years Ago ..., with an introduction by Clarence Cook (New York, 1887). Discussions about femininity appeared with increasing regularity in American magazines and newspapers throughout the Eighteenth Century. Some of these are discussed in Bertha Monica Stearns: "Early Philadelphia Magazines for Ladies", Pennsylvania Magazine of History and Biography LXIV (1940), Pages 479-491.

41. The extent of feminism during and after the Revolution is a puzzle, in need of clearer categories of analysis and more detailed examination. Many individual women expressed discontent with the image. Mary Wollstonecraft was reprinted immediately in Boston and Philadelphia and was widely read. (For one girl's comments on Vindication, see Bowne: A Girl's Life Eighty Years Ago, Pages 58-62.) The novelist Charles Brockden Brown wrote two feminist dialogues in Alcuin, available in paperback. See also David Lee Clark: "Brockden Brown and the Rights of Women", Comparative Literature Series 2, University of Texas Bulletin (1922) for a summary and an assertion of his originality. Thomas Paine published a plea for enfranchisement of women, "An Occasional Letter on the Female Sex", in Conway (editor): Writings of Thomas Paine (New York, 1894), Volume 1. New Jersey "forgot" to include the word "man" in its new constitution. This sort of information is catalogued in a few articles, but is confused in vague intellectual history and in hazy definitions of feminism.

42. Herbert Brown: The Sentimental Novel in America, 1789-1860 (Durham, North Carolina, 1940). Hannah Foster: The Coquette (Boston, 1794). Memoir of Miss Hannah Adams, Written by Herself (Boston, 1832) provides one account of a woman making a career of writing. Rush and Hannah Foster and others expressed distaste for female novel-reading in their proposals for education, but seem not to have made a dent in popularity.

43. Karl Marx: Capital, Volume 1 (Modern Library Edition), Pages 89-90. For a historical overview of pre-industrial conditions and the rise of manufacturing in relation to women, see Edith Abbott: Women in Industry: A Study of American History (New York, 1910, 1969), Chapters 1-3.

44. William R. Taylor: Cavalier and Yankee (New York, 1963), Pages 96-99 and 118-119; David M. Kennedy: Birth Control in America (New

Haven, 1970), Page 40; William Bridges: "Family Patterns and Special Values in America, 1825-1875", American Quarterly XVII (Spring 1965), Pages 3-11.

45. For examples of colonial definitions see Wallace Notestein: "The English Woman, 1580-1650", in J. H. Plumb: Studies in Social History: A Tribute to G. M. Trevelyan (London, 1955), Pages 69-107, describing some of the English Seventeenth Century elements of this image. Anne Firor Scott, in The Southern Lady, from Pedestal to Politics, 1830-1920 (Chicago, 1970), traces the continuation of this ideal of Southern Womanhood in the antebellum period. For counterparts of women's lives in the frontier, see William Sprague: Women and the West (Boston, 1940) and Dee Brown: The Gentle Tamers: Women of the Old Wild West (New York, 1958). Both books contain interesting contrasts with the genteel image of Northeastern urban women.

46. Barbara Welter: "The Cult of True Womanhood, 1820-1860", in the American Quarterly XVIII (Summer 1966), fully delineates this stereotype. Fuller treatment is accorded by Glenda Riley: "Changing Image of the American Woman in the Early Nineteenth Century" (unpublished PhD dussertation, Ohio State University, 1967). A rather interesting although unfairly critical analysis appears in a rarely used source, Fred Vigman's Beauty's Triumph (Boston, 1966). For one of the earliest descriptions of American Victorian women, see an early work by Mary Roberts Coolidge, Why Women Are So (New York, 1912), which traces the notion of femininity from its origins in pre-Victorian settings.

47. Many of these restrictions closely resembled and imitated the British Victorian culture. Two useful, although sexist, sources are Gordon R. Taylor: Sex in History (New York, 1954), and Walter E. Houghton: The Victorian Frame of Mind (New Haven, 1957).

48. One of the most interesting compilations and analyses of fashion can be found in Bernard Rudofshy: Are Clothes Modern? (Chicago, 1947). See also Robert Riegel: "Women's Clothes and Women's Rights", American Quarterly XV (Autumn 1963), Pages 390-401, for a survey of feminists' responses to and description of Victorian fashion. For an excellent critique of Victorian furnishings, see Siegfried Giedion: Mechanization Takes Command (Second Edition, New York, 1949), and Harriet Martineau: Society in America (Anchor Abridged Edition, Garden City, 1962). Barbara Welter: "The Cult of True Womanhood, 1820-1860", previously cited, refers to Americans' reactions to British feminists.

49. Stephen Nissenbaum: "Careful Love: Sylvester Graham and the Emergence of Victorian Sexual Theory in America, 1830-1840" (unpublished PhD dissertation, University of Wisconsin, 1968) fully developed the intellectual rationales of repressive sexuality. Similarly, Sidney Ditzion: Marriage, Morals, and Sex in America (New York, 1953) contains much useful information on male attitudes and theories of sexuality. Ironically, one of the most sexist treatments, Eric Dingwall: The American Woman: A Historical Study (New York, 1956), describes at length women's denial of their own sexuality. Unfortunately Dingwall assigns to women the blame for all the ramifications of the total repressive ethic in America.

50. For a fine but early scholarly treatment, see Norman Himes: A Medical History of Contraception (Baltimore, 1936). David Kennedy: Birth Control in America, previously cited, contains a most useful second chapter: "The Nineteenth Century Heritage: The Family, Feminism, and Sex", Pages 36-76.

51. William O'Neill: Everyone Was Brave..., previously cited, Pages 4-14.

52. William R. Taylor and Christopher Lasch: "Two Kindred Spirits: Sorority and Family in New England, 1839-1946", in the New England Quarterly XXXVI (March 1963), and Keith Melder: "Beginnings of the Woman's Rights Movement in the United States, 1800-1840" (unpublished PhD dissertation, Yale University, 1965).

53. Sources on feminism and women's rights are described in Part 1. For specialized studies on women and abolitionism, see Samuel Sillen: Women Against Slavery (1955), Aileen Kraditor: Means and Ends in American Abolitionism, 1834-1850 (1969), and Helen M. Lewis: The Woman Movement and the Negro Movement — Parallel Struggles for Rights (1949).

54. Mrs. A. J. Graves: Woman in America (New York, 1855), Page 254. Catherine Beecher's best work is The American Woman's Home: Or Principles of Domestic Science (Boston, 1869). Also, Woman's Profession as Mother and Educator (Philadelphia, 1872) is useful. Helen Papasivily: All the Happy Endings (New York, 1956) traces the glorification of the common woman in the popular domestic novels of

the Nineteenth Century. Other contemporary works on domesticity include: Anonymous: The Young Lady's Own Book (Philadelphia, 1832); Lydia Maria Child: The American Frugal Housewife (Boston, 1836); Marie McIntosh: Woman in America: Her Works and Her Reward (1950); Mrs. L. Abele: Woman in Her Various Relations: Containing Practical Rules for American Females (New York, 1851).

55. Changes in theology and church practice are described in Sandford Fleming: Children and Puritanism..., previously cited. The most complete intellectual history of the motherhood literature is Ann L. Kuhn: The Mother's Role in Childhood Education: New England Concepts, 1830-1860 (New Haven, 1947). Neither book pays attention to the possible chasm between ideas and practice, but their sense of development of the ideas is quite good. The elements of the new care are discussed by Monica M. Kiefer: American Children Through Their Books..., previously cited, and in a short but provocative article by Barbara Garlitz, "The Immortality Ode: Its Cultural Progeny", Studies in English Literature VI (1966), Pages 639-649, in which the influence of Wordsworth and the haloed child is the center of discussion. Charles Strickland: "A Transcendentalist Father: The Child-Rearing Practices of Bronson Alcott", Perspectives in American History III (1969), Pages 5-73, tells an interesting tale of a male theoretician setting rules for his wife. Although his ideas were not particularly successful, more telling is the mother's failure to transcend herself and to meet the standards of idealized warmth and understanding toward her difficult daughters. She simply could not avoid hitting her children or making speedy punishments with the pressures she lived with.

56. Thomas Woody: A History of Women's Education in the United States, previously cited, Volume 1; Eleanor Thompson: Education for Ladies, 1830-1860 (New York, 1947); Helen Campbell: Household Economics (New York, 1897); and Albert H. Leake: Vocational Education of Girls and Women (New York, 1918).

57. David Montgomery: "The Working Classes of the Pre-Industrial American City, 1780-1830", Labor History IX (Winter 1968). For some information on women who were wards of the state, indentured servants, or simply trained as laborers, see Edith Abbott: Women in Industry, previously cited; Marcus W. Jernagan: Laboring and Dependent Classes in Colonial America, 1607-1783 (Chicago, 1931); Richard B. Morris: Government and Labor in Early America (New York, 1946); and A. E. Smith: Colonists in Bondage: White Servitude and Convict Labor in America (Chapel Hill, 1947). Abbott is the only one of these authors who deals particularly with women, but the others provide invaluable information about landless residents of the colonies and provide the legal history defining their lives.

58. Helen L. Sumner: History of Women in Industry in the US, IX, Report of the Condition of Woman and Child Wage-Earners in the US, US Senate Document 645, 61st Congress, 2nd Session (Washington, 1911) is an invaluable source. Alice Hyneman Rhine: "Woman in Industry", in Annie Meyer (editor): Women's Work in America (New York, 1891). Edith Abbott assessed Martineau's findings on the extent of occupations open to women: "Harriet Martineau and the Employment of Women in

1836", Journal of Political Economy XIV (December 1906). For an unusual cataloguing of the variety of jobs supposedly open to women at mid-century, see Virginia Penny: Five Hundred Employments, Adapted to Women with Average Rate of Pay in Each (Philadelphia, 1868).

59. Norman Ware: The Industrial Worker, 1840-1860 (Boston, 1924), Chapters 5-9, has much background information on industrialism and its effects on the wage earner, with special reference to the New England mills girls. Hannah Josephson: The Golden Thread: New England Mill Girls and Magnates (New York, 1949); Caroline Ware: Early New England Cotton Manufacture (1931). Lucy Larcom, an early operative, mentions her mill experience in her memoirs, A New England Girlhood (Boston, 1889), Chapters 7-11. She also composed an epic length poem about life in the mill town, An Idyll of Work (Boston, 1875).

60. Elisabeth Dexter: Career Women of America, previously cited, Pages 218-225, talks about the restrictions placed on working women after the Revolution. The best analysis of class stratification in this period is Gerda Lerner: "The Lady and the Mill Girl: Changes in the Status of Women in the Age of Jackson", Midcontinent American Studies Journal, Volume 10, Number 1 (1969), Pages 5-15. For a contemporary account see Helen Campbell: Prisoners of Poverty: Women Wage Workers, Their Trades and Their Lives (Boston, 1887).

61. William Sanger: A History of Prostitution (New York, 1898) is one of the earliest attempts at an investigation and analysis of local conditions. Some interesting contemporary accounts offer insights into the prevalence and forms of prostitution in the Nineteenth Century: G. Ellington: The Women of New York, Or The Underworld of the Great City (New York, 1869), and J. D. McCabe: Secrets of the Great City (Philadelphia, 1968) and New York by Sunlight and Gaslight (Philadelphia, 1882). For attitudes toward prostitution, see David Jay Pivar: "The New Abolitionism: The Quest for Social Purity, 1876-1900" (unpublished PhD dissertation, University of Pennsylvania, 1965); Robert Riegel: "Changing American Attitudes Toward Prostitution, 1800-1920", in the Journal of the History of Ideas 29 (1969), Pages 437-452; Egal Feldman: "Prostitution, the Alien Woman, and the Progressive Imagination, 1910-1915", American Quarterly XIX (1967), Pages 192-206. For an interesting account of the two most famous madams of the period, see Charles Washburn: Come into My Parlor: A Biography of the Aristocratic Everleigh Sisters of Chicago (New York, 1934).

62. Norman Ware: The Industrial Worker, previously cited; John B. Andrews and W. D. P. Bliss: History of Women in Trade Unions, Senate Documents, Number 645, X, 61st Congress, 2nd Session (Washington, 1911); and Alice Henry: Women and the Labor Movement (New York, 1923).

63. Ross M. Robertson: History of the American Economy (New York, 1964), Pages 336, 572. See also Carl N. Degler: "Revolution Without Ideology: The Changing Place of Women in America", in Robert Jay Lifton (editor): The Woman in America (Boston, 1964).

64. Margaret Benston: "Political Economy of Women's Liberation", Monthly Review (September 1969), and E. P. Thompson: "Time, Work Discipline, and Industrial Capitalism", Past and Present (1967).

65. Simon Patten: quoted in Theresa Schmid McMahan: Woman and Economic Evolution (Madison, 1908).

66. The problem of the "nervous housewife" was discussed in a number of works in the early part of the century. See Alice Beal Parsons: Woman's Dilemma (New York, 1924); Abraham Myerson: The Nervous Housewife (Boston, 1920). Christopher Lasch: The New Radicalism in America (New York, 1965) documents the "restlessness" of women in the early part of the century. For early analyses of woman's role as consumer, see Bertha Lucas: The Woman Who Spends: A Study of Her Economic Function (Boston, 1904); Lorinne Pruette: Women and Leisure: A Study of Social Waste (New York, 1924); Olive Schreiner: Women and Labour (New York, 1911); Julia Jessie Taft: The Woman Movement from the Point of View of Social Consciousness (Chicago, 1915); Thorstein Veblen: "The Economic Theory of Women's Dress", Popular Science Monthly (November 1894).

67. US Department of Labor, Women's Bureau, Bulletin Number 46: Facts About Working Women — A Graphic Presentation Based Upon Census Statistics (1925); and Bulletin Number 104: The Occupational Progress of Women, 1910-1930 (1933). More recent studies of women's employment include: National Manpower Council: Womanpower (New York, 1957) and Work in the Lives of Married Women (New York, 1958).

68. See, for example, Laura Baker: Wanted: Women in War Industry (New York, 1943) and Margaret Culkin Banning: Women for Defense (New York, 1942). The amount of material on women's war work is considerable. Works include Mabel Daggett: Women Wanted: The Story Written in Blood Red Letters on the Horizon of the Great World War (New York, 1918); Katharine Anthony: Out of the Kitchen, Into the War (New York, 1943); Mabel Gerken: Ladies in Pants: A Home Front Diary (New York, 1949).

69. Robert W. Smuts: Women and Work in America (New York, 1959), Pages 88-89. Working women's experiences in industry in the early decades of the Twentieth Century are very well documented by working women themselves, social reformers, and middle-class women who worked in industry for a short time and wrote up their experiences. See Dorothy Richardson: The Long Day: The Story of a New York Working Girl as Told by Herself (New York, 1905); Grace Dodge (editor): Thoughts of Busy Girls: Written by a Group of Girls Who Have Little Time for Study, and Yet Find Much Time for Thinking (New York, 1892); Consumers' League of New York: Behind the Scenes in a Hotel (New York, 1922); Edna Dean Bullock: Selected Articles on the Employment of Women (Minneapolis, 1911); Sue Ainslie Clark and Edith Wyatt: Making Both Ends Meet (New York, 1911); Gwendolyn Hughes: Mothers in Industry: Wage Earning by Mothers in Philadelphia (New York, 1925); Hazel Ormsbee: The Young Employed Girl (Bryn Mawr, 1927); Bessie Van Vorst: The Woman Who Toils: Being the Experience of Two Ladies as Factory Girls (New York, 1903).

70. Letter from Frank Carpenter to Agnes Nestor, March 15, 1908 (Chicago Historical Society, Agnes Nestor Papers); also quoted in Philip Foner: History of the Labor Movement in the United States, Volume 3 (New York, 1964).

71. Alice Henry's works are the best single source for women's experiences in unions. See The Trade Union Woman (New York, 1915) and Women and the Labor Movement, previously cited.

72. The most useful discussions of the feminist movement's relation to working-class women are Aileen Kraditor: The Ideas of the Woman Suffrage Movement (New York, 1965) and Up from the Pedestal (Chicago, 1968), and William O'Neill: Everyone Was Brave..., previously cited. Helen Marot: American Labor Unions, by a Member (New York, 1915) also is useful.

73. Charlotte Perkins Gilman: Women and Economics (New York, 1966) and What Diantha Did (New York, 1910). For discussions of the middle-class base of the suffrage movement see Aileen Kraditor: The Ideas of the Woman Suffrage Movement, previously cited, and William O'Neill: Everyone Was Brave..., previously cited. Good primary source material for the consumer orientation of the feminist movement is included in Rheta Childe Dorr: What Eight Million Women Want (Boston, 1910) and in the materials collected about the women's club movement. Jane Cunningham Croly: The History of the Women's Club Movement in America (New York, 1898) is the most readily available source. Jane Addams also was concerned with this aspect of the feminist movement. See "Why Women Are Concerned with the Larger Citizenship", The Woman Citizen's Library, IX (1913), and A Centennial Reader (New York, 1960).

74. The New York Call (December 29, 1909), Page 4 (the special shirtwaist strike edition).

75. The most valuable source of information on the National Woman's Party is its periodical Equal Rights.

76. Equal Rights (August 16, 1924). Gilman's articles during the 1920s include "Toward Monogamy", The Nation, 118 (June 11, 1924) and "Woman's Achievements Since the Franchise", Current History 27 (October 1927). See also Carrie Chapman Catt: "Suffrage Only an Episode in an Age-Old Movement", Current History 27 (October 1927).

77. Secondary materials on the New Woman include James McGovern: "Woman's Pre-World War I Freedom in Manners and Morals", in the Journal of American History LV (September 1968), and Christopher Lasch: The New Radicalism in America, previously cited. 1920s issues of such magazines as The Nation and New Republic have a voluminous amount of material on the New Woman. Also see Phyllis Blanchard: New Girls for Old (New York, 1930), which is particularly useful for information on contemporary sexual attitudes, and Freda Kirchwey (editor): Our Changing Morality (New York, 1924). Mabel Dodge Luhan: Intimate Memories also is a valuable source.

78. See, for example, Kate Chopin: The Awakening (New York, 1899). Useful discussions of the changes in the family and marriage appear in William O'Neill: Divorce in the Progressive Era (New Haven, 1967) and Everyone Was Brave..., previously cited, and in Carl Degler: "Revolution Without Ideology", previously cited.

79. Mirra Komarovsky: Blue Collar Marriage (New York, 1962) and Lee Rainwater: And the Poor Get Children (Chicago, 1960).

80. Betty Friedan: The Feminine Mystique (New York, 1963).

81. Havelock Ellis: Man and Woman: A Study of Human Secondary Sexual Characteristics (New York, 1904).

82. Alice Beal Parsons: Woman's Dilemma, previously cited, Pages 11-32, and "Manmade Illusions About Women", in Samuel Schmalhausen and V. F. Calverton (editors): Woman's Coming of Age (New York, 1931) and Leta Hollingsworth: "The New Woman in the Making", Current History 27 (October 1927).

83. See, for example, Helene Deutsch: The Pschology of Women, A Psychoanalytic Interpretation (New York, 1944); Ferdinand Lundberg and Maryna Farnham: Modern Woman: The Lost Sex (New York, 1947); Marie Robinson: The Power of Sexual Surrender (New York, 1959). This prevalent psychological construct has not gone without refutation. See, for example, Clara Thompson: "Cultural Pressures in the Psychology of Women", Psychiatry V (August 1942), and Mary Jane Sherfey: "The Evolution and Nature of Female Sexuality in Relation to Psychoanalytic Theory", Journal of the American Psychoanalytic Association 14 (January 1966).

84. Benjamin Andrews: "The Home Woman as Buyer and Controller of Consumption", The Annals of the American Academy of Political and Social Science CXLIII (May 1929), Page 41, and Ladies' Home Journal (August 1924), Page 49.

85. Willystine Goodsell: The Education of Women (New York, 1923), Pages 99-110.

86. Iva Peters: Social and Vocational Orientation for College Women (Richmond, 1926).

CAPITALISM, THE FAMILY, AND PERSONAL LIFE

Eli Zaretsky

I. FEMINISM AND SOCIALISM

THE WOMEN'S LIBERATION MOVEMENT, since its emergence in the late 1960s, has posed a series of fundamental challenges to traditional socialist politics. Against the emphasis on the industrial proletariat it raised the needs of women in the home and children, the majority of the population. Against the emphasis on capitalism, women's liberation attacked male supremacy, a form of oppression that certainly antedated capitalism and that has persisted in the socialist countries. Women's

*I wish to express my gratitude for special help from John Judis, Gil Weisman, and Linda Zaretsky, and from the article "On the Proletarian Revolution and the End of Political-Economic Society" by Martin J. Sklar (*Radical America*, May 1969). —E.Z.*

liberation promised to go beyond what it regarded as the narrowly economic perspective of socialists in order to revolutionize the deepest and most universal experiences of life—those of "personal" relations, love, egotism, sexuality, our inner emotional lives. Just as socialists in the nineteenth century had challenged bourgeois liberal politics by rejecting its exclusive focus on the state and by raising the importance of economic relations, so feminists brought into the arena of political discussion the hitherto private life of the family.

The early writings of the women's movement were fragmentary and exploratory, symbolized by the well-worn, mimeographed articles that for several years were the movement's basic texts. The first attempt at an overall synthesis came in 1970 with the publication of Kate Millett's *Sexual Politics*, which the author described as "something of a pioneering effort . . . tentative and imperfect."[1] *Sexual Politics*, as its title indicates, was an attempt to broaden the meaning of politics. It began with an analysis of how three modern novelists had dealt with sexual intercourse: "Coitus of itself appears a biological and physical activity," wrote Millett, but in fact it is a social act, "a charged microcosm of the variety of attitudes and values to which culture subscribes." Sexual encounters had political meaning since they involved "power-structured relationships . . . whereby one group of persons is controlled by another." Millett sought to broaden the meaning of politics to include power relationships of "personal contact and interaction between members of well-defined and coherent groups."[2]

Millett's concern was with male supremacy, the most pervasive of these power relationships. She argued that male supremacy, which presented itself as a natural or biological phenomenon, was in fact socially enforced through ideological conditioning, socialization of early childhood, restriction of

1. Kate Millett, *Sexual Politics* (New York, 1970), p. 24.

2. Ibid., pp. 23–24; other recent pioneering works, which predated the emergence of women's liberation, would include Simone de Beauvoir's *The Second Sex* (New York, 1952), Betty Friedan's *The Feminine Mystique* (New York, 1963), and Juliet Mitchell's "Women: The Longest Revolution," *New Left Review* 40 (1966).

women to the family, the male monopoly on violence, and other institutions. Through such means women were universally subordinated to men. While Millett did not draw explicit political conclusions, her book encouraged the idea that a feminist movement primarily concerned with the abolition of male supremacy in both its social and "personal" manifestations was needed.

Insisting that male supremacy was a social rather than a biological phenomenon, *Sexual Politics* reflected the early stage of women's liberation: the first priority was to establish the validity of its concern. But while describing various ways in which male supremacy operated, Millett did not present a unified theory of male supremacy. As Juliet Mitchell later wrote: "We are left with a sense of the random and chaotic and *equal* contribution of each and all to the maintenance of patriarchy."[3] Millett did not explain what gave rise to male supremacy in the first place nor why, if male supremacy was socially established, it was universally reproduced while other social institutions varied throughout history. Without such an explanation it was impossible for Millett to outline a strategy for ending male supremacy.

ABOUT A YEAR LATER an explanation was attempted in Shulamith Firestone's *The Dialectic of Sex* (1970), the major single statement of radical feminist theory to date. Firestone's great innovation was in accepting the traditional view that it was "natural" for men to rule women, and turning the implications of this fact on their heads. While Firestone agreed with Millett that male supremacy was socially enforced, she insisted that its origins arose before society in the "biological family"—"the basic reproductive unit of male/female/infant." According to Firestone, this is a form of life that dates back to our animal beginnings and persists in the most developed society. As a result of their child-rearing function (and infancy last much longer in humans than in other animal species) women have always been at the "mercy of their biology." The "biological family" has been the cell, the basic social unit,

3. Juliet Mitchell, *Women's Estate* (New York, 1971), p. 83.

"everywhere, throughout time." As society developed, women remained restricted to the family, while men went forth to organize production, politics, and war. Society was divided into "two distinct biological classes" unequal in their social roles. This class division underlies all subsequent history. Explicitly rejecting the Marxist view that the class struggle originates in the "economic development of society" and "in changes of the modes of production and exchange," Firestone urged us to seek "the ultimate cause and the great moving power of all historic events in the dialectic of sex."

In accord with this theory, Firestone tried to show that radical feminism would subsume the major political grievances of our time: economic inequality, race, ecology, etc. The fundamental social imbalance of power that characterizes the biological family—women dependent on men, children dependent on adults—has given rise to a "power psychology," a "psychological pattern of dominance-submission." This ceaseless striving for power shapes our most intimate personal relations (Firestone analyzes the "unequal power" struggle of romantic love) as well as the major transformations of world history.[4] Political movements that attack outward forms of oppression such as racism or capitalism without transforming the family merely skim the surface of society.

Having offered an explanation for the origins of male supremacy, Firestone was able to outline a strategic program for ending it. While male supremacy had originated in nature, it was possible to end it through new technology—contraception and the possibility of producing children outside the womb. The opportunity, she wrote, is finally at hand for men and women to "outgrow nature." But the opportunity must be seized and carried through by a feminist movement.

Firestone's book, along with other products of the women's movement, crystallized many people's dissatisfaction with the traditional politics of the left. Socialism, staking all on a reorganization of the economy, appeared inadequate to the needs of modern men and women. Socialism promised to revo-

---

4. Shulamith Firestone, *The Dialectic of Sex* (New York, 1970), p. 149.

tionize society on the basis of narrow programs that did not touch the inner life of people. Firestone's book spoke to the deep distrust of both bourgeois and radical politics that prevails in our society. Politics promises to affect us in what we share with large numbers of people, but in much of our lives we feel unique or alone. Firestone's stress on the importance of the family evoked a new conception of a political movement: one that would make the inner emotional life of its participants part of its practice. Within the women's movement in this period small "consciousness raising" groups spread with incredible vitality and vigor. Elsewhere on the left this was a period in which collectives, communes, men's groups, radical therapy, and other attempts to integrate personal and political life flourished. Many male radicals now saw in women's liberation the possibility of a new kind of revolutionary movement.

Firestone was able to advance the early attack on male supremacy by pointing to a specific institution that caused it—the family. This gave a concrete—or, as Firestone said, "materialist"—basis to a phenomenon whose very omnipresence made it appear psychologically determined. By focusing on the family, Firestone was able to relate two separate questions—the oppression of women and the place of personal experience within society—in new and exciting ways. The family *is* the primary institution through which women participate in this society. While Firestone ignored the important fact that women also work outside the home, even working women give the family their primary allegiance. Wherever a woman is in this society, it is the family, and the ideology of the family. that contributes most to shaping her beliefs and maintaining her oppression. In addition, the family is the institution in which one's personal uniqueness is central. It is the crucible in which our emotional life first takes shape and throughout life is the major institution in our society in which we expect to be recognized and cared for, for ourselves. Men, and, to a lesser degree, women, gain a social identity through school or work. But even as adults our "personal" life is confined to the family or to relationships—friendships, love affairs, communal life—that closely resemble it or are based upon it.

Firestone tied the liberation of women to an attack on the family. In *The Dialectic of Sex* she distinguished radical feminism, which directly attacked the "sexual class system," from other tendencies: "conservative feminists" (who "concentrate on the more superficial symptoms of sexism—legal inequities, employment discrimination, and the like"), "politicos," "ladies' Auxiliaries of the Left," etc.[5] But in practice the focus on the family and personal relations has proved an insufficient basis for a political movement. During 1971, "consciousness raising" small groups, the most widespread practice of radical feminism, began to decline partly because they could not cohere into an organized movement and partly because of their limitations in helping their members resolve their "personal" problems. Radical lesbianism advanced the attack on the family by urging women to break completely with their "female role"—in love, in living arrangements, and in sexuality. But radical lesbianism also showed how a political focus on the family and personal relations could lead away from building a social movement and toward entirely personal transformations. Firestone's equation of women's oppression with their oppression within the family obscured the special problems of black and brown women, and of industrial working class women. The idea that male supremacy could be ended through an attack on the intimate personal relations of the family alone began to decline. Similarly, small groups and communes began to give way or go back to political action projects which sought public power (over day care, welfare, women's health, etc.) while maintaining a commitment to personal transformation.

THE WOMEN'S MOVEMENT'S next major advance in the critique of the family, Juliet Mitchell's *Women's Estate* (1971), explained many of the limitations in the radical feminist perspective as presented by Firestone. While it was written from English experience, Mitchell's book has an internationalist perspective and raises problems shared by the diverse feminist movements in the developed capitalist countries. Both Millett

5. Ibid., pp. 36–42.

and Firestone are socialists, but they see the relevance of socialism only in relation to strictly economic questions. Mitchell, on the other hand, urges that we develop a socialist theory of women's oppression and of the family: "We should ask the feminist questions, but try to come up with some Marxist answers."[6] Mitchell criticized Millett's concept of patriarchy as a universal political system: "a political system is dependent upon (a part of) a specific mode of production: patriarchy, though a perpetual feature of it, is not in *itself* a mode of production, though an essential aspect of every economy, it does not dominantly determine it."[7] Similarly, Mitchell criticized Firestone's account as ahistorical. While praising Firestone for giving "full weight to the objective physiological sexual differences," she wrote: "To say that sex dualism was the first oppression and that it underlies all oppression may be true, but it is a general, non-specific truth, it is simplistic materialism, no more. After all we can say there has always been a master class and a servant class, but it does matter *how* these function (whether they are feudal landlords and peasants, capitalists and the working class or so on); there have always been classes, as there have always been sexes, how do these operate within any given, specific society?"[8]

Mitchell's contribution to the analysis of women's oppression falls into two parts. The first, largely a reprint of her 1966 article "Women: The Longest Revolution," analyzes the historic failure of the socialist movement to deal with the oppression of women. Mitchell traces this failure to an abstract conception of the family—a "hypostatized entity" she calls it—and she quotes Marx approvingly: "One cannot, in general, speak of the family 'as such.'"[9] Mitchell urged that we resolve the family into the separate "structures" that compose it: sexuality, reproduction, and socialization of the young. These three structures had been condensed within the apparent

6. Ibid., p. 99.
7. Ibid., p. 84.
8. Ibid., pp. 87, 90.
9. Ibid., p. 148.

monolith of the family, which was then portrayed ideologically as a "natural" institution within which women performed "natural" functions: sex, childbirth, and the rearing of children. Mitchell agreed with Firestone that the root of the oppression of women was their exclusion from production and their restriction to the family. The way out, for Mitchell, was not to attack the "family" but to differentiate the structures that compose it. Hence, Mitchell urged revolutionaries to develop a complex, coordinated program for the separate structures that defined women's condition: sexuality, reproduction, socialization, and production (by which Mitchell meant socialized production, outside the family). She emphasized that these structures interacted so that while birth control, for example, had reduced the weight of reproduction in maintaining the oppression of women, this had been offset by the increased attention paid to socialization. But she did not explain how the unity of the family had been constituted nor how the "triptych" of familial functions ("the woman's world") was, as she put it, "embraced by production (the man's world)—precisely a structure that in the final instance is determined by the economy."[10]

The later sections of *Women's Estate* address themselves to this problem. Mitchell describes the unity of the family in three ways. First, it is always formed as an economic unit. In the present, for example, it serves as a means of reproducing the labor force and as an arena of consumption. This economic dimension constantly varies throughout history and is directly dependent upon the mode of production. Second, the family's unity is formed ideologically—for the contemporary family the key idea is private property, a feudal (and early bourgeois) ideal that, like all ideology, "preserves itself across revolutionary changes in the mode of production." The family encapsulates the "most conservative concepts available."[11] Finally, Mitchell explains the relative autonomy of the family from history by its "biosocial" form—the basic mother/father/child relationship that Firestone had made central. In this relation-

10. Ibid., p. 148.

11. Ibid., p. 156.

ship, within the family, the "human animal" is "socially constructed" and male supremacy first takes shape. In the universal repetition of basic patterns of early childhood—which Freud had described as the oedipus complex—the anatomical differences between men and women are given their social meaning. Mitchell urged the value of psychoanalysis for studying "the borderline between the biological and the social, which finds expression in the family" and concluded: "The bio-social universal, the ideological atemporal, the economic specificity all interlock in a complex manner. . . . Psychoanalysis, the scientific method for investigating the first [the bio-social], can be neglected no more than scientific socialism for understanding the last, the economic, and both are needed for developing a comprehension of the ideological."[12]

Radical feminism, as represented by Firestone, had stressed the role of the family in determining the nature of society. Mitchell advanced this perspective by demonstrating that society simultaneously formed the family. Mitchell also showed us how deep and difficult these problems are. But in one respect her account preserved the dualism that characterized Firestone's account. She described the family as divided between its objective economic functions (formed by capitalism) and its inner psychological life (arising from male supremacy as embodied in the oedipus complex), she then posited an intermediate realm—the "ideological"—in which economic and psychological life interact. But this severely limits the value of what Mitchell called for earlier in her book: "the use of scientific socialism as a method of analyzing the specific nature of [women's] oppression."[13] It restricts Marxism to the study of economic and ideological activity, and excludes from Marxist analysis areas of life that are critical to an understanding of women's oppression and of social life generally—the emotions, sexuality, infancy and childhood, and the instinctual life of both sexes, as well as such "bio-social" processes as aging, sickness, and death. Instead of expanding Marxism to include these areas of life (and using the discoveries of psychoanalysis

12. Ibid., pp. 167, 172.
13. Ibid., p. 92.

to do this) Mitchell left Marxism in its traditional place and introduced psychoanalysis as a residual category to deal with the problems Marxists have slighted. Mitchell's formulation threatened to reproduce the very dichotomy between socialism (the economy) and feminism (the family) that she criticized so well. It is clear from Mitchell's rich account that a revolutionary movement that takes seriously the task of ending male supremacy and of transforming psychological life must be variegated and must operate on many different levels at once. But if socialist analysis is not adequate, what principles could unify such a movement?

II. THE FAMILY AND THE ECONOMY

ACCORDING TO FIRESTONE, both the oppression of women and the split in society between intimate personal experience and anonymous social relations are consequences of the sexual division of labor within the family. Firestone terms the family the base and the political economy the superstructure, but links the two realms only vaguely through "power psychology." While Mitchell stresses the complexity of their interaction she retains the conception of the family as a separate realm (socially defined as "natural") outside the economy—indeed she explains the oppression of women, as Firestone does, by their exclusion from social production.[14] In this way, Mitchell and Firestone share with recent socialist movements the idea of a split between the family and the economy. Given this idea, one cannot understand the relation between family life and the rest of society.

The understanding of the family and the economy as separate realms is specific to capitalist society. By the "economy," Firestone and Mitchell mean the sphere in which commodity production and exchange takes place, the production of goods and services to be sold, and their sale and purchase. Within this

14. In an exchange over "The Longest Revolution" Mitchell wrote that the roles performed by women within the family—sexuality, reproduction, and socialization—were all "roles man shares with other mammals. This confirms de Beauvoir's contention that women are relegated to the species while men—through work—transcend it." *New Left Review* 41, p. 82.

framework of thought, a housewife cooking a meal is not performing economic activity, whereas if she were hired to cook a similar meal in a restaurant she would be. This conception of "economic" excludes activity within the family and a political struggle waged by "economic classes" would exclude women, except in their role as wage-earners. Socialist and communist movements in the developed capitalist countries have also understood the "economy" in this way. And when they have talked of a political struggle between "economic classes," they have essentially excluded both the family and housewives from revolutionary politics.

The historic socialist understanding is based upon an important truth about capitalist society. The capitalist class has organized much of material production as a system of commodity production and exchange, and has organized most forms of labor as wage labor—i.e., as a commodity. By paying the laborer less than the value that the laborer produces, the capitalist is able to appropriate surplus value, unpaid labor time. Surplus value is the social basis for the existence of the capitalist class. The sphere in which surplus value is produced and realized (the "economy") determines the imperatives of society as a whole. The family has changed in capitalist society as the needs generated within the sphere of surplus value production—the needs of the capitalist class—have changed. And since this sphere is organized through wage labor, the destruction of the wage labor system is a central, defining task of a revolutionary movement in a capitalist country. But this task cannot be accomplished by wage labor alone, nor does it exhaust the purposes of a revolutionary movement.

The organization of production in capitalist society is predicated upon the existence of a certain form of family life. The wage labor system (socialized production under capitalism) is sustained by the socially necessary but private labor of housewives and mothers. Child-rearing, cleaning, laundry, the maintenance of property, the preparation of food, daily health care, reproduction, etc. constitute a perpetual cycle of labor necessary to maintain life in this society. In this sense the family is an integral part of the economy under capitalism. Furthermore, the functions currently performed by housewives and mothers will be as indispensable to a socialist society as will be many of the forms of material production currently performed by wage labor. A socialist movement that anticipates its own role in organizing society must give weight to all forms of socially necessary labor, rather than only to the form (wage labor) that is dominant under capitalism.

MARX PROBABLY INTENDED the larger conception of the economy when, in the preface to the *Critique of Political Economy*, he defined the "economic structure" as the "real foundation" of society. The "economic structure," he wrote, was "the total ensemble of social relations entered into in the social production of existence." That this conception of economic structure must include the family would have been perfectly clear in any analysis of a pre-capitalist society.[15] In precapitalist society the family performed such present functions as reproduction, care of the sick and aged, shelter, the maintenance of personal property, and regulation of sexuality, as well as the basic forms of material production necessary to sustain life. There were forms of economic activity that were not based upon family units—such as the building of public works, and labor in state-owned mines or industries. But they do not compare in extent or importance to peasant agriculture, labor based upon some form of the family, or upon the village, an extension of one or several families. In the most "primitive" societies—those in which production is least developed socially—the material necessity of the family, its role in sustaining life, was overwhelming. Even putting aside the dependence of children, adults in "primitive" society had no option but to rely upon the cooperative work of the household and particularly on the sexual division of labor, which by

15. By the "family" I mean any grouping of parents or other relatives with children, embodying a sexual division of labor, and distinguishing itself as a unit by legal, economic, and sexual rights and taboos. While such a unit varies endlessly in form, constitution, and relationship to other social institutions, it is also more or less universal in human societies (though not among all strata of a given society). The best introduction I know to the conception of the family as an anthropological (i.e., universal) entity is Claude Levi-Strauss, "The Family," in Arlene and Jerome Skolnick, *Family in Transition* (Boston, 1971).

restricting tasks to one sex or the other insured their reciprocal dependence. In such societies, widows, orphans, and bachelors are scorned or pitied as if they were witches or cripples: their survival is always in doubt.[16]

It is only under capitalism that material production organized as wage labor and the forms of production taking place within the family, have been separated so that the "economic" function of the family is obscured. Both Firestone and Mitchell contrast the "natural" functions of the family to the more "human" world of social production,[17] but sexuality and reproduction, like the production of food and shelter, are basic forms of "economic" or material necessity in any society. Only with the emergence of capitalism has "economic" production come to be understood as a "human" realm outside of "nature." Before capitalism, material production was understood, like sexuality and reproduction, to be "natural"—precisely what human beings shared with animals. From the viewpoint of the dominant culture in previous societies what distinguished humanity was not production but rather culture, religion, politics, or some other "higher" ideal made possible by the surplus appropriated from material production. In ancient Greece, for example, the labor of women and slaves within the household provided the material basis upon which male citizens could participate in the "free" and "democratic" world of the polis. Politics distinguished human life from the animal existence of women and slaves. Similarly, in medieval Europe, the surplus appropriated from peasant families supported the religious and aristocratic orders who together defined the purpose and meaning of the entire society. The serfs toiling in the field were understood as animals; they became human

16. Claude Levi-Strauss described "meeting, among the Bororo of central Brazil, a man about thirty years old: unclean, ill-fed, sad, and lonesome. When asked if the man were seriously ill, the natives' answer came as a shock: what was wrong with him?—nothing at all, he was just a bachelor. [Since] only the married status permits the man to benefit from the fruits of women's work, including delousing, body-painting, and hair-plucking as well as vegetable food and cooked food . . . a bachelor is really only half a human being." "The Family," p. 57.

17. The fullest statement of this viewpoint is probably Simone de Beauvoir's *The Second Sex*.

because they had "souls"—i.e., they participated in religion. Before capitalism the family was associated with the "natural" processes of eating, sleeping, sexuality, and cleaning oneself, with the agonies of birth, sickness, and death, *and* with the unremitting necessity of toil. It is this association of the family with the most primary and impelling material processes that has given it its connotation of backwardness as society advanced. Historically, the family has appeared to be in conflict with culture, freedom, and everything that raises humanity above the level of animal life. Certainly it is the association of women with this realm that has been among the earliest and most persistent sources of male supremacy and of the hatred of women.[18]

Capitalism, in its early development, distinguished itself from previous societies by the high moral and spiritual value it placed upon labor spent in goods production. This new esteem for production, embodied in the idea of private property and in the Protestant idea of a "calling," led the early bourgeoisie to place a high value upon the family since the family was the basic unit of production. While in feudal society the "personal" relations of the aristocracy were often highly self-conscious and carefully regulated, the domestic life of the masses was private and unexamined, even by the church. Early capitalism developed a high degree of consciousness concerning the internal life of the family and a rather elaborate set of rules and expectations that governed family life. This led to a simultaneous advance and retrogression in the status of women. On one hand, women were fixed more firmly than ever within the family unit; on the other hand, the family had a higher status than ever before. But the feminist idea that women in the family were outside the economy did not yet have any basis. As in pre-capitalist society, throughout most

18. H. R. Hays, in *The Dangerous Sex: The Myth of Feminine Evil* (New York, 1972), gives a historical overview of male supremacy that indicates not only its persistence but the recurrence of identical themes. Almost, but not quite, universally, women are portrayed as dirty, bad-smelling, unhealthy, unspiritual, driven by sensuality and instinctual needs, weak, unreasoning and, in general, under the sway of brute necessity. Early myths such as those of Eve and Pandora also link women with both sexuality and the necessity of labor.

of capitalist history the family has been the basic unit of "economic" production—not the "wage-earning" father but the household as a whole. While there was an intense division of labor *within* the family, based upon age, sex, and family position, there was scarcely a division *between* the family and the world of commodity production, at least not until the nineteenth century. Certainly women were excluded from the few "public" activities that existed—for example, military affairs. But their sense of themselves as "outside" the larger society was fundamentally limited by the fact that "society" was overwhelmingly composed of family units based upon widely dispersed, individually owned productive property. Similarly, women had a respected role within the family since the domestic labor of the household was so clearly integral to the productive activity of the family as a whole.

But the overall tendency of capitalist development has been to socialize the basic processes of commodity production—to remove labor from the private efforts of individual families or villages and to centralize it in large-scale corporate units. Capitalism is the first society in history to socialize production on a large scale. With the rise of industry, capitalism "split" material production between its socialized forms (the sphere of commodity production) and the private labor performed predominantly by women within the home. In this form male supremacy, which long antedated capitalism, became an institutional part of the capitalist system of production.

THIS "SPLIT" BETWEEN the socialized labor of the capitalist enterprise and the private labor of women in the home is closely related to a second "split"—between our "personal" lives and our place within the social division of labor. So long as the family was a productive unit based upon private property, its members understood their domestic life and "personal" relations to be rooted in their mutual labor. Since the rise of industry, however, proletarianization separated most people (or families) from the ownership of productive property. As a result "work" and "life" were separated; proletarianization split off the outer world of alienated labor from an inner world of personal feeling. Just as capitalist development gave rise to the idea of the family as a separate realm from the economy, so it created a "separate" sphere of personal life, seemingly divorced from the mode of production.

This development was a major social advance. It is the result of the socialization of production achieved by capitalism and the consequent decline in socially necessary labor time and rise in time spent outside production. Personal relations and self-cultivation have always, throughout history, been restricted to the leisure classes and to artists, courtiers, and others who performed the rituals of conversation, sexual encounter, self-examination, and physical and mental development according to well-developed and socially shared codes of behavior. But under capitalism an ethic of personal fulfillment has become the property of the masses of people, though it has very different meanings for men and for women, and for different strata of the proletariat. Much of this search for personal meaning takes place within the family and is one reason for the persistence of the family in spite of the decline of many of its earlier functions.

The distinguishing characteristic of this search is its subjectivity—the sense of an individual, alone, outside society with no firm sense of his or her own place in a rationally ordered scheme. It takes place on a vast new social terrain known as "personal" life, whose connection to the rest of society is as veiled and obscure as is the family's connection. While in the nineteenth century the family was still being studied through such disciplines as political economy and ethics, in the twentieth century it spawned its own "sciences," most notable psychoanalysis and psychology. But psychology and psychoanalysis distort our understanding of personal life by assuming that it is governed by its own internal laws (for example, the psychosexual dynamics of the family, the "laws" of the mind or of "interpersonal relations") rather than by the "laws" that govern society as a whole. And they encourage the idea that emotional life is formed only through the family and that the search for happiness should be limited to our "personal" relations, outside our "job" or "role" within the division of labor.

Thus, the dichotomies that women's liberation first confronted—between the "personal" and the "political," and between the "family" and the "economy"—are rooted in the structure of capitalist society. All three writers reflect this split, as all three seek to overcome it. The means of overcoming it is through a conception of the family as a historically formed part of the mode of production.

The rise of capitalism isolated the family from socialized production as it created a historically new sphere of personal life among the masses of people. The family now became the major space in society in which the individual self could be valued "for itself." This process, the "private" accompaniment of industrial development, cut women off from men in a drastic way and gave a new meaning to male supremacy. While housewives and mothers continued their traditional tasks of production—housework, reproduction, etc.—this labor was devalued through its isolation from the socialized production of surplus value. In addition, housewives and mothers were given new responsibility for maintaining the emotional and psychological realm of personal relations. For women within the family "work" and "life" were not separated but were collapsed into one another. The combination of these forms of labor has created the specific character of women's labor within the family in modern capitalist society.

THE FOLLOWING DISCUSSION is an attempt to understand the recent history of the family as part of the history of the capitalist mode of production. It describes two related historical transformations: the elimination of private productive property as the basis of the family among the masses of people, and the emergence of a sphere of personal life seemingly independent of the "economy" and of "production."

Historians of the family in Europe and the United States have focused on its internal institutions—the laws of marriage, inheritance and divorce, the social relations of age and sex. Their emphasis has been formal and legalistic Their major theories have stressed the slow, almost imperceptible evolution in the internal constitution of the household from the "extended" to the "nuclear" family. Viewed in this way, the seeming inertia of the family has been in marked contrast to the continuous upheaval of political and economic history, a contrast that lends plausibility to the view that "history" is the realm of politics and economics while the family is confined to "nature."

In contrast, I have tried to understand the family as an integral part of a society that changes continuously and as a whole. I have focused on the continually changing social basis of the family as part of the organization of production. Under feudalism, kinship ties were of extreme importance, but the basic economic unit was the manor or the village economy. With the beginnings of capitalism, the bourgeoisie, in defending private productive property against feudal ties and restrictions, put forth a new conception of the family as an independent economic unit within a market economy. The bourgeois conception of private productive property underlies the "discovery" of the family in the early bourgeois period, the phenomenon described by Philippe Ariès in *Centuries of Childhood.* [19] Based upon private productive property, the ideology of the family as an "independent" or "private" institution is the counterpart to the idea of the "economy" as a separate realm, one that capitalism over centuries wrested "free" of feudal restrictions, customary law, and state and clerical intervention. Protestantism reinforced this conception of the family by making it a center of religious observance.

In the early stages of industrial capitalism the family remained the productive unit, either through the "putting out" system or by bringing the whole family into the early manufacturing institutions. But by the nineteenth century the factory system has eliminated many of the production functions of the family. The bourgeois family was now reduced to the preservation and transmission of capitalist property, while the productive function of the proletarian family lay in the reproduction of the labor force. Hence, through the family each class reproduced its own class function. How did the proletarian family understand itself once it was stripped of private productive property?

To answer this question I have tried to describe the expansion of personal life among the masses of people in the nine-

19. Philippe Ariès, *Centuries of Childhood: A Social History of Family Life.* Translated by Robert Baldick. (New York, 1962).

teenth and twentieth centuries. Some of the origins of this process lie in the history of the family. The development of the bourgeois family encouraged individualism, self-consciousness and a new attention to domestic relations. But bourgeois individualism is inseparably linked to private productive property and economic competition. With the rise of industry, individualism begins to turn against capitalism itself in such movements as romanticism and utopian socialism. But these movements remained petty bourgeois insofar as they were based upon an obsolete ideal of private property. They proclaimed the unity of "personal" and productive life in the form of self-contained cooperative economic units closely resembling the early bourgeois family.

By the twentieth century, a sphere of "personal" life emerged among the proletariat itself. In the absence of a political movement that sought to transform both personal life and production, personal life was characterized by subjectivity—the search for personal identity outside the social division of labor. Having no private property to uphold, contemporary individualism upholds the self as an "autonomous" realm outside society. This new emphasis on one's personal feelings and inner needs, one's "head" or "life style," to use contemporary formulations, gives a continued meaning to family life and at the same time threatens to blow it apart.

If we can understand the family as part of the development of capitalism this can help establish the specific historical formation of male supremacy. This, in turn, would help focus the attack upon it. The establishment of private productive property as the basis of the bourgeois household meant that society was organized into separate households each of which was ruled by the father (and grandfather). In the democratic proclamations of the bourgeois revolutions every defense of natural rights or individual freedom assumes that the (male) head of the household represents the women, children, and servants within. Similarly, women are invisible in the bourgeois exaltation of "private property" or the "yeoman"; the real "yeoman" is the collective labor of the household. The emergence of personal life encouraged a sense of self-assertion and individual uniqueness among men while assigning women to the newly discovered worlds of childhood, emotional sensibility, and compassion, all contained within women's "sphere," the family.

Personal life appears to take place in some private, psychological realm outside society. By its critique of male supremacy and of the family women's liberation has demonstrated its systematic and social character. The family is an important material basis for subjectivity in this society, and for psychological life generally. If we can simultaneously view it as part of the "economy" a step would be taken toward understanding the connection between our inner emotional lives and capitalist development. The social terrain of personal life is the contemporary family within which men and women share so much, and in which their antagonism is so deeply rooted.

III. CAPITALISM AND THE FAMILY

1. Introduction

AN OVERALL TENDENCY toward dissolution has characterized formal kinship relations in Europe and the United States in modern times. In feudal society kinship was integral to the system of vassalage. The ruling aristocracy was organized as a series of "houses" or families, and pre-feudal clan and tribal survivals underlay the village economy of the peasants. Against the aristocratic emphasis on "line" or "blood," the bourgeoisie asserted the right of every son to form his own family. The bourgeois revolution represented the victory "of the family over the family name." [20] With the rise of industrial capitalism in the nineteenth and twentieth centuries the male-dominated bourgeois family began to break up; the family began to be reduced to its individual members, including women and children. Each phase of dissolution has been accompanied by a new attempt at synthesis—for the bourgeoisie the "patriarchal" or "nuclear" family, for the proletariat "personal life."

Part III describes the place the family occupied in the bour-

20. Karl Marx, *Neue Rheinische Zeitung*, 15 December 1848, quoted in C. H. George, "The Making of the English Bourgeoisie, 1500–1750," *Science and Society*, Winter 1971, p. 385.

geoisie's world outlook. Each succeeding ruling class has incorporated and transformed the ideology of its predecessors. The rise of capitalism turned "families" into units of commodity production. In the process, the bourgeoisie, through its ideology of individualism based on private property, redefined such feudal and pre-feudal ideals as male supremacy, family loyalty, and romantic love. But the further development of capitalism destroyed the basis of that ideology by turning private property into capital and wage labor. When socialist, feminist, and other movements sought a new basis for family and personal life, they drew heavily on the bourgeois ideological heritage, often promising to realize the bourgeois ideal. For that reason I have focused on that heritage.

2. *A Note on the Aristocracy*

FAMILY RELATIONS AMONG the aristocracy were viewed and conducted as economic transactions. According to Christopher Hill, in seventeenth-century England "the law of marriage . . . [was] almost the groundwork of the law of property."[21] Marriage was arranged according to the family's rather than the individual's interest. Love and sexual life were sought outside marriage and mostly by men. Arranged marriages necessitated the double standard, mistresses, and illegitimacy. A major theme of the early bourgeoisie (one which was particularly clear in literature) was an attack on the cynical personal relations of the "money power" and a defense of the family as the realm of *both* economic and personal life.

Aristocratic ideals of romantic love and individuality developed in explicit opposition to the family. In the refined society of the court, beyond the realm of goods production, the aristocracy developed an ideology of spiritualized but non-Christian love which prevailed only as adultery and which, in theory, was never consummated. Man, freed from the necessity of labor, were preoccupied with their personal relations and with an ideal of individual self-improvement.[22] Aristocratic

21. Christopher Hill, *Century of Revolution, 1603-1714* (New York, 1961), p. 253.

22. Frederick Heer, *The Medieval World* (New York, 1962), pp. 165-88. Courtly love reflected the Catholic Church's distinction between sacred

women were exalted as spiritual creatures, as they later would be again, in the nineteenth century, when the bourgeois home lost its productive functions. In these respects and in its emphasis on the emotions, on sexuality and physical well-being, and on the free choice of a unique beloved, courtly love anticipated ideals of love and individualism that the bourgeoisie located within the family and that were generalized and transformed in the course of capitalist development.

3. The Early Bourgeois Family in England

THE PREVALENT FORM of family life in England before the rise of industry in the eighteenth and nineteenth centuries was that of an economically independent, commodity-producing unit. Often referred to as the "patriarchal" family, it survives today only among the petit bourgeoisie. It originated between the disintegration of feudalism in the fourteenth century and the rise of capitalism in the sixteenth. During this period peasant families extricated themselves from feudal ties to become tenants or (far less often) landowners. In feudal society separate households were a subordinate part of a larger enterprise, generally the manor. While peasant families often worked as a unit, they had no independent economic initiative. Their holdings were in the form of narrow strips scattered amid those of other peasants "in unfenced or open fields."[23] The peasants shared the fields for cattle grazing; the harvest was gathered collectively. With the decline of feudalism and the commercialization of agriculture some peasants were driven from the land while the holdings of others were consolidated as independent commodity-producing farms. Slowly, the family replaced the

and secular love. Sacred love, like courtly love, existed outside the family and outside the realm of material production. Neither sacred nor courtly love was to be consummated. Similarly, the knightly quest for self-realization mimics the monastic stages of spiritual development, the emphasis on magic parallels the Catholic ritual, the love of the lady parallels Mariolatry, and baptism is secularized in the rebirth of the knight. Heer points out that courtly love anticipates a long tradition of "self-discovery" culminating in psychoanalysis.

23. Barrington Moore Jr., *Social Origins of Dictatorship and Democracy* (Boston, 1966), p. 12.

manor as the lowest social unit the head of which was an active citizen," able to buy and sell in the marketplace.[24]

On the basis of small-scale commodity production a new form of the family developed in the early bourgeois period. The household of a property-owning family in seventeenth-century England was a complicated economic enterprise that included not only children and relatives but servants, apprentices, and journeymen from different social classes. At its head was the *paterfamilias* who worked alongside his wife, children, employees, and wards. He was solely responsible for the economic and spiritual welfare of his family and represented in his person the supposed unity and independence of the family. The domestic relations of the household were an acknowledged part of the production relations of early capitalism.[25]

This bourgeoisie that emerged in England during the sixteenth and seventeenth centuries had many sources, including the landed nobility and the merchant capitalists of the medieval towns. But its most revolutionary sectors came from the class of small producers working their own property. For centuries the bourgeoisie identified itself with this form of production, distinguishing the "industrious sort of people" from both the idle aristocracy and the shiftless poor. While family life differed vastly among different strata and classes, the early bourgeois family—the family as a self-contained productive unit—furnished the basis for a new ideology of the family linked with the newly emerging ideas of private property and individualism. Much of this ideology was expressed through religion, particularly Puritanism, which was an inseparable part of the early bourgeois outlook. Taken together, the changes achieved by the bourgeoisie in seventeenth-century England

---

24. Christopher Hill, *Society and Puritanism in Pre-Revolutionary England* (New York, 1967), p. 449; Marc Bloch, *Feudal Society* (Chicago, 1968), pp. 123–44.

25. Hill, *Society and Puritanism*, pp. 449, 453. Only the *paterfamilias* could wear a hat in his own house. Hill points out that the *paterfamilias's* responsibility for the household foreshadows the paternalism that becomes so nauseating in the impersonal setting of developed capitalism.

established a new form of the family and an ethic of family life integral to the bourgeois system of rule.

The bourgeoisie encouraged a new respect for labor and economic activity. John Locke, writing toward the end of the century, expressed the bourgeois contempt for medieval "otherworldliness": "We are not born in heaven but in this world, where our being is to be preserved with meat, drink, and clothing, and other necessaries that are not born with us, but must be got and kept with forecast, care and labour, and therefore we cannot be all devotion, all praises and hallelujahs, and perpetually in the vision of things above." [26] Locke expressed the view that through labor the individual expressed his own nature: "Whatsoever [a man] removes out of the state that nature hath provided and left it in, he hath mixed his labour with, and joined to it something that is his own, and thereby makes it his property." [27] This new value placed upon private property and productive labor encouraged a new esteem for the family.

The bourgeoisie's acceptance of economic life helped encourage a new acceptance of sexuality, eating, and other noneconomic material processes of the family. The family had been scorned in medieval society as the realm of both production and sexuality. The Catholic Church, anti-sexual and savagely anti-female, had sanctioned family life only reluctantly, as the alternative to damnation, and had forbidden it to the clergy. The right of the clergy to marry had been a basic issue during the Reformation. In seventeenth-century England, Puritanism, with its acceptance of the life of material necessity, embraced the married state and exalted the family as part of the natural (i.e., God-given) order of productive and spiritual activity. Sexuality and emotional expression were encouraged, so long as they occurred within marriage. The Puritans condemned only "unnatural" forms of sexuality such as the profligacy practiced at the court, and homosexuality,

---

26. Quoted in Sheldon Wolin, *Politics and Vision* (Boston, 1960), p. 298.

27. John Locke, *Treatise of Civil Government* (New York, 1937), pp. 18–19.

which they viewed with particular horror.[28] They argued that emotional and sexual expression must be "weaned"—held within the bounds of nature and not carried to artificial excess. In *Paradise Lost,* a Puritan paean to the married state, Milton wrote, "In loving thou dost well in passion not."[29]

In contrast to the pre-capitalist divorce of spiritual and economic life, human meaning and purpose was now to be sought in the mundane world of production and the family. Throughout the Reformation, an ever-increasing proportion or religious instruction and prayer was removed from the church to the home. More important, Protestantism blessed the material labor performed by the family as sacred. Calvin answered the medieval text "Sell all thou hast and give to the poor" by saying "God sets more value on the pious management of a household."[30] The family's economic life was now spiritualized. The Protestant idea of a "calling" allows one to do God's work in a secular craft or occupation.[31]

Underlying these changes was a new conception of human nature, that of possessive individualism. The bourgeoisie condemned the fixed stratification of medieval society as "artificial" and viewed competitiveness based upon economic self-interest as the natural basis of society.[32] As market relations developed, the identification of the individual with a fixed

28. Lawrence Stone, *The Crisis of the Aristocracy, 1558–1641* (New York, 1967), pp. 298–301.

29. Similarly Puritanism upheld the economically "independent" individual (i.e., family) who held his own in the community, but attacked the "unnatural" spirit of acquisitiveness associated with the rise of commerce.

30. Hill, *Society and Puritanism,* p. 449.

31. In Europe at this time the Catholic Church began to recognize the possibility of awarding sainthood to individuals in pursuits outside the clergy. The church began to encourage the laity in activities such as education previously monopolized by the clergy. Ariès, p. 357.

32. Shakespeare's plays, for example, defend the new early bourgeois ideals of love, marriage, and individual freedom on the basis of their being "natural," i.e., outside convention. In *King Lear,* the established loyalties of the social order are posed against the individualism of the daughters, who wish to break away and live their own lives. The supremely egotistical figure in *Lear* is Edmund, who is a bastard, a child

social position began to give way to a commitment to the "individual" (i.e., the individual family) who would rise or fall on the basis of independent efforts. The family came to be seen as a competitive economic unit apart from, and later even opposed to, the rest of society. In the seventeenth century competitiveness and acquisitiveness were still restricted by the corporate ideals of mercantilism; by the eighteenth century they were generally encouraged.

The bourgeois acceptance of a certain degree of selfishness and aggression as part of human nature gave rise to a search for new principles of social order. While it was the vehicle of private ambition, the family was hierarchically organized and strictly disciplined. It forced the "natural" materialism of its members to take a socially acceptable form. The early bourgeoisie understood the family to be the basic unit of the social order—"a little church, a little state"—and the lowest rung in the ladder of social authority. They conceived of society as composed not of individuals but of families, each an indissoluble cell. If they spoke of "individual rights," it was because of the sovereignty of paternal power.

The new social and religious functions of the family led to a deepening consciousness concerning domestic life and to public debate over its form. Among Puritans and other sects it also led to a deepening *self*-consciousness, an awareness of one's internal psychological life. Christianity has always encouraged a certain degree of self-consciousness in the form of the conscience, the major form of subjective experience in Europe and America until the nineteenth century. But Puritans, and other Protestants, viewed social behavior as a sign of inward grace and argued that no church ritual or other outward act could determine for certain whether an individual was "saved." One indication of the expansion of self-consciousness was the proliferation of diaries in the seventeenth century. More broadly, the same period saw the invention of silvered mirrors, the spread of autobiography, the building of chairs instead of benches, the spread of private lodgings, and the rise of self-

---

of "nature," not part of society at all. Cf. Hill, *Society and Puritanism*, pp. 462–63.

portraits. In this period sincerity became a dominant social ideal.[33]

Taken together, these developments shaped a new ideal of family life. Marriage was coming to be understood as a partnership based upon common love and labor; one's wife was a companion or "helpmeet." The early bourgeois family gave rise to a new set of expectations based upon the couple's common destiny—not only love but mutual affection and respect, trust, fidelity, and premarital chastity. As in medieval society, children were quickly integrated into the adult order, but it was understood that when grown they would marry according to their own desires, although listening to their parents' counsel. In keeping with the high value placed upon both productive labor to expand the family's fortune and the weaning of one's emotions over time, maturity and old age were idealized. The symbol of the wise and self-disciplined grandfather now replaced, for a time, the more traditional image of the dotard.[34]

THE BOURGEOIS FAMILIAL IDEAL obscured two contradictions that emerged in the course of capitalist development: the oppression of women and the family's subordination to class relations. The rise of the bourgeoisie entailed a simultaneous advance and retrogression in the position of women. In the economic life of medieval England women were closer to equality with men than they later were under capitalism. For example, women participated as equals in many guilds in the fourteenth century.[35] With the rise of capitalism they were excluded and, in general, economic opportunities for women not in families—such as spinsters or widows—declined. On the other hand women were given a much higher status within the family. For the Puritans, women's domestic labor was a "calling," a special vocation comparable to the crafts or trades of their husbands. Like their husbands, women did God's work.

33. Lionel Trilling, *Sincerity and Authenticity* (Cambridge, 1972), p. 25; Hill, *Century of Revolution*, p. 253.

34. Simone de Beauvoir, *The Coming of Age* (New York, 1972), pp. 178–79.

35. Mary Beard, *Woman as Force in History* (New York, 1946, 1971), p. 234.

As the lesser partner in a common enterprise, a woman was to be treated with respect. According to Robert Cleaver's *A Godly Form of Household Government*, a 1598 Puritan marriage manual, "She was like a judge joined in commission to help rule his household. She was not to be made into a drudge or ordered about like a servant, but the husband was to command her 'as the soul doth the body,'" [36] i.e., through their mutual harmony. Wife-beating was now forbidden. And the Protestant conviction that all believers were spiritually equal rescued women from their medieval limbo of carnality. As in medieval peasant society, women were associated with the "natural" realm of labor, but in contrast to medieval society this realm was highly valued.

Hence, women were encouraged to think of themselves almost as independent persons at the same time that they were imprisoned within the family. During the English Revolution the question of female equality was debated politically for the first time. Within many sects women played leading roles as preachers and organizers. (This was particularly true in sects that downgraded the importance of learning for salvation, since women were so little educated.)[37] These stirrings of women's equality reached a level in the seventeenth century sufficient to call forth a counter-movement among preachers and others that stressed female subordination within the family. One argument made was that the family was the economic property of the husband, and that married women owned nothing in their own right.[38]

So long as the family was considered the "natural" or God-given basis of society, the issue of women's equality could not emerge on a large scale. The bourgeois view that the family (rather than individuals or classes) was the basic unit of society

36. Quoted in M. M. Knappen, *Tudor Puritanism* (Chicago, 1939, 1970), p. 454.

37. Keith Thomas, "Women and the Civil War Sects," in Trevor Aston, *Crisis in Europe, 1560-1660* (New York, 1967), passim. Episcopal documents of the period describe the sects as "chiefly women," "most silly women," and so forth.

38. George, pp. 407-8. In fact, this did not become a legal reality until the middle of the eighteenth century.

reinforced the deeply rooted traditions of male supremacy. And this view persisted as long as the family was a basic unit of social production. The issue of women's equality was largely muted until the late eighteenth and nineteenth centuries when the rise of industry finally destroyed the bourgeois ideal of the family as an independent productive unit.

That ideal had always been ideological, obscuring the class differences among the supposedly "independent" producers of seventeenth-century England. According to the bourgeoisie, "private property" defined the family as an independent unit, guaranteed its political freedoms, and provided a new justification for the rule of the father. By "private property" the seventeenth-century bourgeoisie meant both one's own labor power (i.e., "property in one's person"), and the land or tools one employed. This obscured the fact that labor alone could never make one an "independent" producer: farmers required land, implements, and stock; weavers required materials and the use of a loom.[39] Hence as capitalism developed, "private property" split—into capital on one hand, and labor power on the other.

In the seventeenth and eighteenth centuries this split took the form of "domestic industry"—the family worked as a unit but in direct dependence on the capitalist class. Weavers, for example, were dependent upon merchant clothiers who supplied their wool, monopolized new technical inventions such as the knitting frame, finished the production of cloth by hiring workers, and served as intermediaries between the weaving family and the shopkeepers who sold their cloth. Only the ownership of land bestowed a measure of independence upon the artisan family.[40]

Domestic industry preserved the "unity" but not the "independence" of the original bourgeois ideal. E. P. Thompson somewhat romantically describes the family of weavers: "The

39. C. B. Macpherson, *The Political Theory of Possessive Individualism* (London, 1967), p. 149.

40. Paul Mantoux, *The Industrial Revolution in the 18th Century* (New York, 1961), pp. 59-68. Maurice Dobb, *Studies in the Development of Capitalism* (New York, 1968), pp. 143-51.

young children winding bobbins, older children watching for faults, picking over the cloth, or helping to throw the shuttle in the broad-loom; adolescents working a second or third loom; the wife taking a turn at weaving, in and among her domestic employments. The family was together, and however poor meals were, at least they could sit down at chosen times, A whole pattern of community life had grown up around the loom-shops; work did not prevent conversation or singing."[41] Even the early forms of factory organization often preserved this unity. In the mills and manufacturing workshops of the early eighteenth century families worked as a unit. Family and community relations were part of the hybrid organization of production in these early enterprises. For this reason, the early working class defended child labor, since it preserved the traditional ties between children and their parents (especially fathers, who transmitted a productive skill).[42]

4. *Decline of the Bourgeois Family*

THE RISE OF THE FACTORY system made manifest the subjection of the family to the class relations of its members. Until then, the bourgeoisie had accommodated itself to domestic industry, since this was the most expedient and profitable way of organizing production. Once families were brought together in a common workshop, however, they were no longer supervised by the father but by the master. They no longer worked at their own rhythm, but according to the systematic labor discipline required by a coordinated division of labor. The master-manufacturer of the eighteenth century was obsessed with the necessity of instructing the workers in "'methodical' habits, punctilious attention to instructions, fulfillment of contracts to time, and in the sinfulness of embezzling materials." In this context Methodism became the dominant religion of both bourgeoisie and working class. Unlike Puritanism, which asserted the unity of economic and spiritual life, Methodists

41. E. P. Thompson, *The Making of the English Working Class* (New York, 1963), pp. 306–7.

42. Neil Smelser, *Social Change in the Industrial Revolution* (Chicago, 1965), passim.

preached the rigid division between the repression, discipline, and social subordination of daily life and the ritualized paroxysms of Sabbath emotionalism.[43]

The introduction of machinery was the culmination of this process, requiring human beings to "identify themselves with the unvarying regularity of the complex automaton."[43] Industrial capitalism required a rationalized, coordinated and synchronized labor process undisturbed by community sentiment, family responsibilities, personal relations or feelings. These changes in the organization of production led to the formation of a new ideology of the family. Earlier the bourgeoisie had portrayed the family as the progressive center of individualism, but as industrial production destroyed the basis of the early bourgeois family, the family came to be either scorned as a backward institution or nostalgically romanticized. In either case it was contrasted to "society," the system of social production and administration.

Jean-Jacques Rousseau, an early exponent of this contrast, identified the family with "nature." Like the early bourgeoisie, Rousseau idealized the family based upon private property. But unlike them he contrasted the "spontaneously" developed, even "primeval," division of labor within the family, to "society."[46] "Society," he asserted, creates inequality, but "nature" is inherently egalitarian: "Neither master nor slave belongs to a family, but only to a class."[46] "Society" constricts human understanding within the narrow confines of rationality, which Rousseau calls "philosophy," but within the family emotional life abounds, particularly compassion. "It is philosophy that isolates a man; it is through philosophy that a man will secretly say, on seeing a man suffer: Die if you will, I am safe." In the

---

43. Thompson, pp. 359, 368–69.

44. Andrew Ure, *Philosophy of Manufactures* (1835), quoted in Thompson, p. 360.

45. By "society" Rousseau refers to commerce and urban life rather than to the industrialization then occurring in England. Nevertheless, the overall direction of French and English society is similar.

46. *Emile* (London, 1966), p. 401. Eva Figes, *Patriarchal Attitudes* (New York, 1970), points out the importance of Rousseau.

family the "natural" sense of human solidarity still prevails, while in society it has been destroyed by the calculating egotism of the bourgeoisie. The early bourgeois family had been a microcosm of social authority. For Rousseau the family is held together "voluntarily"[47] or through the "natural" bonds of male supremacy.[48] In this regard he anticipates the modern belief in the internal freedom of the family and its determination by the emotional needs of its members. In contrast to the emotional life of the family, society was a rationalized programmed mechanism. One of the happiest moments of Rousseau's life came when, upon leaving Paris, he threw away his watch.[49] The family, attuned to the "natural" rhythms of eating, sleeping, and child care, can never be wholly synchronized with the mechanized tempo of industrial capitalism.[50]

Rousseau's exaltation of domesticity was a late expression of the egalitarianism rooted in the bourgeois ideal of private property, as well as an early prefiguring of the romantic and utopian socialist critique of capitalism. Rousseau's "family" is the petit-bourgeois household, part of a society of "independent producers." But the bourgeois family was losing its earlier productive role. Even the most basic domestic tasks, such as child-rearing, were being performed by servants. And as production became increasingly socialized, the bourgeoisie lost the illusion of individual autonomy within the sphere of goods production. By the nineteenth century the bourgeoisie had formulated a very different ideal of the family—that of an enclave protected from industrial society. Although this ideal was based upon the *bourgeois* family it also pervaded petit-

47. *Social Contract* (New York, 1971), p. 8. Locke shared this idea. Both used it to combat defenses of monarchical right that were based upon paternal authority within the family such as those by Filmer and Jean Bodin. Cf. Locke, *An Essay Concerning the True Original Extent and End of Civil Government*, part 6, "Of Paternal Power."

48. Though Rousseau already reflects the division of labor between the sexes based upon wage-labor: "Woman, honor your master, he it is who works for you, he it is who gives you bread to eat; this is he!" *Emile*, p. 401.

49. Ernst Cassirer, *The Question of Jean-Jacques Rousseau* (Bloomington, Ind., 1967).

50. E. P. Thompson, "Time, Work-Discipline and Industrial Capitalism," *Past and Present* 38.

bourgeois and proletarian family life and shaped the movements to transform the family that arose in the nineteenth century.

IN THE EARLY NINETEENTH CENTURY, the bourgeoisie saw themselves as alienated from both "society"—the Frankenstein monster they had created—and "nature"—the world they had left behind. Reflecting the brutal, seemingly irresistible, imposition of industrial capitalism, "society" was envisioned as a vast economic machine.

The idea of self-interest now supplanted the idea of conscience and money came to dominate all social relations. According to Jeremy Bentham, "The preparation in the human bosom for antipathy towards other men is, under all circumstances, most unhappily copious and active." The reason? "The boundless range of human desires, and the very limited number of objects. . . . Human beings are the most powerful instruments of production, and therefore everyone becomes anxious to employ the services of his fellows in multiplying his own comforts." According to Bentham it was futile to "dive into the unfathomable regions of motives" since all that was necessary was to know what one wanted. Indeed, man is "by interest diverted from any close examination into the springs by which his own conduct is determined. From such knowledge he has not, in any ordinary shape, anything to gain—he finds not in it any source of enjoyment." In this species of economic determinism men and women would know each other "solely from the outside" and through a busy life of getting and spending would avoid what Bentham called the "painful probe" of introspection.[51]

Because of the need to recycle all wealth into the process of capital accumulation, the nineteenth-century bourgeoisie put forth an ethic of self-abnegation and denial.[52] "Capital," wrote

51. Wolin, pp. 316, 324, 333, 341. The phrase "solely from the outside" is from Wolin, p. 340. The rest are from Bentham.

52. Trilling, pp. 39–41, points out that insofar as the vision of a "good life" existed in the nineteenth century—in Shakespeare's words "quiet days, fair issue, and long life"—it was an ideal associated with the aristocracy. Material abundance and a willingness to accept pleasure were not part of the outlook of the nineteenth-century bourgeoisie.

the political economist N. W. Senior, is "abstinence." According to John Stuart Mill "everything that is produced perishes and most things very quickly. . . . Capital is kept in existence from age to age not by preservation, but by perpetual reproduction." "We economize with our health, our capacity for enjoyment, our forces," wrote Sigmund Freud in 1883, "we save up for something, not knowing ourselves for what."[53] Nature now appeared cruel and alien. Malthus's theory of population summed up the nineteenth-century belief that nature, in some sort of vicious joke, had instilled men and women with a sexual instinct that led them to produce offspring while simultaneously limiting the potential subsistence it would supply. In this context of scarcity, mutual suspicion, and a deep sense of the inner worthlessness of the world they had created, the Victorian bourgeoisie came to idealize the new, protected family, outside nature and outside production.

THE FAMILY, to the Victorian bourgeoisie, was a "tent pitch'd in a world not right,"[54] "This is the true nature of home," wrote John Ruskin; "it is the place of peace; the shelter, not only from all injury, but from all terror, doubt, and division. . . . So far as the anxieties of the outer life penetrate into it . . . it ceases to be a home; it is then only a part of the outer world which you have roofed over and lighted fire in."[55] It stood in opposition to the terrible anonymous world of commerce and industry: "a world alien, not your world . . . without father, without child, without brother."[56] The Victorian family was distinguished by its spiritual aspect: it is remote, ethereal and unreal—"a sacred place, a vestal temple."[57] As in the middle ages, so now with the bourgeoisie, the domain of the spirit had once again separated off from the realm of production.

---

53. Ernest Jones, *The Life and Work of Sigmund Freud* (New York, 1953), vol. 1, pp. 190–91.

54. Coventry Patmore, "The Angel in the House," quoted in Walter Houghton, *The Victorian Frame of Mind* (New Haven, 1957), p. 345.

55. John Ruskin, "Of Queens Gardens," quoted in Millett, pp. 98–99.

56. Thomas Carlyle, *Past and Present*, quoted in Houghton, p. 345.

57. Ruskin, quoted in Millett, p. 99.

Reflecting this separation, the belief in separate "spheres" for men and women came to dominate the ideology of the family in the epoch of industrial capitalism. As the family was now idealized, so was the familial role of women. According to one of the domestic manuals that began to flourish in the 1830s and '40s, "that fierce conflict of worldly interests, by which men are so deeply occupied, [compels them] to stifle their best feelings."[58] Men, according to Ruskin, are "feeble in sympathy."[59] But women, by contrast, whose "everyday duties are most divine because they are most human," nurture within the family the "human" values crushed by "modern life."[60] Earlier, the feudal aristocracy had idealized women for their delicate beauty. In the eighteenth century the bourgeoisie had stressed their role as practical and intelligent housewives. Now the dominant image of women was that of the mother who, freed from domestic labor by the abundance of servants could devote herself wholly to her child.[61] "A woman when she becomes a mother should withdraw herself from the world," instructed an 1869 domestic manual.[62] In the nineteenth century, childhood was first assigned a separate identity and exalted as the time of life untainted by the roughness of material necessity.[63] To a large extent sexual interest was removed from the bourgeois family and assigned to prostitutes,

58. S. Ellis, *The Daughters of England* (London, 1845), pp. 22–23. quoted in J. A. and Olive Banks, *Feminism and Family Planning in Victorian England* (New York, 1964, 1972), p. 59; see also p. 22.

59. Quoted in Millett, p. 105.

60. Houghton, p. 347, quoting Charles Kingsley, *Letters and Memories*.

61. Ruth Alexander, "Sex and the Sexes in 18th Century American Magazines," unpublished manuscript. Ruth Alexander made several suggestions of major importance for changing an earlier version of this article.

62. S. A. Sewall, *Women and the Times We Live In*, quoted in Banks, p. 60.

63. Describing a parallel transformation in American life, Ralph Waldo Emerson expressed the paradoxical quality of the nineteenth-century exaltation of childhood through the remark of a friend who recalled the hardships of his own youth: "It was a misfortune to have been born when children were nothing and to live till men were nothing." "Historic Notes of Life and Letters in New England," in Perry Miller, ed., *The American Transcendentalists* (New York, 1957), p. 5.

an important group among working-class women. Filial relations were intensified and charged with unsuspected emotions by the sexual repression and prudery characteristic of the period of capital accumulation. As Freud soon demonstrated, the Victorian bourgeois family was a cauldron of anger, jealousy, fear and guilt—not to mention sexuality. But its internal, subjective life was masked by the stark contrast between its protective warmth and the "universal thirst for power"[64] that prevailed in society. Even men could find their "true self" in the family, "no longer stained by contact with the . . . petty spite and brutal tyranny of an office."[65] This vision of the family was incorporated and systematized within the realm of moral philosophy. John Stuart Mill, for example, praised its "loving forgetfulness of self"[66] and Hegel argued that it was the "naturally ethical" antithesis to the brutal competition of civil society.[67]

Victorian idealism represented a decline from the early bourgeois conception of the family. Just as the bourgeoisie was being transformed into a parasitic class within the system of production, so its ideology of the family was becoming abstract and idealized. Within this decline the bourgeois family was called into question by the new social movements of the late eighteenth and nineteenth centuries.

BEGINNING IN THE EIGHTEENTH century a series of writers and artists attacked the bourgeois ideal of the family on behalf of free love. Drawing upon the arguments of William Godwin, Percy Shelley wrote, "Love withers under constraint: its very essence is liberty: it is compatible neither with obedience, jealousy, nor fear." Shelley urged the abolition of marriage, and expected that the result would be unions "of long duration," marked by generosity and self-devotion, since "choice

64. Bentham again, quoted in Wolin, p. 342.

65. *Mark Rutherford's Deliverance*, ch. 8, pp. 106-7, quoted in Houghton, p. 346.

66. Quoted in Houghton, p. 347.

67. Shlomo Avineri, *The Social and Political Thought of Karl Marx* (Cambridge, 1969), p. 90.

and change will be exempted from restraint."[68] In its origins, the support for free love was closely related to an attack on the social repression of women.

Feminism in England had two different sources. Among middle-class women it represented a protest against the enforced domesticity brought about by the rise of industry. The withdrawal of commodity production from the home radically separated women from men; the creation of a separate "sphere" for women also laid the basis for a separate women's movement. Women attacked the genteel idleness of the "doll's house" and demanded entry into education, the professions, and public life. Simultaneously, working-class women were being drawn into large-scale industry. Demands for female suffrage and related reforms were raised within the proletarian movement generally—for example, among the National Union of the Working Classes and the Chartists. Both groups of women often reconciled their demands with support for the traditional domestic values of the bourgeois household.

The Victorian opposition to female equality was bitter and furious, reflecting the idea that the family had become the last refuge from the demands of capitalist society. The emancipation of women threatened to degrade all society to a common level of cynical manipulation (i.e., economic competition in the marketplace). Within the same bourgeois view, feminists argued that bringing women into society would humanize it. Nineteenth-century feminism was closely involved with movements of moral reform such as temperance and the abolition of prostitution. Their participation in these movements supported the idea that women were the guardians of society's morals. Similarly, on the basis of their special capacity for service, certain occupations, for example schoolteaching and nursing, were largely restricted to women, and downgraded.

To the feminist attack on the Victorian ideal the socialists' voice was added. The rise of industrial capitalism had created a new form of the family among the bourgeoisie, but it had

68. Percy Bysshe Shelley, *Complete Poetical Works* (London, 1881), p. 223; Kenneth Neill Cameron, *The Young Shelley: Genesis of a Radical* (New York, 1950), p. 270.

eliminated the economic basis of the family—private productive property—among the working class. As Engels wrote in his 1844 description of the English working class, "Family life for the worker is almost impossible under the existing social system. . . . The various members of the family only see each other in the mornings and evenings, because the husband is away at his work all day long. Perhaps his wife and the older children also go out to work and they may be in different factories. In these circumstances how can family life exist?"[69] Marx and Engels rejected the nineteenth-century idealization of the bourgeois family, which they viewed as the retrograde preserve of private wealth. In contrast to Hegel and Mill they insisted that "civil society" or "political economy"—capitalism—directly infected family life. "On what foundation is the present family, the bourgeois family, based?" they wrote in the *Communist Manifesto*. "On capital. On private gain. . . . The bourgeois sees in his wife a mere instrument of production" whereas, among the proletariat, "all family ties . . . are torn asunder." According to Marx and Engels the early bourgeois ideals of the family—love, equality, and common work—could not be realized so long as society was organized around private property. The family under capitalism, ostensibly private, was in fact continually transformed by the needs of the dominant class. Communism would liberate the family from its subjection to capital and "will make the relations between the sexes a purely private affair, which concerns only the two persons involved."[70] Hence in the nineteenth century a series of movements arose directed at "private" or family life. Part IV describes their social basis.

---

69. *The Condition of the Working Class in England* (Stanford, 1968), p. 145.

70. This quote is from the 1847 *Communist Credo* by Engels, which preceded the Communist Manifesto. Dirk Struik, ed., *Birth of the Communist Manifesto* (New York, 1971), p. 185.

IV. PROLETARIANIZATION AND PERSONAL LIFE

1. The Transformation of Bourgeois Individualism and the Rise of Subjectivity

IN FEUDAL SOCIETY, men and women occupied a fixed position within a stratified division of labor—they owed allegiance to a particular lord and worked on a particular plot of land rather than being "free" to sell their labor or property. Explicit and direct relations of authority defined people's sense of individual identity. Catholicism provided them with a common purpose outside themselves.

Private property freed the early bourgeoisie from a fixed social role within the feudal order. On the basis of private property the bourgeoisie has defended "individual rights" throughout history—first against feudal prerogative, more recently against labor unions and "state intervention." The bourgeoisie has consistently defended the right of individuals to rise and fall within the marketplace through their own efforts, rather than on the basis of birth; the bourgeoisie originated the idea of a contradiction between the individual and society.

But bourgeois individualism also serves as a basis for social order within capitalist society. Based upon private property, bourgeois individualism was identified with a particular activity—commodity production—and a predetermined inner life—the Christian conscience and self-interest. Major bourgeois social theories such as liberalism or rationalism posit a society of individuals (i.e., families) who, acting in their own self-interest, advance the social purpose by expanding private wealth: while individuals compete against one another, the marketplace guarantees a coherent social whole. Similarly, bourgeois moral ideals combine an emphasis on being true to oneself—direct, unashamed—with an emphasis on performing one's social obligations. In this view the property owner and his authoritarian family ("a little commonwealth") are the center of a well-ordered society.

The development of large-scale industrial production destroyed this unity. In a process that lasted several centuries but that culminated in the nineteenth century in England and the United States, productive property was virtually monopolized by a small centralized ruling class. The center of social authority shifted from the property-owning family to remote centers of power. The British radical Thomas Cobbett wrote in the early nineteenth century that industry had drawn "the resources of the country unnaturally together into great heaps." [71] Work, in the form of wage-labor, was removed from the center of family life, to become the means by which family life was maintained. Society divided and the family became the realm of "private life."

At the same time the conflict between the individual and society took on a new meaning. On one side appeared "society"—the capitalist economy, the state, the fixed social core that has no space in it for the individual; on the other, the personal identity, no longer defined by its place in the social division of labor. On one side the objective social world appeared, perceived at first as "machinery" or "industry," then throughout the nineteenth century as "society" and into the twentieth as "big business," "city hall," and then as "technology" or "life," as the domination of the proletariat by the capitalist class became more difficult to perceive. In opposition to this harsh world that no individual could hope to affect, the modern world of subjectivity was created.

This sense of an isolated individual ranged against a society he or she cannot affect, distinguishes social life in developed capitalist society. The major tradition of modern bourgeois social thought, as exemplified in the work of Freud and Weber, portrays the conflict between the "individual" and "society" as the "human condition" and thereby encourages "mature" acquiescence to the demands of capital. But there is also a tradition of protest. Its earliest expression did not come from the proletariat but from the petit-bourgeois and artisan classes who, as society divided between capital and wage labor, resisted proletarianization. Beginning in the late eighteenth and early nineteenth centuries petit-bourgeois individualism per-

71. Quoted in Raymond Williams, *Culture and Society* (New York, 1958), p. 15.

petually ranged itself against the emerging bourgeoisie, and perpetually lost. But political and economic weakness was accompanied by ideological strength. Petit-bourgeois individualism defended what was most progressive in the bourgeois past while articulating what was most oppressive in the condition of the emerging proletariat. It spoke for the whole individual before the deformations of the capitalist division of labor. It argued that one's work should be an expression of oneself rather than just a means to survival. Petit-bourgeois individualism continually threatened to burst and overflow the private property integument that enclosed it and to envision the individual as an end in him or herself.

In the nineteenth century the romantic artist was the great symbol of the individual posed against society. Before the rise of industrial capitalism artists occupied a fixed place within an explicit division of labor. Writers lived on "pensions, benefices and sinecures," composers were "court musicians, church musicians or town musicians," artists were commissioned by patrons.[72] In this regard the production relations of artists were similar to those of other pre-industrial artisans whose income and position were based less on supply and demand than on custom, social prestige, and traditional standards of pay and workmanship.[73] By the early 1800s the artist was producing commodities for newly arisen industries: commercial publishing, popular periodicals, newspapers, galleries and commercial concerts. The artist's defense against proletarianization lay in a new emphasis on the originality of the artist and the uniqueness of the work of art. Beginning with romanticism, artists declared that art was the product less of a particular craft or discipline than of the artist's inner life. "What information does a poet require?" asked Wordsworth in 1800; unlike "a lawyer, a physician, a mariner, an astronomer, or a natural philosopher" only that which he possesses "as a man"—"the

72. Arnold Hauser, *The Social History of Art*, vol. 3 (New York, 1958), pp. 53, 81; Williams, "The Romantic Artist," in *Culture and Society*; Eric Hobsbawm, *The Age of Revolution, 1789-1848* (New York, 1964), p. 307.

73. E. P. Thompson, *Making of the English Working Class*, passim.

sympathies of our daily life."[74] Wordsworth spoke for the artist, but it was the universality of the experience of pitting oneself, one's inner feelings, private thoughts, and dreams, against "society" that inspired the modern image of the artist.

Wordsworth looked back to "humble and rustic life" in which "the essential passions of the heart find a better soil." But this ideal had lost its social basis with the rise of industrial capitalism. Throughout the nineteenth century the romantic tradition conjured up a series of figures who allegedly stood apart from society on the basis of their own personal uniqueness: the hero, the virtuoso, the mystic, the world traveler, the wandering Jew, the mountain climber; figures who constantly threaten to disappear from society.[75] The idea of the genius also comes from this period, as well as the idea of the dandy who turns his personal life into art. But dandyism, according to Charles Baudelaire, depends on people "free from the need to follow any profession. They have no other purpose than to . . . satisfy their desires, and to feel and think."[76] Romantic individualism's final expression, in twentieth-century art, would confine the individual to an entirely subjective and psychological realm, wholly divorced from the rest of society.

The defense of the subjective individual against "science," "industry," or "modern society" continued throughout the nineteenth century. Its characteristic tone was one of protest: for example, Thomas Carlyle in 1829: "Not the external and physical alone is now managed by machinery but the internal and spiritual also. . . . Men are grown mechanical."[77] Against the general rationalization of life the romantic tradition upheld the view that men and women were feeling beings. It saw in "nature" (which eventually came to include sexuality) "the

---

74. William Wordsworth, "Observations Prefixed to 'Lyrical Ballads,'" in Mark Schorer, Josephine Miles, and Gordon McKenzie, eds., *Criticism: The Foundations of Modern Literary Judgment* (New York, 1958), p. 36. Ideas similar to those of the romantics were expressed within evangelical and millenarian groups.

75. Morse Peckham, *The Triumph of Romanticism* (Columbia, S.C., 1970), pp. 36–46. Peckham refers to these as "anti-roles."

76. Charles Baudelaire, "The Painter of Modern Life," in Peter Quennell, ed., *The Essence of Laughter* (New York, 1956), p. 52.

77. Quoted in Williams, *Culture and Society*, p. 73.

repository of [those] inner tendencies opposing the growth of mechanisation, dehumanisation and reification."[78] In its emphasis on the emotions, on innocence and childhood, on love and on beauty, romanticism invoked a world in which human beings were no longer dominated by the daily discipline of production. In this way, a tradition deeply rooted in the bourgeois ideal of individualism also came to stand for a qualitatively different way of life.

The socialist movement, which arose in the nineteenth century, was closely linked to this romantic tradition, particularly through its utopian forebears. The concept of alienation derives from the same milieu as the artist's assertion that one's product is a part of oneself. Marx invokes a conception of human activity closely related to the romantic vision: "The ancient conception in which man always appears (in however narrowly national, religious, or political a definition) as the aim of production, seems very much more exalted than the modern world in which production is the aim of man and wealth the aim of production. In fact, however, when the narrow bourgeois form has been peeled away, what is wealth, if not the universality of needs, capacities, enjoyments, productive powers, etc. of individuals, produced in universal exchange?"[79]

On the other hand, socialism developed in the nineteenth century by defining itself off from this romantic and utopian tradition. Romanticism represented an ideological understanding of capitalist society, and throughout the nineteenth century aligned itself as easily with conservative and reactionary political currents as with socialism. Socialists downgraded the split it portrays between the "individual" and "society" as the expression of a declining class whose productive function was being eliminated. The romantic tradition exalted the "lone individual" at a time when society was dividing irrevocably into two classes. And, indeed, it is likely that the romantic tradition of individualism would have dwindled into obscurity

78. Georg Lukács, *History and Class Consciousness* (Cambridge, Mass., 1972), p. 136.

79. Karl Marx, *Pre-Capitalist Economic Formations* (New York, 1964), pp. 84–85.

if the rise of capitalism had not created a new social basis for it in the proletarian family.

Proletarianization created a new form of the family among the masses of people—one "separated" off from the sphere of goods production. Within it, new needs began to take shape. For those reduced to proletarian status from the petit bourgeoisie, one's individual identity could no longer be realized through work or through the ownership of property: individuals now began to develop the need to be valued "for themselves." Proletarianization gave rise to subjectivity. The family became the major sphere of society in which the individual could be foremost—it was the only space that proletarians "owned." Within it, a new sphere of social activity began to take shape: personal life. The nineteenth century Victorian ideology of the family as the repository of "human values" converged with the tradition of romantic revolt. The proletariat itself came to share the bourgeois ideal of the family as a "utopian retreat." Although this development did not emerge clearly until the twentieth century, its preconditions were established in the early stages of industrial capitalism.

2. *The Proletarian Family*

WITH THE RISE of industrial capitalism wages replaced productive property as the economic basis of the family. "Private property" was redefined among the proletariat to refer to objects of consumption: food, clothing, domestic articles, and later, for some, a home. The traditional division of labor within the family was threatened as women and children joined men in the factories. Meanwhile, capital was accumulated by restricting domestic consumption and diverting any surplus into industry. The bourgeois ethic of repression and abstinence was extended to the proletariat through the force of material circumstances. The family's internal life was dominated by the struggle of its members for their basic material needs.

This understanding underlay the politics of nineteenth-century socialists and reformers. Many feared that by turning women and children into wage-earners, industrial capitalism was destroying the family. The goal of "saving" the family underlay such nineteenth-century reforms as protective legislation and child labor laws. Over time a series of private and public institutions arose—schools, savings banks, insurance companies, welfare agencies—whose function was to mediate between capitalist production and the fragmented realm of private life. The great trade union struggles through which the nineteenth-century working class both resisted and accommodated itself to industrial capitalism were also intended to establish a new basis for the proletarian family. Women were commonly excluded from trade unions and male trade unionists demanded a wage that could support the entire family.

When the socialist movement took up the question of the family in the nineteenth century it expected that a revolution in commodity production would simultaneously transform the family; early socialists did not experience the family as a "separate" political problem. The major critique of the family came from within romantic and utopian socialist currents and from feminists. The great effect that Marx and Engels had on nineteenth-century socialism was to demonstrate the centrality of the sphere of commodity production (the sphere in which surplus value was produced and realized) to all areas of life. This gave the romantic and utopian critique a theoretical basis that it lacked, and encouraged a focus on collective political action rather than on individual transformation. But it also led away from the emphasis on subjective or personal life that distinguishes the petit-bourgeois tradition. Reflecting the struggle for survival that characterized the nineteenth-century proletarian family, Marx and Engels saw no need for a separate program for "personal" life, including the oppression of women by men within the family. Instead they believed that if individuals were freed from economic exploitation they would arrange their private lives according to earlier ideals of domestic and personal fulfillment, unrealizable under conditions of industrial capitalism.

THE DEVELOPMENT OF capitalism destroyed this hope and to a great extent "separated" the socialist movement from the subsequent development of the family and of personal life among the proletariat. The reduction of the economically "independent" family to a houseworker and a factory worker was part of a process that led to greatly expanded productivity of labor. In the face of a growing labor movement, European and American capitalists began to meet some trade union demands, while diverting the working class from its attack against capitalist production.

By the middle of the nineteenth century in England and America bourgeois economists had begun to argue that the development of leisure time among the workers coupled with a rise in wages would benefit capital by greatly expanding the domestic market for consumer goods. This argument was also adopted by the labor movement. In 1863, for example, an American labor spokesman, Ira Steward, called for *A Reduction of Hours, An Increase of Wages* which jointly would encourage "the workers, through their new leisure, to unite in buying luxuries now confined to the wealthy."[80] In the second half of the nineteenth century the great industries of domestic consumption arose in England: clothing, food, furniture, housing.[81] By the end of the century bourgeois spokesmen were proclaiming that workers were becoming "capitalists," since a frugal and fortunate working family could in some cases eventually purchase its own home. Along with this, the bourgeoisie encouraged the belief that human meaning could be found primarily within the sphere of consumption.

At the same time, women and children lost the central place they had occupied in the early proletariat. Child labor was slowly eliminated and women were transformed into a marginal labor force in relation to capitalist production, with their primary loyalty to the home. The housewife emerged, alongside the proletarian—the two characteristic laborers of developed capitalist society. Her tasks extended beyond the material labor of the family to include responsibility for the "human values" which the family was thought to preserve: love, personal happiness, domestic felicity. In contrast, the working-class husband's primary responsibility was understood to be earning a wage, whether or not his wife worked. The

80. Jurgen Kuczynski, *The Rise of the Working Class* (New York, 1967), p. 115.

81. Eric Hobsbawm, *Industry and Empire* (New York, 1968), p. 73.

split in society between "personal feelings" and "economic production" was integrated with the sexual division of labor. Women were identified with emotional life, men with the struggle for existence. Under these conditions a new form of the family developed—one that understood itself to be operating in apparent freedom from production, and that placed a primary emphasis on the personal relations of its members. A separate sphere of personal life began to develop among the proletariat. This development can be seen most clearly in the twentieth-century United States.

3. Personal Life and Subjectivity in the Twentieth-Century United States

AS CAPITALISM DEVELOPED the productive functions performed by the family were gradually socialized.[82] The family lost its core identity as a productive unit based upon private property. Material production within the family—the work of housewives and mothers—was devalued since it was no longer seen as integral to the production of commodities. The expansion of education as well as welfare, social work, hospitals, old age homes, and other "public" institutions further eroded the productive functions of the family. At the same time the family acquired new functions as the realm of personal life—as the primary institution in which the search for personal happiness, love, and fulfillment takes place. Reflecting the family's "separation" from commodity production, this search was understood as a "personal" matter, having little relation to the capitalist organization of society.

The development of this kind of personal life among the masses of people was a concomitant of the creation of a working class in capitalist society. Peasants and other pre-capitalist laborers were governed by the same social relations "inside" and "outside" work; the proletarian, by contrast, was a "free" man or woman outside work. By splitting society between

82. Although much of the following also applies to black and other "third world" families, there are also enormous differences that I do not discuss. A good starting place for such a discussion is Angela Davis, "Reflections on the Black Woman's Role in the Community of Slaves," *Black Scholar*, December 1971.

"work" and "life," proletarianization created the conditions under which men and women looked to themselves, outside the division of labor, for meaning and purpose. Introspection intensified and deepened as people sought in themselves the only coherence, consistency, and unity capable of reconciling the fragmentation of social life. The romantic stress on the unique value of the individual began to converge with the actual conditions of proletarian life, and a new form of personal identity developed among men and women, who no longer defined themselves through their jobs. Proletarianization generated new needs—for trust, intimacy, and self-knowledge, for example—which intensified the weight of meaning attached to the personal relations of the family. The organization of production around alienated labor encouraged the creation of a separate sphere of life in which personal relations were pursued as an end in themselves.

But the creation of a separate sphere of personal life was also shaped by the special problems of the capitalist class in the early twentieth century. Increasing proletarianization, along with deepening economic crises, created increasing labor unrest and class conflict, as well as the growth of the socialist movement. Beginning in the early twentieth century a significant minority of American capitalists saw the possibility of integrating labor within a capitalist consensus through raising its level of consumption. Besides expanding the market for consumer goods, such a strategy would divert the working class from socialism and from a direct assault on capitalist relations of production. Edward Filene, for example, a Boston department store owner, urged his fellow capitalists to recognize unions and raise wages as a way of extending "industrial democracy" and "economic freedom" to the working class. "The industrial democracy I am discussing," he explained, "has nothing to do with the Cubist politics of class revolution." Instead, he urged that workers be free to "cultivate themselves" in the "school of freedom" which the modern marketplace constituted. "Modern workmen have learned their habits of consumption . . . in the school of fatigue," but mass production was transforming the consumer market into a "civilizing" experience for the working class.[83] The emphasis on consumption was an important means through which the newly proletarianized, and still resisting, industrial working class was reconciled to the rise of corporate capitalism, and through which the enormous immigrant influx of the late nineteenth and early twentieth centuries was integrated with the industrial working class.

The extraordinary increases in the productivity of labor achieved during the nineteenth century, along with increasing American dominance within the world market, made it possible for capitalists to pursue this course. By the 1920s many firms had acceded to the sustained demand for a shorter workday. This demand, probably the most persistent trade union demand of the nineteenth century, was the necessary prerequisite to the establishment of personal life among the proletariat: it freed life-time from the immediate demands of capital. In the nineteenth century, socialists had emphasized the eight-hour day, since it would free the working class for self-education and political activity. But with the decline of American socialism after World War I, this issue receded. In the 1930s the eight-hour day and the forty-hour week became the standard in mass-production industry. Work time has been fixed at these levels ever since, in spite of subsequent technological progress. The capitalist class has extended "leisure" to the proletariat, but only within the limits set by the capitalists' need to retain control of the labor force.

Similarly, the capitalist class has raised wages in accord with its overall interests. Monopoly control of the market made it possible for capitalists to "compensate" themselves for wage increases by simultaneously raising prices. Beginning in the 1930s state programs such as welfare and unemployment insurance financed a minimum level of consumption among the entire working class by taxing its better-paid sectors. Along with these measures corporate capitalists created a sales force and employed the new media of radio and television to spread the ethic of consumerism into every home.

83. Stuart B. Ewen, "Advertising as Social Production," *Radical America*, May 1969, pp. 46–47.

The family, no longer a commodity-producing unit, received a new importance as a market for industrial commodities. Mass production forced the capitalist class to cultivate and extend that market, just as it forced it to look abroad for other new markets. As a result, American domestic and personal life in the twentieth century has been governed by an ethic of pleasure and self-gratification previously unknown to a laboring class. Working people now see consumption as an end in itself, rather than as an adjunct to production, and as a primary source of both personal and social (i.e., "status") identity. This is symbolized within the "middle class" as "lifestyle," a word that is used to defend one's prerogatives regardless of the demands of "society."

The rise of "mass consumption" has vastly extended the range of "personal" experience available to men and women while retaining it within an abstract and passive mode: the purchase and consumption of commodities. Taste, sensibility, and the pursuit of subjective experience—historically reserved for leisure classes and artists—have been generalized throughout the population in predetermined and standardized forms by advertising and other means. This is reflected in the modern department store in which the wealth, culture, and treasures of previous ruling classes now appear in the form of cheap jewelry, fashions, and housewares.[84]

On one hand there has been a profound democratization of the idea that it is good to live well, consume pleasurably, and enjoy the fruits of one's labor. On the other hand, "mass consumption"—within the context of capitalism—has meant the routinization of experience and the deepening of divisions within the proletariat. The deep material deprivation that still characterizes the lives of most Americans— bitter inadequacies of housing, food, transportation, health care, etc.—has taken on added emotional meanings. The "poor" feel personally in-

---

84. Honoré de Balzac noted a similar phenomenon in the Paris arcades of the 1820s and 1830s, perhaps the earliest form of the department store: "The magic columns of these palaces show to the connoisseur on every side in the articles which their portals display that *industry rivals the arts.*" Quoted in Walter Benjamin, "Paris—Capital of the Nineteenth Century," *New Left Review*, March 1968, p. 77. Italics added.

adequate and ashamed, while the more highly educated and better-paid sectors of the working class experience guilt toward the "less fortunate."

IN DEVELOPED CAPITALIST SOCIETY, the enhancement of personal consumption has been closely related to the devaluation of labor. Like the rise of mass consumption, the idea that labor is worthless results from its vastly expanded productivity. Expanded production of necessary goods—for example, food, clothing, and housing—without expanding the labor time spent in such production, began in agriculture after the Civil War and in manufacturing during the 1920s.[85] As a result, the sphere of necessary goods production has shrunk in relation to other spheres of production. To counteract the effects of this tendency—particularly rising unemployment—and to maintain a level of "scarcity" in consumer goods, corporate capitalism has fostered inflation, waste, planned obsolescence, and underutilization of productive capacity. It has vastly expanded "non-productive" industries such as advertising and finance, and used the state to subsidize the production of useless or destructive goods, such as armaments. A great amount of labor time in capitalist society is spent in activities that have the purpose of perpetuating capitalist relations of production, rather than producing necessary goods. This deepening irrationality of capitalist production has obscured the place of production within our society.

In the nineteenth century, every sacrifice to the engine of capital accumulation was justified in the name of "material necessity," the driving force of all previous human history.

85. Martin J. Sklar, "On the Proletarian Revolution and the End of Political-Economic Society," *Radical America*, May 1969, terms this tendency "disaccumulation" to contrast it with the accumulation process of industrial capitalism. In some way every attempt to describe what has changed in capitalism since the nineteenth century must make this tendency central. For example, Paul Baran and Paul Sweezy's *Monopoly Capital* (New York, 1966) refers to it as the tendency of the surplus to rise. Other examples include Maurice Dobb, "Some Features of Capitalism since the First World War," in *Capitalism, Development and Planning* (New York, 1970), pp. 38–39, and Tom Nairn and Angelo Quattrocchi, *The Begining of the End* (London, 1968), pp. 156–73.

Similarly, socialists defined their revolution in terms of taking over the productive capacity as it had been developed under capitalism. But in the twentieth century the center no longer holds. Most people see no meaning or value in their work. In addition, marginal employment and unemployment characterize major groups in American society—youth, housewives, "hippies," the black "lumpenproletariat." Within these groups, which are themselves marginal to the sphere of commodity production, the idea has developed that production is itself marginal to social life.

This tendency has also been reinforced within the sphere of goods production. In the nineteenth century the capitalist class and its representatives directly supervised the labor process. By contrast, capitalists are often physically absent in the modern corporation. Instead the labor process appears to be governed by neutral, scientific laws such as centralization, efficiency, the imperatives of technology, etc. This appearance reflects the increasing rationalization of the labor process and reinforces the tendency to understand modern society in terms of the domination of the individual by anonymous, impersonal forces. Rather than encountering the capitalist class, the proletariat is faced by abstract, scientific laws and "countless, immediate oppressors."[86]

The combination of waste, underemployment, and rationalization has come close to destroying people's understanding of their part in an integrated system of social production. It has reinforced the tendency to look to personal life for meaning, and to understand personal life in entirely subjective terms. The isolation of so much of modern life from the sphere of necessary goods production gives it its "abstract" character. Both "society" and personal life are experienced as formless, with no common core, in inexplicable disarray.

THE CHANGING CHARACTER of developed capitalist production has expanded personal life in constricted, capitalist forms. As opportunities for capital investment have declined within

86. Il Manifesto, "Technicians and the Capitalist Division of Labor," *Socialist Revolution* 9 (May–June 1972), pp. 66–69. This sense is even more pronounced within bureaucracies.

the sphere of necessary goods production, capital has spread to the sphere of personal life. Whole new industries—the "services"—have developed in this way.[87] Examples include the media and other forms of culture, travel, sports, psychotherapy, health, and commercial religions. Since production no longer integrates social life, the capitalist class has sought new means of social solidarity. In particular the education system has been assigned the function of teaching people to "get along" with one another.[88] The increasing role of mental labor within the process of production has entailed the creation of new skills such as "imagination" and "sensitivity," which have in turn shaped personal life.

Both the emphasis on salesmanship, integral to the rise of mass production, and the emphasis of the services and the state on "working with people" have encouraged an attention to psychology and new forms of sensitivity. Insight into the personal lives of others, gained to a large extent through self-awareness, has been taught to large sectors of the working class: it has become a productive skill necessary to capitalist development. Similarly the working class and petit bourgeoisie have been urged to shed the "selfish individualism" associated with laissez-faire capitalism, in favor of cooperation, sociability, and tolerance.[89] But "cooperation" and "sociability" are enforced through authoritarian institutions such as the public schools that have the responsibility—and power—to make people get along with one another.

Similarly, the increasingly technological character of modern production has created a need for workers with abilities of self-expression, independence, and creativity. But the educational system has cloaked these skills in an ideology of

---

87. Many services are direct adjuncts of goods production. Further, a large component of all service industries can be resolved into goods production—consider the health industry as an example.

88. The best introduction to this function of the modern state is James O'Connor, "The Fiscal Crisis of the State," *Socialist Revolution* 1 and 2 (January-February and March-April 1970).

89. This ideal ("the family of man"), like the ideals generated by mass consumption, takes the form of a conflict between the "new middle class" and the rest of the proletariat.

personal development rather than presenting them as necessary skills of production. As a result men and women (but particularly men) have been encouraged to dwell upon their own uniqueness and to understand themselves in terms of chimeras such as "brightness" or "talent" supposedly innate in certain individuals. In fact "brightness" and "talent" are developed as alienable forms of mental labor. Nevertheless, the aspirations toward self-expression, like those toward "cooperation," continually threaten to go beyond the specific form they take within capitalist production. While these tendencies are more pronounced among highly educated sectors of the work force, the ideology that underlies them is spread to all sectors.

A collective consciousness of great diversity has been created. Experienced personally as individual and unique, it is simultaneously integral to and shaped by capitalist development. Non-Marxist thinkers have always understood this development ideologically, abstracting either the pole of personal aloneness or the pole of social control. Their theories of the twentieth century portray either "mass society," "other-directed man," "men without qualities," "organization man," "conformism," the "rise of the masses," or, the polar opposite, "existential man," "irrational man," "psychological man," "post-industrial" or "post-scarcity" man, man for whom hell is other people. In fact, developed capitalism has mass-produced specific forms of personal life, and of individuality, which simultaneously reinforce and threaten capitalist hegemony.

INCREASINGLY CUT OFF from production, the contemporary family threatens to become a well of subjectivity divorced from any social meaning. Within it a world of vast psychological complexity has developed as the counterpart to the extraordinary degree of rationalization and impersonality achieved by capital in the sphere of commodity production. The individualist values generated by centuries of bourgeois development—self-consciousness, perfectionism, independence—have taken new shape through the insatiability of personal life in developed capitalist society. The internal life of the family is dominated by a search for personal fulfillment for which there seem to be no rules.[90] Much of this search has been at the expense of women.

Already in the late nineteenth century American women were consumed with a sense of their own diminished role and stature when compared with their mothers and grandmothers,[91] women who labored within the productive unity of the family defined by private property. In a letter to Jane Addams in the early twentieth century, Charlotte Gilman described the married woman's sense of living second-hand, of getting life in translation, of finding oneself unready and afraid in the "face of experience."[92] By 1970 this fear had become a desperate sense of loss. Meredith Tax describes the "limbo of private time and space" of the housewife: "When I am by mvself, I am nothing. I only know that I exist because I am needed by someone who is real, my husband, and by my children. My husband goes out into the real world. . . . I stay in the imaginary world in this house, doing jobs that I largely invent, and that no one cares about but myself. . . . I seem to be involved in some sort of mysterious process."[93]

Just as the rise of industry in the eighteenth and nineteenth centuries cut women off from men and gave a new meaning to male supremacy, so the rise of mass education has created the contemporary form of youth and adolescence. The "generation gap" is the result of the family lagging behind the dominant tendencies of the culture and of the transformation of productive skills which children learn in school and through the media. Parents now appear "stupid" and "backward" to their children, representing, as they do, an earlier stage of

90. Asked for an explanation for the proliferation of clinics for sex therapy William Masters (of Masters and Johnson) gave as one reason "a man and a woman need each other more now than ever before. People need someone to hold on to. Once they had the clan but now they only have each other." *New York Times*, 29 October 1972.

91. Gail Parker, ed., *The Oven Birds: American Women on Womanhood, 1820–1920* (New York, 1972), pp. 4 ff.

92. Christopher Lasch, *The New Radicalism in America, 1889-1963: The Intellectual as a Social Type*.

93. Meredith Tax, *Woman and Her Mind: The Story of Daily Life* (Cambridge, Mass., 1970), pp. 7, 17.

capitalist development. Beginning in the early twentieth century the family began to appear to young people as a prison cut off from reality.[94]

At the same time, in the form of "public opinion," the imperatives of capitalist production have been recreated within the family, particularly in the "expectations" through which parents bludgeon themselves and their children into submission.[95] Fathers, like school teachers or policemen, appear to stand for the whole bourgeois order. Hence, the split between the public and the private is recreated within the family. As in the "outside world," people feel they are not known for themselves, not valued for who they really are.

While serving as a refuge, personal life has also become depersonalized; subjective relations tend to become disengaged, impersonal, and mechanically determined. Introspection has promised to open a new world to men and women, but increasingly the inner life reverberates with the voices of others, the imperatives of social production. This is inevitable because the expansion of inner and personal life has been as integral to capitalist expansion in the modern epoch as has the spread of capitalism throughout the world.

But this process has also given shape to the revolutionary possibilities of our time. In previous centuries only a handful of individuals were prized for their special qualities of mind or character; the mass of men and women were ground down to an approximate sameness in the general struggle for existence. What distinguishes developed capitalist society is that the stress on individual development and uniqueness has become a tendency characterizing all of society.

The bourgeoisie made its revolution on behalf of a specific property form—private property—which it already possessed. But the only "property" that the proletariat possesses lies

94. At this point, "What is the meaning of life?" becomes a pervasive question among youth. Eugene Gant in *Look Homeward Angel* is a good example.

95. Aaron Esterson, *The Leaves of Spring* (Harmondsworth, 1970), a study of a schizophrenic family, distinguishes between "public opinion" which dominates the family's collective life and "God" who operates primarily when the individual is alone, especially in the toilet, the only room within the family in which privacy actually prevails.

within itself: our inner lives and social capabilities, our dreams, our desires, our fears, our sense of ourselves as interconnected beings. Reflecting the "separation" of personal life from production, a new idea has emerged on a mass scale: that of human relations, and human beings, as an end in themselves.

This idea as it currently prevails is ideological. It presents human beings as an end in themselves only insofar as they are abstracted from the labor process. These ideas flourish within the worlds of modern art, psychology, and communes, and in such utopian authors as Norman O. Brown who envision a society passing totally beyond the realm of necessity. But in themselves they cannot supply the basis for a transformation of society, since a new society—whether socialist, communist, or anarchist—would necessarily be based upon a new division of labor and a new mode of production.

But these ideas also express what is realistic: the possibility of a society in which the production of necessary goods is a subordinate part of social life and in which the purposes and character of labor are determined by the needs of the individual members of society. It is appropriate that the family, in which so many of the most universal and impelling material processes of society have so far taken place, should also indicate the limited ability of capitalism to subordinate human needs to its own empty aggrandizement. The latest and most democratic form of an old hope can be discerned in the often tortured relations of contemporary personal life: that humanity can pass beyond a life dominated by relations of production. In varying forms this hope has given shape to radical and revolutionary movements since the nineteenth century.

CAPITALISM, THE FAMILY, AND PERSONAL LIFE

PART 2

Eli Zaretsky

V. POLITICS AND PERSONAL LIFE

1. Introduction

AS THE RISE OF INDUSTRIAL capitalism progressively removed goods production from the home, men and women came to see the family as separate from the economy, and personal life as a separate sphere of life divorced from the larger society. Revolutionary movements against capitalism have tended to recreate this separation through their failure to challenge it. The most recent—and extreme—expression of this tendency has been the polarization between radical feminism and traditional American socialist and Communist politics.

Radical feminism, as presented in Firestone's *Dialectic of Sex,* identifies the root cause of war, exploitation and racism as the "power psychology," the ceaseless striving to dominate others, that originates in the rule of men within the family.[1] Economic exploitation, which Marxists identify as the motor of history, is merely one form of domination. For Firestone the family operates independently of the economy; by shaping the psychological life of men and women it shapes the economy and the rest of society. Unlike previous movements which focused on outward manifestations of social control such as the economy or the state, radical feminism would go deeper and transform men and women directly.

The American Communist Party and most other socialist organizations have stood at the opposite pole from radical feminism. These groups have focused on the immediate relations of workers and capitalists within the sphere of commodity production to the exclusion of other areas of society. They have assigned women a secondary role within the socialist movement, except insofar as they were members of the working class, and have downgraded the radical feminist attention to family life as a "petit-bourgeois" or "subjective" preoccupation. Personal life and the family, they argued, would be changed more or less automatically through a revolution within the sphere of commodity production.

As I have sought to show, this polarization is rooted in the social structure of developed capitalist society. Firestone portrays the division between women in the family and men in the economy as a natural or biological condition that antedates history; in fact it arose at a relatively recent stage of capitalist development. Until the rise of industry both personal life and commodity production were organized within a family unit based upon private property. In the United States, because of the relatively wide diffusion of small private property, this way of life was particularly pervasive and persistent. White Americans and, after the Civil War, black Americans too, continually aspired to be small, independent, property-owning producers—farmers, shopkeepers, home manufacturers, mechanics and artisans who owned their own tools. As in Europe, this ideal was always belied by the bourgeoisie that inspired it. Beginning in the colonial settlements, American capitalists forced small

1. Shulamith Firestone, *The Dialectic of Sex* (New York, 1970). I am repeating some material in this section that was covered in the first part.

producers into economic dependence. By 1840 the rise of the New England textile industry had socialized a major form of women's domestic labor.[2] Throughout the nineteenth century industrial capital spread into the South and West. Nevertheless, the ideal of competitive individualism was sustained through economic and territorial expansion, which Americans came to see as natural—just as private property was natural. As a result the transformation caused by proletarianization occurred later than in Europe and has been particularly drastic. Even though by 1870 two out of every three productively engaged Americans, excluding housewives, were hired workers,[3] many of these workers were close to artisan status and could expect to own property. And employers were small and rural and, in contrast to the big merchants and financiers, were often grouped together with their employees under the term "free labor."

During the last third of the nineteenth century, and particularly after 1890, the slow inevitable tendencies of capitalist development produced a qualitative transformation. American society polarized between a small, centralized bourgeoisie in control of the "trusts" and a mass of dispossessed proletarians who owned only their own labor-power and household goods. By World War I, the emerging corporate capitalist class had won the American people to a new epoch. Such phrases as "the end of American innocence" and "America's coming of age" symbolize the acquiescence of Americans in the demise of private productive property and their entry into a vast army of labor that, every morning, goes to work, and evenings and weekends, recovers from it.

This same transformation gave rise to a new form of the family, one with no apparent connection to the rest of society. The production of exchange value was removed from the family and vested in large-scale, "impersonal" corporate units. But rather than destroying traditional bourgeois family life this transformation gave it a new meaning as the realm of happiness, love, and individual freedom. With the rise of corporate capitalism, the family became the major institution in society

2. Barbara Easton, unpublished manuscripts.

3. David Montgomery, *Beyond Equality* (New York, 1967), p. 28.

given over to the personal needs of its members. Society divided between an inner and an outer world. At one pole the individual was central and a sometimes desperate search for warmth, intimacy, and mutual support prevailed. At the other pole social relations were anonymous and coerced; the individual was reduced to an interchangeable economic unit.

This same transformation mystified and obscured the place of the housewife within capitalist production. The specific class position of the housewife under capitalism now lay in her "classlessness"[4]—i.e., the absence of a direct relation to the capitalist class. Socialists and others understood her class position to be that of her husband, since her relation to the outside world was mediated through him. But the creation of a separate sphere of personal life among the proletariat entailed the creation of a separate class of housewives and mothers whose physical and mental labor reproduced this separate sphere. In contrast to the proletarian who worked in large socialized units and received a wage, the housewife worked alone and was unpaid. Rather than working for a corporation the housewife worked for a particular man, for herself, and for their children and relatives. Housework and child-rearing came to be seen as natural or personal functions performed in some private space outside society.

Twentieth-century socialist movements failed to challenge this ideological view of personal life and of women's labor within the home. The basis for this ideology is in seeing production and the economy as restricted to the sphere of commodity production and exchange. According to Marx, any society, if it is to survive, requires that its members organize themselves into a system of social production in order to meet their basic material needs. The form in which social labor is distributed changes from society to society and is determined by the dominant mode of production. Capitalist production takes the form of the production of surplus value. The fact that housewives and mothers do not produce surplus value

4. Selma James and Mariarosa Dalla Costa described this condition more specifically as the housewife's *wageless state* in talks in San Francisco and Berkeley during June, 1973. See also their *The Power of Women and the Subversion of the Community* (Bristol, England, 1972).

has obscured their participation with wage labor in an interdependent system of production. Thus, when socialists spoke of the economy as the determining force in society and restricted the meaning of economy to the sphere of surplus value, they lost the sense of capitalism as an integrated social system.

By excluding the family from their conception of capitalist production, socialists could not distinguish the specific oppression of women from the general oppression of the working class. Focusing on the rise of industry and the growth of the proletariat they missed its complement—the isolation of women and children from socialized production and the emergence of a separate sphere of personal life that veiled women's labor in the home. Every program developed by socialists for female liberation depended upon the entry of women into the wage labor force. Similarly, feminists, before the emergence of the current women's movement, sought to liberate women through an emphasis on jobs, equal pay, education, and, above all, through the ballot. The result, as in the Russian Revolution or in early twentieth century American feminism, has been to transform the position of women as wage laborers and professionals or in political life, while leaving women's place within the family relatively intact. Socialist movements have also lost touch with the development of modern personal life. Excluding the family from their conception of social production, socialists tended to accept the ideological portrayal of personal life that prevails in bourgeois society—that personal life is an entirely subjective phenomenon, having meaning only for the individual.

Against and outside the twentieth-century socialist movement an important modern tradition has developed based upon the emergence of a sphere of personal life not directly subordinate to capital. Utopians, hippies, existentialists, bohemians, psychoanalytically oriented radicals, communitarians, and sexual freedom advocates have stressed the key role of inner psychological change and of immediate personal relations in transcending if not transforming society. These currents have tended to distrust socialism in particular and politics in general as superficial or external responses to problems they see as rooted more deeply in the human condition. This is a tradition upon which radical feminism drew and against which it has fought. In common with this tradition radical feminism attempts to defend the personal and restore trust in subjectivity. But against psychoanalysis and similar currents radical feminism insists upon the necessity of waging a systematic political struggle.

But the radical feminist defense of subjectivity has not challenged, but assumed, the view of the family and personal life as a separate sphere ruled by its own laws. Rather than viewing the contemporary family as specific to developed capitalism, radical feminism takes it to be a universal form of oppression. "Beneath economics," wrote Firestone, "reality is psychosexual." Marxism's failure was that "it did not dig deep enough to the psychosexual roots of class." [5] These roots were the domination of women by men and of children by adults, essentially within the family. Basing its politics on the predominance of women within the personal sphere, radical feminism leaves uncontested the capitalist domination of society as a whole.

WHILE THE OPPOSITION between radical feminism and socialism is rooted in the divided structure of capitalist society, it was not inevitable that political movements would recapitulate this division. Part V is a history of how the division developed. In the nineteenth century, socialists envisioned a revolution that would transform every area of life. This was clearest among utopian socialists who based much of their outlook upon the petit-bourgeois family in which production and personal life were still integrated. Nineteenth-century individualism and utopian socialism defended the whole individual against the fragmentation of capitalist society. Similarly, Marxian socialists understood themselves to be extending the limited political democracy achieved by the bourgeois revolutions (particularly the French Revolution) to the "private" economic realm of civil society and the family. Throughout most of the nineteenth century the relation between commodity

5. Firestone, pp. 6, 12.

production and the rest of society had not yet become problematic and veiled. In Europe and the United States the question of the emancipation of women played a much larger part in the nineteenth and early twentieth century socialist movements than it has since the Russian Revolution. In the United States, currents of artistic modernism, bohemia, and sexual freedom were more closely associated with socialism before the 1920s than after. This was a period in which radicals anticipated an imminent social revolution.

In the United States the split between the traditions of personal liberation and of social transformation began to occur in the early twentieth century. The rise of corporate capitalism led to the emergence of forms of personal life that were seen as independent of the mode of production. The split was accelerated by the domination of the American left by the Soviet Union and the emergence of a model of socialism based simply on the planned expansion of goods production. Currents based upon the new sphere of personal life such as psychoanalysis and bohemia tended to play down or ignore the importance of the economy. For this reason the Communist movement has downgraded these currents as "petit-bourgeois" or "middle class." But the idea that personal life could be transformed directly through the transformation of production had its major relevance in pre-industrial societies like Russia and China where the family as a whole was still a unit of commodity production. The development of corporate capitalism in the United States, where the overwhelming majority of the population depends on wages in order to survive, entails the development of a separate personal life. This in turn sets new tasks for a socialist movement—tasks that the Communist Party barely began to address, and that have only recently begun to take political form.

2. *The Politics of Individualism: Charles Fourier*

THE DEFENSE OF THE INDIVIDUAL against capitalism began amid the petit-bourgeois movements of artisans, peasants, and tradesmen opposed to the rise of large-scale capital in the early nineteenth century. Within these movements the defense of small-scale private property was often intermingled with a defense of the individual as an end in him- or herself. Since private property and the self-sufficient family were the bases of these movements the split between the personal and the political was not part of their outlook. Utopian socialists, reformers, and radical artists in the period following the French Revolution discussed morality and the family as easily as politics and economics.[6] They saw the enhancement of the individual as the end of political change, and saw the individual's self-transformation as its means. The Marquis de Sade, whose personal and sexual experiments represent one of the many blind alleys of the new individualism, articulated a widely felt sentiment: "Frenchmen! You are too enlightened not to feel that a new government will necessitate a new way of living."[7] A similar emphasis underlies transcendentalism, communalism, abolitionism, civil disobedience, educational reform, perfectionism, and the campaigns of moral suasion of the Jacksonian United States.

Many of the liberating potentialities of early nineteenth century individualism as well as its limitations can be seen in the work of Charles Fourier, who, writing during and after the French Revolution, produced an extraordinarily comprehensive critique of capitalist society on behalf of a new conception of the individual and the possibilities of social life. Against the competitive egotism based upon private property upheld by the prevailing Jacobin ideology, Fourier argued that men and women were emotional beings who expressed themselves through social interaction. In common with the romantic poets Fourier affirmed the subjective self, but unlike them he never ceased to stress that the self could only be realized with and through others. As with the romantics, the basis of Fourier's outlook was the conflict between "human nature" or "the individual" and society.

While every individual was unique, Fourier argued, all individual character developed through the combination of a limited number of basic passions, which "remain invariable among

6. This they shared with the bourgeois thinkers of the period—economics, for example, used to be studied as "political economy" and "moral philosophy."

7. Frank and Fritzie Manuel, *French Utopias* (New York, 1966), p. 219.

all nations of men."[8] Under the reign of "civilization," Fourier's term for competitive capitalism, the natural impulses of men and women were repressed and distorted by "morality," the mortal enemy of "passional attraction." People were forced into constant warfare with themselves so they might conform to some bloodless ideal. Fourier argued that a passion was neither good nor bad in itself. Any passion might be beneficial in the proper social combination. Society must be organized in self-sufficient communities designed to enhance the expression and combination of the passions. To advance this goal, Fourier compiled an obsessive catalogue of social needs and instinctual passions—a "calculus of passional attraction." For instance, he would capitalize on children's attraction to dirt by having them manage the community's waste.

In such a society, production and consumption would not be severed, as in capitalism, but would be unified. In this way, human needs would dictate economic development: "Our starting point is that a general perfection in industry will be attained by the universal demands and refinement of the consumers." Agriculture under civilization, for example, is onerous labor partly because "people are too poor to participate in the consumption of choice foods."[9] At the same time, "the epicure is not a cultivator, his epicurism lacks a *direct* bond with cultivation; it is nothing but sensuality."[10] In the future state of civilization, production would be guided by the "generalization of epicureanism" while consumption would be an integrated part of active social life.

---

8. The passions range from those arising from the senses to love, ambition, friendship, and consanguinity to the passion for intrigue, complexity, variety, and the desire to share one's life with others. These go through endless permutations. Charles Fourier, *Design for Utopia* (New York, 1971). All quotations from Fourier are from this book unless otherwise noted. Mark Poster's "Fourier's Concept of the Group" (unpublished manuscript) was also of great help to me.

9. Fourier's range is indicated by his unusual sensitivity to the importance of eating in daily life: "Questions regarding love and gourmandise are treated facetiously by the Civilized, who do not understand the importance that God attaches to our pleasures." Jonathan Beecher and Richard Bienvenu, *The Utopian Vision of Charles Fourier* (Boston, 1972), p. 265.

10. Fourier, *Design*, p. 65.

Fourier's commitment to communities that would unify the personal and social needs of people is related to his unusual sensitivity to the problems of the family and to the oppression of women. While some utopian socialists exalted the petit-bourgeois family and its "natural" division of labor,[11] others, like Fourier and the Saint-Simonians, advocated free love or other measures as a means of attacking traditional patriarchy. In this way the cause of the emancipation of women came to be linked, in the early nineteenth century, with the defense of individualism against the bourgeois ideal of the family.[12]

Fourier wrote that the "extension of privileges to women is the general principle of all social progress." His main charge against the French Revolution was its failure to abolish the family. A traveling salesman and a bachelor, Fourier wrote, "I have witnessed closely many families. I have not found a single one joyful on the inside. . . . In general, every family seems to say, like Dido: I want to flee, I want to escape from myself." [13] The bourgeois family "brought domestic society to the highest degree of isolation and egoism by dividing it into sexual couples or exclusive married households. Would it be possible to push unsociability farther?" [14] Sexuality, to which Fourier assigned a central place in human life,[15] was trapped and deformed by the family. The central problem of the utopian communities of the early nineteenth century became on one hand "the extension of family union beyond the little man-and-wife circle to large corporations" and, on the other, "whether the existence of the marital family is compatible with that of the universal family, which the term 'Community' signifies." [16]

---

11. For example, Proudhon: "Marriage is the union of two heterogeneous elements, *power* and *grace*." *Selected Writings*, (New York, 1969), p. 254.

12. In Britain the circle of Shelley, Godwin, and Mary Woolstonecraft represents a related development.

13. Quoted in Nicholas Riasanovsky, *The Teaching of Charles Fourier* (Berkeley, 1969), p. 216.

14. Ibid., p. 149.

15. "Voluptuousness is the sole arm which God can employ to master us and lead us to carry out his designs; he rules the universe *by Attraction and not by Force*." *Design*, p. 61.

16. The first quote is from John Humphrey Noyes, *American Socialisms*;

Fourier's work indicates the psychological range and depth of early nineteenth century individualism, as well as the limitations of an outlook that takes the individual, rather than an overall conception of social development, as its starting point. Fourier brilliantly attacks the repression, guilt, and narrow egotism characteristic of competitive capitalism[17] but he does so on the basis of an abstract conception of human nature that ends paradoxically by replicating the bourgeois individualism he abhors. In emphasizing the emotions and criticizing bourgeois morality Fourier goes far beyond the calculating individualism of Jacobinism, but his model of human nature remains the isolated family working a piece of private property on which personal and economic life are integrated. Fourier would simply extend this mode of life to include a large number and variety of communitarians. His conception of socialist property relations is really a form of private property shared by the community—as private property is shared within the family. Moreover, the passions that Fourier takes as permanent and unchanging—love, ambition, intrigue—are the frustrated social relations of competitive capitalist society; Fourier proposes to fulfill them through association, rather than to transform them. Indeed, the Fourierist phalanxes, like other utopian communities, invariably reproduced the social relations of the society they sought to escape. Fourier's view of human nature is necessarily dualistic; the passions rise upward from men and women while civilization thwarts and distorts them from above. He calls for a society in which needs dictate economic development but does not recognize that economic development has already dictated particular needs.

Fourier's commitment to the individual or "human nature," abstracted from its class position, gives his work great force. He reminds us that all people are "poor" under capitalism, whatever class they belong to. Their desires are unfulfilled, their senses stunted, their complex social sensibilities pitifully

---

the second from Charles Lane, "Brook Farm," *Dial*, January 1844; both cited in John Thomas, "Romantic Reform in America, 1815–1865," *American Quarterly*, Winter 1965, pp. 656–81.

17. Actually, of *commercial* capitalism, more developed than industrial capitalism in France, and the sector Fourier worked in.

constricted. But the same vision severely limits the scope of Fourier's conception of revolution. For Fourier, socialism will be achieved through small bands of believers who take deliberate and purposeful control of their immediate social relations. From the point of view of petit-bourgeois private property it would make no sense to call that an "individual" solution. So long as private productive property remained dispersed, all solutions were individual.

3. Friedrich Engels and the Politics of Class

FOURIER'S VISION of a world organized around the emotional and sensual relations of men and women at first glance contrasts sharply with Marx and Engels' consistent focus on the outer historical world of politics and economics. Yet when Engels considered the question of the family in *The Origin of the Family, Private Property and the State,* he originally intended to place Fourier's "brilliant critique of civilization" side by side with his own historical account.[18]

By the time Marx and Engels began their collaboration, utopian socialism had devolved into a series of squabbling sects. In attempting to provide a theoretical and political basis for the romantic critique of capitalism, Marx and Engels discovered the role of commodity production and class relations in determining the character of all other social relations, and of the working class as the only group capable of making the revolution. This gave Marxian socialists a unified perspective that other social movements lacked. Engels' *Origin of the Family,* written in 1884 and incorporating Marx's notes, is the major Marxist attempt to situate the family, and the oppression of women, in relation to the historical development of production. According to Engels, personal oppression within the family results from its place within a mode of production based upon private property and class divisions.

Primitive society, Engels argues, was characterized by organic unity. The gens or primitive community was simultaneously

18. Frederick Engels, *The Origin of the Family, Private Property and the State* (1884) in Marx and Engels, *Selected Works* (Moscow, 1962), vol. 2, p. 326, fn. 1. Lack of time prevented him from doing so. See also Marx and Engels, *Selected Correspondence* (Moscow, 1965), p. 373.

family and society. Membership was through kinship; property was held in common. Engels links the emergence of the family to the emergence of the state.[19] In primitive society no separate "public" sphere stood over and above the members of society. "There was as yet no distinction between [private] rights and [public] duties; the question of whether participation in public affairs, blood revenge or atonement for injuries was a right or a duty never confronted the Indian; it would have appeared as absurd to him as the question of whether eating, sleeping or hunting was a right or a duty." [20]

In such a society, the fact that women had responsibility for child-rearing and for the household economy signified not their oppression but, in Engels' words, their "free" and "highly respected" position. The household economy "was just as much a public, a socially necessary industry as the providing of food by the men." [21] Engels concludes: "That woman was the slave of man at the commencement of society is one of the most absurd notions that have come down to us from the period of the Enlightenment of the eighteenth century." [22]

According to Engels, woman's oppression arose through the creation of a separate sphere of private life—the "family"—based upon the private appropriation of communal property. Private property was made possible by the production of a surplus above what was immediately necessary to sustain life. Engels is vague in describing this transformation, but he stresses the emergence of new productive forces (particularly domesticated animals) that could not be contained within the limited social structure of the household-centered gens. Traditional kinship ties now began to break down as families separated off from the gens, basing their new identity on private property. Engels implies, but does not explain, that "private property" had its own dynamic of expansion. For example, slavery now

19. Similarly, Marx wrote: "The abstraction of the state as such belongs only to the modern era, because the abstraction of private life belongs only to the modern era." *Werke*, vol. 1, pt. 1, p. 437, quoted in Karl Löwith, *From Hegel to Nietzsche* (New York, 1967), p. 242.

20.,,*Origin*, p. 308. Engels' account is largely based on Lewis Henry Morgan's study of the Iroquois.

21. Ibid., p. 240.

22. Ibid., p. 209.

developed, made possible since labor could now produce more than its cost of maintenance.

The rise of private property spelled the downfall of women. Production outside the household expanded far more rapidly than production within the household. As a result the traditional division of labor between men and women, which had arisen out of the physiological differences between the sexes, took on a new social meaning. As the household dwindled in importance, so too did the role of women. In the gens kinship had been matrilineal, but men now sought to overthrow traditional kinship forms so that property could be preserved within the "private" family. Engels calls the development of patrilineal kinship the "world-historic defeat of the female sex." Basing himself upon the ownership of property, "the man seized the reins in the house also, the woman was degraded, enthralled, the slave of man's lust, a mere instrument for breeding children."[23] "The wife became the first domestic servant pushed out of participation in social production."[24] Her oppression was fixed by her restriction to the household. Away from women arose the state, "a special public authority separated from the totality of those concerned."[25] Its purpose was "to safeguard the newly acquired property of private individuals against the communistic traditions of the gentile order."[26] The existence of the state was an admission that society had "become entangled in an insoluble contradiction with itself."[27]

Since the domestic sphere is based wholly upon private property, Engels would end the oppression of women by abolishing private property. "The predominance of the man in marriage," he writes, "is simply a consequence of his economic predominance and will vanish with it automatically."[28] Politically this involved a dual program. "Private housekeeping," along with child-raising, must be "transformed into a social industry." Conversely, the spread of industry into the family was to be accompanied by the entry of women into industry: "The emancipation of women becomes possible only when

23. Ibid., p. 225. 24. Ibid., p. 240. 25. Ibid., p. 252. 26. Ibid., p. 263. 27. Ibid., p. 318. 28. Ibid., p. 240.

women are enabled to take part in production on a large, social scale."[29]

The Origin of the Family has often been criticized for its inconsistencies, unilinear historical scheme, and factual inaccuracies.[30] While these criticisms are valid, they do not dispel the power of Engels' work. As a historical speculation on the origins of class society *The Origin of the Family* successfully ties together the oppression of women and the existence of the family with the economic organization of society.[31] The book's major theoretical weakness lies in tracing the oppression of women to private property in general, without any attempt to indicate that both private property and women's oppression have different meanings in different modes of production. In fact, what Engels has done is to project the split between socialized production and the family, as it developed under capitalism, back upon all previous society. In doing so he fails to be specific about either the impact of *capitalist* private property or the continuous, and continuously changing, ideology and structure of male supremacy.

As a result, Engels fails to specify the place of women, as housewives and mothers, in relation to capitalist production. Although in his preface to *The Origin of the Family* Engels portrays the family in all societies as an integral part of the mode of production, he never returns to this critical insight.[32]

29. Ibid., p. 311.

30. Two excellent and balanced discussions of *The Origin of the Family*, both, I believe, still in manuscript, are Ann J. Lane, "Women in the Industrial Process: A Critique of Frederick Engels," and Rosalind Delmar, "Some Comments on Engels' *Origin of the Family*."

31. *The Origin of the Family* can be viewed as an attempt to describe the basic character of human history by a sort of myth of its origins. It can be compared to Freud's *Totem and Taboo* in this regard. Another related book, far more historical, is Fustel de Coulanges, *The Ancient City* (1864).

32. Engels wrote: "According to the materialistic conception, the determining factor in history is, in the last resort, the production and reproduction of immediate life. But this itself is of a twofold character. On the one hand, the production of the means of subsistence . . . on the other, the production of human beings themselves, the propagation of the species. . . . Social institutions . . . are conditioned by both kinds of production: by the stage of development of labour, on the one hand, and of the family, on the other." *Origin*, pp. 170–71.

While he terms the family the "economic unit" of society, he restricts this term to its role in the transmission of private property. He reinforces the bourgeois equation of production with the production of surplus value, and of work with wage labor, and therefore portrays women's labor within the home as marginal to society. This idea reinforces the exclusion of housewives and mothers, and their concerns, from socialist politics.

Engels wrote at a time when the proletarian family had not yet been stabilized and when its life was dominated by the struggle for survival. Changes in the nature of the family and of society since then raise additional problems. Writing before a separate sphere of personal life had emerged within the proletariat, Engels does not examine the ideological, psychological, and emotional life of the family. For Engels private property is the material reality upon which the family exists as a subjective contingency. Engels was convinced that proletarian family life was being obliterated by the rise of capital. His description of the family is bare and external, as if the inner, subjective life of the family either did not exist or was of little consequence.

In addition, Engels does not challenge the natural or biological basis of the family insofar as it has persisted into the present.[33] That basis is the sexual division of labor—for example, the responsibility of women for child care—and heterosexuality. Heterosexuality is the precondition for the sexual division of labor; the division of labor, by insuring the reciprocal dependence of the sexes, gives rise to the "bias toward heterosexuality."[34] Engels portrays the sexual division of labor as a natural or spontaneous phenomenon that derives its oppressive meaning only through the growth of commodity production. He assumes that under socialism the family will embody the traditional division of labor (to the extent that its productive functions have not been fully socialized) and that it will be based upon heterosexuality. But the development of contraception, changes in the technology of reproduc-

33. This entire paragraph derives from Delmar's article, though her argument is different.

34. Delmar.

tion, and the declining need for laborers make it possible to challenge the original biological imperatives.[35] Engels accepts the perpetuation of natural conditions into a period when they are no longer compelling.

These weaknesses influence Engels' solution. He would resolve the contradiction between women and men simply by integrating women into the industrial proletariat; he would eliminate the contradiction between the family and the economy by industrializing the functions of the home. Engels was right to emphasize the centrality of the sphere of socialized production, but wrong in believing that changes within this sphere would necessarily transform, as if by reflex, the sphere of private and family life. Entry into modern industrial production did bestow a certain independence upon working women in relation to men, but rather than eliminating oppression within the family this independence exacerbated and deepened the contradiction between the "public" and "private" spheres of life. Engels' account encourages the view that the social relations of personal life can be transformed without selfconscious political struggle. He did not believe that the psychological life of the family, its ancestral division of labor, and its historically developed sentiments and emotional relations could persist through a transformation of the mode of production. He believed that male supremacy will "vanish automatically" along with its original cause—private property. His vision of emancipation is rooted in the nineteenth-century proletarian family's struggle for survival. He assumes that under socialism the functions currently performed by the family will be socialized, but that something very much like the bourgeois family, based upon individual sex love and embodying the sexual division of labor, will flourish.

Within the socialist movement Engels' book was taken not as a beginning but as the final word. Within the Second International women's entry into the labor force determined their role in the revolution. The needs of women were thereby assimilated to the needs of the industrial proletariat. Domesticity, wrote Rosa Luxemburg, "is but the private affair of the

35. Firestone, pp. 3–15.

worker, his happiness and blessing, and for this reason non-existent for our present society."[36] Not only was women's labor within the home considered marginal, but so were all other "private" concerns. In his famous conversation with Clara Zetkin, Lenin expressed dismay at what he considered bourgeois influence on socialist women: "I have been told that at the evenings arranged for reading and discussion with working women, sex and marriage problems came first . . . I could not believe my ears when I heard that."[37] The solitary emphasis on production allowed party members to remain staunchly puritanical while spurning the hypocrisy of the Victorian bourgeoisie. Free love, and other varieties of sexual reform, were relegated to the tradition of "personal emancipation." Along with Engels socialists assumed that the only problem with the working-class family was that it was driven by economic necessity and that under socialism the family based upon love would automatically come into its own.[38]

4. *Russia and China: Revolution Based upon Economic Development*

BOTH THE STRENGTHS and the weaknesses of Engels' theory of the family can be seen in the Russian and Chinese revolutions. In Russia and China, the transformation of the family, and of the oppression of women, has been both a consequence and a component of the overall development of the productive forces. Both revolutions began by destroying feudal and slave social relations, in which women were mired, in order to create a relatively egalitarian and homogeneous body of citizens and workers. The establishment of legal equality through marriage

36. Rosa Luxemburg, "Women's Suffrage and the Class Struggle," in *Selected Political Writings*, edited by Dick Howard (New York, 1971), p. 220. Luxemburg's purpose in this passage was to point out the absurdity of a society in which surplus value determined social needs, but her argument is that only women's entry into the labor force establishes a basis for socialist response.

37. V. I. Lenin, *On the Emancipation of Women* (Moscow, 1968), p. 101.

38. Karl Kautsky, *The Class Struggle* (New York, 1971), pp. 26, 127–29; Bruce Dancis, "The Attitudes of Male Leaders of the Socialist Party of America toward Women and Women's Suffrage, 1907–1912," unpublished manuscript.

and divorce codes, the abolition of polygamy, and other reforms, along with the entry of women into industry, raised women in both countries from a position close to slavery to membership in the working class. Hence the early phases of these revolutions accomplished a transformation that Engels expected capitalism to accomplish. "Industry," Lenin wrote in an early study, "creates a new position for the woman in which she is completely independent of her family and husband. . . . This is the equality of the proletarian." [39]

Soviet policy since the revolution has been based on the principle that women and family life would be liberated through the development of production. In the early years of the revolution the Bolsheviks promulgated the most advanced program of European and American feminism: abolition of ecclesiastical marriage; women's right to property, legal abortion, and contraception; marriage and divorce codes based upon the equality of men and women; recognition of de facto marriage; and equal rights for illegitimate children. They regarded these measures as part of the bourgeois phase of their revolution, recognizing that these rights were purely formal. Real equality would come through the entry of women into the labor force and thereby into political life.

While ideas concerning free love, the "new woman," and the abolition of the family were initially important, especially in the cities, such concerns had begun to be postponed or downgraded by the 1920s as diversions from the single-minded focus on economic growth. Russian Marxists and earlier intellectuals had introduced the romantic tradition of personal liberation into a country in which a separate sphere of personal life scarcely existed except among the aristocracy and bourgeoisie. While most Bolsheviks felt that the family, like the state, would eventually "wither away," this was not a subject of mass political discussion. As Trotsky wrote in 1923, "The party did not and could not afford specific attention to questions of the everyday life of the working masses. . . . We have never thrashed out these questions . . . as we have the questions of wages, fines, the length of the working day, police

39. *Emancipation of Women*, p. 16, fn.

prosecution, the form of the state, the ownership of land and so on."[40] During the period of War Communism problems of acute food shortages and homeless children led to the establishment of collective dining, nurseries, and settlements.[41] Hence the pressures of material survival contributed to the belief that the family was being abolished. But by the NEP period the reconstruction of domestic life, after its devastation by war and revolution, was valued more highly than experiments in collective living.[42] By the 1930s, while the question of the family remained a major social question, the European heritage of "personal liberation" had been completely eliminated from Soviet life.[43]

Soviet policy went beyond the romantic concern with the family as a moral issue and began to make explicit the role of the family in economic life. State planning of the family was integrated with and subordinated to economic planning, population policy, and the control of crime. In 1935 the Soviet government sought to strengthen traditional family life by making abortion and divorce more difficult and by forbidding homosexuality. A major purpose was to utilize the labor of grandmothers for child-rearing in order that both parents might work. In addition the government sought to raise the birthrate to strengthen the Soviet position in world politics.[44] World War II and twenty million dead added the special problem of repeopling the country; in 1944 the formal bonds of the family were further strengthened to counter its wartime dissolution.

40. Quoted in H. Kent Geiger, *The Family in Soviet Russia* (Cambridge, Mass., 1968), p. 77.

41. E. H. Carr, *Socialism in One Country*, vol. 1 (Baltimore, 1970), p. 39.

42. Leon Trotsky, *Women and the Family* (New York, 1970), pp. 32–35.

43. The idea that Bolshevik policy during the 1930s represented a radical reversal probably arose with Wilhelm Reich's *The Sexual Revolution* (New York, 1972), first published in 1945, and has been popularized in Kate Millett's *Sexual Politics* (New York, 1970). There was certainly change but there was also an underlying continuity. The conservative counterpart to Reich's polemic is the academic opinion that the Bolsheviks first attempted to abolish the family, and then learned it couldn't be done.

44. Rudolf Schlesinger, ed., *The Family in the USSR* (London, 1949), passim.

The social transformation accomplished in Russia is similar to the path traversed by capitalist development over the past two centuries: universal proletarianization and the rise of large-scale industry. One result of this transformation has been a split between public and private life comparable to the one that prevails in developed capitalist society. But the private or personal sphere, rather than being idealized as in the West, has been downgraded; the state continually intrudes upon the "autonomy" of the family, eroding its promise of comfort, privacy, and individual freedom. Much of the current protest activity in the Soviet Union is in part an appeal for the enhancement of the private sphere: personal liberty; increased consumption; freedom of speech, travel, artistic expression, etc. For the first time in Soviet history there is a social basis for these demands.

The Bolshevik revolution began with a deep commitment to the emancipation of women. The eventual limits of that emancipation are instructive. The tradition of personal liberation had little meaning in a pre-industrial society in which the family was still the basic hub of production, and in which production and personal life were integrated. It was difficult for the Bolsheviks to see whether and in what form personal life could become a progressive political issue. Soffia N. Smidovich, a feminist and Bolshevik, explained: "We are inclined . . . to close our eyes about a lot, when the matter concerns so-called personal life. . . . We are apprehensive lest we fall into dogmatism, carry on like the priests, and so on."[45] Nor was the tradition of personal liberation, free love, and abolition of the family integrated with a commitment to feminism. As in Europe and the United States, personal liberation and sexual liberation primarily benefited men. During the Russian Revolution this was known as the "mutuality problem." The ease of divorce, for example, when children were involved meant "the women remains tied with chains to the . . . ruins of the family hearth. The man, happily whistling, can leave it."[46] In this context, it was possible to reconcile the strengthening of the traditional family with the goal of emancipating women.

45. Quoted in Geiger, pp. 61–62.

46. Ibid., p. 71.

Revolution through economic development left intact a major part of women's oppression. The psychosocial heritage of male supremacy was scarcely challenged by the entry of women into industry, while the strengthening of the family encouraged a resurgence of traditional patriarchal ideals, such as the exaltation of motherhood.[47] Perhaps most important, the division of labor within the family retained all its force; as Firestone wrote, "the roles of women were enlarged rather than redefined."[48] Because housework and child-rearing had never been granted full status as forms of social production, the commitment to equality never extended to labor performed within the home. This in turn restricted the attack on the sexual division of labor in industry. The emancipation of women in the Soviet Union has been subordinated to the overall development of the productive forces. Women benefited from their proletarianization and from the general betterment of life, but the issue of women's liberation, as a separate issue, was eliminated from Soviet politics.

THE CHINESE AND RUSSIAN revolutions share many similarities. As in the Soviet Union, the Chinese Communists destroyed feudal and slave kinship relations that the Chinese bourgeoisie had only challenged. Chinese communism abolished wife purchase, footbinding, polygamy, concubinage, and ancestor worship, and put in their place monogamous marriage based upon the free choice of man and woman. As in the Soviet Union, the party stresses the entry of women into social production as the key to their emancipation. The emphasis on women's equality has waxed and waned in relation to overall questions of economic development.

During periods in which the Chinese followed the Soviet plan of development—hierarchical division of labor, relatively greater stress on material incentives, capital-intensive production, and an emphasis on developing heavy industry—the issue of women's liberation has been played down and women

47. The ideal of motherhood was associated with the re-emergence of Great Russian nationalism and the idea of the "Motherland" during the 1930s.

48. Firestone, p. 248.

have even been encouraged to remain in the home. But the Chinese have also learned from the inadequacies of the Soviet model. Beginning with the Great Leap Forward (which was in part prompted by the Hungarian Revolution of 1956), the Chinese Communists have periodically stressed the integration of economic development with the creation of anti-authoritarian social relations. In such periods the Chinese encouraged labor-intensive industry, the creation of more egalitarian social relations in industry, and the development of medium and light industry in the countryside. As part of the effort to mobilize all available labor power, the Chinese stressed the participation of women in social production. Similarly, support for birth control has been associated with the entry of women into production as well as with the equality of women.[49] The different character of Chinese economic policy in these periods has accented the issue of women's liberation and is one reason for the relatively deeper and more thoroughgoing transformation of the family in the course of the Chinese Revolution.

Another difference between the Russian and the Chinese experience lies in the greater importance attached to culture and ideology in the Chinese revolution. Colonial revolutions against imperialism have generally paid much attention to the culture or way of life of the people. Stokely Carmichael represented many third world revolutionaries when he wrote, "Colonization is not just the economic raping of someone, not merely taking a lot of money away. Colonization deals with destroying the person's language, his history, his identification, his total humanity."[50] Contact with imperialism throws the traditional culture on the defensive and forces the revolutionary movement either to defend or to supplant it. Family relations and the position of women are integral to the traditional

49. Birth control teams speak against "the repeated desire to have at least one son." Soong Ching Ling, "Women's Liberation in China," *Peking Review*, 11 February 1972, p. 7. For the rest of this paragraph see Laurie Landy, *Women in the Chinese Revolution* (New York, n.d.), passim; C. K. Yang, *Chinese Communist Society: The Family and the Village* (Cambridge, Mass., 1959, 1968), pp. 3–21, 208 ff.; Maria Antonietta Macciocchi, *Daily Life in Revolutionary China* (New York, 1972), pp. 348–78.

50. Stokely Carmichael, "Pan-Africanism—Land and Power," *Black Scholar*, November 1969, pp. 36–37.

culture of any colonial nation.[51] But particularly in China the family was at the center of a highly coherent and deeply rooted social philosophy that united all aspects of traditional society. According to Confucianism, the traditional culture of China, society was organized through a set of five primary relations: father-son, sovereign-minister, husband-wife, old-young, and friendship.[52] The place of the family was closely tied to the world position of China, the role of the emperor, and the authority of the gentry—all social relations challenged by the presence of imperialism. The Chinese Communists were forced to struggle against this Confucian world view, including its view of the family, in order to supplant the traditional ruling class.

While the Russian revolution was anti-imperialist, Russia was itself an imperialist power. Questions of either preserving or transforming traditional cultural institutions were more important for the subject nationalities freed by the 1917 revolution than for the Soviet nation as a whole. In China, on the other hand, traditional Confucian culture had been forced on the defensive by its inability to resist imperialism for at least a century before the rise of the Communist Party. This was not a debate restricted to the intellectuals but was expressed in a series of mass social movements beginning with the Taiping Rebellion (1853–1868), extending through the Boxer Rebellion (1898–1900) and May 4th Movement (1919), and culminating in the Chinese Communists. In all of these movements the viability of Confucianism in the context of imperialism was a continued question. Similarly, conservative movements such as Chiang Kai-shek's argued that Confucianism could continue to serve as a basis of social order. The Western tradition of romantic individualism, free love, and personal liberation

51. This has often encouraged a defense of male supremacy against "imported Western" ideas such as feminism. For example in Algeria the secretary-general of the FLN has written, "The way of life of European women is incompatible with our traditions and our culture. . . : We can only live by the Islamic morality"; and an Algerian woman attacking feminism wrote that in the choice between "the freaks of a super-civilization and . . . tradition, I choose tradition." David C. Gordon, *Women of Algeria: An Essay on Change* (Cambridge, Mass., 1972), pp. 67, 74.

52. These are Mencius's categories. Yang, p. 7.

played even less role in China than in Russia and was associated with the bourgeois rather than the Communist phase of the Revolution.[53] But the prolonged struggle against Confucianism has given the question of culture a centrality in the Chinese Revolution and helps explain the intensity and persistence with which that question recurs.

Finally, the revolutionary process in China took much longer and penetrated more deeply into the life of the people. In Russia the Bolsheviks took power when they were little known outside the industrial centers. The transformation of society followed the seizure of state power. In China the revolutionary movement ruled large sections of the country for over a decade before winning state power. In this process the integration of village and familial life with socialist production and with party organization was prepared for. Communist production has often accommodated itself to traditional social organization such as the village.[54] This has facilitated the introduction of day care, feeding stations (at work), and other communal institutions. The same writings intended to regulate social production and political life—for example, the Red Book—are read by couples as manuals of family life. There does not seem to be the same tension between public and private space that characterizes developed capitalism and that has emerged in the Soviet Union.[55] Far more than in the Soviet Union, family life has been discussed at political meetings. In fact, the question of women's liberation has come to the fore in periods of mass political participation—such as after the seizure of power and during the Great Leap Forward and the Cultural Revolution—and has receded as political activity has receded.[56]

53. Particularly with the May 4th Movement.

54. Franz Schurmann, *Ideology and Organization in Communist China* (Berkeley, 1970), pp. 423 ff.

55. William Hinton, *Fanshen* (New York, 1968); Committee of Concerned Asian Scholars, *China!: Inside the People's Republic* (New York, 1972), pp. 266–92; Charlotte Bonny Cohen, "Experiment in Freedom," in Robin Morgan, ed., *Sisterhood Is Powerful* (New York, 1970), pp. 385–420.

56. Landy; Macciocchi, pp. 348–78.

The Chinese experience, even more than the Soviet, demonstrates the relevance of Engels' emphasis on entry into social production to the emancipation of women. But women in China have had a historically different set of needs than women in the developed capitalist countries. China was an overwhelmingly peasant country in which a separate sphere of personal life had scarcely emerged. In art and in other areas the Chinese have sought to show that the modern Western emphasis on subjective or psychological life is an illusion and that so-called "personal" questions can be resolved into questions of one's objective class position. For example, in a 1969 attack on Stanislavsky, the Chinese condemn the idea that an actor should act out of inner emotions or project a divided consciousness. Instead, drama should portray the clash of idealized representatives of different classes. Stanislavsky's system, they charge, would replace "the analysis of objective things with one's subjective imaginary bourgeois feelings."[57] In addition sexual life is governed by a puritanism characteristic of countries in the early stage of industrial development. In part this is probably a reaction against the sexual degradation of women in imperial China.[58]

In both Russia and China women have been emancipated as part of the "emancipation" of the productive forces of society. The basic idea was classic Marxism: the social order of the past is destroyed through the expansion of material production. Engels applied this idea to women: male supremacy resulted from the "backwardness" of the family, its isolation from socialized production. The liberation of women would occur when socialism unblocked the forces of production developed by capitalism, bringing women into industry and industrializing housework. Both Russia and China sought to "raise" familial life to the level attained by socialist production. Both revolutions have begun to recognize that the family performs critical economic functions which the state can either socialize or reward. The redefinition of the problem of the

57. Shanghai Revolutionary Mass Criticism Writing Group, "On Stanislavsky's 'System'" (Peking, 1969), pp. 5, 6, 8, 22. Another charge made against Stanislavsky concerned his reliance on the "subconscious."

58. Mitchell, p. 121.

family from a moral to an economic problem marks a great advance. But as economic problems, questions of the family and of the emancipation of women have been bound by the overall context of material impoverishment. In both countries the vision of "personal" emancipation—the "new man," the "new woman"—has been subsumed by the goal of developing production. The idea of life no longer dominated by relations of production has scarcely emerged.

5. *The Emergence of a Separate Sphere of Personal Life*

IN CONTRAST TO the Soviet Union and China, Engels' vision of resolving the oppressiveness of the family by revolutionizing the mode of production has appeared less and less plausible in the twentieth-century United States. With the development of industry a sphere of life emerged divorced from any direct relation to social production. By World War I a diverse series of social movements (e.g., family reform), social and psychological milieus (bohemia, "youth"), and theoretical advances (psychoanalysis) indicated the coming into existence of a new area of social life, the personal. Most Americans continued to see their personal fates as inextricably tied to the development of commodity production; this idea underlay their struggles for better food, shelter, recreation, a shorter workday, education, and culture. At the same time, the rise of corporate capitalism created the possibility of liberating society from the constant constraint of economic necessity. A small but growing number of Americans began to see their personal lives as wholly apart from the sphere of production. In the realm of personal relations, emotional and sexual life, and creative expression, they exercised the "freedom" denied them within the sphere of alienated labor.

In the nineteenth century, artists and romantic intellectuals proclaimed the emergence of the subjective self, no longer bound by the division of labor. In the early twentieth century, psychologists, educators, progressives, and reformers continued this tradition, reflecting the extension of personal life on a larger social scale. The rise of modern industry centralized private productive property and thus eliminated the economic basis for the patriarchal family. But radicals and reformers held that industrialization was creating a new form of the family based upon the personal freedom of its members. They believed, with Engels, that the entry of women into industry and the industrialization of the productive functions of the family would eliminate the subordination of women. New theories of psychological life, childhood, adolescence, progressive education, and sexuality contributed to a new ideology of personal freedom and individualism based upon wage labor. In this newly discovered realm of personal life Americans in the twentieth century have expressed a constricted vision of freely determined social relations, no longer dominated by the imperatives of production.

Arthur Calhoun, an evolutionary socialist who saw the rise of corporate capitalism as a basically benign step toward socialism, reflected the general optimism of pre–World War I America. "Industrialism," he wrote, has led to the "general democratization of society" and the "waning of domestic monarchy." As women gained "economic opportunity outside of marriage," they became freer and more independent within the home. Through her "formal education, working experience and the development of household economics into a technical pursuit" she confronts man as an equal, and indeed superior, as the man becomes a mere "earning mechanism." The passing of society "into the regime of surplus . . . brings with it the lengthening of infancy and the elevation of childhood." "The father cannot comprehend what his children are learning" and so paternal power wanes. "Society lays claim to the child and refuses to recognize the parent's property right." "The family," he concludes, "experiences individuation, ceases to be a forced grouping, and develops toward ethical unity and spontaneous democracy." [59]

Charlotte P. Gilman's feminism was based upon a similar analysis. "The growing individualization of democratic life brings inevitable change to our daughters as well as to our sons," she wrote. Until the rise of industry the family was the basic "social group, an entity, a little state." Its basis was eco-

59. W. Arthur Calhoun, *A Social History of the American Family*, vol. 3 (Cleveland, 1919), pp. 157–58.

nomic necessity. In its origins "it moved over the earth, following its food supply, and fighting occasionally with stranger families for the grass or water on which it depended." But industry made possible the "economic independence" of the members of the family—i.e., as wage laborers. In place of the family, Gilman upholds "marriage": "although made by us an economic relation, it is not essentially so, and will exist in much higher fulfillment after the economic phase is outgrown." On a new basis of equality between men and women marriage will become a "personal union for life of two well-matched individuals."[60] For both Calhoun and Gilman, wage labor established the potential for a new form of family life based upon the personal freedom of its members.

As the family lost its function as the basic unit of commodity production, the laws and traditions that had regulated the conduct of its members were thrown into question. The birth control and divorce movements demanded that the family's internal relations should be entirely determined by its members. Throughout the nineteenth century the birth rate declined while divorces steadily rose.[61] The birth control movement now promised to liberate women from the tyrannical cycle of reproduction. In the nineteenth century the exclusive purpose of female sexuality was understood to be procreation; doctors commonly advised upper-class women to have intercourse only the five or six times in their lives necessary for conception. With birth control, sexuality promised to become an end in itself rather than serving the social imperative of procreation. Similarly, divorce, the very symbol of marriage freely entered into and freely given up, was attacked by conservatives because it placed the rights of individuals above those of society.[62]

The belief in an internally emancipated family encouraged new conceptions of childhood and of adolescence. In the

60. Charlotte Perkins Gilman, *Women and Economics* (New York, 1966), pp. 213-16.

61. David Kennedy, *Birth Control in America: The Career of Margaret Sanger* (New Haven, Conn., 1970), p. 37, fn. 1.

62. William O'Neill, *Divorce in the Progressive Era* (New Haven, Conn., 1967), p. 260.

United States the idealization of childhood and the child-centeredness of the family had begun with the rise of industrial capitalism. Ralph Waldo Emerson, for example, commented on a new "tenderness" that emerged in the period 1820–1840: "Children had been repressed and kept in the background; now they were considered, cosseted and pampered."[63] Childhood, in addition to being the period in which the child was shaped to adult (i.e., social) requirements, was coming to be seen as an end in itself. By the 1890s a series of reform movements arose—child study, the kindergarten movement, the Herbartians—that argued that the child's natural fund of spontaneity, inventiveness, and imagination should be respected rather than constricted by "society." "Teaching," wrote Maria Montessori, "shall be rigorously guided by the principle of limiting to the greatest possible point the active intervention of the educator."[64] Progressive education, arising partly out of the changing educational requirements of corporate capitalism, similarly sought to liberate the child from adult constraints. G. Stanley Hall, rejecting the traditional view of children's play as preparation for the tasks of later life, stressed the radical disjuncture between the child's world and the adult's.[65]

As childhood became understood not only as preparation for adult society but also as a period of unspoiled virtues opposed to it, the transition from child to adult became problematic. In 1904, in *Adolescence*, the culmination of decades of work, Hall invented the concept of a new zone of life half integrated with and half antagonistic to the adult social order. He described adolescence as the "passionate stage of life," and assigned to it the qualities of moral idealism and intense emotionality that the Victorians had assigned to upper-class women, isolated within the home. Americans, following Hall, have romanticized and prolonged the period of adolescence,

---

63. Emerson, "Historic Notes of Life and Letters in New England," in Perry Miller, ed., *The American Transcendentalists* (New York, 1957), p. 5.

64. Quoted in Elizabeth Lawrence, *The Origins and Growth of Modern Education* (Baltimore, 1970), p. 331.

65. Dorothy Ross, *G. Stanley Hall: The Psychologist as Prophet* (Chicago, 1972), pp. 299–300, 307.

unable to incorporate these qualities into their conception of adult social activity.[66]

An emphasis on sexuality added a special depth to the twentieth-century conception of personal life. Sexuality was coming to be understood as the basis of human individuality, the natural life of men and women outside society's domination. As with the study of the child, positivistic science went hand in hand with romantic idealization. Most late nineteenth century studies of sexuality before Freud involved the detailed cataloguing of "perversions." On the other hand, Margaret Sanger, exemplar of a frank and scientific attitude toward sex, memorialized Havelock Ellis as follows: "We owe [to him] our concept of that Kingdom of God within us, that inner world. . . . Thanks to him we realize that happiness may be the fruit of an attitude toward life."[67] Freud's view of human activity as divided between the world of instinctual pleasure that is an end in itself (play) and the world of social reality in which activity is shaped by extrinsic purposes (work) is the culmination of all these tendencies.

Finally, and most important, the emergence of personal life was linked to a reformulated view of individuality. It was no longer possible to identify the individual simply with his or her place within the social division of labor. The development of an important zone of personal life cut off from commodity production provoked the discovery and investigation of the interior or psychological life of men and women. The ideas of consciousness, in anything like our contemporary formulation, and of the unconscious, developed at the end of the nineteenth

66. Ibid., p. 339. Here is a characteristic quote from Hall's *Adolescence* (book 2, p. 624): "Woman at her best never outgrows adolescence as man does, but lingers in, magnifies and glorifies this culminating stage of life with its all-sided interests, its convertibility of emotions, its enthusiasm, and zest for all that is good, beautiful, true and heroic." A contemporary linking of women and adolescence is found in Meredith Tax, *Woman and Her Mind: The Story of Daily Life* (Cambridge, Mass., 1970), p. 2: "It is in adolescence that we first learn how immensely we are impinged on by the world, and how easily it can destroy us. Our incredibly painful self-consciousness may be exaggerated, but it is based on a true perception of how we are constantly judged, how our very being is assaulted."

67. Margaret Sanger, *Autobiography* (New York, 1938, 1971), p. 141; see also O'Neill, pp. 89–167.

century. Earlier psychologies had all assumed an isomorphic correspondence between the elements of the mind and the elements of the social and material world. In the early 1880s William James, reflecting the advanced thought of his time, repudiated the view that consciousness was composed of discrete elements that combined like building blocks into complex ideas or associations. Instead, he put forth the idea of the stream of thought, according to which everyone's ideas were uniquely personal and different, ideas and emotions were in constant interaction, and the mind was in dialectical relation with external reality. This new emphasis on introspection, on individual uniqueness, and on the emotions reflected in theory the psychological dimension of the emergence of personal life.

6. *Toward a Politics of Personal Life*

IN THE EARLY twentieth century a large socialist movement existed in the United States, along with a widespread conviction that the United States was heading toward a major social transformation. In this context two groups were strategically placed to raise questions of personal life both as separate concerns and in conjunction with the socialist movement: feminists and young radical intellectuals.

No group experienced the subjective isolation of personal life so deeply as women, trapped as they were within the family, blamed for its egregious faults, or forced to negotiate the limbo between it and the world of wage-labor. As housewives, and particularly as mothers, women became a focus of the modern aspiration for personal happiness. The newly emerged areas of personal life were the housewife's responsibility—in particular childhood, but also sexuality, emotional expression, and the family's pattern of consumption. Far from being a refuge for women the family was a workplace. As Charlotte Gilman pointed out, neither women nor children had any private space within the home; the father alone might have a study.

The new ideologies of personal life encouraged the illusion that women were outside the dominant material processes and class relations of their time. The social responsibility of women for personal life was masked as a return to "natural" affections, a return dependent upon the historic equation of women with the realm of intuition and sensuality. Lacking an explicit connection to social production, the housewife's labor was viewed as her personal expression. The "new mother," wrote Havelock Ellis in 1933, "regards motherhood as a relationship of loving and natural intimacy." No longer guided "by obedience to outworn traditions she has learnt how to become the friend of her children."[68] Later, Benjamin Spock began his child care manual with the hard injunction "Trust yourself."[69] Failures in such labor cannot be salvaged by retreat to yet another private realm.[70]

Feminists believed that the way out for women was entry into the world of wage labor. From 1880 to 1910 the number of women working outside the home rose from 2.6 million to 8 million.[71] Educated women entered professions such as teaching, nursing, and social work, which were in large part defined by the new ideologies of personal life; service, melioration, and respect for the rights of others. As Jane Addams pointed out, middle-class women's need to be of use (in her case through social settlements) was based upon a "subjective necessity": the need of women to link up with the rest of society.[72] Most women, however, became office workers, domestics, or factory operatives. They entered the sphere of commodity production as the rising productivity of labor was leading to declining opportunities for employment. This encouraged the consignment of female employment to the lower-paid and less unionized sectors of the economy: the services where labor was similar to that performed within the home and the production of domestic consumption goods, beginning with textiles in the nineteenth century. The really large-scale

68. Havelock Ellis, *Of Life and Sex* (New York, 1922, 1957), p. 128.

69. Benjamin Spock, *Baby and Child Care* (New York, 1970), p. 3.

70. Not surprisingly, nervous breakdowns and similar crises around the time of marriage amounted to a social epidemic among educated women in the period of transition to the modern family.

71. Meta Stern Lilienthal, *From Fireside to Factory* (New York, 1916), p. 42; Eleanor Flexner, *Century of Struggle* (New York, 1971), p. 230.

72. Jane Addams, "The Subjective Necessity of Social Settlements," in Christopher Lasch, ed., *The Social Thought of Jane Addams* (Indianapolis, Ind., 1965), pp. 28–43.

entry of women into socialized production has taken place since the 1920s at a time when unemployment and underemployment have become structural features of the capitalist economy. Women's experience as wage laborers was predicated upon and encouraged the idea that their real place was within the home.

Both within industry and within the family the division of labor between men and women was widening drastically at a time when the growth of mass production was eliminating the historic justification ("nature" or economic necessity) for that division. But the creation of a separate sphere of personal life created a new justification. The family, and the subordination of women within it, was necessary to preserve a refuge of spiritual and emotional life against the dehumanization of capitalist society. To a significant extent feminists acquiesced in this conception, and supported the suffrage and female employment as reforms that would humanize public life. One manifestation of this impulse was the genteel women's club, which extended the ideals of domesticity into community life. The major feminist achievement—the suffrage—left the family intact.

Emma Goldman was one of the few feminists who criticized the shrinking of women's politics to the limit of the suffrage. "Merely external emancipation," she wrote, "has made of the modern woman an artificial being." Goldman argued that the emphasis on winning careers for women while ignoring their personal relations had produced "mere professional automatons."[73] But Goldman's comments were based upon her sentimentalizing of the traditional domestic relations of the patriarchal family rather than on any attempt to extend the range of politics into the personal sphere.[74] After winning the suffrage women's politics went into abeyance until the 1960s. During the intervening years women's desire for personal emancipation was expressed through psychoanalysis, bohemia, sexual freedom and other currents of cultural radicalism—

73. Emma Goldman, "The Tragedy of Women's Emancipation," in Alix Kates Shulman, ed., *Red Emma Speaks* (New York, 1972), p. 176.

74. A sentimentalizing that accompanied her belief in free love, personal emancipation and anarchism.

currents that accepted personal life as a question outside politics.

THE OTHER GROUP whose concern for personal life arose from their ambivalent relation to social production were intellectuals, artists, radicals, and feminists, centered in Greenwich Village, and close to the Socialist Party or the IWW in the early 1900s. The development of a radical intellectual culture reflected the proletarianization of petit-bourgeois occupations such as art, journalism, and teaching, as well as the resistance of young people to life as industrial workers. Early twentieth century radical intellectuals represent a transition between nineteenth-century petit-bourgeois individualism and the mass educated labor force of today—which is commonly called the middle class. This group encompassed all those who were able to restrict the role of alienated labor in their lives and to define their major activity outside immediate capitalist production relations: free-lance writers, artists and intellectuals, bohemians and vagabonds, radicals and revolutionaries, "the men and women without a productive or market function traditional to economic society."[75]

The American tradition of romantic individualism began with the rise of industrial capitalism in the Jacksonian era. According to Emerson "mind had become aware of itself . . . the young men were born with knives in their brain, a tendency to introversion, self-dissection, anatomizing of motives."[76] Transcendentalism, like European romanticism, upheld the self-sufficient individual (or utopian community) against "society." But in the early twentieth century radical intellectuals began to combine the romantic defense of individualism with a critique of capitalism itself. Van Wyck Brooks, for example, pointed out that Emerson's "really equivocal individualism . . . asserted the freedom and self-reliance of the spirit [as easily as] of the business man."[77] Brooks distinguished bourgeois

75. Martin J. Sklar, "On the Proletarian Revolution and the End of Political Economic Society," *Radical America*, May–June 1969.

76. Emerson, pp. 5, 7.

77. Brooks, "America's Coming of Age," in Claire Sprague, ed., *Van Wyck Brooks: The Early Years, A Selection from His Works, 1908–1921* (New York, 1968), p. 99.

individualism which "was essentially competitive" from the "new individualism which finds its gospel in self-expression." The "new individualism," he wrote, "is individualistic only by default." It is the barrenness of capitalist society that forces the new individualism back into the sectarian world of private pursuits. The initial impulse of individualism is "filled with an intense, confused eagerness to identify itself with the life of the whole people."[78] By offering it only alienated labor and economic acquisitiveness, the United States was "breeding a race of Hamlets."[79]

Inspired by feminism, and by psychoanalysis, young intellectuals castigated traditional family life for what Randolph Bourne called its "blind jealousy toward any assertion of individual ideals."[80] They anticipated that the new forms of personal life developing in bohemia would spread throughout the population as a result of politics and propaganda. Floyd Dell's *Love in the Machine Age*, which synthesized much of this thought, traced male supremacy to the fact that in "pre-industrial" society the family was practically the sole economic unit. Women and children had been dependent upon the patriarch for their livelihood. The rise of industry eliminated this dependence but social relations based upon it had persisted. According to Dell, "patriarchal customs [had] become modern neuroses." "Neuroses," Dell explained, were not the result of "individual shortcomings" but were due "to our general social-economic backwardness."[81]

According to Van Wyck Brooks "the center of gravity in American affairs has shifted wholly from the plane of politics to the plane of psychology and morals."[82] Therefore a new kind of politics was required—one that addressed itself to the problems of personal life. The young intellectuals were almost universally socialists who rejected any politics that did not encompass a "program for spiritual and artistic libera-

78. Brooks, "Toward a National Culture," in Sprague, p. 190.

79. Ibid., p. 188.

80. Quoted in Christopher Lasch, *The New Radicalism in America, 1889-1963: The Intellectual as a Social Type* (New York, 1965).

81. Floyd Dell, *Love in the Machine Age* (London, 1930), pp. 5, 404.

82. Brooks, "America's Coming of Age," in Sprague, p. 151.

tion."[83] They identified art, psychoanalysis, bohemia, and other forms of personal revolt with the impending social revolution. They anticipated no conflict between their individual aspirations and the practical needs of a movement. Dell wrote in his autobiography, "As a bohemian, I did not ask of myself any regular, practical propaganda duties; my contribution to the revolution would be such truth-telling as I could manage to do . . . as an artist."[84] According to Brooks, self-assertion had been antisocial so long as it was based upon economic gain. But self-assertion expressed through politics or "through science, or literature, or mechanics or industry itself" was a "directly social activity" in which one fulfilled oneself through and with others.[85]

7. *The Separation of the Personal . . .*

MUCH OF THE STRENGTH of nineteenth-century romantic individualism derived from its association with the French Revolution and with currents such as abolitionism in England and America. Similarly, the possibility in the United States of basing a program of action (a "politics" broadly conceived) upon the new sphere of personal life was rendered plausible by the vitality and momentum of the socialist and feminist movements. World War I, the Nineteenth Amendment, and the split in the socialist movement after the Russian Revolution, however, destroyed these movements and with them the general mood of impending revolution within which individual liberation and social transformation were reconciled. The Bolshevik Revolution helped refocus the political attention of European and American socialists exclusively on the question of state power just as "personal" questions were assuming widespread significance. Following the Russian example the goal of socialism was presented purely in terms of economic development. The Communist Party wrote off the pre–World War I currents of personal radicalism as "petty bourgeois" and rejected as a

83. Henry May, *The End of American Innocence* (New York, 1969), p. 304.

84. Floyd Dell, *Homecoming: An Autobiography* (n.p., n.d.), pp. 147–48.

85. Brooks, "America's Coming of Age," in Sprague, p. 94.

whole the legacy of romantic individualism and art. Correspondingly, the various ideologies of personal life began to reject socialist politics as "irrelevant" to the changing needs of the American people. Beginning in the 1920s bohemians looked to France for inspiration while socialists looked to the Soviet Union. A gulf opened between the radicalism of personal liberation and the radicalism of political revolution that remained largely unchallenged until the 1960s.

In the absence of any connection to a concrete social movement the culture that arose on the new terrain of personal life was plunged into subjectivity. Movements such as progressive education, psychoanalysis, and sexual freedom reflected the illusion that personal life could be transformed without a transformation of the mode of production. Lacking any analysis of how capitalism formed personal life, such movements were easily co-opted and integrated into the corporate capitalist system. They have supplied much of the élan in our changing patterns of commodity consumption. Alternatively, these movements resisted "selling out," but they did so on behalf of the lone individual—the "genius," the hipster, the beatnik artist. Cut off from production and from the life of the masses of people, cultural radicalism survived in the form of protest movements whose radical content was increasingly esoteric, abstract, and utopian.

Educational reformers around 1900 opposed the child's world of play and imagination to the adult regimen of alienated labor. On this basis reformers criticized traditional education but failed to criticize the capitalist order that produced it. The twentieth century corporate economy demands "creativity," "inventiveness," and "imagination" as constituent elements in the process of production. It requires a more cooperative and socially oriented labor force and a more flexible and diversified curriculum than nineteenth-century capitalism required. Through the work of John Dewey and others the romantic idealization of the child was combined with a program of social adjustment. Unlike previous reformers Dewey stressed the *continuity* between play and work, and between childhood and society. Respect for the child's innate capabilities was combined with the need to educate the child to what

Dewey called a "socialized disposition."[86] In this way the emphasis on the child's spontaneity and freedom was integrated with the reformed and stratified educational system of corporate capitalism.

The liberating potential of modern art has also been dissipated. Since the rise of romanticism the artist has symbolized the free individual who brought to society not the performance of an assigned function but his or her own self.[87] This image spoke to the situation of proletarianized individuals who felt that their real, inner being was not engaged by their social function. Its peril, however, lay in the artist's unawareness of his or her own social relations and place, as an artist, in the capitalist system of production. With the rise of mass-produced art in the twentieth century—publishing, magazines, movies, etc.—the artist's conception of him or herself as a unique individual, a "genius," became the artist's major defense against proletarianization. The subjectivity of modern art became elitist and mystified. Many currents repudiated romanticism in a search for objective and impersonal disciplines. In either case, rather than symbolizing universal feelings and experience, modern art has become obscurantist and remote from actual human concerns.

Similarly, psychoanalysis has been both integrated into

86. Dewey argued that the decline in the productive functions of the family had undermined its educational role. The schools were to fill this vacuum. On the model of the earlier bourgeois family he urged that the school be a collective productive enterprise in which learning proceeded by doing. Lawrence A. Cremin, *The Transformation of the School* (New York, 1961), pp. 125, 154-57.

87. In the romantic tradition the image of the artist or "genius" as a figure outside the division of labor originally had a democratic aspect. According to Emerson: "He that is once admitted to the right of reason is made a freeman of the whole estate. What Plato has thought, he may think; what a saint has felt, he may feel." Ralph Waldo Emerson, "History," in *The Portable Emerson* (New York, 1968), p. 139. Similarly Wordsworth asks, "What is a Poet?" and answers, "He is a man speaking to men. . . . The Poet thinks and feels in the spirit of human passions. How then can his language differ in any material degree from that of all other men who feel vividly and see clearly?" William Wordsworth, "Observations Prefixed to Lyrical Ballads," in Mark Schorer, Josephine Miles, and Gordon McKenzie, eds., *Criticism: The Foundations of Modern Literary Judgment* (New York, 1958).

capitalist production and has survived as an esoteric rebellion against it. Originally, psychoanalysis was a time-consuming and expensive treatment restricted to the European and American middle classes. In the form of therapy, counseling, social work, and other institutions this treatment has been extended to large sectors of the working class. The growth of psychotherapy parallels the rise of higher education; both reflect the development of a diversified and educated working class that looks to life outside production for its sense of personal meaning. Once it was integrated into the system of production and administrative control, psychoanalysis could easily be adapted to the prevailing ideology of adjustment, social conformity, and cynical self-confidence. In this context the radical component of Freudian theory appeared to be the instinct theory, the sphere of sexuality and instinctual needs that could not be contained within "one-dimensional" society. The popularity of psychoanalysis during the 1950s among American intellectuals such as Norman Mailer lay in the idea that the instinctual or sexual component of human life could never be subdued by social imperatives. Similarly, in the early twentieth century, such ideas as vitalism, the life force, the struggle for existence, the *élan vital* and creative evolution were linked to the individual's protest against the existing order. As with the artist, the tradition of psychoanalytic rebellion survives as a defense of the rebel or hipster who stands against the mass.[88]

So long as the realm of personal life was understood as divorced from production, the radicalism to which it gave rise would be forced back upon itself in an ever-narrowing circle of self-concern. The 1920s saw a new literature emerge amid a new social movement—emigration. As capitalism continued to expand, what was there outside capitalism? Novelists like Hemingway contributed to a cult of "experience" and of the individual. Personal radicalism gravitated toward irrationality, violence, and mystery. From the surrealists through R. D. Laing, a series of movements have arisen to uphold madness as the positive alternative to oppression.

88. John Judis, "The Social Meaning of Psychoanalysis," unpublished manuscript.

In this context perhaps we can understand the mysterious significance of sexuality in the lives of modern men and women. It is almost as if sexuality has been invested with all the mystery of society itself. Sex has appeared as the ultimately asocial act, the one in which men and women were the most "natural," in the dark without clothing. As the other world of capitalist society, ignored, denied, and lied about, sexuality stood for the real life of men and women as opposed to the artificial constraints of society. Seen in this way, the most personal and intimate of experiences is, paradoxically, also the most universal and natural.

Yet, sex is also the supremely social act, a human exchange of love and power. As such it is a social relation of capitalist society: male supremacy, authoritarianism, and the need for social connection are integral parts of sexuality. The twentieth-century assertion of sexuality has been an abstract one; it has not included a critique of the social relations of sexuality. The birth control movement, for example, was initially supported by socialists and anarchists because they saw its potential for liberating women from the tyranny of endless reproduction. But no critique of male supremacy was ever sustained within the birth control movement. Instead the movement confined itself to the purely private rights of individuals to choose the sexual life they wished. By 1916 Margaret Sanger was presenting birth control as the solution to working-class misery and as a means of controlling the birth rate of the "unfit." [89] A similar fate befell all other forms of sexual radicalism. Sex was "liberated" (i.e., it became a commodity, an ideology, and a form of "leisure") but men and women were not. The same dualism applies to Wilhelm Reich, who made the most important effort to integrate sex with politics. Reich accepted genital heterosexuality as a fact of nature and held it up as an ideal against capitalist social relations; he did not subject sexuality to a social critique. Sexuality in our time has been infused with the most complex and intense social meaning, and yet is understood as the realm of pure and private individualism. No wonder that it is in the experience of sex that

89. Kennedy, pp. 112 ff.

men and women today so often encounter their own solitude and confusion.

8. . . . and the Political

IN NINETEENTH-CENTURY AMERICA, personal life entered politics primarily through conservative movements such as prohibition and censorship. Progressives and liberals believed that personal life should simply be left to the individual. Most socialists agreed, adding that a revolution in which the working class took power would free the individual to choose the private life he or she wanted. The socialist respect for individual freedom was important, but it also tended to reinforce the ideology that governs modern personal life—that it is entirely an individual matter. Throughout our century this ideology has given rise to a program of abstract individualism—personal liberation within capitalist society. And it has encouraged the idea that the oppression of women within the family was not a matter for politics. But this ideology also reflected a profound truth: commodity production had become a restricted part of social life. For socialists to address the questions of personal life, therefore, it was necessary for them to break with the idea that socializing the means of production would revolutionize all society. Or, alternately, socialists had to redefine the meaning of production.

The Communist Party, the dominant force on the left between the Russian Revolution and the 1960s, did neither. In regard to women's liberation and the family, as in so many other regards, Communists perpetuated the best and deepest nineteenth-century understanding into the transformed conditions of corporate capitalism. As the possibility arose for a society no longer organized around alienated work, the Communist Party defined socialism primarily as a more efficient form of economic development. Beginning in the second half of the 1920s the major public issues the party addressed were support for the Soviet Union and the inability of the capitalist class to provide for economic stability and growth. Communists did not address the question of the purposes of production or the place of production in society as a whole. In the absence of a comprehensive critique of capitalist society on behalf of the alternative of socialism, the Communist Party was unable to develop a sustained public politics concerning personal life.

In the 1920s currents of personal emancipation and cultural radicalism flourished on a larger scale than ever before, but now, and for the first time, almost entirely isolated from the left. Against contemporary currents of free love the party upheld the ideal of sex within marriage. At the same time the Communist Party did pay attention to the transformation of personal relations among its members.[90] Inspired by the Soviet Union, a Spartan ideal of female equality and a subculture of "red weddings" and "Komsomols" (youth groups) arose. The party stressed the political participation of women and the sharing of housework among party members. However, as the party moved toward a reformist politics in support of existing trade union and "progressive" struggles, questions of personal life were increasingly seen as irrelevant and even divisive.

The Depression nearly destroyed the spontaneous impulse toward personal and cultural radicalism that characterized the teens and twenties. The 1930s was a period of conservative return to traditional values—the nation, rural America, and the family. The rise of new mass media, commercial sports, popular religion, and the psychological and political triumph of the New Deal reinforced the general rallying around "the American Way of Life." The family was portrayed as the bulwark of the new community achieved by mass culture. The 1930s witnessed the birth of "scientific" marriage counseling, a new emphasis on child-rearing, and, in a time of unemployment, the return of women to the home.[91]

The Popular Front policy arose out of the isolated position of the Soviet Union in the face of the rise of fascism. But the Communist emphasis on uniting all "democratic" and "progressive" tendencies against fascism fed into the conservative

90. Information on the Communist Party from conversation with James Weinstein, June 1973.

91. Warren Susman, ed., *Culture and Commitment, 1929–1945* (New York, 1973), introduction, p. 16.

nationalism of the 1930s. Communism, proclaimed the party in the 1936 presidential election, is "Twentieth Century Americanism." According to Earl Browder, "all of the immediate measures proposed by the Communists are aimed to protect the home."[92] The party sought and won a new respectability. As one organizer has written, the "proletarian garb favored by functionaries was replaced by the business suit."[93] Since the party did not consider socialism to be an issue during the Great Depression, Communists concentrated more and more on separate reforms and less and less on changing social relations as a whole. The Communist emphasis on joining the mainstream of American life is shown in the following remarks from a 1939 *Young Communist League Bulletin* from the University of Wisconsin:

> Some people have the idea that a YCL'er is politically minded, that nothing outside of politics means anything. Gosh, no. They have a few simple problems. There is the problem of getting good men on the baseball team this spring, of opposition from other pingpong teams, of dating girls, etc. We go to shows, parties, dances and all that. In short, the YCL and its members are no different from other people except that we believe in dialectical materialism as the solution to all problems.[94]

World War II and the Cold War continued and intensified the social conservatism of the 1930s. In the absence of a general struggle for socialism any challenge to prevailing personal or familial mores appeared as an esoteric or sectarian diversion. The decline of American feminism reinforced the party's submersion in traditional and popular social ideals. Partly in response to the isolation of the party in the Cold War period, but also because of a "left turn" after 1945, the party did recreate an internal party culture within which new social relations, including women's equality, were upheld. But this culture prevailed primarily among youth; when people entered

92. Earl Browder, *The People's Front* (New York, 1938), p. 201.

93. George Blake Charney, *A Long Journey* (Chicago, 1968), p. 74.

94. Quoted in Hal Draper, "The Student Movement of the Thirties: A Political History," in Rita James Simon, ed., *As We Saw the Thirties* (Urbana, Ill., 1967), p. 181.

the world of work there was great pressure on them to be the same as everyone else and to live like "real" workers.

The Communist Party believed that it was basing its politics on the needs of the industrial proletariat. In fact it based its politics on those needs only as they were expressed by the trade union movement. The party's greatest effort went into building the trade union movement, but it submerged the public struggle for socialist revolution in this effort. Among industrial workers a critique of family and personal life did not emerge spontaneously. Because Communists left unquestioned people's lives as alienated workers they did not see that questions of the family and personal life were integral to every issue they dealt with, from wages and hours, to industrial safety, housing, racism, etc. They left the question of the family, like the question of socialism, for an indefinite and always receding future.

Beginning in the 1920s the number of industrial workers began to decline relative to the overall growth of the working class. Major new sectors developed, particularly after World War II—technical, administrative, and non-manual workers. The number of students grew drastically; between 1940 and 1970 the college population in the United States quintupled.[95] Among these groups the long-suppressed currents of personal radicalism began to re-emerge, first in the late 1950s and then explosively in the 1960s. These tendencies have taken an individualist form that has been easily contained: beatniks, hippies, freaks, communes, consciousness III, rock music, etc. At the same time the new left and the women's movement have raised questions of personal life as political issues—issues related to the organization of society as a whole. The emergence of these movements, along with the black revolt, reflects the exhaustion of the Communist tradition and the possibility of a new socialist movement in the United States.

VI. A NOTE ON PSYCHOANALYSIS

PSYCHOANALYSIS AROSE at the point of capitalist development at which the family had ceased to be a unit of

95. Robert Carson, "Youthful Labor Surplus in Disaccumulationist Capitalism," *Socialist Revolution* 9, p. 35.

commodity production, and was increasingly being seen as a refuge from the "economy" and "society." Its subject matter is the internal life of the family and of personal relations abstracted from political economy. It comprehends the family as an autonomous institution subject to its own laws of functioning. On the basis of those laws it attempts to construct a science of the family and of personal identity. But psychoanalysis has no theory of how the family is itself socially determined—instead it explains the family in terms of itself. As a result, psychoanalysis cannot distinguish what is universal in the family (a biological unit after all as well as a social one) from what is specific to the family of a particular mode of production. It cannot distinguish what in the human condition is subject to historical transformation and what should be seen as "civilization and its discontents." It tends to project the family of developed capitalist society onto all previous history.

The psychoanalytic movement arose along with the possibility of a society in which goods production was no longer the central human activity. Its initial members were intellectuals, doctors, artists, and scientists, who saw themselves as outside the productive process. The needs to which psychoanalysis speaks—for intimacy, self-understanding, sensual and emotional gratification—are needs that have arisen historically. Its mass appeal since World War II reflects the turn of large sectors of the population from a search for private productive property to a search for fulfillment in their personal lives. Psychoanalysis reflects the new social need to be valued for oneself. It invokes the sensual and instinctual life of men and women at a time when their animal energies are no longer given over entirely to production and reproduction. It would moderate asceticism, sexual repression, and self-denial at a time when these traits were becoming less functional to the process of capital accumulation.

Socialists have approached psychoanalysis mainly from two perspectives. Most have viewed it as a rationale for bourgeois unhappiness and a theory of "individual solutions"—a guide to getting by in capitalist society. This approach tends to perpetuate the exclusion of the family and personal life from politics. Other socialists, including Herbert Marcuse, Juliet

Mitchell, Louis Althusser, and Wilhelm Reich, have viewed psychoanalysis as a science whose valid content could be annexed to Marxism. But this approach, similarly, reflects the split between commodity production (which Marxism studies) and personal life (psychoanalysis). Viewed as separate sciences, Marxism and psychoanalysis contain elements that are irreconcilable. Before they can be integrated, important elements in both will have to be critically redefined.

The potential point of contact between Marxism and psychoanalysis lies in a conception of the family and of personal life as concrete social institutions, integral to and shaped by the prevailing mode of production. Freud, like Marx, began his study with concrete social behavior. In contrast to psychiatry, which reduced behavior to its organic causes, or to philosophical psychology, which posited a separate "mind" or "reason," Freud attempted to bring into scientific discussion a new area of social life: "what is most intimate in mental life, everything that a socially independent person must conceal."[96] Its most important social content was the family:

> It follows from the nature of the facts which form the history of psychoanalysis that we are obliged to pay as much attention in our case histories to the purely human and social circumstances of our patients as to the somatic data and the symptoms of the disorder. Above all, our interest will be directed toward their family circumstances—and not only, as will be seen later, for the purpose of inquiring into their heredity.[97]

Freud's most important theories, that of the instincts of drives, and that of the unconscious, derive their greatest value when they are situated as part of a theory of the family. At the same time, their ideological character derives from the fact that Freud has no theory of how the family itself has been, and is, continually remade by society.

Freud's theory of the instincts illustrates both the continuity and the contrast between psychoanalysis and Marxism. Like

---

96. Sigmund Freud, *The Complete Introductory Lectures on Psychoanalysis* (New York, 1966), p. 18.

97. Sigmund Freud, *Dora: Fragment of an Analysis of a Case of Hysteria* (New York, 1969), p. 32.

Marx, Freud sees human society as part of nature. But unlike Marx, he does not explain how human beings, through history, transform nature (including their own nature, themselves). For Marx, this is accomplished through social labor. The natural or biological condition of human beings—for example, their need for food or shelter—gives rise to forms of social organization and production that transform those conditions. This constant self-transformation of nature constitutes the Marxian dialectic. Freud's conception of the instincts potentially extends this dialectic to include our "inner nature," the instinctual life of men and women.

Before Freud, the instinctual (or natural or animal) component of human life was not generally seen as subject to historical or social modification. Scientists, doctors, and moralists viewed the biological realm as autonomous, subject to laws independent of those that governed social activity. Humanity was understood to be irretrievably divided between lower and higher functions, body and mind, sex and love, organic and functional illnesses, science and morality. To inspire progress, a higher ideal, above and beyond human needs themselves, was necessary. This was tied to political conservatism, for such an ideal could only be realized by an elite free from the imperatives that drove other human beings.[98]

Freud removed the human instincts from the autonomous realm of biology and plunged them into the social world of the family. Freud distinguished between *Instinkt* which is preadapted to reality and *Trieb* which is shaped in a definite social context.[99] Depending upon the influence of this context over time, the instincts express themselves in social activity, fantasy, creativity, etc. Beginning with his early work on hysteria, Freud sought to show how similar mechanisms of instinctual control could express themselves either somatically or psychologically. Before Freud the sexual instinct was thought to have a predetermined object (heterosexuality) and aim (genital sexuality); sexual behavior that did not conform was "unnatural." The sexual drive that Freud describes can take many forms,

98. O. Mannoni, *Freud* (New York, 1971), passim.

99. Generally translated "instinct," *Trieb* is Freud's normal usage.

depending upon the social, biological, and psychological conditions under which it operates.

Freud's thought opens the way for an understanding of the role that instinctual sexuality plays in social life. It makes it possible to talk about transforming our sexual lives as we now talk about transforming our economic and political systems. At the same time psychoanalysis considers sexuality only as it takes shape within the family, and considers the family a relatively unchanging social form. As a result, this potential social dimension in Freud's thought has scarcely been explored.

Similarly Freud's theory of the unconscious opens a new dimension to our understanding of society but remains abstract in the absence of a historical view of the family. The Freudian unconscious is created in the course of the "humanization" of the infant, the transition from the purely neurological state of the newborn to the social state of the child. This process occurs in every society and is different in every society. The social life of the family—acceptance, rejection, presence, absence, feeding, hygiene, etc.—imposes its rhythm and structure upon the child. A later and essential phase of this process is the learning of language, through which the child enters the social universe of discourse: mother, father, I, he, she, me, mine, we. . . . The psychic life of the child is superseded as we become conscious of our social relations, but persists to shape those relations. The existence of an unconscious is a bio-social necessity: primary instincts and needs must be integrated within a definite social formation. But its content and meaning varies historically according to the actual social relations and ideology contained within the family.[100]

Because the social content of psychoanalysis is restricted to its theory of the family, and because the family is conceived of as a relatively unchanging unit, attempts to develop a broader social theory on the basis of psychoanalysis have failed. Efforts to explain the origins of guilt, the meaning of culture and religion, and the beginning of human society end up as metaphors that project the model of the family onto the

100. Louis Althusser, "Freud and Lacan," in Althusser, *Lenin and Philosophy* (New York, 1971), pp. 189–220.

screen of history. The absence of a broader social theory, in turn, limits and distorts the psychoanalytic explanation of the family. This can be seen in the theory of the oedipus complex.

It was not the idea of infantile sexuality alone that made the Freudian theory of the family so disquieting. In contrast to the Ruskinesque idyll of the nineteenth-century imagination, the oedipus complex portrays anger, resentment, jealousy, fear, and guilt as normal components of the relations between and among parents and children. Psychoanalysis, far from promising a cure, threatened to take the lid off, which is why, crossing the Atlantic in 1909 to his first major public recognition, Freud remarked ironically, "We are bringing them—a plague."

How did this searing and incestuous family life arise? The oedipus complex presents a critical component of the answer: it is within the family that instinctual sexuality is first constrained and socially formed. But how were the social relations of the family, between men and women and between adults and children, themselves formed? To answer this, psychoanalysis is forced back upon itself and explains the social relations of the family in terms of instinctual sexuality. The way out of this circle is through a conception of the family as a historical unit as well as a biological one. Recently social movements have arisen, focusing on the family, which have begun such an analysis. The "youth revolt" has been expressed theoretically by R. D. Laing, David Cooper, and others, who re-explain the family in terms of the authority relations between adults and young people.[101] And Firestone's attempt to re-explain the oedipus complex in terms of the sexual division of labor reflects the experience of women's liberation.

For socialists, psychoanalysis is critical for including the family within the scope of revolutionary politics. Marxists have rightly pointed out that any society must organize the production of food, clothing, and shelter, but they have forgotten that it must equally organize the sexual and instinctual life of its members, and the process of human reproduction. Under capitalism these related imperatives are carried out separately

101. Mitchell, p. 165.

—socialized commodity production within the factory and domestic labor and sexuality within the family. At present psychoanalysis is the only social theory that gives due weight to the importance of sexuality and reproduction in the organization of society.

Socialists view labor (by which they mean wage labor under capitalism) as the central human activity, and as the practice that distinguishes human from animal life.[102] This idea has been taken over by feminists who contrast the tasks of sexuality and reproduction to the more "human" labor performed in the sphere of commodity production. But what distinguishes human from animal life is not labor—it is *conscious* labor. According to Marx: "A bee puts to shame many an architect in the construction of her cells. . . . But . . . the architect raises his structure in imagination before he erects it in reality. . . . He not only effects a change of form in the material on which he works, but he also realizes a purpose of his own." [103] Similarly, what distinguishes human sexuality from animal, and human reproduction from animal, is consciousness too—fantasy, imagination, love, purpose. By this definition the labor performed by the proletariat is no more "human" than the labor performed by women within the home. We need a movement that will transform both forms of labor consciously, deliberately and in accord with human ends.

Finally, the psychoanalytic emphasis on what has been relatively permanent and unchanging in human experience helps put into perspective the tasks of a socialist movement. History does not begin with capitalism. Many of the social relations that a socialist movement must confront—and specifically male supremacy—antedate capitalism. Some aspects of male supremacy originate in feudalism, some in slave society, some in taboos of primitive society. As Freud argued in a passage

102. The same distinction between our "human" and "animal" activities underlies the puritanism endemic to the socialist movement. Women's liberation has perpetuated this puritanism—for example, by attacking sexual exploitation or pornography without defending some principle of sexual freedom—and has repudiated it—for example, by its defense of homosexuality and masturbation.

103. Karl Marx, *Capital*, vol. 1 (Moscow, 1965), p. 178.

that once again brings out the social content of his theory:

> It seems likely that what are known as materialistic views of history err in underestimating [the force of past traditions]. They brush it aside with the remark that human "ideologies" are nothing other than the product and superstructure of their contemporary economic conditions. That is true but very probably not the whole truth. Mankind never lives entirely in the present. The past—the tradition of the race and of its people—lives on in the ideologies of the superego, and yields only slowly to the influences of the present and to new changes.[104]

What is important is not to posit male supremacy or any other social relation as arising in a "state of nature," but to understand that "ideologies" arise because of definite social conditions (including those of primitive society) and persist in definite social forms. Only in this way can we avoid binding ourselves to some myth of the past and begin to understand that our social relations are subject to our collective intervention. In this sense, a socialist movement confronts not only capitalism, but the entire prehistory of humanity: primitive, feudal, slave, etc. What we face are our own antecedents and the causes of our own development—not some universal dilemma.

104. Freud, *Complete Introductory Lectures*, p. 531.

The New Woman: Changing Views of Women in the 1920s

ESTELLE B. FREEDMAN

In his suggestive article, "What Happened to the Progressive Movement in the 1920's," Arthur S. Link analyzed the legacy of the pre-World War I "progressive coalition" of businessmen, farm groups, labor unions, and "advocates of social justice."[1] However, he neglected to mention the fate of feminists, either those women active in the suffrage movement or those involved in broader areas of social reform. Despite Link's inattention to women reformers, the question he posed about the progressive movement in the 1920s should be asked of the women's movement as well. What happened to feminism during the decade after the political goal of suffrage had been achieved?

Failure to consider the women's movement in the 1920s is not an uncommon oversight among historians. Even students of women's history, including Eleanor Flexner, Andrew Sinclair, and Aileen Kraditor, conclude their accounts with the passage of the nineteenth amendment.[2] Until recently, this tendency to ignore post-1920 women's history has fostered the repetition of a standard image of American women in the 1920s. Frederick Lewis Allen's account is representative:

> The revolution [in manners and morals] was accelerated . . . by the growing independence of the American woman. She won the suffrage in 1920. She seemed, it is true, to be very little interested in it once she had it; she voted, but

Estelle B. Freedman is an instructor of history in Princeton University.

[1] Arthur S. Link, "What Happened to the Progressive Movement in the 1920's?" *American Historical Review*, LXIV (July 1959), 833-51.

[2] Eleanor Flexner, *Century of Struggle: The Woman's Rights Movement in the United States* (Cambridge, Mass., 1959); Andrew Sinclair, *The Better Half: The Emancipation of the American Woman* (New York, 1965); Aileen S. Kraditor, *The Ideas of the Woman Suffrage Movement, 1890-1920* (New York, 1965). See also Page Smith, *Daughters of the Promised Land: Women in American History: Being an examination of the strange history of the female sex from the beginning to the present with special attention to the women of America, illustrated by curious anecdotes and quotations by divers authors, ancient and modern* (Boston, 1970); and Ishbel Ross, *Sons of Adam, Daughters of Eve* (New York, 1969).

mostly as the unregenerate men about her did. . . . Few of the younger women could rouse themselves to even a passing interest in politics: to them it was a sordid and futile business, without flavor and without hope. Nevertheless, the winning of the suffrage had its effect. It consolidated woman's position as man's equal.[3]

William E. Leuchtenburg reached a similar conclusion nearly three decades later:

The new woman wanted the same freedom of movement that men had and the same economic and political rights. By the end of the 1920's she had come a long way. Before the war, a lady did not set foot in a saloon; after the war, she entered a speakeasy as thoughtlessly as she would go into a railroad station. . . . In the business and political worlds, women competed with men; in marriage, they moved toward a contractual role. . . . Sexual independence was merely the most sensational aspect of the generally altered status of women.[4]

These and other accounts have attributed several characteristics to the "New Women" of the 1920s: they failed to vote as a block or in greater numbers than did men; their manners and morals differed sharply from those of previous generations; and their legal and economic position had so improved that for the first time in history women had become the social and economic equals of men.

An examination of the record, however, reveals that historians have repeated these descriptions not because research and analysis have confirmed their validity, but because no new questions have been asked about women in the 1920s since the initial impressionistic observations were made. The fact that these interpretations have been handed down for forty years with very little modification makes them suspect, and closer analysis confirms that several important historical questions have remained unanswered. Who precisely was the new woman; what was her fate after 1920; and how does her history relate to that of the women's movement? Specifically, historians need to clarify when and why the organized women's movement lost its influence; whether enfranchisement affected women's efforts for social reform and for equal rights for their sex; precisely what economic gains women made; and how widely and deeply the moral revolution extended.

Original and creative use of primary resources is necessary to answer these questions. But before this research is undertaken, it is essential to understand what has already been written about women in the 1920s. This essay seeks to provide such a historiographical framework by tracing inter-

[3] Frederick Lewis Allen, *Only Yesterday: An Informal History of the Nineteen-Twenties* (New York, 1931), 95-96.

[4] William E. Leuchtenburg, *The Perils of Prosperity: 1914-32* (Chicago, 1958), 159.

pretations of the new woman from the 1920s to the present. The influence of historical events and the emphases on political and legal rights as opposed to broader feminist goals is of central concern.[5] But of even greater significance is the shift of conceptual frameworks from the contemporary analysis of the 1920s to the current quasi-feminist approach.

For years, historians agreed with Mary Beard's claim that women have been a positive "force in history." They praised the post-1920 woman as an active participant in American politics and economic life, as if trying to correct what Arthur Meier Schlesinger had termed "the pall of silence which historians have allowed to rest" over women's "services and achievements."[6] Women's history was merely an effort to include more women and their successes in the history books. In later years, after social scientists rediscovered the "woman question" in the 1950s, historians groped toward a feminist view which holds that women have been unable to contribute fully to American society—even after suffrage—because they have remained the oppressed victims of history.[7] If the latter view prevails, women's history must become the study of a unique interest group, a study which requires new forms of research and new conceptual models.

Since historians were relatively silent on the question of the new woman during all but two periods—from approximately 1927 to 1933 and from 1964 to the present—broad accounts and textbooks must suffice as evidence for a review of the literature. Toward the end of the long period of neglect, scholars in other disciplines began to question the validity of the image of the post-World War I woman in America. By the time that a revival of interest in the subject had reached popular dimensions (coincident with but not necessarily related to the 1963 publication of Betty Friedan's *The Feminine Mystique*), historians too had begun to review their conceptions of the new woman. Numerous revisionist interpretations can now be ex-

[5] Gerda Lerner, "Women's Rights and American Feminism," *American Scholar*, 40 (Spring 1971), 235-48. Gerda Lerner's distinction between the women's rights movement and the broader women's emancipation movement has been adopted in the following discussion. She defines the former as a quest for political and legal equality and the latter as a search for "freedom from oppressive restrictions imposed by sex; self-determination and autonomy . . . financial and cultural independence, freedom to choose one's own life-style regardless of sex." *Ibid.*, 237.

[6] Arthur Meier Schlesinger, *New Viewpoints in American History* (New York, 1922), 126.

[7] Mary R. Beard, *Woman as Force in History: A Study in Traditions and Realities* (New York, 1946). For a discussion of historiographical approaches to women's history and the distinction between Beardian and feminist views, see Gerda Lerner, "New Approaches to the Study of Women in American History," *Journal of Social History*, 3 (Fall 1969), 53-62. Lerner rejects both approaches; she contends that women are too complex to be considered as a single group, although she recognizes that they have been the victims of group discrimination.

pected; from what historiographical traditions do they proceed?

Social commentators of the late 1920s and early 1930s reached mixed conclusions in their evaluation of the first decade of woman suffrage. Concentrating on political and economic measures of emancipation, they praised women's participation in American society, in spite of strong indications that women had not achieved equality.

As might be expected, many analyses reflected pre-suffrage positions. In a 1927 *Current History* symposium on "The New Woman," Charlotte Perkins Gilman found extensive evidence of women's political, literary, and economic achievement since enfranchisement, and Carrie Chapman Catt wrote that the vote had been used profitably to remove discrimination on the state level and to improve legislation for women and children.[8] Former opponents of woman suffrage expressed discontent in articles decrying "Woman's Encroachment on Man's Domain," and the "Evils of Woman's Revolt Against the Old Standards."[9] Ida Tarbell, an opponent of suffrage in the early debate, wrote in 1930, "I don't feel that women have contributed anything new or worthwhile . . . I maintain that this ten years experience has proved that women have become the tools of party leaders, just as men have."[10]

Positive but apologetic evaluations of women's progress appeared in a special issue of the *Annals of the American Academy of Political and Social Science* devoted to "Women in the Modern World." A regional director of the League of Women Voters argued that it would take more than eight years to break a tradition of exclusion from public affairs and that the contribution of women could not be measured by the size of their vote. Another contributor proclaimed that already "women have successfully stepped from social life into the political realm," even as she felt it necessary to assure her readers that women politicians did not shirk their domestic duties.[11]

Journalists, too, concentrated on political progress. Although generally favorable, their analyses were usually qualified by an apologetic tone. "Not

[8] Charlotte Perkins Gilman, "Woman's Achievements Since the Franchise," *Current History*, XXVII (Oct. 1927), 7; Carrie Chapman Catt, "Woman Suffrage Only an Episode in Age-Old Movement," *ibid.* See also, "Ten Years of Woman Suffrage," *Literary Digest*, 105 (April 26, 1930), 11.

[9] Anthony M. Ludovici, "Woman's Encroachment on Man's Domain," *Current History*, XXVII (Oct. 1927), 21-25; Hugh L. McMenamin, "Evils of Woman's Revolt Against the Old Standards," *ibid.*, 30-32.

[10] "Ten Years of Woman Suffrage," 11.

[11] Marguerite M. Wells, "Some Effects of Woman Suffrage," *Annals of the American Academy of Political and Social Science*, CXLIII (May 1929), 209; Dorothy Ashby Moncure, "Women in Political Life," *Current History*, XXIX (Jan. 1929), 639-43.

many of our editors seem enthusiastic over the showing made under the Nineteenth Amendment," a *Literary Digest* survey found; "Yet on the other hand, few are pessimistic." A representative editorial comment appeared in the Winston-Salem *Journal*:

> The women have acquitted themselves well during this first ten years of their political enfranchisement. But even greater results will be expected during the next decade. During the ten years just passed the women have been laying a foundation. The superstructure of achievement now remains to be built.[12]

Social scientists whose early evaluations reported few substantive gains for women were not without sympathy for the problems the new voters faced. The authors of a statistical study of the 1920 election found that women had not utilized the ballot to the same extent as men, nor had they voted predictably; however, they suggested that women were politically handicapped—not by a psychological incapacity for politics, as some critics claimed, but only by lack of experience. "When participating in politics has become through habit as natural to women as to men . . . women will undoubtedly participate in all phases of political life on a basis of actual as well as nominal equality with men."[13]

Although most writers stressed political rights, a few surveyed women's progress in finding new economic and social roles. Radical editor V. F. Calverton believed that "woman's economic independence has been a far more important item in her emancipation than [has] her political enfranchisement." He was impressed by the increasing number of married women who were working and by the effects of the growing women's labor force in fortifying single women's desires for independence. However, Calverton duly noted the pervasive discrimination against women workers, particularly that of organized labor against married women in industry.[14]

Other writers who explored the possibilities of social and cultural emancipation of women in the 1920s found, like Calverton, that antifeminist attitudes persisted. George Britt wrote that "it is possible for the Southern girl now to an extent never permitted before to . . . become a person and not just another woman." But, after citing individual examples of professional women in the South, the growth of women's clubs during

[12] "Ten Years of Woman Suffrage," 11.

[13] Stuart A. Rice and Malcolm M. Willey, "American Women's Ineffective Use of the Vote," *Current-History*, XX (July 1924), 641-47.

[14] V. F. Calverton, "Careers for Women—A Survey of Results," *ibid.*, XXIX (Jan. 1929), 633-38; V. F. Calverton and Samuel D. Schmalhausen, eds., *Woman's Coming of Age: A Symposium* (New York, 1931), xi-xx.

the 1920s, changes in personal habits such as smoking, and the involvement of women in social reform, Britt concluded: "The Southern girl may like to earn a little money and have her fling, but the ideal in the back of her head is a nice house in the home town and a decorative position in society."[15] Former Judge Ben Lindsey drew on his experiences counseling youth in the 1920s to make ample references to signs of the moral revolution: premarital sex, birth control, drinking, contempt for older values. Yet almost every case he cited revealed a strong conflict between the appeal of flamboyant freedom and the sense of sin it still engendered. Beneath it all Lindsey suspected that in a few years the lively flapper would become "a happy, loyal wife with several children."[16]

In spite of indications that only limited women's rights and not broader feminist goals had been advanced, the optimistic writers of the 1920s generally hailed the participation of women in American society and the end of discrimination. Typical of their strained efforts was Chase Going Woodhouse's overly enthusiastic tone, even as his evidence wore thin. Women had made significant advances in education, Woodhouse wrote, particularly "outstanding improvements in nursing education," but Harvard still refused to train women for law and medicine; employment figures "increased steadily," he claimed, although for the period after 1919 he had to juggle figures to include housewives among the "gainfully employed"; women achieved professional advances, he noted, adding, however, that they were mainly in teaching and mostly before 1920. Despite the fact that in education, industry, and politics "despair and resentment" characterized women's responses, Woodhouse claimed "steadily gained recognition" for women.[17]

Certainly women had made some advances by the end of the 1920s, although few commentators explained how their economic and political gains compared to previous decades or with the broader social and cultural goals of feminists. In politics, women writers claimed significant progress, while men graciously excused women's supposedly poor voting record, and most writers ignored entirely women's legislative achievements of the early 1920s. A few writers recognized the limitations in women's roles, but most strained to emphasize the positive, although often superficial, aspects of women's history in the 1920s—slight increases in political officeholding

[15] George Britt, "Women in the New South," Calverton and Schmalhausen, eds., *Woman's Coming of Age*, 409-23.

[16] Ben B. Lindsey, "The Promise and Peril of the New Freedom," *ibid.*, 447-71.

[17] Chase Going Woodhouse, "The Status of Women," *American Journal of Sociology*, XXXV (May 1930), 1091-96.

and nonprofessional jobs and greater sexual freedom. Nevertheless they confidently portrayed the period as one in which feminist goals were well on their way to fulfillment.[18] By proclaiming emancipation a *fait accompli* and denying the existence of discrimination, they only helped to discourage further feminist efforts for deeper social change.

Meanwhile, historians began to incorporate the 1920s into their works, and they too stressed positive roles and women's increased participation in American life. Although published in the early 1930s, the first histories reflected the tone of the years before the crash rather than the Depression. Charles and Mary Beard, Allen, and Preston William Slosson echoed the feelings of the generation that had seen both the pre-suffrage woman and the new woman, and their accounts emphasized the changes in woman's social position during the 1920s.

"Women," wrote the Beards, "now assumed an unquestioned role in shaping the production of goods, material, humanistic, literary, and artistic." The ballot had enlarged women's influence in politics, while economic power, education, and social freedom had made women "powerful arbiters in all matters of taste, morals, and thinking." The Beards seemed pleased with these successes, but they were also apprehensive about some of the consequences of women's emancipation—the decline in the authority of fathers, defiant and divorce-prone women, and the "more intransigent" demand for " 'absolute and unconditional equal opportunity' in every sphere" of an equal rights amendment.[19]

Slosson reported the "complete acceptance of American women in political life" and even greater progress, if that was possible, in economic status and social prestige. But Slosson's main concerns centered on areas traditionally defined as women's spheres. In a chapter entitled "The American Woman Wins Equality," Slosson devoted six pages to economic and political developments and twenty-two pages to the family, home, and fashions. Shorter skirts, more comfortable undergarments, shorter hair, the use of cosmetics, smoking, drinking, and the "breezy, slangy, informal" flapper characterized the era for him. As suffrage "disappeared from politics," women became content, he wrote, with the exception of "the more doctrinaire type" who pressed for equal rights.[20] Women's history was reverting to women's spheres of home, fashions, and sex and finding there little or no oppression.

[18] A similar confidence among social scientists in the 1920s has been described by Henry F. May, "Shifting Perspectives on the 1920's," *Mississippi Valley Historical Review*, XLIII (Dec. 1956), 405-27.

[19] Charles A. and Mary R. Beard, *The Rise of American Civilization: The Industrial Era* (New York, 1930), 753-58.

[20] Preston William Slosson, *The Great Crusade and After: 1914-1928* (New York, 1930), 130-61.

According to Allen, women did not vote in the 1920s, but they did work, if not in offices or factories, then in the professional job of homemaking. But the job, or the potential for earning, created a feeling of comparative economic independence in women, which, for Allen, threatened husbandly and parental authority. Even with all of this, woman wanted more: "She was ready for the revolution"—sexual freedom, as enhanced by Sigmund Freud, the automobile, and Hollywood. Changes in fashion, Allen implied, were signs of deeper changes in the American feminine ideal.[21]

With these three historical views, women in the 1920s began to be presented as flappers, more concerned with clothing and sex than with politics. Women had by choice, the accounts suggested, rejected political emancipation and found sexual freedom. The term feminism nearly disappeared from historical accounts, except in somewhat pejorative references to the Woman's party. While critics claimed that women had achieved equality with men, they issued subtle warnings of moral and family decay.

At the same time, women writing about the 1920s remained more concerned about political and economic equality than about the flapper and the moral revolution. In 1933, Inez Haynes Irwin offered *Angels and Amazons*, an all too glowing chronicle of the advancement of women in American history. Looking back over the first decade of new freedom, Irwin found four organized feminist activities "worth remembering": work for child welfare, self-education as voters, influence on world peace, and the struggle for equal legal status for women.[22] None of these subjects had been discussed yet by historians, and Irwin left the moral revolution entirely to them.

In the same year, Sophonisba Breckinridge offered a more sophisticated approach to women's history in a monograph which Henry F. May has called "a monument of the chastened social science of the thirties."[23] Entitled *Women in the Twentieth Century*, her volume was a statistical survey accompanied by analytical comment on women's organizations, occupations, and political life. It is an invaluable aid for the study of American women, in sobering contrast to the superficial treatment of women in other works.

Breckinridge's conclusions suggested that perhaps women were not the emancipated, satisfied participants in American society that historians were describing. While an increasing number of women worked, she found that

[21] Allen, *Only Yesterday*, 97-109.

[22] Inez Haynes Irwin, *Angels and Amazons: A Hundred Years of American Women* (Garden City, 1933), 411.

[23] Sophonisba P. Breckinridge, *Women in the Twentieth Century: A Study of the Political, Social and Economic Activities* (New York, 1933); May, "Shifting Perspectives on the 1920's," 410.

they were severely restricted in their range of employment. In the realm of public activity, Breckinridge reported that "the moment seems an unhappy one at which to attempt to take account of stock." Women had become disillusioned with the ballot and had turned to government agencies and educational institutions for bases of emancipation, but they had not as yet been successful in obtaining political power. Breckinridge described women's lobbying efforts and their roles in the national parties, but her picture is nowhere as promising as either Irwin's account of public life or the "progress" implied in Slosson's or Allen's descriptions of the flapper. The Breckinridge study provided the data which might have prompted historical revisions on women's emancipation in the 1920s. On the contrary, with one exception in the mid-1930s, her work seems to have been unconsulted for several decades, and the new woman remained an assumption rather than a subject for historical inquiry.

The one writer who did examine Breckinridge's work was Ernest R. Groves, a sociologist of marriage and the family who stressed the economic roots of feminist activity. Groves outlined the effects of industrial employment during World War I in raising women's expectations and in a "heightening of the feelings of self-interest." Groves was aware that the growth of a female labor force did not automatically change attitudes toward working women and the family, and he suggested that the continued existence of a temporary female work force contributed to an exploitative double standard of wages geared to nonpermanent help. While the vote had quickened the trend to legal equality and reinforced lobbying activities, women were not yet, in Groves' view, active and equal subjects in history. Later writers would agree with him that women were a special class, treated unequally, the "feminine side of a masculine civilization."[24]

From the mid-1930s through the late 1940s feminism was not a popular subject among historians, just as women's rights was not one of the raging issues of the day. A country struggling through a prolonged depression saw woman's emancipation and her entry into the job market in a very different light than had an earlier, more prosperous society. Working women were being asked, if not forced, to leave their newly acquired positions and return to the home, either to allow men to take up their jobs or at least to

[24] Ernest R. Groves, *The American Woman: The Feminine Side of a Masculine Civilization* (New York, 1937), 364, 377. Legislative victories included the Women's Bureau, which became a permanent agency in 1920, and the Sheppard-Towner Act of 1921, which funded welfare and hygiene centers for maternity and infancy care. Ernest R. Groves also connected the sexual revolution with economic roots: because women's motives for marrying had become less economic, he reasoned, women had begun to "demand from the experience a fulfillment of personality which more and more includes satisfactory sexual relationships." *Ibid.*, 389.

offer moral support to families in a time of crisis.[25] When rearmament and the war provided new jobs for women, American society had ample reason to readjust to working women; but by no means had a consensus been reached on the proper place of women in American society, for the postwar years witnessed renewed debate over women's roles.

It is not surprising that during these crisis-ridden years, historians were either silent or ambivalent about the emancipation of women. The only sense one can get of their interpretations must come from textbooks and broad surveys of American thought, most of which contained brief sections on the new woman.[26] While no one seemed to doubt that emancipation had occurred, several historians were unsure whether to welcome or denounce the new woman.

Historians often cited the relationship between urbanization and the emancipation of women to explain economic opportunities in the 1920s: a rising standard of living, more household appliances, and compulsory public education provided women with unprecedented leisure time which enabled them to join women's clubs or to enter the work force.[27] These developments in turn influenced family life, the texts claimed, as evidenced by a declining birth rate and a climbing divorce rate. At this point historians often highlighted woman's new role of "professional homemaker." For example, Dwight Lowell Dumond's 1937 college text explained that feminists in the nineteenth century had made only small gains, but "Since then household electrical appliances have done more to emancipate women than all the generations of agitation by militant suffragettes." Consequently, "women were living in a new and happier world. . . . The joy of homemaking replaced the drudgery of housekeeping. . . ."[28] Merle Curti's image

[25] According to Robert and Helen Lynd, the need for women to work to supplement reduced family incomes during the Depression confused traditional roles and placed renewed emphasis on femininity and on the value of women as homemakers. Robert S. Lynd and Helen Merrel Lynd, *Middletown in Transition: A Study in Cultural Conflicts* (New York, 1937), 102-43. E. Wight Bakke noted that although women worked during the Depression, their employment was always considered a necessity, and their proper place remained in the home. E. Wight Bakke, *The Unemployed Worker: A Study of the Task of Making a Living without a Job* (London, 1940), 118.

[26] Jeannette P. Nichols, *Twentieth Century United States: A History* (New York, 1943); Samuel Eliot Morison and Henry Steele Commager, *The Growth of the American Republic* (2 vols., New York, 1942); John D. Hicks, *The American Nation: A History of the United States from 1865 to the Present* (Boston, 1949).

[27] Harold Underwood Faulkner, *American Political and Social History* (New York, 1937), 651-52; Foster Rhea Dulles, *Twentieth Century America* (Cambridge, Mass., 1945), 176-77; Dwight Lowell Dumond, *Roosevelt to Roosevelt: The United States in the Twentieth Century* (New York, 1937), 35; Merle Curti, Richard Shryock, Thomas Cochran, and Fred Harvey Harrington, *An American History* (New York, 1950), 452-60; Louis M. Hacker and Helene S. Zahler, *The United States in the 20th Century* (New York, 1952), 355-56.

[28] Dumond, *Roosevelt to Roosevelt*, 35.

of women in the 1920s displayed ambivalance toward working women. While he found that women's magazines devoted space to careers "in the big world outside the home," he added that they "naturally" gave more space to the efficient management of the home.[29] Foster Rhea Dulles' one page on the emancipation of women related increasing opportunity in business and professions to divorce rates, as well as to the development of independent social lives for women.[30] Harvey Wish discussed women's employment outside the home and then cited Robert and Helen Lynd's Middletown study to demonstrate the weaknesses in modern marriage—the loss of companionship in marriage, the use of birth control, and the new manners (smoking, drinking, and masculinized fashions) of women.[31]

These authors may not have intended to link working women with family decline, but often the proximity of the two statements, if not an explicitly drawn connection, brought them together in the mind of the reader. Similarly, historians in the 1930s and 1940s viewed the "moral revolution" in more negative terms—as a threat to the family—than it had been seen in the late 1920s, when the short skirt and bobbed hair were likely to be used as symbols of emancipation.

Once again, historians disagreed about the political effects of enfranchisement. Some believed that voting rights for women had little or no effect.[32] Others claimed that women had won total equality, as in John D. Hicks' statement that even before 1920 "Legal discriminations against women, aside from suffrage, were brought near the vanishing point."[33] Similarly, Henry Steele Commager wrote that while the emancipation of women had begun in the 1890s with the typewriter, telephone exchange, and labor saving devices, it was "dramatized by the vote, and guaranteed by birth control."[34] Dumond pointed to women's political roles in the Women's Joint Congressional Committee and stated that "Their success in securing

[29] Merle Curti, *The Growth of American Thought* (New York, 1943), 700. Merle Curti left the reader with the impression that women remained at home in the 1920s as efficient homemakers, occasionally glancing up from the card table to take note of the world. But during his discussion of the 1930s, Curti looked back on the decade as a time of "expanding economic opportunities from which so many ambitious women had profited. . . ." The 1930s, he claimed, "dealt blow after blow at women in the professions, in the arts, and in business. Feminists regretted that the new turn of events undermined the progress women had been making. . . ." *Ibid*., 721. When this progress had been made is unclear.

[30] Dulles, *Twentieth Century America*, 176.

[31] Harvey Wish, *Society and Thought in Modern America: A Social and Intellectual History of the American People from 1865* (New York, 1952), 445-47.

[32] Hacker and Zahler, *United States in the 20th Century*, 356; Faulkner, *American Political and Social History*, 651-52.

[33] Hicks, *American Nation*, 408.

[34] Henry Steele Commager, *The American Mind: An Interpretation of American Thought and Character Since the 1880's* (New Haven, 1950), 46.

state legislation for child welfare, women's legal rights, social hygiene and education have been little less than phenomenal."[35] A 1950 textbook by Curti, Richard Shryock, Thomas Cochran, and Fred Harvey Harrington also acknowledged women's fight for progressive legislation and local good government in the 1920s, but contrary to Dumond claimed that women rarely joined political parties.[36]

Throughout the 1930s and 1940s, then, historians briefly portrayed post-1920 women as emancipated by the vote and by an urbanized, industrialized society, but choosing to remain for the most part in the home. Their portrayals of satisfied professional housewives or unstable career women were doubtless both products of and reinforcements for the Depression psychology which sought to bring women out of the work force. While legal and political equality were praised, social and cultural emancipation evoked gentle reproaches. In no sense, however, did historians acknowledge the persistence of discrimination in all realms.

Post-World War II American society faced a dilemma of women's roles: would the many women who had gone to work during the war return to their homes? Popular literature on "woman's place" abounded after 1947,[37] and scholars, too, began to question women's roles in a way that would eventually change the direction of historical writing on the new woman. Once the existing discrimination against women was exposed, historians would have to reexamine their portrayal of the past decades as periods of emancipation.

Evidence of a reemerging intellectual curiosity about women can be found in the publications and reviews of the early 1950s. Alfred Kinsey's report on *Sexual Behavior in the Human Female* raised dormant issues of women's sexuality.[38] More provoking, perhaps, was the 1953 English translation of Simone de Beauvoir's *The Second Sex*, which produced new hopes and fears of a revitalization of feminism.[39] In the same year, Mirra

[35] Dumond, *Roosevelt to Roosevelt*, 60. The Women's Joint Congressional Committee worked for passage of the Sheppard-Towner Act (1921), the Cable Act (1922), which guaranteed the right of independent citizenship for married women, and dozens of other bills.

[36] Curti, Shryock, Cochran, and Harrington, *An American History*, 462.

[37] On the postwar confusion over women's roles, see William Chafe, "From Suffrage to Liberation: The Changing Roles of American Women, 1920-1970" (doctoral dissertation, Columbia University, 1971), especially chapter ten. William Chafe cites, for example, Frances Levison, "American Woman's Dilemma," *Life*, 22 (June 16, 1947), 101-16.

[38] Alfred Kinsey and others, *Sexual Behavior in the Human Female* (Philadelphia, 1953).

[39] Simone de Beauvoir, *The Second Sex* (New York, 1953). The generally favorable reviews ranged in opinion from "a very lively thesis" (New York *Times*, Feb. 22, 1953) to ". . . borders on the paranoid" (Charles J. Rollo, "Reader's Choice," *Atlantic*, 191 [April 1953], 86). Two reviewers predicted that the book would dispel myths about women and encourage reform. Patrick Mullahy, "Woman's Place," *Nation*, 176 (Feb. 21, 1953), 171-

Komarovsky defended equal education for women, and another sociologist, Sidney Ditzion, published *Marriage, Morals, and Sex in America: A History of Ideas*. If these offerings were not sufficient to bring women to the attention of the intellectual community, the very title of Ashley Montagu's essay, *The Natural Superiority of Women*, must have raised a few eyebrows (though probably not much consciousness).[40]

These precursors of the new feminism appeared in the 1950s for several reasons. American women were ready for a revival of feminism. They had weathered the years of the Depression and war without making new demands for equality. They now lived in an increasingly affluent society which was beginning to turn its attention to the question of racial equality, a subject which has historically heightened feminist concerns. Furthermore, the generation of women which came to maturity in the 1950s had not lived through and tired of an earlier feminist movement. These women were at a crossroads; would they return to the long interrupted battle for equality, or would they be seduced by the security promised to homemakers? Scholars looked back to the 1920s for clues, and although they considered women's political life, they placed more emphasis on social and cultural forces and explored the social roles open to women.

In 1950, for example, sociologists Arnold W. Green and Eleanor Melnick asked "What Has Happened to the Feminist Movement?" They found that feminism had achieved specific goals of suffrage and job opportunity, as well as contributing to broader change by giving impetus to "the steady nurturing of the philosophy of the service state." But the feminist movement, they believed, had in a larger sense failed, for "about thirty years ago, in both politics and the job world, a fairly stable level was reached which the further passage of time has only indeterminately altered." Three factors hampered women's efforts for further advancement: the "residue of prejudice against working women," especially in non-traditional women's occupations; feminists' ignorance "of the fundamental changes in social structure which must precede women's assuming positions of leadership . . ."; and class cleavages in the women's movement as exacerbated by the conflict over the equal rights amendment (the National

72; and Ashley Montagu, New York *Herald Tribune*, Feb. 22, 1953. Elizabeth Hardwick bitterly criticized the book as one which filled her "with a kind of shame and sadness." Elizabeth Hardwick, "The Subjection of Women," *Pa tisan Review*, 20 (May 1953), 321-31. Joint reviews on women's literature included S. Rudikoff, *Hudson Review*, IX (Summer 1956); and Robert Bierstadt, "The Women Books," *Antioch Review*, XIV (June 1954).

[40] Mirra Komarovsky, *Women in the Modern World: Their Education and their Dilemmas* (Boston, 1953); Sidney Ditzion, *Marriage, Morals, and Sex in America: A History of Ideas* (New York, 1953); Ashley Montagu, *The Natural Superiority of Women* (New York, 1953).

Woman's party of upper-class and professional women supported the amendment, while proletarian and middle-class women wanted protective legislation).[41]

The view that women had not yet achieved full equality and that social prejudices were at least partially responsible found even fuller expression in 1951 in a pivotal article by sociologist Helen Mayer Hacker. Elaborating on Gunnar Myrdal's comparison of woman's social position with that of Negroes, Hacker viewed women as a minority group that suffered collective discrimination, received separate socialization, and generally fit sociological definitions of minority group status and behavior.[42] Of particular interest to historians was Hacker's conceptualization of a "sex relations cycle," comparable to the race relations cycle hypothesized by Robert Park. She believed that the latter stages of the cycle of competition, conflict, accommodation, and assimilation had been reached with the passage of the suffrage amendment, and she suggested prophetically that a new era of women's dissatisfaction was approaching.

The analogy of women with minority groups later appeared elsewhere, including Ditzion's *Marriage, Morals, and Sex* and in a reinterpretation of the flapper by B. June West. Rejecting the traditional view that women's fads and fashions in the 1920s were manifestations of freedom, West's literary analysis suggested that women's fashions were an apeing of men, "as minority groups have always done . . . to the so-called superior group." Although the plays and novels of the 1920s depicted women in a variety of masculinized roles—the aggressor in sex, the divorcee—West cautioned that the literature "implied a moral disintegration that was quite likely more publicized than actually existent."[43]

Another reinterpretation of changes in women's roles in the 1920s which questioned historians' assertions of sex equality was *Women and Work in America* by Robert W. Smuts. The legal status of women, he found, shifted not after World War I but earlier with the passing of the frontier, and by the end of the war the feminist movement was "rapidly subsiding." The war had led to a "remarkable liberalization of views about women's abilities and the propriety of their working outside the home," but the postwar decades were marked by women's lack of interest in many of the vic-

[41] Arnold W. Green and Eleanor Melnick, "What Has Happened to the Feminist Movement?" Alvin W. Gouldner, ed., *Studies in Leadership: Leadership and Democratic Action* (New York, 1950), 83, 296, 301.

[42] Helen Mayer Hacker, "Women as a Minority Group," *Social Forces*, 30 (Oct. 1951), 60-69. The definitions she used are those of Louis Wirth and Kurt Lewin.

[43] B. June West, "The 'New Woman,'" *Twentieth Century Literature*, I (July 1955), 55-68.

tories they had won. As evidence Smuts described a low level of interest in politics, a small increase in women working for pay, retirement from work at marriage, indifference of young women to feminism, and a failure to make significant gains in careers other than teaching and nursing. His explanation for this demise of feminism in the 1920s was that feminists, never more than a small minority of women to begin with, had won their primary goals; their demands became less important as the status of men and women became less differentiated. Thus the women's rights movement had failed only in succeeding too well, and women turned from a search for political and economic equality to one for sexual and social identity.[44]

How did historians respond to the postwar interest in the social roles of women? A few studies appeared, some inspired by the centennial of the Seneca Falls Convention, some worthless, such as Eric J. Dingwall's survey of women in American history, and some very suggestive, such as Carl N. Degler's article on Gilman.[45] For the most part, however, historians maintained the older views that women had lost interest in politics after attaining legal equality. Historians' interests in social emancipation remained confined to the "revolution in morals" concept.

Eric Goldman's 1952 history of reform, *Rendezvous with Destiny*, stated little more than that women's suffrage had made no difference, women failed to use the ballot, and when they did vote they did not vote as women.[46] Link's 1955 text repeated the story of the revolution in manners and morals, claimed that women had achieved political and economic equality after 1920, and seemed relieved to announce that the "revolution in morals and customs had run its full course by 1930 [when] . . . [t]here seemed to be certain signs of returning sanity."[47] Leuchtenburg argued that "women's suffrage had few consequences, good or evil"; although millions voted and some held office, "the new electorate caused scarcely a ripple in American political life." Yet in business and social life, Leuchtenburg described a period of accomplishment.[48]

These accounts are not necessarily mistaken, but they are glaringly inconsistent in their evaluations of the progress toward women's emancipation that was made in the 1920s. What is most interesting is that histo-

[44] Robert W. Smuts, *Women and Work in America* (New York, 1959), 142-43.

[45] Eric John Dingwall, *The American Woman: An Historical Study* (New York, 1956); Carl N. Degler, "Charlotte Perkins Gilman on the Theory and Practice of Feminism," *American Quarterly*, VIII (Spring 1956), 21-39.

[46] Eric F. Goldman, *Rendezvous with Destiny: A History of Modern American Reform* (New York, 1952), 292-93.

[47] Arthur S. Link, *American Epoch: A History of the United States since the 1890's* (New York, 1955), 274-75.

[48] Leuchtenburg, *Perils of Prosperity*, 160.

rians had not yet defined and attempted to resolve the controversies over the women's movement and the history of women after suffrage. Previous writers had claimed all things and nothing for women in the 1920s: that the vote was not used, that it had brought equality; that women became men's equals in the world of work, that they had remained in traditionally feminine occupations; that the sexual revolution had changed women's lives, that the revolution was more a literary than an actual occurrence. Either historians were indifferent to these issues in the early postwar years, or, perhaps, while other scholars pointed to new conceptual frameworks for viewing women's history, historians were contemplating the issues and beginning to design the research which was to take form in the next decade. If the latter was the case, it was a long time before their thoughts actually reached the public, for one must skip to the early 1960s to find them in print. By this time, concern about discrimination against minority groups was widespread; President John F. Kennedy had established a Commission on the Status of Women and several states and localities had followed suit; civil rights legislation was being applied to women's rights; the Negro rights movement was about to turn toward black power; and, in 1963, Friedan published *The Feminine Mystique*, a journalistic polemic which was to sell over a million copies and help spark a revival of feminism in America.[49]

As if to mark the beginning of serious interest in women in American history, two established historians published essays on the subject in 1964.

[49] Betty Friedan, *The Feminine Mystique* (New York, 1963). Although Betty Friedan's book is not a historical study, it does offer several hypotheses on the history of women after 1920 which require clarification. Friedan dated the end of the era of the new woman—the woman who searches for her own identity—around 1950, when a change in emphasis to "femininity" created the feminine mystique of housewife-mother. Her argument is based in large part on analyses of short stories in women's magazines, in which she finds career girl heroines predominant in the 1930s and housewife-mother heroines, who forsake careers for husband, home, and family, characteristic of the 1950s. One explanation for the shift, Friedan asserted, was that career women editors of these magazines were either being replaced by men or were so embarrassed by their own success that they tried to make other women accept a more traditional feminine role. "Did women really go home again as a reaction to feminism?" she asked; "The fact is that to women born after 1920 [and thus coming to maturity in the post-World War II period] feminism was dead history. It ended as a vital movement in America with the winning of that final right: the vote." *Ibid.*, 93. After 1945, the sexual sell of advertising further encouraged the role of homemaker-consumer. *Ibid.*, 200-05. Friedan's argument overlooked the realities of women's history. She hypothesized a generation of liberated career women in the 1920s and 1930s, largely based on one short story published in 1939. She offered some basis for the 1950s model from the magazine literature but had no reason to suggest that the homemaker-consumer had not originated in the 1920s. After World War II, she admitted, statistics on working women show increased female employment. For another use of the women's magazine literature, see Chafe, "From Suffrage to Liberation," 190-201, which finds domesticity and an attack on feminism in the 1930s, if not earlier.

Both works indicated a significant shift away from the view that women's emancipation had been completed in the 1920s and toward one that recognized the persistence of discrimination against women.

David Potter's comments on "American Women and the American Character" credited the city, the business office, and mechanization with the promotion of sexual equality but noted the barriers to full equality remaining, notably the dualism of career and domestic roles which made emancipation of women different from that of other oppressed groups.[50] Degler also traced feminism to industrialization and urbanization. At first, Degler agreed with earlier commentators about the advances women had made. However, he retreated from unqualified congratulations by noting that no permanent increase in the female labor force was made after World War I, that women's occupational gains were not great in the professions, that sexual divisions of labor remained, and that women's educational position later regressed. Why, a historian finally asked, did feminism fail to consolidate and increase its gains after the 1920s? Changes in women's status, he explained, had occurred more through chance of war, depression, and technological change than through planned efforts.[51] American women, "like American society in general, have been more concerned with individual practice than with a consistent feminist ideology."[52] Thus, he concluded, only a strong ideological stand would enable feminists to recognize their goals consistently and continuously.

At the time that Degler and Potter made these generalizations about women, a small number of historians began investigating more closely women's political and social activities in the post-World War I decade. They discovered that there was more to the new woman than the image of the flapper had revealed, and their works offered compensatory balance to former interpretations. Harking back to the emphasis on women's political activities during the late 1920s, the new studies still did not elaborate on the theme of women as an oppressed group, but they did present valuable discussions of women's political efforts and incidentally acknowledged the social barriers impeding emancipation.

One revision was implicit in Clarke A. Chambers' study of social service. Chambers did not discuss feminism *per se*, but he did find women in the 1920s actively working in settlement houses, lobbying for wages and hours

[50] David M. Potter, "American Women and the American Character," John A. Hague, ed., *American Character and Culture: Some Twentieth Century Perspectives* (DeLand, Fla., 1964), 65-84.

[51] Carl N. Degler, "Revolution Without Ideology: The Changing Place of Women in America," Robert Jay Lifton, ed., *The Woman in America* (Boston, 1964), 197.

[52] *Ibid.*, 207.

regulations and for safeguards for earlier protective legislation, and educating women workers. Chambers proposed that progressive thought did not end in the 1920s but was tempered, to be drawn on heavily by the New Deal.[53] Anne Firor Scott's study of southern women confirmed that women advanced progressivism in the 1920s and weakened historians' monolithic interpretation of the new woman as flapper. Suffrage, she found, greatly encouraged the political life of southern women and prompted efforts for social and political reform. In several states Scott found women's organizations investigating labor conditions, securing children and women's legislation, and even organizing for interracial cooperation. In Georgia, Tennessee, Virginia, and Kentucky, women's groups pursued state and municipal government reform. At odds with entrenched politicians, southern women's political progress was "not one to gladden Mrs. Catt's heart," yet their efforts persisted through the decade. However, the 1920s did not witness a new morality in the South: "Through it all the outward aspect of the Southern lady was normally maintained as the necessary precondition of securing a hearing."[54]

James Stanley Lemons' study of postwar women cited successes such as the Sheppard-Towner Act, new marriage and divorce laws, independent citizenship (the Cable Act), and municipal reform, as well as organizations such as the National Women's Trade Union League, the National League of Women Voters, and the National Consumer's League and various professional women's groups as proof that "the woman's rights movement advanced progressivism in the period from World War I to the Great Depression."[55] The list of legislation which the Women's Joint Congressional Committee influenced successfully is a lengthy one, but most of its entries are dated before 1925, for as Lemons shows, forces of reaction after 1925 shifted the emphasis of women's activities from goals of social justice to goals of efficiency.[56] Red-baiting, the defeat of the child labor amendment, decisions of the Supreme Court barring protective legislation, and the rejection of the Progressive party in the 1924 election placed progressive women on the defensive. The equal rights amendment, Lemons believed, was "the hallmark of impatience in the 1920's, and it was an issue

[53] Clarke A. Chambers, *Seedtime of Reform: American Social Service and Social Action, 1918-1933* (Minneapolis, 1963), 82-83.

[54] Anne Firor Scott, "After Suffrage: Southern Women in the Twenties," *Journal of Southern History*, XXX (Aug. 1964), 298-318; Anne Firor Scott, *The Southern Lady: From Pedestal to Politics 1830-1930* (Chicago, 1970).

[55] James S. Lemons, "The New Woman in the New Era: Woman Movement from the Great War to the Great Depression" (doctoral dissertation, University of Missouri, 1967), v, vi, 72-73.

[56] *Ibid.*, 77, 90-91, 100.

which helped fragment the women's movement and weaken the progressive impulse."[57] Although the newly enfranchised sex had achieved no great political gains in public office or party politics, women had continued to push for reforms, laying the groundwork for the New Deal.

Not unrelated to these new interpretations of women in the 1920s was an essay by James R. McGovern, which called into question earlier historians' periodization of the revolution in morals. Citing Breckinridge's statistics on the prewar occupational status of women, pre-1910 advertisements depicting women, changing hair and cosmetic styles in the Progressive era, dance crazes, the practice of birth control, and use of automobiles, McGovern showed that the flapper had been predated by events of the first decades of the century. If, as McGovern suggested, a moral revolution occurred before World War I, were the 1920s as "revolutionary" as they had been depicted, or in fact had a reaction taken place in which women returned to home and family?[58]

The works of Scott on the southern woman's new political awareness, Chambers and Lemons on progressivism and women in the 1920s, and the reinvestigations of the moral revolution by McGovern and others may differ on many counts, but they all point to a new attitude toward women's history. Prompted in part by the political and social movements of the 1960s, these authors looked more closely at the political lives of post-World War I women and more critically at the supposed moral revolution. While they were eager to praise the role women had played in political movements, their researches laid the foundation for recent works which are critical of the failures of the women's movement to achieve lasting reform. Two current studies are evidence of the shift in view from woman as emancipated participant to woman as the victim of discrimination. William O'Neill places the bulk of the blame for feminism's demise on women; William Chafe faults American society for oppressing the "second sex."

Everyone Was Brave, O'Neill's history of feminism, was subtitled *The*

[57] *Ibid.*, 302. Another positive interpretation of women's political progress in the 1920s is found in Martin Gruberg, *Women in American Politics: An Assessment and Sourcebook* (Oshkosh, Wisc., 1968), 9-26.

[58] James R. McGovern, "The American Woman's Pre-World War I Freedom in Manners and Morals," *Journal of American History*, LV (Sept. 1968), 315-33. See also, Robert E. Riegel, "Women's Clothes and Women's Rights," *American Quarterly*, XV (Fall 1963), 390-401; William L. O'Neill, *Divorce in the Progressive Era* (New Haven, 1967); and Henry F. May, *The End of American Innocence: A Study of the First Years of Our Own Time 1912-1917* (Chicago, 1959). Kenneth A. Yellis noted that "The new woman seemed to go into eclipse during the period of anxiety [the Depression], but the changed circumstances of World War II, including a manpower shortage, brought her out again." Kenneth A. Yellis, "Prosperity's Child: Some Thoughts on the Flapper," *American Quarterly*, XXI (Spring 1969), 64.

Rise and Fall of Feminism in America, a phrase indicative of the author's view of the 1920s:

The women's rights movement expired in the twenties from ailments that had gone untreated in its glory days. Chief among them was the feminists' inability to see that equal suffrage was almost the only issue holding the disparate elements of the woman movement together.[59]

O'Neill found that politicians abandoned the women's movement when no women's voting bloc appeared, and he offered several criticisms of women's political activity. The author quoted—and made clear his agreement with—a blatantly antifeminist assessment of women's suffrage which claimed that the vote had done little more than to bring out such undesirable traits of women as fussiness, primness, bossiness, and the tendency to make unnecessary enemies. He further claimed that although the radicals of the Woman's party correctly understood the discrimination against women which existed after 1920, their "knowledge did them little good because the passions that led them to demand a feminist revival kept them from effecting it."[60]

In nonpolitical realms, as well, O'Neill noted little progress toward emancipation after 1920. The moral revolution had been rooted in the prewar years, and "sexual freedom had little effect on the life styles of most women," who still preferred the stability of home and family to the life of the flapper. Professionalism among women declined by the mid-1920s, he explained, because the novelty and "glamour" of the career experience was wearing out, discrimination in salaries and promotions became apparent to women, and the struggle between home and career exhausted working women.[61]

O'Neill believed that the feminine mystique of fulfillment through motherhood and home originated in the 1920s, when "feminism" came to mean merely sexual liberation within the confines of domesticity. Home economics became woman's professional realm, and femininity became the

[59] William O'Neill, *Everyone Was Brave: The Rise and Fall of Feminism in America* (Chicago, 1969), 264. For a summary of William O'Neill's distinction between "social feminism" and "hard-core feminism," see William L. O'Neill, "Feminism as a Radical Ideology," Alfred F. Young, ed., *Dissent: Explorations in the History of American Radicalism* (DeKalb, Ill., 1968), 273-300. Another study which contributes to post-1920 women's history but does not explicitly deal with the decline of feminism is David M. Kennedy's *Birth Control in America: The Career of Margaret Sanger* (New Haven, 1970). If Margaret Sanger is representative, which is unlikely, women activists rejected radicalism and left-wing allegiances to pursue the acceptance of their activities by middle-class women. Could a toning down of radicalism in the 1920s account for the view that feminism, "disappeared?"

[60] O'Neill, *Everyone Was Brave*, 270-73, 291.

[61] *Ibid.*, 306.

watchword for the "privatized young women."[62] Although the ideas of earlier feminists were kept alive by individuals such as Gilman, Dorothy Bromley, Alice Beal Parsons, and Suzanne La Follette, by 1930 feminism had fallen, to remain dormant until the present revival.

The second recent interpretation and one of greater usefulness is Chafe's study of the changing roles of American women from 1920 to 1970. In an effort to correct what Degler called the "suffrage orientation of historians of women's rights," Chafe began after suffrage, and he has provided a broad and preliminary investigation of women in politics, industry, the professions, and other aspects of American life. Drawing on several of the studies discussed above, he explored the progressive legislative successes of women in the early 1920s and acknowledged the individual accomplishments of women in the peace movement, in the struggle for social welfare legislation, and in municipal government reform. But in general, Chafe found that women had failed to achieve political equality. After surveying the political and sociological literature on voting behavior, he attempted to explain women's political failure in terms of social forces —cross-group pressures on women, discrimination rooted in the authoritarian family structure and the sexual division of labor, and the absence of a strong women's issue for the new voters to focus on. Chafe acknowledged that economic advances by women were minimal. Although he believed that sexually women had "substantially increased the amount of equality," he realized that "shifts in manners and morals did not interfere with the perpetuation of a sexual division of labor." He dated the shift in emphasis from careers to homemaking at 1930 and suggested that the Depression merely wielded the final blow to feminist hopes for equality. Although Chafe placed part of the blame for the decline of feminism on the feminists themselves, especially their factionalism over the equal rights amendment, his analysis emphasized social barriers to emancipation. "For economic equality to become a reality," he wrote, "a fundamental revolution was required in the way men and women thought of each other, and in the distribution of responsibilities within marriage and the family."[63]

In the last few years, the literature on women in the 1920s has reached a new level of historical inquiry. Historians are now trying to understand the decline of feminism rather than to deny the need for further emancipation. Although the revised version finds that women were politically active in lobbying for reforms in spite of failures at the polls, the latest accounts recognize that the 1920s were not the years of economic prosperity

[62] *Ibid.*, 313.

[63] Chafe, "From Suffrage to Liberation," 56, 120, 185, 211-12. See also Mari Jo Buhle, Ann G. Gordon, and Nancy Schrom, "Women in American Society: An Historical Contribution," *Radical America*, 5 (July-Aug. 1971), 3-66.

for women described so proudly earlier: professional gains were minimal, industrial wages discriminatory, and unionization difficult. Marriage and motherhood brought most women out of the labor force and, supposedly, home to domestic and sexual fulfillment. Historians have generally retained the notion of the revolution in manners and morals, although research on the prewar years and on literary stereotypes may indicate a need for revision. How the social freedom in clothing, manners, and sex contributed to deeper social change must be questioned further in light of the new view of women's history. Rather than proclaiming the contributions of "woman as force" in recent history, historians now explain feminism's decline in terms of societal forces, such as family structure and political trends, the weaknesses inherent in the pre-1920 suffrage coalition, and legal and social discrimination against women as a group.

By further investigations of women's lives, historians can continue to correct their past errors, not only for the sake of historical accuracy, but also to begin to compensate for the disservice which earlier writings have rendered. The portrayal of the 1920s as a period of full equality, when in fact discrimination in education, hiring, salaries, promotions, and family responsibilities was abundant, has perpetuated a myth of equality, one which has helped undermine women's attainment of group consciousness. Similarly, to write and teach—on the basis of unsubstantiated observations—that women were politically apathetic but sexually active during the 1920s is to create sexually stereotyped historical roles for women. Historians' use of the "sexual revolution" as an explanation for women's history in the 1920s was perhaps an extension of their own inability to conceive of women outside of sexual roles. Furthermore, if the admittedly minimal evidence on writings in the 1930s and 1940s is substantiated, American historians' emphasis on woman's place in the home rather than her capacities for non-domestic careers may have contributed to the perpetuation of cultural stereotypes which helped weaken feminism since 1920.

The work of recent historians begins the long overdue revision of historical attitudes toward women. The most serious of the problems which recent studies manifest is that of excessive generalization—the tendency to write about *the* American woman, when race, class, region, and ethnicity have significantly divided women in twentieth-century America. Perhaps by studying the lives of countless individual women during the 1920s and after scholars will begin to discover patterns of response to both opportunities and discrimination. Only after extensive research has been completed can historians generalize successfully about the new woman. Only then can they begin to certify whether women were active participants or struggling victims in American history.

PLACING WOMEN IN HISTORY: DEFINITIONS AND CHALLENGES

Gerda Lerner

In the brief span of five years in which American historians have begun to develop women's history as an independent field, they have sought to find a conceptual framework and a methodology appropriate to the task.

The first level at which historians, trained in traditional history, approach women's history is by writing the history of "women worthies" or "compensatory history."[1] Who are the women missing from history? Who are the women of achievement and what did they achieve? The resulting history of "notable women" does not tell us much about those activities in which most women engaged, nor does it tell us about the significance of women's activities to society as a whole. The history of notable women is the history of exceptional, even deviant women, and does not describe the experience and history of the mass of women. This insight is a refinement of an awareness of class differences in history: Women of different classes have different historical experiences. To comprehend the full complexity of society at a given stage of its development, it is essential to take account of such differences.

Women also have a different experience with respect to consciousness, depending on whether their work, their expression, their activity is male-defined or woman-oriented. Women, like men, are indoctrinated in a male-defined value system and conduct their lives accordingly. Thus, colonial and early nineteenth-century female reformers directed their activities into channels which were merely an extension of their domestic concerns and traditional roles. They taught school, cared for the poor, the sick, the aged. As their consciousness developed, they turned their attention toward the needs of women. Becoming woman-oriented, they began to "uplift" prostitutes, organize women for abolition or temperance and sought to upgrade female education, but only in order to equip women better for their traditional roles. Only at a later stage, growing out of the recognition of the separate interests of women as a group, and of their subordinate place in society, did their consciousness become woman-defined. Feminist thought starts at this level and encompasses the active assertion of the rights and grievances of women. These various stages of female consciousness need to be considered in historical analysis.

The next level of conceptualizing women's history has been "contribution history": describing women's contribution to, their status in, and their oppression by male-defined society. Under this category we find a variety of questions being asked: What have women contributed to abolition, to reform, to the Progressive movement, to the labor movement, to the New Deal? The movement in question stands in the foreground of inquiry; women made a "contribution" to it; the contribution is judged first of all with respect to its effect on that movement and secondly by standards appropriate to men.

The ways in which women were aided and affected by the work of these "great women," the ways in which they themselves grew into feminist awareness, are ignored. Jane Addams' enormous contribution in creating a supporting female network and new structures for living are subordinated to her role as a Progressive, or to an interpretation which regards her as merely representative of a group of frustrated college-trained women with no place to go. In other words, a deviant from male-defined norms. Margaret Sanger is seen merely as the founder of the birth control movement, not as a woman raising a revolutionary challenge to the centuries-old practice by which the bodies and lives of women are dominated and ruled by man-made laws. In the labor movement, women are described as "also there" or as problems. Their essential role on behalf of themselves and of other women is seldom considered a central theme in writing their history. Women are the outgroup, Simone de Beauvoir's "other."

Another set of questions concern oppression and its opposite, the struggle for woman's rights. Who oppressed women and how were they oppressed? How did they respond to such oppression?

Such questions have yielded detailed and very valuable accounts of economic or social oppression, and of the various organizational, political ways in which women as a group have fought such oppression. Judging from the results, it is clear that to ask the question—why and how were women victimized—has its usefulness. We learn what society or individuals or classes of people have done to women, and we learn how women themselves have reacted to conditions imposed upon them. While inferior status and oppressive restrains were no doubt aspects of women's historical experience, and should be so recorded, the limitation of this approach is that it makes it appear either that women were largely passive or that, at the most, they reacted to male pressures or to the restraints of patriarchal society. Such inquiry fails to elicit the positive and essential way in which women have functioned in history. Mary Beard was the first to point out that the ongoing and continuing contribution of women to the development of human culture cannot be found by treating them only as victims of oppression.[2] I have in my own work learned that it is far more useful to deal with this question as one aspect of women's history, but never to regard it as the *central* aspect of women's history. Essentially, treating women as victims of oppression once again places them in a male-defined conceptual framework: oppressed, victimized by standards and values established by men. The true history of women is the history of their ongoing functioning in that male-defined world, *on their own terms*. The question of oppression does not elicit that story, and is therefore a tool of limited usefulness to the historian.

A major focus of women's history has been on women's-rights struggles, especially the winning of suffrage, on organizational and institutional history of the women's movements, and on its leaders. This, again, is an important aspect of women's history, but it cannot and should not be its central concern.

Some recent literature has dealt with marriage and divorce, with educational opportunities, and with the economic struggles of working women. Much of recent work has been concerned with the image of women and "woman's sphere," with the educational ideals of society, the values to which women are indoctrinated, and with gender role acculturation as seen in historical perspective. A separate field of study has examined the ideals, values, and prescriptions concerning sexuality, especially female sexuality. Ron Walters and Ben Barker-Benfield has tended to confirm traditional stereotypes concerning Victorian sexuality, the double standard, and the subordinate position of women. Much of this material is based on the study of such readily available sources as sermons, educational tracts, women's magazines, and medical textbooks. The pitfall in such interpretation, as Carl Degler has pointed out in his recent perceptive article, is the tendency to confuse prescriptive literature with actual behavior. In fact, what we are learning from most of these monographs is not what women did, felt, or experienced, but what men in the past thought women should do. Charles Rosenberg, Carroll Smith-Rosenberg, and Carl Degler have shown how to approach the same material and interpret it from the new perspective of women's history.[3] They have sharply distinguished between prescription and behavior, between myth and reality.

Other attempts to deduce women's status from popular literature and ideology demonstrate similar difficulties. Barbara Welter is an early and highly influential article, found the emergence of "the cult of true womanhood" in sermons and periodicals of the Jacksonian era. Many historians, feminists among them, have deduced from this that Victorian ideals of woman's place pervaded the society and were representative of its realities. More detailed analysis reveals that this mass media concern with woman's domesticity was, in fact, a response to the opposite trend in society.[4] Lower-class women were entering the factories, middle-class women were discontented with their accustomed roles, and the family, as an institution, was experiencing turmoil and crisis. Idealization is very frequently a defensive ideology and an expression of tension within society. To use ideology as a measure of the shifting status of women, it must be set against a careful analysis of social structure, economic conditions, institutional changes, and popular values. With this caution society's attitudes toward women and toward gender role indoctrination can be usefully analyzed as manifestations of a shifting value system and of tensions within patriarchal society.

"Contribution" history is an important stage in the creation of a true history of women. The monographic work which such inquiries produce is essential to the development of more complex and sophisticated questions, but it is well to keep the limitations of such inquiry in mind. When all is said and done, what we have mostly done in writing contribution history is to describe what men in the past told women to do and what men in the past thought women should be. This is just another way of saying that historians of women's history have so far used a traditional conceptual framework. Essentially, they have applied questions from traditional history to women, and tried to fit women's past into the empty spaces of historical scholarship. The limitation of such work is that it deals with women in male-defined society and tries to fit them into the categories and value systems which consider *man* the measure of significance.

Perhaps it would be useful to refer to this level of work as "transitional women's history," seeing it as an inevitable step in the development of new criteria and concepts.

Another methdological question which arises frequently concerns the connection between women's history and other recently emerging fields. Why is women's history not simply an aspect of "good" social history? Are women not part of the anonymous in history? Are they not oppressed the same way as racial or class or ethnic groups have been oppressed? Are they not marginal and akin in most respects to minorities? The answers to these questions are not simple. It is obvious that there has already been rich cross-fertilization between the new social history and women's history, but it has not been nor should it be a case of subsuming women's history under the larger and already respectable field of social history.

Yes, women are part of the anonymous in history, but unlike them, they are also and always have been part of the ruling elite. They are oppressed, but not quite like either racial or ethnic groups, though some of them are. They are subordinate and exploited, but not quite like lower classes, though some of them are. We have not yet really solved the problems of definition, but it can be suggested that the key to understanding women's history is in accepting—painful though that may be—that it is the history of the *majority* of mankind. Women are essentially different from all the above categories, because they are the majority now and always have been at least half of mankind, and because their subjection to patriarchal institutions antedates all other oppression and has outlasted all economic and social changes in recorded history.

Social history methodology is very useful for women's history, but it must be placed within a different conceptual framework. For example, historians working in family history ask a great many questions pertaining to women, but family history is not in itself women's history. It is no longer sufficient to view women mainly as members of families. Family history has neglected by and large to deal with unmarried and widowed women. In its applications to specific monographic studies, such as the work of Philip Greven, family history has been used to describe the realtionships of fathers and sons and the property arrangements between them.[5] The relationships of fathers to daughters and mothers to their children have been ignored. The complex family-support patterns, for example, whereby the work and wages of daughters are used to support the education of brothers and to maintain aged parents, while that of sons is not so used, have been ignored.

Another way in which family history has been interpreted within the context of patriarchal assumptions is by using a vaguely defined "domestic power" of women, power within the family, as a measure of the societal status of women. In a methodologically highly sophisticated article, Daniel Scott Smith discovers in the nineteenth century the rise of something called "domestic feminism;" expressed in a lowered birth rate from which he deduces an increasing control of women over their reproductive lives.[6] One might, from similar figures, as easily deduce a desire on the part of men to curb their offspring due to the demands of a developing industrial system for a more highly educated labor force, hence for fewer children per family. Demographic data can indeed tell us something about female as well as male status in society, but only in the context of an economic and sociological analysis. Further, the status of women within the family is something quite different and distinct from their status in the society in general.

I learned in studying the history of black women and the black family that relatively high status for women within the family does not signify "matriarchy" or "power for women," since black women are not only members of families, but persons functioning in a larger society. The status of persons is determined not in one area of their functioning, such as within the family, but in several. The decisive historical fact about women is that the *areas* of their functioning, not only their status *within* those areas, have been determined by men. The effect on the consciousness of women has been pervasive. It is one of the decisive aspects of their history, and any analysis which does not take this complexity into consideration must be inadequate.

Then there is the impact of demographic techniques, the study of large aggregates of anonymous people by computer technology based on census data, public documents, property records. Demographic techniques have led to insights which are very useful for women's history. They have yielded revealing data on fertility fluctuations, on changes in illegitimacy patterns and sex ratios, and aggregate studies of life cycles. The latter work has been done very successfully by Joseph Kett, Robert Wells, Peter Laslett and Kenneth Keniston.[7] The field has in the United States been largely dominated by male historians, mostly through self-imposed sex-role stereotyping by women historians who have shared a prejudice against the computer and statistics. However, a group of younger scholars, trained in demographic techniques, have begun to research and publish material concerning working-class women. Alice Harris, Virginia McLaughlin, Judith and Daniel Walkowitz, Susan Kleinberg and Tamara Hareven are among those who have elicited woman-oriented interpretations from aggregate data.[8] They have demonstrated that social history can be enriched by combining cliometrics with sophisticated humanistic and feminist interpretations. They have added "gender" as a factor for analysis to such familiar concepts as class, race and ethnicity.

The compensatory questions raised by women's history specialists are proving interesting and valuable in a variety of fields. It is perfectly understandable that after centuries of neglect of the role of women in history, compensatory questions and those concerning woman's contribution will and must be asked. In the process of answering such questions it is important to keep in mind the inevitable limitation of the answers they yield. Not the least of these limitations is that this approach tends to separate the work and activities of women from those of men, even where they were essentially connected. As yet, synthesis is lacking. For example, the rich history of the abolition movement has been told as though women played a marginal, auxiliary, and at times mainly disruptive role in it. Yet female antislavery societies outnumbered male societies; women abolitionists largely financed the movement with their fundraising activities, did much of the work of propaganda-writing in and distribution of newspapers and magazines. The enormous political significance of women-organized petition campaigns remains unrecorded. Most importantly, no historical work has as yet taken the organizational work of female abolitionists seriously as an integral part of the antislavery movement.

Slowly, as the field has matured, historians of women's history have become dissatisfied with old questions and old methods, and have come up with new ways of approaching historical material. They have, for example, begun to ask about the actual *experience* of women in the past. This is obviously different from a description of the condition of women written from the perspective of male sources, and leads one to the use of women's letters, diaries, autobiographies, and oral history sources. This shift from male-oriented to female-oriented consciousness is most important and leads to challenging new interpretations.

Historians of women's history have studied female sexuality and its regulation from the female point of view, making imaginative use of such sources as medical textbooks, diaries, and case histories of hospital patients. Questions concerning women's experience have led to studies of birth control, as it affects women and as an issue expressing cultural and symbolic values; of the physical conditions to which women are prone, such as menarche and pregnancy and women's ailments; of customs, attitudes, and fashions affecting women's health and women's life experience. Historians are now exploring the impact of female bonding, of female friendship and homosexual relations, and the experience of women in groups, such as women in utopian communities, in women's clubs and settlement houses. There has been an interest in the possibility that women's century-long preoccupation with birth and with the care of the sick and dying have led to some specific female rituals.[9]

Women's history has already presented a challenge to some basic assumptions historians make. While most historians are aware of the fact that their findings are not value-free and are trained to check their biases by a variety of methods, they are as yet quite unaware of their own sexist bias and, more importantly, of the sexist bias which pervades the value system, the culture, and the very language within which they work.

Women's history presents a challenge to the periodization of traditional history. The periods in which basic changes occur in society and which historians have commonly regarded as turning points for all historical development, are not necessarily the same for men as for women. This is not surprising when we consider that the traditional time frame in history has been derived from political history. Women have been the one group in history longest excluded from political power as they have, by and large, been excluded from military decision making. Thus the irrelevance of periodization based on military and political developments to their historical experience should have been predictable.

Renate Bridenthal's and Joan Kelly-Gadol's articles in this volume confirm that the history of women demands different periodization than does political history.[10] Neither the Renaissance, it appears, nor the period during which women's suffrage was won, were periods in which women experienced an advance in their status. Recent work of American historians of women's history, such as Linda Kerber's work on the American Revolution and my own work, confirms this conclusion. For example, neither during nor after the American Revolution nor in the age of Jackson did women share the historical experience of men. On the contrary, they experienced in both periods status loss, a restriction of options as to occupations and role choices, and certainly in

Jacksonian America, there were restrictions imposed upon their sexuality, at least in prescriptive behavior. If one applies to both of these cases the kind of sophisticated and detailed analysis Kelly-Gadol attempts—that is, differentiations between women of different classes and comparisons between the status of men of a given class and women of that class—one finds the picture further complicated. Status loss in one area—social production—may be offset by status gain in another—access to education.

What kind of periodization might be substituted for the periodization of traditional history, in order for it to be applicable to women? The answer depends largely on the conceptual framework in which the historian works. Many historians of women's history, in their search for a unifying framework, have tended to use the Marxist or neo-Marxist model supplied by Juliet Mitchell and recently elaborated by Sheila Rowbotham.[11] The important fact, says Mitchell, which distinguished the past of women from that of men is precisely that until very recently sexuality and reproduction were inevitably linked for women, while they were not so linked for men. Similarly, child-bearing and child-rearing were inevitably linked for women and still are so linked. Women's freedom depends on breaking those links. Using Mitchell's categories we can and should ask of each historical period: What happened to the link between sexuality and reproduction? What happened to the link between child-bearing and child-rearing? Important changes in the status of women occur when it becomes possible through the availability of birth control information and technology to sever sexuality from inevitable motherhood. However, it may be the case that it is not the availability and distribution of birth control information and technology so much as the level of medical and health care which are the determinants of change. That is, when infant mortality decreases, so that raising every child to adulthood becomes the normal expectation of parents, family size declines.

The above case illustrates the difficulty that has vexed historians of women's history in trying to locate a periodization more appropriate to women. Working in different fields and specialities, many historians have observed that the transition from agricultural to industrializing society and then again the transition to fully developed industrial society entails important changes affecting women and the family. Changes in relations of production affect women's status as family members and as workers. Later, shifts in the mode of production affect the kinds of occupations women can enter and their status within them. Major shifts in health care and technological development, related to industrialization, also affect the lives of women. It is not too difficult to discern such patterns and to conclude that there must be a causal relationship between changes in the mode of production and the status of women. Here, the Marxist model seems to offer an immediately satisfying solution, especially if, following Mitchell, "sexuality" as a factor is added to such factors as class. But in the case of women, just as in the case of racial castes, ideology and prescription internalized by both women and men, seem to be as much a causative factor as are material changes in production relations. Does the entry of lower-class women into industrial production really bring them closer to "liberation"? In the absence of institutional changes such as the right to abortion and safe contraception, altered child-rearing arrangements, and varied option for sexual expression, changes in economic relations may become oppressive. Unless such changes are accompanied by changes in consciousness, which in turn result in institutional changes, they do not favorably affect the lives of women.

Is smaller family size the result of "domestic freedom" of choice exercised by women, the freedom of choice exercised by men, the ideologically buttressed coercion of institutions in the service of an economic class? Is it liberating for women, for men, or for corporations? This raises another difficult question: What about the relationship of upper-class to lower-class women? To what extent is the relative advance in the status of upper-class women predicated on the status loss of lower-class women? Examples of this are: the liberation of the middle-class American housewife in the mid-nineteenth century through the availability of cheap black or immigrant domestic workers; the liberation of the twentieth-century housewife from incessant drudgery in the home through agricultural stoop labor and the food-processing industry, both employing low paid female workers.

Is periodization then dependent as much on class as on gender? This question is just one of several which challenge the universalist assumptions of all previous historical categories. I cannot provide an answer, but I think the questions themselves point us in the right direction.

It appears to me that all conceptual models of history hitherto developed have only limited usefulness for women's history, since all are based on the assumptions of a patriarchal ordering of values. The structural-functionalist framework leaves out class and sex factors, the traditional Marxist framework leaves out sex and race factors as *essentials*, admitting them only as marginal factors. Mitchell's neo-Marxist model includes these, but slights ideas, values, and psychological factors. Still, her four-structures model and the refinements of it proposed by Bridenthal, are an excellent addition to the conceptual working tools of the historian of women's history. They should be tried out, discussed, refined. But they are not, in my opinion, the whole answer.

Kelly-Gadol offers the useful suggestion that attitudes toward sexuality should be studied in each historical period. She considers the constraints upon women's sexuality imposed by society a useful measure of women's true status. This approach would necessitate comparisons between prescribed behavior for women and men as well as indications of their actual sexual behavior at any given time. This challenging method can be used with great effectiveness for certain periods of history and especially for upper- and middle-class women. I doubt that it can be usefully employed as a general criterion, because of the difficulty of finding substantiating evidence, especially as it pertains to lower classes.

I raised the question of a conceptual framework for dealing with women's history in 1969,[12] reasoning from the assumption that women were a subgroup in history. Neither caste, class, nor race quite fit the model for describing us. I have now come to the conclusion that the idea that women are some kind of a subgroup or particular is wrong. It will not do—there are just too many of us. No single framework, no single factor, four-factor or eight-factor explanation can serve to contain all that the history of women is. Picture, if you can, an attempt to organize the history of men by using four factors. It will not work; neither will it work for women.

Women are and always have been at least half of mankind and most of the time have been the majority of mankind. Their culturally determined and psychologically internalized marginality seems to be what makes their historical experience essentially different from that of men. But men have defined their exeprience as history and have left women out. At this time, as during earlier periods of feminist activity, women are urged to fit into the empty spaces, assuming their traditional marginal, "sub-group" status. But the truth is that history, as written and perceived up to now, is the history of a minority, who may well turn out to be the "subgroup." In order to write a new history worthy of the name, we will have to recognize that no single methodology and conceptual framework can fit the complexities of the historical experience of all women.

The first stage of "transitional history" may be to add some new categories to the general categories by which historians organize their material: sexuality, reproduction, the link between child-bearing and child-rearing; role indoctrination; sexual values and myths; female consciousness. Further, all of these need to be analysed, taking factors of race, class, ethnicity and, possibly, religion into consideration. What we have here is not a single framework for dealing with women in history, but new questions to all of universal history.

The next stage may be to explore the possibility that what we call women's history may actually be the study of a separate women's culture. Such a culture would include not only the separate occupations, status, experiences, and rituals of women but also their consciousness, which internalizes partiarchal assumptions. In some cases, it would include the tensions created in that culture between the prescribed patriarchal assumptions and women's efforts to attain autonomy and emancipation.

The questions asked about the past of women may demand interdisciplinary approaches. They also may demand broadly conceived group research projects that end up giving functional answers; answers that deal not with slices of a given time or society or period, but which instead deal with a functioning organism, a functioning whole, the society in which both men and women live.

A following stage may develop a synthesis: a history of the dialectic, the tensions between the two cultures, male and female. Such a synthesis could be based on close comparative study of given periods in which the historical experience of men is compared to that of women, their tensions and interactions being as much the subject of study as their differences. Only after a series of such detailed studies can we hope to find the parameters by which to define the new universal history. My guess is that no one conceptual framework will fit so complex a subject.

Methods are tools for analysis—some of us will stick with one tool, some of us will reach for different tools as we need them. For women, the problem really is that we must acquire not only the confidence needed for using tools, but for making new ones to fit our needs. We should do so relying on our learned skills and our rational scepticism of handed-down doctrine. The recognition that we had been denied our history came to many of us as a staggering flash of insight, which altered our consciousness irretrievably. We have come a long way since then. The next step is to face, once and for all and with all its complex consequences, that women are the majority of mankind and have been essential to the making of history. Thus, all history as we now know it, is merely prehistory. Only a new history firmly based on this recognition and equally concerned with men, women, the establishment and the passing away of patriarchy, can lay claim to being a truly universal history.

NOTES

This article, in an earlier version, was presented at the panel, "Effects of Women's History Upon Traditional Concepts of Historiography" at the Second Berkshire Conference on the History of Women, Cambridge, Mass., October 25-27, 1974. It was, in revised form, presented as a paper at the Sarah Lawrence College Workshop-Symposium, March 15, 1975. I have greatly benefitted from discussion with my co-panelists Renate Bridenthal and Joan Kelly-Gadol, and from the comments and critique of audience participants at both conferences.

[1]For the term "women worthies," I am indebted to Natalie Zemon Davis, Stanford University.
For the terms "compensatory history" and "contribution history" I am indebted to Mari Jo Buhle, Ann G. Gordon and Nancy Schrom, "Women in American Society: An Historical Contribution," *Radical America* 5, no. 4 (July-August 1971): 3-66.

[2]Mary Beard, *Woman as Force in History* (New York: Collier Books, 1972).
See also a further discussion of this question in Gerda Lerner, "New Approaches for the Study of Women in American History," *Journal of Social History* 3, no. 1 (Fall 1969): 53-62. Also available in Bobbs-Merrill, Reprint, number H432.

[3]Ronald G. Walters, ed., *Primers for Prudery* (Englewood Cliffs, New Jersey: Prentice-Hall, 1974); Ben Barker-Benfield, "The Spermatic Economy: A Nineteenth Century View of Sexuality," *Feminist Studies* 1, no. 1 (1972): 45-74; Carl Degler, "What Ought To Be and What Was: Women's Sexuality in the Nineteenth Century," *American Historical Review* 79, no. 5 (December 1974): 1467-1490. For a different approach see also: Carroll Smith-Rosenberg and Charles Rosenberg, "The Female Animal: Medical and Biological Views of Women in Nineteenth Century America," *Journal of American History* 60, no. 2 (September 1973): 332-56; Carroll Smith-Rosenberg, "The Hysterical Woman: Some Reflections on Sex Roles and Role Conflict in 19th Century America," *Social Research* 39, no. 4 (December 1972): 652-78; Charles Rosenberg, "Sexuality, Class and Role," *American Quarterly* 25, no. 2 (May 1973): 131-53.

[4]Barbara Welter, "The Cult of True Womanhood, 1820-1860," *American Quarterly* 18, no. 2 (Summer 1966): 151-57; Gerda Lerner, "The Lady and the Mill Girl: Changes in the Status of Women in the Age of Jackson," *Midcontinent American Studies Journal* 10, no. 1 (Spring 1969): 5-15.

[5]Philip J. Greven, Jr., *Four Generations: Population, Land and Family in Colonial Andover, Massachusetts* (Ithaca: Cornell University Press, 1970). For a good sampling of recent work in family history, see Michael Gordon, ed., *The American Family in Social-Historical Perspective* (New York: St. Martin's Press, 1973).

[6]Daniel Scott Smith, "Family Limitation, Sexual Control and Domestic Feminism in Victorian America," *Feminist Studies* 1, no. 3/4 (Winter-Spring 1973): 40-57.

[7]See *Journal of Interdisciplinary History* 2, no. 2 (Autumn 1971) for articles by Joseph Kett, Robert Wells, Peter Laslett, and Kenneth Keniston.

[8]Virginia Yans McLaughlin, "Patterns of Work and Family Orgnaization: Buffalo's Italians," ibid., pp. 219-314. Tamara Hareven, "The History of the Family as an Interdisciplinary Field," ibid., pp. 399-414; Susan Kleinberg, University of California San Diego, "Women's Work: The Lives of Working Class Women in Pittsburgh, 1870-1900" (unpublished paper); and Alice Harris, Sarah Lawrence College, "Problems of Class and Culture in Organizing Women Workers, 1900-1920," (unpublished paper).

[9]For a good overview of this work see the papers of the Second Berkshire Conference on the History of Women, Radcliffe College, 1974, some of which are published in this issue and in *Feminist Studies* 3, no. 3/4. See especially, Carroll Smith-Rosenberg, "The New Woman and the New History."

[10]See forthcoming papers by Bridenthal and Kelly-Gadol in *Feminist Studies* 3, no. 3/4 (1975).

[11]Juliet Mitchell, *Woman's Estate* (New York: Pantheon Books, 1972); Sheila Rowbotham, *Woman's Consciousness, Man's World* (Baltimore: Penguin Books, 1973); Rowbotham, *Women, Resistance and Revolution* (New York: Pantheon Books, 1972).

[12]Gerda Lerner, "New Approaches to the Study of Women in American History," *Journal of Social History* 3, no. 1 (Fall 1969): 53-62.

History and Historiography: The Treatment in American Histories of Significant Events Concerning the Status of Women

By

MARGRIT EICHLER

and

CAROL ANN NELSON*

It has been a recognized fact ever since Francis Bacon wrote about the various idols that rule the thoughts of people in different areas of social life that knowledge is neither acquired nor transmitted in a social vacuum. According to Karl Marx, the ideology of each era is always the ideology of the ruling class. Recently, several writers have applied this dictum to the relationship of the sexes. Starting from the observation that men are the dominant group in society, the social sciences and humanities have been criticized with respect to their treatment of women. The criticisms usually run along the following lines: Theoretical models of society that underlie and guide data collection and interpretation are structured in such a way that they consider women only insofar as they are attached—in some capacity or another—to men. Consequently, significant factors or events that pertain primarily to women are underrepresented or entirely ignored in both empirical and theoretical treatises.[1]

*Dr. Eichler is Associate Professor at the Ontario Institute for Studies in Education. Ms. Nelson is a law student at Osgoode Hall Law School, York University.

[1] In recent years, several critiques have appeared concerning the way in which women in the social sciences have been treated. The most important among these include several of the articles contained in the special issue on "Sexism in Family Studies" of the *Journal of Marriage and the Family* 33 (August 1971); Marcia Millman and Rosabeth Moss Kanter, eds., *Another Voice* (New York, 1975); several articles in Vivian Gornick and Barbara K. Moran, eds., *Woman in Sexist Society* (New York and London, 1971); several articles in the special issue on "Changing Women in a Changing Society" of the *American Journal of Sociology* 78 (January 1973); Mary R. Beard, *Woman as Force in History* (New York, 1971); Inge K. Broverman et al., "Sex Role Stereotypes and Clinical Judgments of Mental Health," *Journal of Consulting and Clinical Psychology* 34 (1970): 1-7; Margrit Eichler, "Women as

As far as history's treatment of women is concerned, Mary Beard asked herself in 1946 whether the men who write history "do consider women something even less important than subjects of men—exactly nothing,"[2] and she concluded in her book that indeed women have received very scarce attention from historians. More recently, Ruth Rosen has charged that "sexism in historical writing is much like sexism in daily life. For the most part women are made invisible."[3]

In this paper we wish to examine systematically the extent to which historians pay attention to one of the most crucial events in American history concerning the status of women: woman's suffrage. To do so, we have taken two complementary approaches: first, we conducted an index search concerning suffragism in general history books and compared the frequency of mention with comparable, contemporaneous items. Second, we examined a number of major reform histories with respect to their treatment of woman's suffrage—which was clearly a major reform when it was finally achieved. The results are discussed below.

Index Search of Suffragist Items in General History Books

Sixty-one general American history books were examined with respect to their index listings pertaining to suffragism and populism (as control items). The books were selected as follows: All the books in a Canadian University library[4] which, according to the Library of Congress cataloguing system, fell into the category of generalized American history constituted the original population of books. Of these, all those which were published prior to 1925 were eliminated. (Women were enfranchised in 1920, and the five-year lag allows for the time gap between the occurrence of an event and its discussion in print.) Further, the book had to cover the period from 1890 to 1920. It had to have an index, and edited books were excluded. Finally, the book had to have at least one reference in the index to one of the check items listed below. Of all the books, sixty-one met these criteria.[5]

The suffragist items selected for analysis were the following:

Personal Dependents," in *Women in Canada*, ed. Marylee Stephenson (Toronto, 1973); Ellen Rosen, "Sex Role Stereotypes as Reflected in the Work of Female Sociologists," *The Human Factor* 10 (1970): 1-20; and Sally Linton, "Woman as Gatherer: Male Bias in Anthropology," in *Women in Cross-Cultural Perspective*, comp. Sue-Ellen Jacobs (University of Illinois, 1971), 9-21.

[2] Beard, *Woman as Force in History*, 64.

[3] Ruth Rosen, "Sexism in History, or Writing Women's History is a Tricky Business," *Journal of Marriage and the Family* 33 (August 1971): 541-44.

[4] University of Waterloo, holdings of 1974.

[5] See Appendix for a complete list of the books.

Woman's Suffrage, Woman's Party, Susan B. Anthony, and Elizabeth C. Stanton.[6] As a control event we utilized the populist movement, selecting the following items for analysis: Populism, the Grange or the Granger movement,[7] the Farmer's Alliance, Henry George, and James B. Weaver.

We are not attempting here to give a new evaluation of either suffragism or populism or a detailed comparison of the two, but only a rough estimate of their relative importance. The importance that is accorded to social movements and historical figures is, of course, partially dependent on an arbitrary judgment by specific writers which varies with different viewpoints. Nevertheless, there are some objective indicators of the historical significance of a movement or personality, such as the number of adherents to a movement, its geographical spread, its length of duration, etc. Since the point we are trying to make here is that there is a lack of congruence between historiography and history as far as women's history is concerned, we shall briefly compare suffragism and populism in terms of objective factors rather than in terms of subjective evaluations of selected historians.

Discussion of Importance of Suffragism Compared with Populism

Length of duration of movements. In 1869 the woman's suffrage movement constituted itself formally in the National Woman's Suffrage Association and the American Woman's Suffrage Association. The formal associations were preceded by a period of general social unrest which included demands for female enfranchisement dating back to the Seneca Falls Convention in 1848. The National American Woman's Suffrage Association (which was the successor organization to the two earlier associations) continued to exist and to work actively for its goals until 1920, when the Nineteenth Amendment granting women the vote was ratified. We can therefore calculate the length of duration of the Woman's Suffrage Movement as at least half a century.

In contrast, the Populist Party was in existence for approximately five years (1891 to 1896). The Farmer's Alliance was active between 1880 and 1892. As a precursor to the Farmer's Alliance, the Grange was most active in the decade preceding it.

[6] In order to ensure that we covered all possible references to woman's suffrage, three other items were also checked: woman's rights, Seneca Falls, and feminism. These items were found to be unnecessary as they added no books that did not already have direct suffragist items. Since the three latter items are only tangentially related to woman's suffrage, they were dropped from the analysis.

[7] The Grange still exists today as a fraternal organization. To ensure that index notations to the Grange actually referred to the Granger movement of the 1870s, the content of the references was examined.

Altogether, we can therefore count a period of approximately twenty-five years in which the populist movement and its direct precursors were of import. This means that the Woman's Suffrage Movement had approximately double the duration of the Populist Movement.

Numbers of participants. Kraditor estimates the *minimum* number of members in the National American Woman's Suffrage Association in 1917 at two million.[8] This counts only fee-paying members; the figure does not take into account any other support that the NAWSA may have had.

In comparison, Pollack estimates the *maximum* Populist vote at 1.5 million[9]—this is considerably higher than the one million votes which the Populist presidential candidate James B. Weaver received in the 1892 federal election. Even allowing for estimate errors, it seems safe to assume that the Woman's Suffrage Association at its height had more participants than did the Populist Party at its height.

Geographical spread. The Suffrage Associations were national in scope, organization, and support, with state affiliates in all parts of the country. The Nineteenth Amendment was ratified in thirty-six states.

In comparison, the populist movement was essentially sectional. Kansas, Nebraska, North Dakota, and South Dakota were the centers of its activities, and even in these states the Populist Party received less than 50 percent of the votes in the 1892 election. Therefore, in terms of geographical spread, the suffrage movement clearly had a larger range of activities than did the populist movement.

Assessment of overall importance of the two movements. Traditionally, scholars have seen populism as the "root of reform." More recently, many historians have regarded populism as simply a rural-based movement "concerned only with gaining a greater portion of the national wealth for farmers."[10] Our intention here is not to assess the "real" importance of populism but only to utilize it as a convenient comparison point in assessing the importance of suffragism.

Suffragism constituted the first organized, collective, persistent attempt of women in American history to gain equal rights with men. Within its framework the first political mass actions of

[8] Aileen Kraditor, *The Ideas of the Woman Suffrage Movement 1890-1920* (Garden City, N.Y., 1971), 5.

[9] Norman Pollack, ed., *The Populist Mind* (Indianapolis, 1967), xxxix.

[10] Daniel Levine, *Varieties of Reform Thought* (Madison, 1964), vii. See also Leonard W. Levy and Alfred Young in Foreword to Pollack, *The Populist Mind.*

American women took place. At stake was a basic democratic right that had been withheld from the largest minority ever—namely, a numerical majority. The writings that were inspired by the struggle are still to a large extent valid today—witness the large number of new editions and reprints that suffragette writers experience currently. Finally, the people directly affected by the passing of the Nineteenth Amendment comprised more than half the population.

Therefore, if we judge the importance of suffragism in comparison with that of populism, it seems that suffragism was at least as important for the history of the country as populism if not more so. And if historians try to deal with such events as are of vital importance to the entire nation, then we would expect to find at least as much discussion of suffragism as we find of populism in general American history books.

The Importance of Henry George and James B. Weaver Compared with the Importance of Susan B. Anthony and Elizabeth C. Stanton

Henry George became famous through his book *Progress and Poverty* which was published in 1879. In it he advocated a single 100 percent tax to be imposed on all landowners which would replace all other taxes currently being levied. His book penetrated the ideology of the populists, and it is for this reason that he is here considered. The *Encyclopedia Britannica* evaluates his overall importance as follows:

> George's specific remedy had no significant practical result, and economists of reputation who supported it were rare. His economic analysis, though more sophisticated than that of most of his contemporaries, is crude by modern standards. His forceful emphasis, however, on "privilege" and the demand for equality of opportunity, coupled with a systematic analysis, proved a stimulus to orderly reform.[11]

James B. Weaver was twice a presidential candidate: in 1880 for the Greenback Party and in 1892 for the Populist Party. On the latter occasion, he won twenty-two electoral votes. He was twice elected as a representative to Congress. This secures him a modest place in history, but he did not leave any intellectual legacy.

By comparison, the work of both Anthony and Stanton did have concrete practical results (the Nineteenth Amendment was called the Susan B. Anthony Amendment in recognition of her path-breaking, half-a-century labor toward its adoption). In ad-

[11] *Encyclopedia Britannica*, 1973 ed., s.v. "Henry George."

dition, along with their co-workers, they were pioneers in the formulation of thoughts concerning sex equality and the rejection of "privileges" based on being born male. Both Anthony and Stanton were in and out of the public limelight for about half a century, devoting much of their energy to woman's suffrage but also to other issues, such as abolition and prohibition. In the late 1870s, Stanton and Anthony began to work on their monumental *History of Woman's Suffrage,* still the best primary document on the movement. (If for no other reason, they should at least be given credit as historians.)

In terms of their long-range effects on American history, Anthony and Stanton can be considered to be at least as important, if not more so, than George and Weaver. We would therefore expect that they receive at least as much if not more attention from historians of general American histories.

Index Search Results and Discussion

Based on an assessment of the importance of suffragism and populism, our expectation would be that the general American histories selected would have at least as many if not more references to the suffragist items as to the populist items. The results of the index search do not substantiate this hypothesis.

As can be seen from tables 1 and 2, populism is listed in the indexes of 80 percent of the books, while woman's suffrage is listed in only 56 percent of the books. In other words, 44 percent of the examined books do not mention woman's suffrage at all although they purport to be *general* American histories! Even more astonishing, not a single book mentions the Woman's Party! The Woman's Party represents a drastically different style of political action from what has been (and still is) customarily considered typical for women. It was the first sustained organized collective *militant* effort of women to fight for their rights. It was also a driving force behind the less militant NAWSA. In general terms, the Woman's Party included the first group of people ever to picket the White House for an extended period of time in order to draw public attention to their cause. If for no other reason, it deserves mention on the grounds that the Woman's Party engaged in behavior that challenged many of the established notions of female nature.

Henry George is mentioned in 59 percent of the books, James B. Weaver likewise. By contrast, Susan B. Anthony *or* Elizabeth C. Stanton, or both, are mentioned in only twenty-two books, i.e., 35 percent of the total. Most of the books which mention the one also mention the other, and 65 percent of the books do not once mention either one. If we combine all the suffragist items, we

TABLE 1

FREQUENCY OF MENTION OF SUFFRAGIST ITEMS BY NUMBER OF REFERENCES AND NUMBER OF BOOKS (TOTAL NO. OF BOOKS EXAMINED, 61)

Item	Total No. of Page References	No. and Percent of Books with References	No. and Percent of Books without References
Woman's Suffrage	104	34 (56%)	27 (44%)
Woman's Party	0	0 (0%)	0 (100%)
Susan B. Anthony	23	16 (26%)	45 (74%)
Elizabeth C. Stanton	26	20 (33%)	41 (67%)

TABLE 2

FREQUENCY OF MENTION OF POPULIST ITEMS BY NUMBER OF REFERENCES AND NUMBER OF BOOKS (TOTAL NO. OF BOOKS EXAMINED, 61)

Item	Total No. of Page References	No. and Percent of Books with References	No. and Percent of Books without References
Populism	335	49 (80%)	12 (20%)
Farmer's Alliance	76	28 (46%)	33 (54%)
The Grange	142	42 (69%)	19 (31%)
Henry George	93	36 (59%)	25 (41%)
James B. Weaver	79	35 (59%)	24 (41%)

find that 61 percent have a reference to *either* Anthony or Stanton or Woman's Suffrage, and 39 percent have not a single reference to any of the suffragist items. This compares to an 80 percent mention of populism alone, without the other populist items. In terms of numbers of references, populism alone has more than double the number of references (335) that *all* the suffragist items have combined (153).

Clearly, then, there is a serious lack of concern with suffragism and the leading suffragists in general history books which can in no way be related to the real importance of the movement and its exponents. In other words, there is undoubtedly an intentional or unintentional oversight in the examined history books of one of the major events in American history for American women and the country at large.

Examination of Reform Histories with Respect to Their Treatment of Woman's Suffrage

After discovering such a dramatic lack of concern with suffragism in general history books, our next concern was to examine specific reform histories in the expectation of finding more information about suffragism there. The books were selected for analysis as follows: As in the index search project, only books which had been published in 1925 or later were considered. All edited books were omitted. The books had to cover at least a twenty-five-year period which had to include the year 1920. This resulted in twelve books, which are discussed one by one below.

Our procedure consisted in first checking the index and the table of contents for any possible suffrage-related issues (e.g., woman's suffrage, women's rights, feminism, female votes, etc.). We then read the entire section. If it pertained to woman's suffrage, we quoted the entire passage, with the exception of a few longer passages which we summarized. In the following, therefore, we are quoting in most cases the sum total of the author's comments about suffragism, and in all cases we are giving a comprehensive picture of the treatment of woman's suffrage. We will now give a book-by-book summary of their treatment of woman's suffrage.

Chamberlain, in *Farewell to Reform,*[12] has not a single reference to woman's suffrage.

Likewise, Ekirch in *The Decline of American Liberalism,*[13] has not a single mention of woman's suffrage. However, in his later book, *The Challenge of American Democracy,* he lists three entries under woman's suffrage. The first of these reads, "Although the adoption of a constitutional amendment for national woman's suffrage was deferred until after World War I, a number of states in the 1900s followed the earlier example of Wyoming, Colorado, Idaho, and Utah in providing partial or equal suffrage. The advocates of woman's suffrage felt that with this right secured, other undemocratic restrictions on their sex could soon be voted away."[14] Woman's suffrage is mentioned again in the context of Wilson withholding support "from a model bill for a federal child labor law . . . and from the agitation to enact woman's suffrage."[15] Finally, Ekirch discusses in approximately a half page the effects of the ratification of the Nineteenth Amendment (which is incorrectly dated as June 1919 rather than August 1920).[16] He mentions that women were slow to use the ballot at first but that they gradually assumed a larger role in political life, especially through the League of Women Voters. He concludes, "If women were sometimes guilty of political apathy and indifference, they could point to the example of American males."[17] While this is

[12] John Chamberlain, *Farewell to Reform: The Rise, Life and Decay of the Progressive Mind in America* (Chicago, 1965).

[13] Arthur A. Ekirch, Jr., *The Decline of American Liberalism* (New York, London, and Toronto, 1955).

[14] Ekirch, *The Challenge of American Democracy: A Concise History of Social Thought and Political Action* (Belmont, Cal., 1973), 169.

[15] *Ibid.,* 180.

[16] *Ibid.,* 211.

[17] *Ibid.*

more of a discussion than in either Chamberlain or Ekirch's other book, it is still less than a page of printed material for the entire subject of woman's suffrage (or 1/336 of the book). This is especially surprising in the context of a book which mentions in its introduction that "in particular the younger radicals condemn the failure of American democracy to include equally in its benefits ethnic groups and other disadvantaged minorities—women, black people, and poor individuals."[18] Thus women are (by implication) one of the groups which have "given fresh meaning to some of John Dewey's older concepts of community and participatory democracy"[19] and should obviously be credited for it.

Filler, in *Crusaders for American Liberalism,* refers to woman's suffrage in the following sentence: "*The Ladies Home Journal* carried on a sober controversy about woman's suffrage—Bok soberly concluding that women did not want it."[20] He has another reference to it in the context of discussing the activities of Rheta Dorr, "the women's muckraker," who concerned herself among other things with "the fight for suffrage and against the double standard."[21] In a third reference to woman's suffrage, he introduces Sarah Platt Decker, of Colorado, as "a militant suffragist,"[22] but, as with the other two references, he does not discuss any suffragist activities.

Goldman, in *Rendezvous with Destiny,* has the following references to suffragism in his book: "The men of Cincinnati were to concern themselves with nothing so bizarre as woman suffrage."[23] Further on he comments, in somewhat more than a page, that "woman suffrage made the most spectacular lack of difference."[24] He comes back to this same subject once more for a brief consideration later in the book.[25]

Greer, in *American Social Reform Movements,* has one reference to Susan B. Anthony: "Susan B. Anthony, famous suffragist, was one of the first women delegates [to the National Labor Union], as was Mrs. Mary Kellog Putnam, daughter of a prominent labor reformer."[26]

[18] *Ibid.,* 5.

[19] *Ibid.*

[20] Louis Filler, *Crusaders for American Liberalism* (Yellow Springs, Ohio, 1961), 262.

[21] *Ibid.,* 273.

[22] *Ibid.,* 261.

[23] Eric F. Goldman, *Rendezvous with Destiny: A History of Modern American Reform* (New York, 1955), 19.

[24] *Ibid.,* 226.

[25] *Ibid.,* 338.

[26] T. H. Greer, *American Social Reform Movements: Their Pattern Since 1865* (Port Washington, N.Y., 1965), 14.

Hart, in *The Liberal Tradition in America,*[27] has no reference whatsoever to woman's suffrage.

Hofstadter, in *The Age of Reform,* mentions woman's suffrage once, in the following sentence: "To attend to the terms in which the various reforms intended to promote direct democracy were debated—and to these one should add the proposal for woman's suffrage—one might think that the issue was utopia versus apocalypse.[28] Hardly an adequate discussion of one of the major reforms of "the age of reform."

Lasch, in *The New Radicalism in America,* has a whole chapter on "Women as Alien"—in which woman's suffrage has exactly one mention, namely, that *Harper's Bazaar* favored woman suffrage and other progressive reforms whereas *Good Housekeeping* and the *Ladies' Home Journal* did not.[29]

Lens, in *Radicalism in America,* mentions woman's suffrage twice. It is referred to once in a relative clause: "There were other reformers plowing the fields: those who were disillusioned with the Republican Party and proposed a labor party; the suffragists of Susan B. Anthony; the producer cooperative zealots; and many more";[30] and once in a caption under a picture of Susan B. Anthony: "Sufragette Susan B. Anthony created a stir among delegates by attending the National Labor Union convention in 1868. She was seated only after labor leaders made it clear that they would not endorse her 'peculiar ideas'."[31] This nontreatment of woman's suffrage must be seen in the context of a book whose author says, "The radical has been a motor force of history"[32] and "The strain of radicalism runs deep in the saga of the United States. It is neither legend nor footnote, but an integral part of American history. Without it, indeed, there is no American history."[33]

Madison, in *Critics and Crusaders,*[34] takes a biographical approach to social history. Although among the twenty-one personal-

[27] Louis Hart, *The Liberal Tradition in America: An Interpretation of American Political Thought since the Revolution* (New York, 1955).

[28] Richard Hofstadter, *The Age of Reform: From Bryan to F.D.R.* (New York, 1955), 265.

[29] Christopher Lasch, *The New Radicalism in America 1889-1963: The Intellectual as a Social Type* (New York, 1965), 49.

[30] Sidney Lens, *Radicalism in America* (New York, 1969), 133.

[31] *Ibid.*, 180.

[32] *Ibid.*, 1.

[33] *Ibid.*, 40.

[34] Charles A. Madison, *Critics and Crusaders: A Century of American Protest* (New York, 1934).

ities discussed there are two women (Margaret Fuller as a representative of transcendentalism and Emma Goldman as a representative of anarchism), there is no mention of a suffragist at all. In contrast, Henry George is considered important enough to be accorded a twenty-eight-page section.

Symes and Clement, in *Rebel America,* have precisely one reference to woman's suffrage, in the following sentence "To its [the National Labor Union's] congresses were coming delegates from two new elements in the labor movement: the women's unions, organized and led in the main by intellectual, leisure-class women like Elizabeth Cady Stanton, who were also leaders of the suffrage cause, and the new Negro unions." [35] This exhausts the discussion of the contribution of women in "The Story of Social Revolt in the United States" (subtitle of the book).

Discussion of the Treatment of Woman's Suffrage in Reform Histories

Of the twelve reform histories that qualified for inclusion in our sample, four have not a single reference to woman's suffrage (Chamberlain, Ekirch [1955], Hart, and Madison). The others have one to three references to woman's suffrage, often in one sentence each. They include insignificant references which merely utilize suffrage concerns as character attributes (e.g., Decker, "the militant suffragist"). Some references even appear in a satirical context (e.g., "The men of Cincinnati were to concern themselves with nothing so bizarre as woman suffrage"). The two longest discussions are in Goldman and Ekirch [1973]. Goldman is the only author who spends somewhat more than a page on woman's suffrage, but it is interesting to note that this comparatively lengthy discussion is entirely centered on the topic of the failure of woman's suffrage to produce the exaggerated results that some people had expected. Ekirch, who, comparatively speaking, has the best discussion of woman's suffrage, puts this failure to produce dramatic election results into perspective by comparing it with the apathy of male voters. Nevertheless, this comparatively better discussion still considers woman's suffrage of sufficiently little import so that a mistake on the date of the ratification of the Nineteenth Amendment could slip in.

If we consider that the authors of the examined books concern themselves by self-declaration with such issues as the history of political action, radicalism in America, American social reform movements, etc., then the systematic exclusion of all pertinent

[35] Lillian Symes and Travers Clement, *Rebel America: The Story of Social Revolt in the United States* (New York, 1934), 132.

discussions of woman's suffrage as a reform movement, of the Woman's Party as a unique form of political action, and of the writings of the suffragists as some of the most outspoken radicals of their times can only be explained in two ways: either by a profound ignorance or by a serious underevaluation of female political action. It seems that ignorance can be canceled out as a sufficient explanation—after all, the six volumes of the *History of Woman Suffrage* have been available since 1922, and since the sixties other excellent studies have appeared.[36] If we cancel out ignorance, we are left with a serious underevaluation of the importance of significant events in American history—and the only explanation for that is sexual bias on the part of those historians we have examined.

Conclusion

The attention paid by American historians to one of the most significant events for the status of women in American history has been examined in two different ways: by an index search of suffragist items in general American histories and by an examination of the way in which specific reform histories treat woman's suffrage. In both cases, we found either that the historians examined totally ignored woman's suffrage or that they dealt with it in an inadequate manner. Since lack of data cannot be used to explain this inadequacy, it has been inferred that we are dealing instead with a sexual bias on the part of the historians involved.

If this is at all representative of the way in which American historians treat events that pertain to women, we must conclude that they have not lived up to their responsibilities to the female part of the population. The accusations that Beard and Rosen raised against historians in general have been substantiated, as far as the treatment of woman's suffrage is concerned, by the historians examined here.

Events become history because they happened—but, in addition, they also need to be recorded and passed on from generation to generation. We have found a significant discrepancy between history and historiography as far as woman's suffrage is concerned. It can only be hoped that this discrepancy will be overcome in the future.

[36] See Eleanor Flexner, *Century of Struggle: The Woman's Rights Movement in the United States* (New York, 1971); Kraditor, *Woman's Suffrage Movement 1890-1920;* Kraditor, ed., *Up From the Pedestal: Selected Writings in the History of American Feminism* (Chicago, 1968); William L. O'Neill, *The Woman Movement* (New York, 1962); and many others.

APPENDIX

General American History Books Examined

[1] Adams, James Truslow. *The American: The Making of a New Man.* New York: Charles Scribner's Sons, 1943.

[2] ——. *The Epic of America.* Garden City, N.Y.: Blue Ribbon Books, 1941.

[3] ——. *The March of Democracy.* 2 vols. New York: Charles Scribner's Sons, 1932-33. Vol. 2: *From Civil War to World Power.*

[4] Agar, Herbert. *The Price of Union.* Boston: Houghton Mifflin Co., 1950.

[5] Bailey, Thomas Andrew. *The American Pageant: A History of the Republic.* Boston: D.C. Heath & Co., 1956.

[6] Baldwin, Leland Dewitt. *The Stream of American History.* 2nd ed. New York: American Book Co., 1957. Vol. 2.

[7] Barnes, Harry Elmer. *History and Social Intelligence.* New York: Alfred A. Knopf, 1926.

[8] Bates, Ernest Sutherland. *American Faith: Its Religious, Political, and Economic Foundations.* New York: W. W. Norton & Co., 1940.

[9] Beals, Carlton. *American Earth: The Biography of a Nation.* Philadelphia: J. B. Lippincott Co., 1939.

[10] Beard, Charles A, and Beard, Mary R. *The Rise of American Civilization.* New York: Macmillan Co., 1930.

[11] Beard, Charles A.; Beard, Mary R.; and Beard, William. *The Beards' New Basic History of the United States.* Garden City, N.Y.: Doubleday & Co., 1960.

[12] Beard, Mary R., ed. *America Through Women's Eyes.* New York: Macmillan Co., 1933. Reprint. New York: Greenwood Press, 1969.

[13] Billington, Ray Allen. *Westward Expansion: A History of the American Frontier.* 2nd ed. New York: Macmillan Co., 1963.

[14] Blum, J. M., et al. *The National Experience: A History of the United States.* New York: Harcourt, Brace & World, 1963.

[15] Carman, Harry James. *Social and Economic History of the United States.* Boston: D. C. Heath & Co., 1934. Reprint. New York: Johnson Reprint Co., 1968. Vol. 2: *The Rise of Industrialism, 1820-1875.*

[16] Caughey, John Walton, and May, Ernest R. *A History of the United States.* Chicago: Rand McNally & Co., 1964.

[17] Cole, Donald B. *Atlas of American History.* Boston: Ginn & Co., 1963.

[18] Craven, Avery Odelle. *Democracy in American Life: A Historical View.* Chicago: University of Chicago Press, 1941.

[19] Curti, Merle Eugene. *The Roots of American Loyalty.* New York: Columbia University Press, 1946.

[20] Degler, Carl N. *Out of Our Past: The Forces that Shaped Modern America.* New York: Harper & Bros., 1959.

[21] Dulles, Foster R. *The United States Since 1865.* Ann Arbor: University of Michigan Press, 1959.

[22] Farr, David M.; Morr, J. S.; and Mealing, S. R. *Two Democracies.* Toronto: Ryerson Press, 1963.

[23] Faulkner, Harold Underwood. *American Political and Social History.* 7th ed. New York: Appleton-Century-Crofts, 1957.

[24] Fielding, R. Kent. *The United States: An Interpretive History.* New York: Harper & Row, 1964.

[25] Fish, Carl Russell, and Wilson, Howard E. *History of the United States.* New York: American Book Co., 1936.

[26] Garraty, John Arthur. *The American Nation: A History of the United States.* New York: Harper & Row, 1966.

[27] Golden, Harry Lewis, and Rywell, Martin. *Jews in American History: Their Contribution to the United States of America.* Charlotte, N.C.: H. I. Martin Co., 1950.

[28] Graff, Henry Franklin, and Krout, John A. *The Adventure of the American People: A History of the United States.* Chicago: Rand McNally & Co., 1964.

[29] Hacker, Louis Morton. *The Triumph of American Capitalism: The Development of Forces in American History to the End of the Nineteenth Century.* New York: Columbia University Press, 1947.

[30] Handlin, Oscar. *The Americans: A New History of the People of the United States.* Boston: Little, Brown & Co., 1963.

[31] Harlow, Ralph Volney. *The Growth of the United States.* 2 vols. Rev. ed. New York: Henry Holt & Co., 1951. Vol. 2: *The Expansion of the Nation, 1865-1943.*

[32] ———. *The United States: From Wilderness to World Power.* 4th ed. Revised by Nelson M. Blake. New York: Holt, Rinehart & Winston, 1964.

[33] Hicks, John Donald, and Mowry, George E. *A Short History of American Democracy.* 2nd ed. Boston: Houghton Mifflin Co., 1956.

[34] Hofstadter, Richard; Miller, William; and Aaron, Daniel. *The American Republic.* 2 vols. Englewood Cliffs, N.J.: Prentice-Hall, 1959. Vol. 2: *Since 1865.*

[35] ———. *The Structure of American History.* Englewood Cliffs, N.J.: Prentice-Hall, 1964.

[36] ———. *The United States: The History of a Republic.* Englewood Cliffs, N.J.: Prentice-Hall, 1957.

[37] Hofstadter, Richard, and Wallace, Michael, eds. *American Violence: A Documentary History.* New York: Alfred A. Knopf, 1970.

[38] Huberman, Leo. *We, the People.* Rev. ed. New York: Harper & Bros., 1947.

[39] Jernegan, Marcus Wilson; Carlson, Harry Ellsworth; and Ross, A. Clayton. *Growth of the American People.* 1941 ed. New York: Longmans, Green, 1941.

[40] McNaught, Kenneth W., and Cook, Ramsey. *Canada and the United States: A Modern Study.* Toronto: Clarke, Irwin, 1964.

[41] McNaught, Kenneth W.; Ricker, John C.; and Saywell, John T. *Manifest Destiny: A Short History of the United States.* Toronto: Clarke, Irwin, 1965.

[42] Maurois, André. *The Miracle of America.* Trans. by Denver and Jane Lindley. New York and London: Harper & Bros., 1944.

[43] Morison, Samuel Eliot. *The Oxford History of the United States.* 2 vols. London: Oxford University Press, 1928. Vol. 2.

[44] Morison, Samuel Eliot, and Commager, Henry Steele. *The Growth of the American Republic.* 4th ed., rev. and enl. New York: Oxford University Press, 1956.

[45] Nevins, Allan, and Commager, Henry Steele. *America: The Story of a Free People.* Oxford: The Clarendon Press, 1942.

[46] ———. *A Short History of the United States.* New York: Modern Library, 1945.

[47] Ostrander, Gilman Marston. *A Profile History of the United States.* New York: McGraw-Hill, 1964.

[48] Perkins, Dexter, and Van Deusen, Glyndon G. *The American Democracy: Its Rise to Power.* New York: Macmillan Co., 1964.

[49] Rae, John Bell, and Mahoney, Thomas H. D. *The United States in World History: From its Beginnings to World Leadership.* 3rd ed. New York: McGraw-Hill, 1964.

[50] Rosenkrantz, Barbara Gutman, and Koelsch, William A., comps. *American Habitat: A Historical Perspective.* New York: The Free Press, 1973.

[51] Rugg, Harold Ordway. *A History of American Government and Culture: America's March Toward Democracy.* Boston: Ginn & Co., 1931.

[52] Schlesinger, Arthur Meier. *Paths to the Present.* New York: Macmillan Co., 1949.

[53] ———. *Political and Social Growth of the United States, 1852-1933.* Rev. ed. New York: Macmillan Co., 1936.

[54] Sellers, Charles, and May, Henry. 2nd ed. *A Synopsis of American History.* Chicago: Rand McNally & Co., 1969.

[55] Sinclair, Andrew. *A Concise History of the United States.* Rev. ed. London: Thames & Hudson, 1970.

[56] Smith, Theodore Clarke. *The United States as a Factor in World History* New York: Henry Holt & Co., 1947.

[57] Thistlewaite, Frank. *The Great Experiment: An Introduction to the History of the American People*. Cambridge: The University Press, 1955.

[58] Turner, Frederick Jackson. *The Frontier in American History*. New York: Henry Holt & Co., 1958.

[59] ——. *The Significance of Sections in American History*. Gloucester, Mass.: Peter Smith, 1959.

[60] Wilson, Woodrow. *A History of the American People*. 10 vols. New York and London: Harper & Bros., 1903. Reprint. New York: W. H. Wise, 1931. Vol. 5.

[61] Woodward, William E. *A New American History*. New York: The Literary Guild, 1936.

William H. Chafe

Sex and Race: The Analogy of Social Control

> "Prejudice against color, of which we hear so much, is no stronger than that against sex. It is produced by the same cause, and manifested very much in the same way. The Negro's skin and the woman's sex are both prima facie evidence that they were intended to be in subjection to the white Saxon man."
>
> —Elizabeth Cady Stanton, 1860

PROBABLY NO ANALOGY has been used more frequently by both scholars and women's rights advocates than that between sex and race. Yet the comparison has also stirred controversy and anger. Although some scholars and activists continued to draw the parallel during the 1960's, many observers —especially Black male activists—dissented vigorously. To equate the experience of manacled slaves with that of comfortable homemakers, they argued, was an insult to Black people and a travesty of historical analysis. The issue was complicated even further during the civil rights movement when volatile feelings about the issues of sex and race became embroiled in the politics of interracial sex and the emergence of Black Power. By the end of the 60's as much emotional energy was expanded denouncing the analogy as defending it.

Clearly, the comparison of sex and race evokes strong reactions and touches themes which run deep in the culture. But for that very reason it may be worthwhile to take another look at it. It may also be timely to ask whether the relationship of sex and race can be seen in alternative ways which might illuminate how American society has functioned to keep both women and Black people in their "place." The real lesson of the comparison may be what it teaches about the process and forms of social control in America, not what it tells about the condition of women and Blacks.

THE ARGUMENTS FOR THE ANALOGY fall essentially into two categories: both women and Blacks have shared a collective experience of being assigned a set of attributes and responsibilities on the basis of a physical characteristic; and as a result of this, each has a history of being denied fundamental rights of citizenship, including access to political, economic and educational opportunity.

The evidence for these propositions is incontrovertible. Through much of American history, the vast majority of women and Blacks have been denied recognition as persons under the law. As slaves, African-Americans were chattel, their work habits, family life and physical survival were controlled completely by the white master. For the most part, they could neither own property, sue in court, nor move about without permission. Although the constraints on women were less severe, they too were denied legal control over their earnings, the right to enter most professions, or the freedom to move their residence without permission if they were married. (As late as 1948 a Georgia law required a married woman to accompany her husband to a primitive rural cabin—against her wishes.) Under the common law, a woman ceased to exist legally as a person once she took a husband. At that point her identity became submerged in his. Elizabeth Cady Stanton spoke poignantly about the consequences for each group. "The Negro has no name," she remarked in 1860. "He is Cuffy Douglass, or Cuffy Brooks, just whose Cuffy he may chance to be. The Woman has no name. She is . . . Mrs. John Doe, just whose Mrs. she may chance to be." In both cases the absence of legal standing testified vividly to the lack of control over one's destiny.

Even more pernicious than disability under the law was a pattern of informal discrimination which suffused nearly all areas of life. Although Black men and all women won the nominal right to vote with the 15th and 19th Amendments, neither group was permitted to enter the inner circle of political influence or to wield independent political power. Both groups were also denied access to many of the social clubs, elite colleges and professional associations where networks of power were perpetuated. It was in the realm of economic opportunities, though, that discrimination took its greatest toll. In most cases, it was simply assumed that Blacks and women belonged in the lowest level of occupations, particularly domestic and service work. As Catharine Stimpson has observed, "the tasks of women and Blacks are usually grueling, repetitive, slogging and dirty." [1]

Each of these manifestations of subservient status has been rooted in the fact that women and Blacks were assigned a "place" on the basis of a physical characteristic rather than having the opportunity to achieve a position through individual ability. Stated in another way, neither Blacks nor women could aspire to the American dream of upward mobility and individual accomplishment because each group had an ascribed status which carried with it an automatic set of duties and obligations. Although most ethnic groups also suffered significant discrimination, it was possible for individuals from each group to overcome effective ethnic prejudice, especially in the second generation. For both women and Blacks, on the other hand, there was a visible, physical symbol of difference which immediately triggered a series of responses that limited the opportunities open to the individual.

A number of corollaries accompany the phenomenon of being assigned an ascribed status, each of which reinforces the analogy between women and Blacks. Both groups have been characterized as "ineffectual," "frivolous," "naturally passive" and incapable of performing effectively in the white male world. According to the historian Barbara Welter, nineteenth century middle class white women (and in many cases twentieth

[1] Catharine Stimpson, "'Thy Neighbor's Wife, Thy Neighbor's Servants': Women's Liberation and Black Civil Rights," in Vivian Gornick and Barbara Moran, eds., *Woman in Sexist Society* (New York, 1971).

century women) were judged according to how well they conformed to cultural norms of submissiveness and domesticity.[2] Blacks frequently were judged by the same criteria. Both groups, Carl Degler points out, have been depicted as a different order of human being, people whose intrinsic aspirations and abilities are different from, and less than, those of the "master class."[3] Since it has been assumed that these qualities were innate, a second corollary is that any Black or woman who deviated from them could be dismissed as an aberration, someone who was unrepresentative and unnatural. Historically, women were thought to have been born for the sole purpose of becoming wives and mothers. Hence any woman who chose to remain childless and single, or to pursue a career similar to that of a man could be perceived as "non-feminine" or "pseudo-masculine." "The independent woman," Ferdinand Lundberg and Marynia Farnham announced in their 1947 bestseller, *Modern Woman: The Lost Sex*, "is a contradiction in terms." In the same way, Blacks supposedly were born to be happy as domestics and to enjoy serving white people. Thus any protest from the Black community could only be viewed as the result of "outside agitation" or of some pathology on the part of the individual protestor. The "uppity nigger" was as much a contradiction in terms as the "independent woman." Both were seen as acting in violation of nature.

Finally, because of this ascribed status and supposed passivity, women and Blacks have been placed in the position of being politically and economically dependent upon white men. In sociological terms, this has meant that they derived their influence from association with those above them, rather than from their own independent effort. Similarly, in most cases where women exercised influence in a community, it was attributed to the men they were married to. In like manner, the

---

[2] Barbara Welter, "The Cult of True Womanhood: 1820–1860," *American Quarterly*, XVIII (Summer, 1966).

[3] Carl Degler, "Introduction," in Carl Degler, ed., Charlotte Perkins Gilman, *Women and Economics* (New York, 1966). See also Degler, *Neither Black nor White* (New York, 1973).

status of Blacks has frequently depended on their connection with white people, particularly the white imprimatur that they are "good" and "can be trusted." As W. E. B. DuBois learned when he sought a teaching job in the Tennessee countryside during the 1880's, success required satisfying a white superintendent about one's "manners." Indeed, the language used to describe such relationships testifies to the possessiveness and dependency implicit in them. A woman might achieve prestige because of being "Mr. Jones's secretary" or a Black author singled out for attention because of being Carl Van Vechten's "protégé," but not because of their intrinsic qualities. The patron-protégé relationship, with its implicit requirements of dependency, gratitude, and deference, is one which runs throughout the history of women and Blacks.

The strongest parallel between women and Blacks, then, has been their ascribed status and shared relationship of dependency and powerlessness vis-à-vis white men. Clearly, not all white men tyrannize women and Blacks, and some women and Blacks occupy positions of greater power and status than many white men. Nevertheless, a system of power and influence exists from which some white males benefit greatly and in which most women and Blacks (as well as some white men) are consigned to roles which are subservient and inferior. Within this system there has long been a perverse dynamic at work which causes women and Blacks, almost as a matter of automatic response, to be treated as outsiders and inferiors, thereby giving all those who are not women and Black some sense of being superior.

POWERFUL PARALLELS EXIST between the condition of women and that of Blacks, but there may be even stronger arguments against the analogy. The most obvious is that there can be no comparison between Blacks and women in the actual suffering experienced by both. Blacks have endured more collective oppression, physically and psychologically, than white women. They have been forced to live in the worst areas of every community, consigned to the poorest educational facilities, limited to the worst-paying jobs, subject to poor housing, widespread disease, and above all, consistent violence. Throughout American history, Black people have been the victims of terrorism, including lynchings, beatings and riots. In contrast, all women are not oppressed in the same way, many of them believe they are not oppressed at all, and some are distinctly more oppressed than others. The slaveholder's wife may have suffered some disabilities, Gerda Lerner points out, but she herself participated in the victimization of her female slaves. Thus, "to equate her oppression with that of the slave woman is to ignore the real plight of the slave."[4] Although many women also have been subject to consistent patterns of violence, particularly in the threat and reality of rape, it is not valid to conclude that women as a group have suffered from physical oppression and brutality in the same way as Blacks.

This, in turn, is a function of the fact that women live in intimacy with men while Blacks, for the most part, are physically distant from their white oppressors of both sexes. As Alice Rossi has pointed out, the most striking and ironic fact about women's experience is that they live closer to the group holding power over their lives than they do to each other.[5] Women are distributed throughout the social structure and do not share as a group the physical experience of economic deprivation, poor housing and widespread disease which characterizes the lives of most Blacks. Even though white women do not ordinarily exercise power in their own right, their intimacy with men gives some of them a closer connection to the sources of power in society than is generally available to Blacks. At the very least, they have the opportunity for vicarious gratification. In addition, it is clearly important to most males that the women in their lives not be thoroughly alienated. Many whites on the other hand, do not care if Blacks are disaffected. Thus the very nature of the intimate relationship between

[4] Gerda Lerner, "The Feminists: A Second Look," *The Columbia Forum*, XIII, 3, Fall, 1970.

[5] Alice Rossi, "Equality Between the Sexes: An Immodest Proposal," in Robert J. Lifton, ed., *The Woman in America* (Boston, 1967).

women and men ensures that *white* women, at least, will suffer less violence than Blacks, will be more acceptable to the society at large, and will be in a better position to influence, at least indirectly, the decisions of those in power.

Black women, of course, occupy a position which amounts to double jeopardy. As Blacks they suffer all the burdens of prejudice and mistreatment which fall on anyone with dark skin. As women they bear the additional burden of having to cope with white and Black men. The Black female, the poet Maya Angelou has observed, endures not only the natural stresses of growing into adolescence and adulthood, but is also "caught in the tripartite crossfire of masculine prejudice, white illogical hate, and Black lack of power."[6] It is perhaps not surprising that Black women earn least of any occupational group, although they have been more likely than either Black men or white women to hold service jobs. Because of their blackness, they have been denied the vicarious satisfactions which at least some white women receive through sharing in the prestige and power of their well-off husbands.

The difference between Black and white women runs even deeper. As Angela Davis has noted, the Black woman has never shared any of the "alleged benefits of femininity. . . . She was not sheltered or protected; she would not remain oblivious to the desperate struggle for existence unfolding outside the 'home.' "[7] Although much the same thing might have been said of many white women in colonial America, by the late nineteenth and twentieth centuries middle and upper class white women had entered a different type of existence, far removed from that of nearly all Black women. While many white daughters were raised in genteel, refined circumstances, most Black daughters were forced to deal with poverty, violence and a hostile outside world from childhood on. Though white mothers frequently were free to spend long hours in play with their children, Black mothers rarely had the time to give their children the "advantages" of Spock-like attention.

[6] Maya Angelou, *I Know Why the Caged Bird Sings* (New York, 1973).
[7] Angela Davis, "Reflections on the Black Woman's Role in the Community of Slaves," *The Black Scholar*, III, 3, December, 1971.

When Hannah Peace, a character in Toni Morrison's novel, *Sula,* asked if her mother loved her, the mother responded: "what you talkin' 'bout did I love you girl. I stayed alive for you can't you get that through your thick head. . . ." When dying or running away or surrender might have been the easier alternative, staying alive was a fundamental manifestation of love. But it grew out of, and created, a situation for Black women which differed from that of most white women.

One of the consequences has been a sense of distance and suspicion among Black women toward white women. Not only did blue eyes, blonde hair and white skin represent a hostile force, used by the dominant culture to accuse the Black woman of inferiority; but the women who possessed those attributes frequently were part of the problem, acting as though Black women were dirt. When Maya Angelou first went to work in the home of a white woman, she felt a bond of sympathy and compassion for her employer because she could not bear children; but the employer refused to call her by her proper name, demeaned her worth as a person, and provoked an angry reprisal. Mary Helen Washington, a student of Black literature, has found that nearly all Black women writers portray white women as callous, snobbish, and, even if liberal, condescending. Given the relative comfort, leisure, and freedom of the middle class white woman's life, it has been difficult for Black women to identify with white women's anger or sense of oppression.

As a result, Black women have perceived racial oppression as much more basic to their lives than sex oppression. Black women have chosen their priorities clearly, tracing many of the conflicts with their men to a racist social structure which denies the Black male the chance to realize his own ambitions. Furthermore, the economic realities of the Black community have never permitted a rigid polarization of sexual spheres and roles. Black women, for the most part, have not experienced the full-time homemaking and suburban domesticity which has given rise to discontent among white women. (Many, in fact, would welcome a chance to share in the life which many middle-class white feminists reject.) Thus Black women have approached the entire issue of sex liberation with a different perspective from whites. As Frances Harper, a Black woman and an abolitionist, said over a century ago, if it came to choosing between race and sex, "the lesser question of sex must go. Being Black is more precarious and demanding than being a woman; being Black means that every white, including every white working-class woman, can discriminate against you."

This difference between Black and white women points to another major shortcoming of the sex/race analogy: Black people of both sexes come from a different historical experience than white women. Before being carried to America, Afro-Americans—men and women—shared an autonomous, culturally distinctive, geographically separate existence. At the root of their identity in America, especially prior to the twentieth century, has been a collective, if diffuse, sense of this historic experience of freedom and independence. Black Americans under slavery had a point of reference, a starting place, a memory of something better, which gave added dimension to their experience of suffering here. White women, in contrast, lack a collective history as a separate group in another place where freedom, autonomy, and distinctive cultural forms existed. The absence of this collective geographical and cultural past is crucial in distinguishing women's oppression from that of Blacks.

The most profound argument against the analogy is the differing level of consciousness about one's oppression which has characterized women and Blacks. One of the primary themes of those who have defended the analogy is that both women and Blacks thoroughly internalized the stereotypes circulated about them by the dominant culture. Thus Judith Bardwick and Elizabeth Douvan have commented on how disturbing it is "to review the extent to which women perceive their responsibilities, goals, their very capacities as inferior to males." [8] Similarly, it was argued during the late 1950's that Black slaves had internalized the Sambo image and, in effect, become

[8] Judith Bardwick and Elizabeth Douvan, "Ambivalence: The Socialization of Women," in Gornick and Moran, *op. cit.*

the docile, subservient, ineffectual personalities which their masters talked about to visitors and needed to believe in for their own psychic well-being. If both women and Blacks had in fact identified wholly with the roles they played for their respective audiences, there would be an overpowering case for the analogy.

It has become increasingly clear, though, that Black Americans never were unconscious of their oppression, and never ceased, in whatever way possible, to express their rage. The memory of the African past, handed down through oral tradition, provided a strong alternative frame of reference for loyalty and identity. The separate life of the slave quarters made it possible to retain distinctive cultural forms, an independent group of "significant others" for children to look up to, and a relatively autonomous system of values. Whether through plantation sabotage, such as destroying farm tools, or through verbal expressions of resentment at masters, Black Americans even in the ante-bellum South showed a keen awareness of their condition.

This is not to say that the Sambo "image" was unreal or that the role had no consequence for those playing it. The fact of having to behave in a certain way in the presence of whites exerted a crucial influence on the entire spectrum of Afro-American life, including one's image of self. Among other things, it meant that the presence of a white-skinned person automatically acted as a constraint on self-expression and symbolized the limitations on one's sense of possibilities for self-realization.

But the research of social scientists has shown that there are many different kinds of roles, and that they vary remarkably in saliency, intensity, and identification. The role of mother, lover, preacher or conjurer is likely to have been more significant and emotionally compelling than the role of cotton-picker. Research also having shown that surveillance is an important force in inducing behavioral conformity, there was probably a vast difference between complying externally in the presence of an overseer and identifying internally with such behavior.

Field hands on the plantation might play a role perfectly on demand (warned through the verse of their work song that "master's in de field") and just as quickly drop the role when the audience had left. Life in a slave quarters or ghetto provided the opportunity to engage in other roles which bolstered an alternative, and more internally consistent, sense of self. Although Blacks frequently *appeared* quiescent under the watchful eyes of whites, and though this behavior inevitably affected in some ways their sense of self, the evidence suggests strongly a very different, and much more rebellious syndrome of attitudes and expressions on home ground.

The experience of white women seems to have been different, with much less evidence of a collective consciousness of oppression or commitment to a change in status. Conceivably, historians as well as contemporary observers have been deceived by the appearance of conformity to their "place" by most American women, just as historians in the past misperceived the state of conformity or resistance among Blacks; but on the basis of what we now know, only a minority of women resisted overtly their condition or traced their grievances in life to the belief that women—as a social group—were oppressed in society. Through most of history, the sense of sisterhood which existed among women seems to have consisted of a shared commitment to nurturant, compassionate roles rather than a collective awareness of injury and oppression. Women believed in giving support, comfort, and sympathy to the aggrieved, but do not appear to have seen themselves as political victims whose shared response should be anger. While public opinion polls indicate that most Black Americans have supported the civil rights movement, only a minority of women said that they supported the fight for sex equality prior to the 1970's. For a host of complicated reasons it seems that women have experienced less *conscious* resistance to their "place" than Blacks have.

The differential in consciousness and protest symbolizes the underlying weakness of the sex/race analogy—the absence of a consistent and collective geographical and physical base for women. In twentieth century terms, the fact that Blacks have lived in ghettoes and women have been dispersed throughout the entire culture seems crucial to the dissimilarity of collective protest against discrimination. It was almost impossible for Blacks living together not to share a common hostility toward whites or a common awareness of how white Americans controlled their lives and limited their chances for self-fulfillment. Living with men, in contrast, white women especially were denied the kind of incubator environment which automatically raised the consciousness of Blacks to their plight. As Betty Friedan pointed out in the *Feminine Mystique*, most women believed that whatever problems they experienced were a product of their individual situation rather than of their social condition. The issue of resistance testifies to the difference between Blacks and women, and to the importance of the ghetto as a social environment conducive to protest.

For these and other reasons, recent observers have questioned the direct comparison of women as a class and Black people as a class. Although the analogy helps to illuminate differences, that seems an insufficient justification for pursuing it. Catharine Stimpson, among others, has written that those using the analogy are seeking to exploit the passion and energy of the civil rights movement without coming to grips either with the differences between women and Blacks, or the fact of white women's racism.[9] There are important contrasts in the historical experiences of white women and Afro-Americans which makes difficult the establishment of categorical links between the two groups.

THE GREATEST PROBLEM HAS been that those using the analogy have attempted to prove a likeness between the *substantive condition* of women and Blacks. What if the question were posed in different terms? Comparisons need not be exact to be fruitful, and analogies should not be limited to conditions of substance alone. According to Webster, an analogy

[9] Stimpson, *op. cit.*

is "a relation of likeness . . . consisting in the resemblance not of the things themselves but of two or more attributes, circumstances or effects." Throughout the preceding discussion, the strongest parallels involved the use of stereotypes and ascribed attributes to define the respective position of women and Blacks in the society. What if we look at women and Blacks instead as examples of how social control is exercised in America? What if the nature of the analogy is not in the *substance* of the material existence which women and Blacks have experienced, but the *forms* by which they are "kept in their place" and prevented from challenging the status quo?

The virtues of such an approach are many. It provides greater flexibility in exploring how the experience of one group can illuminate the experience of another. It has the potential of developing insights into the larger processes by which the status quo is perpetuated from generation to generation. And it can teach us about the operation of society as a whole and the way in which variables like sex and race are made central to the division of responsibilities and power within the society. If the forms of social control used with Blacks and women resemble each other in "two or more attributes, circumstances or effects," then it may be possible to learn something both about the two groups and the society.

In his brilliant autobiographical novel, *Black Boy*, Richard Wright presents a poignant description of growing up Black in the Jim Crow South. Using his family, the church, his classmates, his jobs, and his fantasies as stage-pieces for his story, Wright plays out the themes of hunger, fear, and determination which permeated his young life. He provides a searing account of how white Southerners successfully controlled the lives and aspirations of Blacks. A series of concentric circles of social control operated to limit young Blacks to two life options —conformity to the white system, or exile.

The outermost circle of control consisted of physical intimidation. When Richard asked his mother why Black men did not fight white men, she responded, "the white men have guns and the black men don't." Physical force, and ultimately the threat of death, served as a constant reminder that whites held complete power over Black lives. Richard saw that power manifested repeatedly. When his Uncle Hoskins dared to start his own saloon and act independently of the white power structure, he was lynched. The brother of one of Richard's schoolmates suffered a similar fate, allegedly for fooling with a white prostitute. When Richard worked for a clothing store, he often saw the white manager browbeat or physically attack Black customers who had not paid their bills on time. When one woman came out of the store in a torn dress and bleeding, the manager said "that's what we do to niggers when they don't pay their bills." The result was pervasive fear. "The things that influenced my conduct as a Negro," Richard wrote, "did not have to happen to me directly; I needed but to hear of them to feel their full effects in the deepest layers of my consciousness. Indeed the white brutality that I had not seen was a more effective control of my behavior than that which I knew . . . . as long as it remained something terrible and yet remote, something whose horror and blood might descend upon me at any moment, I was compelled to give my entire imagination over to it, an act which blocked the springs of thought and feelings in me."

The second circle of control rested in total white domination of the economic status of Black people. If a young Black did not act the part of "happy nigger" convincingly, the employer would fire him. Richard was repeatedly threatened with the loss of work because he did not sufficiently suppress his anger and independence. "Why don't you laugh and talk like the other niggers?" one employer asked. "Well, sir, there's nothing much to say or smile about," Richard said. "I don't like your looks nigger. Now git!" the boss ordered. Only a limited number of economic roles were open to Blacks, and if they were not played according to the rules, the job would be lost. A scarce supply of work, together with the demand that it be carried out in a deferential manner, provided a powerful guarantee that Blacks would not get out of line.

Significantly, the highest status jobs in the Black community—teachers, ministers, civil servants—all depended ultimately upon acting in ways which pleased the white power structure. One did not get the position at the post office, or in the school system without being "safe"—the kind of person who would not make trouble.

The third circle of control consisted of the psychological power of whites to define and limit the reach of Black aspirations. The verbal cues, the discouragement or encouragement of authority figures, the picture of reality transmitted by friends, or teachers—all of these help to shape how people think of themselves and their life chances. Within this realm of social psychology, white Southerners exerted a pervasive and insidious control upon Blacks. When Richard took his first job in a white household, he was given a bowl of molasses with mold on it for breakfast, even as his employers ate eggs and bacon. The woman he worked for asked what grade he was in, and when he replied the seventh, she asked, "then why are you going to school?" When he further answered, "well, I want to be a writer," she responded: "you'll never be a writer. . . who on earth put such ideas into your nigger head?" By her response, the woman had defined the outer boundaries of a Black person's reality. As Richard noted, "she had assumed that she knew my place in life, what I felt, what I ought to be, and I resented it with all my heart . . . . perhaps I would never be a writer; but I did not want her to say so." Richard Wright was able to defy the limits set upon his life by white people; but for the overwhelming majority of his fellow Blacks, the ability of whites to intimidate them psychologically diminished the chance that they would be able to aspire realistically to a life other than that assigned them within a white racist social structure.

The most devastating control of all, though, was that exercised by the Black community itself out of self-defense. In the face of a world managed at every level by white power, it became an urgent necessity that Black people train each other to adapt in order to survive. The most profound and effective socialization toward accepting the racial status quo came from Richard's own family and peer group. It was Richard's mother who slapped him into silence "out of her own fear" when he asked why they had not fought back after Uncle Hoskin's murder. Even to ask the question posed a threat to safety. Similarly, it was Richard's Uncle Tom who insisted that Richard learn, almost by instinct, how to be accommodating. If Richard did not learn, the uncle said, he would never amount to anything and would end up on the gallows. Indeed, Richard would survive only if somebody broke his spirit and set the "proper" example.

Instances of social control exercised by the Black community abound in Wright's *Black Boy*. Almost every Black he knew opposed Richard's writing aspirations. "From no quarter," he recalls, "with the exception of the Negro newspaper editor, had there come a single encouraging word . . . I felt that I had committed a crime. Had I been aware of the full extent to which I was pushing against the current of my environment, I would have been frightened altogether out of my attempts at writing." The principal of his school insisted that Richard give a graduation speech written by the principal rather than by Richard himself so that the proper tone of accommodation could be struck; the reward for going along was a possible teaching job. Griggs, Richard's best friend, was the most articulate in demanding that Richard control his instincts. "You're Black and you don't act a damn bit like it." When Richard replied, "Oh, Christ, I can't be a slave," Griggs responded with the ultimate lesson of reality: "But you've got to eat . . . when you are in front of white people, think before you act, think before you speak . . . you may think I'm an Uncle Tom, but I'm not. I hate these white people, hate 'em with all my heart. But I can't show it; if I did, they'd kill me." No matter where he went or whom he talked to in his own community, Richard found the warning that he must behave externally in the manner white people expected. Whatever the hope of ultimate freedom, survival was the immediate necessity. One could not fight another day if one was not alive.

Paradoxically, even the outlets for resistance within the system provided a means of reinforcing it. There were many ways of expressing unhappiness with one's lot and all were essential to let off steam. The gang on the corner constantly verbalized resentment and anger against the white oppressor. Yet the very fact that the anger had to be limited to words and out of the earshot of whites meant that in practical terms, it was ineffectual. Humor was another form of resistance. Richard and his friends joked that if they ate enough black-eyed peas and buttermilk, they would defeat their white enemies in a race riot with "poison gas." But the end of the joke was an acknowledgement that the only way in reality to cope with the "mean" white folks was to leave.

Indeed, the most practical form of resistance—petty theft —almost seemed a ploy by white people to perpetuate the system. Just as modern-day department store owners tolerate a certain degree of employee theft as a means of making the workers think they are getting away with something so they will not demand higher wages, so white employers of Black people appeared to have intentionally closed their eyes to a great deal of minor stealing. By giving Blacks a small sense of triumph, white employers were able to tie them even more closely into the system, and prevent them from contemplating outright defiance. As Wright observed:

> No Negroes in my environment had ever thought of organizing . . and petitioning their white employers for higher wages. . . They knew that the whites would have retaliated with swift brutality. So, pretending to conform to the laws of the whites, grinning, bowing, they let their fingers stick to what they could touch. And the whites seemed to like it.
>
> But I, who stole nothing, who wanted to look them straight in the face, who wanted to talk and act like a man, inspired fear in them. The southern whites would rather have had Negroes who stole work for them than Negroes who knew, however dimly, the worth of their own humanity. Hence, whites placed a premium upon black deceit; they encouraged irresponsibility, and their rewards were bestowed upon us blacks in the degree that we could make them feel safe and superior.

From a white point of view, a minor exercise of indirect and devious power by Blacks was a small price to pay for maintaining control over the entire system. Whites held the power to define Black people's options, even to the point of controlling their modes of resistance.

The result of all this was a system which functioned smoothly, with barely a trace of overt protest or dissension. Everyone seemed outwardly content with their place. At a very early age, Wright observed, "the white boys and the Black boys began to play our traditional racial roles as though we had been born to them, as though it was in our blood, as though we were being guided by instinct." For most people, the impact of a pervasive system of social control was total: resignation, a lowering of aspirations, a recognition of the bleakness of the future and the hopelessness of trying to achieve major change. In Wright's image life was like a train track, and once headed in a given direction, there was little possibility of changing course.

Wright was the exception. "Somewhere in the dead of the southern night," he observed, "my life had switched onto the wrong track, and without my knowing it, the locomotive of my heart was rushing down a dangerously steep slope, heading for a collision, heedless of the warning red lights that blinked all about me, the sirens and the bells and the screams that filled the air." Wright had chosen the road of exile, acute self-consciousness, and alienation. For most Blacks of his era the warning red lights, the sirens, the bells, and the screams produced conformity to the status quo. In the face of forms of social control which effectively circumscribed one's entire life, there seemed no other choice.

OBVIOUSLY, WOMEN have not experienced overtly and directly the same kind of consistent physical intimidation which served so effectively to deter the Black people of Richard Wright's childhood from resisting their condition. On the other hand, it seems clear that the physical strength and alleged dominance of men has been an important instrument of controlling women's freedom of action. The traditional image of the male as "protector" owes a great deal to the notion that women cannot defend themselves and that men must therefore take charge of their lives physically. The same notion of male strength has historically been responsible for restricting jobs involving heavy labor to men. Nor is the fear with which women view the potential of being struck by a male lover, husband, or attacker an insignificant reality in determining the extent to which women have accepted the dominance of the men in their lives. Richard Wright observed that "the things that influenced my conduct . . . did not have to happen to me directly; I needed but to hear of them to feel their full effect . . . ." Similarly, women who have grown up with the image of powerful and potentially violent men need not have experienced a direct attack to share a sense of fear and intimidation. "Strength," the psychologist, Jerome Kagan, has observed, "is a metaphor for power." Despite the substantive difference in the way women and Blacks have been treated, the form of social control represented by physical strength has operated similarly for both groups.

An even stronger case can be made for the way in which economic controls have succeeded in keeping Blacks and women in their place. In 1898, Charlotte Perkins Gilman argued in *Women and Economics* that the root of women's subjection was their economic dependence on men. As long as females were denied the opportunity to earn their own living, she argued, there could never be equality between the sexes. The fact that women had to please their mates, both sexually and through other services, to ensure their survival made honest communication and mutual respect impossible. The prospects of a "present" from a generous husband, or a new car or clothes, frequently served to smooth over conflict, while the implicit threat of withholding such favors could be used to discourage carrying conflict too far.

In fact, the issue of women not controlling their own money and having to petition their husbands for funds to buy food and clothing has long been one of the most painful and humiliating indices of inequality between the sexes. Money symbolizes power; having to ask others for it signifies subservience and an inferior status. Carol Kennicott, the heroine of Sinclair Lewis' *Main Street*, recognized the problem. After begging prettily for her household expenses early in her marriage, she started to demand her own separate funds. "What was a magnificent spectacle of generosity to you," she told her husband, "was a humiliation to me. You *gave* me money—gave it to your mistress if she was complaisant." Beth Phail, a character in Marge Piercy's novel *Small Changes*, experienced the same conflict with her husband, who was immediately threatened by the idea of her economic autonomy. Few examples of psychological control seem more pointed than those represented in husbands treating their wives as not mature enough to handle their own money.

Even the women who held jobs reflected the pattern by which economic power was used to control women's freedom of action. Almost all women workers were concentrated in a few occupations delineated as "women's work." As secretaries, waitresses, cooks, and domestic workers, women on the job conformed to the "service" image of their sex. Significantly, the highest status jobs available—nurses and teachers—tended to reinforce a traditional image of women and the status quo between the sexes, just as the highest jobs available within the Black community—teachers and ministers—reinforced a pattern of accommodation with the existing white power structure. Any woman who chose a "man's job" automatically risked a loss of respect, if not total disdain. For most, the option simply did not exist.

Even those in the most prestigious positions illustrated how money could be used as an instrument of social control. Frequently, college administrators in Black and women's schools found that they had to shape their programs in conformity to social values which buttressed the status quo if they were to succeed in raising funds. Booker T. Washington represented the most outstanding example of this phenomenon. Repeatedly, he was forced to appease white racist presumptions in order to get another donation for Tuskegee. As the funnel through which all white philanthropic aid to Blacks was channeled, Washington had to ensure that no money would be spent in a way which might challenge the political values of his contributors. But he was not alone. During the 1840's Mary Lyons, head of Mt. Holyoke Seminary, agreed not to attend board meetings lest she offend male sensibilities, and Mary Alice Baldwin, the very effective leader of the Woman's College of Duke University, consistently paid homage to the conservative tradition of "the southern lady" in order to sustain support for women's education at Duke.

In all of these instances, economic controls functioned in parallel ways to limit the freedom of women and Blacks. If a group is assigned a "place," there are few more effective ways of keeping it there than economic dependence. "I don't want to be a slave," Richard Wright observed. "But you have to eat," Griggs replied.

The strongest parallel, however, is the way in which Blacks and women alike have been given the psychological message that they should be happy with their place. This form of control has effectively limited members of the respective groups from aspiring to nonconventional roles. Although Beth Phail of *Small Changes* wanted to go to college and law school, her family insisted that her highest aspiration should be marriage and homemaking. A woman should not expect a career. Similarly, when Carol Kennicott told her college boyfriend, "I want to do something with my life," he responded eagerly: "What's better than making a comfy home and bringing up some cute kids. . . ." The small-town atmosphere of Gopher Prairie simply reinforced the pressure to conform. Carol was expected to be a charming hostess, a dutiful wife, and a good homemaker, but not a career woman. As Sinclair Lewis observed, she was a "woman with a working brain and no work." The messages Carol received from her surroundings were not designed to give her a sense of high self-esteem. Her husband called her "an extravagant little rabbit."

Although Carol's personality was atypical, her social experience was not. When high school girls entertained the possibility of a career, they were encouraged to be nurses, not doctors. The qualities which received the most praise were those traditionally associated with being a "lady," not an assertive individual ready to face the world. Significantly, both women and Blacks were the victims of two devices designed to discourage nonconformity. Those who sought to protest their status, for example, were subjected to ridicule and caricature. The Black protestor was almost certain to be identified with subversive activity just as the woman's rights advocate was viewed as unsexed and a saboteur of the family. (Ordinary Blacks and females were subject to a gentler form of humor, no less insidious, as in the characters of "King Fish" or "Lucy.") In addition, it was not uncommon for Blacks to be set against Blacks and women against women in a competition which served primarily the interests of the dominant group. According to Judith Bardwick and Elizabeth Douvan, girls are socialized to use oblique forms of aggression largely directed at other females, while men's aggression is overt.[10] The stereotype of women doing devious battle over an attractive man is an ingrained part of our folk tradition. Nor is the "divide and conquer" strategy strange to the history of Black people, as when white workers sowed seeds of suspicion between Richard Wright and another Black worker in order to make them fight each other for the entertainment of whites.

In both cases, the psychological form of social control has operated in a similar fashion. The aspirations, horizons, and self-images of Blacks and women have been defined by others in a limiting and constrictive way. More often than not, the result historically has been an acceptance of the dominant society's perception of one's role, and the willingness to set aside aspirations for a different life. The prospect of becoming an architect, an engineer or a carpenter is not easy to sustain in an environment where the very idea is dismissed as foolish or unnatural. Instead of encouragement to aspire to new achieve-

---

[10] Bardwick and Douvan, *op. cit.*

ments, the message transmitted to Blacks and women has been the importance of finding satisfaction with the status quo.

But in the case of women, as with Blacks, the most effective instrument of continued control has been internal pressure from the group itself. From generation to generation, mothers teach daughters to please men, providing the instruction which prepares the new generation to assume its roles as mothers and housewives. Just as Blacks teach each other how to cope with Whitey and survive within the system, women school each other in how to win a man, how to appear charming, where to "play a role" in order to avoid alienating a potential husband. When Beth in *Small Changes* rebelled against her husband and fought the idea of tying herself down with a child, it was the other women in her family who urged her to submit and at least give the appearance of accepting the role expected of her. Indeed, dissembling in order to conform to social preconceptions has been a not infrequent theme in women's history. As Mirra Komarovsky has demonstrated, college women in the 1940's were taught to hide their real ability in order to make their male friends feel superior. "My mother thinks that it is very nice to be smart in college," one of Komarovsky's students noted, "but only if it doesn't take too much effort. She always tells me not to be too intellectual on dates, to be clever in a light sort of way." [11] It is not difficult to imagine one woman saying to another as Griggs said to Richard Wright, "when you are around white people [men] you have to act the part that they expect you to act."

The most effective device for maintaining internal discipline has been that of ostracizing those who do not conform. Richard Wright found himself singled out for negative treatment because he refused to accept authority and to smile and shuffle before either his teachers or white people. Beth Phail was roundly condemned by her sisters and mother for not pleasing her husband, and above all for not agreeing to have a child.

[11] Mirra Komarovsky, "Cultural Contradictions and Sex Roles," *American Journal of Sociology*, LII, November, 1946.

The disapproval of her female peers was the strongest weapon used to keep her in line.

The pressure of one's own group represented a double burden. In an environment where success was defined as marriage, and fulfillment as being a happy homemaker, it was hard enough to fight the tide in the first place. If one did, though, there was the additional problem of being seen as a threat to all the other members of the group who had conformed. The resistance of Blacks toward Richard Wright and of women toward Carol Kennicott becomes more understandable in light of the fact that in both cases, the individual protestors, through their refusal to play the game according to the rules, were also passing judgment against those who accepted the status quo. Historically, women and Blacks have kept each other in line not only as a means of self-defense—protecting the new generation from harm and humiliation—but also as a means of maintaining self-respect by defending the course which they themselves have chosen.

For women, as for Blacks, even the vehicles for expressing resentment became reinforcements of the status quo. For both groups, the church provided a central emotional outlet—a place where solidarity with one's own kind could be found, and where some protest was possible. Women's church groups provided not only a means of seeking reform in the larger society, but also for talking in confidence to other women about the frustrations of being a woman in a male-dominated society. What social humorists have called "hen-sessions" were in fact group therapy encounters where women had a chance to voice their gripes. Humor was frequently a vehicle for expressing a bitter-sweet response to one's situation, bemoaning, even as one laughed, the pain of being powerless. But as is the case with Blacks, venting one's emotions about a life situation—although necessary for survival—was most often an instrument for coping with the situation, rather than changing it.

Perhaps the most subversive and destructive consequence of a pervasive system of social control is how it permeates every action, so that even those who are seeking to take advantage of the "enemy" end up supporting the system. When Shorty, the elevator man in *Black Boy* who was known for his wit and hostility to whites, needed some money for lunch one day, he told a white man he would not move the elevator until he got a quarter. "I'm hungry, Mr. White Man. I'm dying for a quarter," Shorty said. The white man responded by asking what Shorty would do for a quarter. "You can kick me for a quarter," Shorty said bending over. At the end of the elevator ride, Shorty had his quarter. "This monkey's got the peanuts," he said. Shorty was right. He had successfully used racial stereotypes and his own role as a buffoon to get himself some lunch money. In the process the entire system of racial imbalance had been strengthened.

Similar patterns run throughout the history of women's relationship to men. The coquette's role is only the most extreme example of a type of manipulative behavior by women which seems to confirm invidious stereotypes. In the classic case of a wife trying to persuade her husband to go along with a desired course of action, the woman may play up to a man's vanity and reinforce his stereotypes about being strong and in control. Similarly, a female employee wishing advancement may adopt a flirtatious attitude toward a male superior. By playing a semi-seductive role and implying a form of sexual payoff for services rendered, she may achieve her immediate goal. But in each of these cases, the price is becoming more frozen in a set of distorted and unequal sex role stereotypes. The fact that overt power and the ability to express oneself honestly and openly has been denied leads to the use of covert and manipulative power. The result is pathological power which simply perpetuates the disease. The irony is that even in trying to outwit the system of social control, the system prevails.

Basic to the entire system, of course, has been the extent to which a clearly defined role was "woven into the texture of things." For Blacks the crucial moment might come as soon as they developed an awareness of whites. In the case of women, it more likely took place at puberty when the need to begin pleasing potential husbands was emphasized. In either case, what Richard Wright said about the process of socialization could be said of both groups. "I marveled," he wrote:

> at how smoothly the black boys [women] acted out the role. . . mapped out for them. Most of them were not conscious of living a special, separate, stunted way of life. Yet I knew that in some period of their growing up—a period that they had no doubt forgotten—there had been developed in them a delicate, sensitive controlling mechanism that shut off their minds and emotions from all that the white race [society] had said was taboo. Although they lived in America where in theory there existed equality of opportunity, they knew unerringly what to aspire to and what not to aspire to.

The corollary for both women and Blacks, at least metaphorically, has been that those unable or unwilling to accept the role prescribed for them have been forced into a form of physical or spiritual exile. Richard Wright understood that continued accommodation with the white southern system of racial oppression would mean the destruction of his integrity and individuality. "Ought one to surrender to authority even if one believes that that authority was wrong," Wright asked. "If the answer was yes, then I knew that I would always be wrong, because I could never do it. . . . How could one live in a world in which one's mind and perceptions meant nothing and authority and tradition meant everything?" The only alternative to psychological death was exile, and Wright pursued that course, initially in Chicago, later in Paris. In her own way Carol Kennicott attempted the same journey. "I've got to find out what my work is," she told her husband. "I've been ruled too long by fear of being called things. I'm going away to be quiet and think. I'm—I'm going. I have a right to my own life." And Beth Phail finally fled her home and family because it was the only way to grow up, to find out what "she wanted," to learn how to be a person in her own right in the world.

Although in reality only a few Blacks and women took the exact course adopted by Richard Wright, Carol Kennicott, and Beth Phail, all those who chose to resist the status quo shared to some extent in the metaphor of exile. Whether the person was a feminist like Charlotte Perkins Gilman, a pioneer career woman such as Elizabeth Blackwell, a runaway slave like Frederick Douglass, or a bold race leader like W. E. B. DuBois, the act of challenging prevailing norms meant living on the edge of alienation and apart from the security of those who accepted the status quo. Until and unless protest generated its own community of support which could provide a substitute form of security and reinforcement, the act of deviance promised to be painful and solitary.

This condition, in turn, reflected an experience of marginality which many Blacks and women shared. In sociological terms, the "marginal" personality is someone who moves in and out of different groups and is faced with the difficulty of adjusting behavior to the norms of those different groups. By definition, most Blacks and most women have participated in that experience, especially as they have been required to accommodate the expectations of the dominant group of white males The very fact of having to adopt different modes of behavior for different audiences introduces an element of complexity and potential conflict to the lives of those who are most caught up in a marginal existence. The house slave for example, faced the inordinately difficult dilemma of being part of an oppressed group of slaves, yet at the same time living in intimacy with and under the constant surveillance of the white master-class, thereby experiencing in its most extreme form the conflict of living in two worlds.

Ordinarily, the tension implicit in such a situation is deflected, or as Richard Wright observed, "contained and controlled by reflex." Most house slaves seemed to learn how to live with the conflict by repressing their anger and uneasiness. Coping with the dilemma became a matter of instinct. But it is not surprising that many slave revolts were led by those house slaves who could not resolve the conflict by reflex, and instead were driven to alienation and protest. For the minority of people who misread the cues given them or learned too late how to cope, consciousness of the conflict makes instinctive conformity impossible. As Richard Wright observed, "I could not make subservience an automatic part of my behavior. . . . while standing before a white man. . . I had to figure out how to say each word. . . I could not grin . . . I could not react as the world in which I lived expected me to." The pain of self-consciousness made the burden almost unbearable. As Maya Angelou has written, awareness of displacement "is the rust on the razor that threatens the throat."

Dissenting Blacks and women have shared in common this experience of being "the outsider." Unable to accept the stereotyped behavior prescribed for their group, they have, in Vivian Gornick's words, stood beyond the embrace of their fellows. With acute vision, Gornick writes, the outsider is able to "see deeply into the circle, penetrating to its very center, his vision a needle piercing the heart of life. Invariably, what he sees is intolerable."[12] On the basis of such a vision, exile is the only alternative available. Yet, ironically, it too serves to reinforce the status quo by removing from the situation those most likely to fight it. Until the numbers willing to resist become great enough, the system of social control remains unaltered.

ON THE BASIS OF THE PRECEDING DISCUSSION, it seems fair to conclude that a significant resemblance does exist in the forms of social control used to keep women and Blacks in their "place." Both groups occupy an ascribed status. A physical characteristic has been the basis for assigning to each a network of duties, responsibilities and attributes. And for both, a relationship of subservience to the dominant group has been perpetuated by varieties of physical, economic, psychological and internal controls which have functioned in a remarkably similar way to discourage deviancy and place a premium on conformity. Notwithstanding the substantial differences between women and Blacks, and white women and Black women, the underlying process of control has been to take away the power to define one's own aspirations, destiny and sense of self. "It was

[12] Vivian Gornick, "Woman as Outsider," in Gornick and Moran, *op. cit.*

brutal to be Negro and have no control over my life," Maya Angelou has written in her autobiography. "It was brutal to be young and already trained to sit quietly. . . ." From a feminist perspective, the same words describe the situation facing most women.

The analogy provides a potential insight into the strategies and possibilities of social change. If women and Blacks have been kept in their "place" by similar forms of social control, the prerequisites for liberation may consist of overcoming those forms of social control through a similar process. In the case of both women and Blacks, the fundamental dilemma has been that others have controlled the power to define one's existence. Thus, to whatever extent women and Blacks act or think in a given way solely because of the expectation of the dominant group rather than from their own choice, they remain captive to the prevailing system of social control. The proto-typical American woman, Vivian Gornick writes, is perceived as "never taking, always being taken, never absorbed by her own desire, preoccupied only with whether or not she is desired." Within such a context, the "other" is always more important than the "self" in determining one's sense of individual identity. It is for this reason that efforts by Blacks and women toward group solidarity, control over one's own institutions, and development of an autonomous and positive self-image may be crucial in breaking the bonds of external dominance.

Yet such a change itself depends on development of a collective consciousness of oppression and a collective commitment to protest. As long as social and political conditions, or the reluctance of group members to participate, precludes the emergence of group action, the individual rebel has little chance of effecting change. Thus the issue of social control leads inevitably to the question of how the existing cycle is broken. What are the pre-conditions for the evolution of group protest? How do external influences stimulate, or forestall, the will to resist? And through what modes of organization and action does the struggle for autonomy proceed? For these questions too, the analogy of sex and race may provide a useful frame of reference.

Whatever the case, it seems more productive to focus on forms of control or processes of change than to dwell on the substantive question of whether Blacks and women have suffered comparable physical and material injury. Clearly they have not. On the other hand when two groups exist in a situation of inequality, it may be self-defeating to become embroiled in a quarrel over which is more unequal or the victim of greater oppression. The more salient question is how a condition of inequality for both is maintained and perpetuated —through what modes is it reinforced? By that criterion, continued exploration of the analogy of sex and race promises to bring added insight to the study of how American society operates.

Linda Gordon What Should Women's Historians Do: Politics, Social Theory, & Women's History*

I want to focus in this talk on the kinds of questions we women's historians are working on and how we choose them. Since choices must be made within our political context, whether or not we know it, it may be appropriate to begin with the reminder that the feminist movement, and the gains women have made because of it, are today facing a strong and possibly growing resistance and backlash. Primarily, we face a strong, new, rightwing political movement, ranging from such single-issue campaigners as antiabortionists to ideological fascists. To some extent this rightwing resurgence is an international phenomenon, paralleled in England, Germany, and other European countries as well as in the Third World. But the Right in the United States alone has made antifeminism its central concern and rallying cry.[1] The character of the Right in this country in part reflects the power of the women's movement, just as in the last century feminism reached its greatest strength here.

The women's movement has produced another kind of backlash among liberals and even leftists, among intellectuals and professionals. This antifeminist response, like that of the Right, is being conditioned by economic recession and the return to a scarcity mentality after the optimism of the 1960s. But, while it is the Right that adopts the direct-action techniques of the New Left—witness the recent sit-ins at abortion clinics—and even threatens us with a taste of gang violence (fire-bombings, gang beatings of gays), Left and liberal antifeminism have moderation, caution, and calm as their standards. We are experiencing a return to the myth of academic objectivity; a return to unanalyzed empiricism and narrow focus in scholarship; a return to the fetish of strict boundaries not only between the disciplines but within them—e.g., social, political, and intellectual history.

These and other changes have spurred me to rethink the relationship of scholars who work in women's studies to the feminist movement. What seemed an adequate relationship eight years ago will no longer do. During the

*Speech at the International Conference in Women's History, Nov. 16-18, 1977, University of Maryland, sponsored by Conference Group in Women's History and the Women's Research and Resource Center, London.

late 1960s the women's historians with whom I met and talked in Boston imagined ourselves simply propagandists for the women's liberation movement. I myself wrote some polemical pieces that I do not like very much now and, indeed, soon came to reject. We quickly recognized that we could not serve up history upon demand or produce heroines, inspirationals, or laments for victims to serve immediate tactical needs, especially as the women's movement's own lack of clarity and unity became clear. But we should also note the importance of some of those ill-founded early polemics about women in history. That kind of world-turned-upside-down thinking, suggesting that everything was really its opposite, has been characteristic of many powerful social movements. This turning of reality inside-out is a way of supplying the vision of a changed future, even if it is described in fantasies about the past.

Needed now, however, is a more complex relationship of commitment to the feminist movement, with a relative autonomy as scholars. One characteristic of this relationship might be that we should take our questions from the movement but not our answers. Certainly, we recognize that the questions do not always emerge from the research itself—that without radical political demands we may not dare to wonder the things we should be wondering. At the least, women's history may dry up if its practitioners lose touch with the polemical and theoretical writings of activists. We will get our answers primarily from the analysis of historical data, but if our questions are dictated by the methods and procedures of our profession, they may not be the most revealing. Obvious as this may seem, we do not always discipline ourselves to choose our topics thoughtfully. The availability of a cache of source material, and of a method for analyzing it, often creates our topics for us.

But this distinction—questions from one place, answers from another—is too simple. We cannot, after all, prepare a list of questions and categories of analysis and then apply it to data, as some social scientists do. We need a mutual relation between our historical era and our subjects and their era. If you listen quietly and intently to the people who appear in your historical source material, it sometimes happens that they begin to speak to you. It is a surprising experience at first, for, as one stares at these women of the past, one is often taken aback at their strange ways: Their language seems incomprehensible, their manners odd, their responses bewildering; and then they suddenly reach out to offer a new word, a new concept, a new phrase or analogy, to explain themselves. Now this experience, at least for me, is most of what is wonderful about being a historian, and I should not like to smother those voices. Approaching them with preformed questions will do just that, will prevent them from speaking, whether the preformed questions come from methodological or political determinism.

Still, historical material, dead people, will not dictate to us what to write. We must bring to it not only questions but also hunches, even theories, based on other parts of our knowledge. And, let us be honest, we are also usually and unavoidably hoping for certain answers. The idea is to keep our expectations and contributions flexible, to remain humble about what we know, and to expect and learn to love surprises.

The small degree of feminist academic success achieved in the United States—and nowhere else I might add—has both advantages and disadvantages for those who want to attempt this two-sided task. It is a great victory that so many of us teach women's history and some of us even sponsor Ph.Ds. We should understand the history of our own professionalization and see that our work rests, both intellectually and professionally, on the bases of work done by at least a century and a half of previous feminist scholars. In this regard I would like to recommend Kathryn Sklar's article about women's historians of the nineteenth-century United States.[2] She shows that material need—that of "respectable" women who had to earn their own livings—provided a much greater impetus for serious historical research and writing than pure conviction did. To recall the circumstances that propelled Mary Wollstonecraft into her career as a writer is to notice an important part of material conditions for the birth of modern feminism.

Thus, for most of us professionalization is not a political choice but an economic, and now social, necessity. While women's history remains at the fringes of the discipline—indeed, still outside it in the view of most historians—many of us were trained in the more central concerns and methods of the discipline of history from which we have gained some methodological and critical rigor. But professionalization has also encouraged among us an increasing specialization that makes it harder and harder to relate to a social movement which, after all, demands opinions about everything. Professionalism makes us busier and busier. It is all we can do to keep up with the scholarship in our "field," let alone read about or participate in social action. Professionalism makes us more and more antiutopian, practical, modest in our demands, as it makes us more estranged from the situation of the majority of women.

Let me make explicit the conclusions inherent in a historical understanding of our professionalization. We cannot, nor should we, reject it. We are stuck with it and are lucky to be stuck with it at this historical moment. We should learn everything possible from this elite, male-dominated discipline called history. But we can also support and maintain confidence in those women trying to do similar work without the advantages and limitations of membership in the profession. A good beginning, at least intellectually, towards that humility might be some critical reading about professionals in general: C. Wright Mills has a lot to say in his *White Collar* and in his essay, "The Professional Ideology of the Social Pathologists";[3] more recently Barbara and John Ehrenreich offered a post-1960s view—one I disagree with but think essential to consider—in their essay "The Professional-Managerial Class."[4]

To move now from the general to the specific, how do professional women's historians try to maintain a living, tense, and stubborn relationship to the women's movement in our intellectual work? I have argued that our historical questions ought to be formed in relation to current politics as well as to open-minded exploration of the past "as it really was." A difficult double task, but let me offer three thoughts about useful questions.

First, we need to be concerned with both objective and subjective reality. We have recently experienced great advances in the availability of objective data: family size and structure, fertility, employment, criminal activity, health, consumption. As a result, we are experiencing a sort of bottleneck in the study of subjective experience, especially since it is difficult to find the historical voices of the common people. But, to resign oneself to this difficulty can lead to dreadful distortions. In contrast to some of the great traditional biographies and intellectual histories of the elite, some "social" historians have recently produced studies of working people who seem to have no emotional or mental life, no cravings for "higher" things. The product is historically false and has a conservative political impact. The point is not that it is illegitimate to collect and analyze objective data, but that the neglect of subjectivity, politics, and intellectual history can create a misleading impression of the totality and a distorted interpretation of reality.

Perhaps some examples may illuminate these problems. We know that in the United States there has been a rather steady shift from the employment of daughters to that of mothers, but we know little about the attendant intrafamily conflict. Similarly, subjective material can lead to misinterpretation if not set in the context of objective conditions. Thus, we would be puzzled by nineteenth-century women's effusive expressions of love for each other if we could not set those feelings within the context of women's family and friendship networks.

Sources that reveal subjective experience among common people may remain scarce. We will have to squeeze them hard and to refine our systems of interpretation. Cultural anthropology has offered useful methods of analysis as illustrated by Natalie Davis' use of the complex and indirect meanings of cultural symbols.[5] We can also turn "psychohistory" to our use. Kathryn Sklar's biography of Catharine Beecher[6] demonstrates that, without detaching the individual from her social and intellectual context, it is possible to enter ego conflicts to illuminate the situation of womanhood at a specific historical moment.

Second, we need to ask questions about change over time. This problem increases as we collect more objective data, which almost always pertains to particular moments. Even comparison of data from two points in time remains an observation of two static points. Change can only be inferred, and a common inference in liberal capitalist society is that it happened gradually. In fact, social change often occurs in bursts. Its study requires close observation and analysis of the process of transformation itself: moments of revolution or of other social disturbances, and social and ideological movements themselves. We shall lose a great deal if the static, conflict-denying myths that now dominate some social sciences—e.g., modernization theory—begin to determine historical research.

So, at least part of women's history must remain committed to an older tradition of social history—the study of social conflict. We can use some insights of other recent social history—e.g., that social conflict is part of culture, often invisible to the outsider. Nevertheless, I am still convinced that the moments of overt conflict express, condense, and ever clarify the conflict latent at other times. They do so not only through struggle, but through the social ideologies they both use and create. Underestimation of the importance of ideology in women's past encourages, and is encouraged by, over-objectivism.

Third, I do not see how one can study social conflict without doing what has been called political history. Since social change only happens through power conflict, it cannot be apprehended without attention to politics. A social history that excludes politics risks becoming ahistorical.

This third observation remains abstract because it immediately encounters a large theoretical problem: the definition of politics, one of the greatest concerns for Marxism at this time. Much current Marxist writing about the State, and the Genoveses' article "The Political Crisis of Social History,"[7] seem to me to miss one of the lessons of the New Left and the women's movement—that one can no longer define politics only in terms of struggle for the State. The State is central to political power in modern society, and political strategies must ulitmately focus upon it; but groups can also wield political power through structures and processes distant from government. I suspect that on this question confusion may be more correct than clarity at the current time, and that an important reconceptualization is in process. But the necessity to include politics in social history still holds. Social findings about women must be situated in relation to political structures or they lose significance.

The Marxist tradition has offered the most accurate analysis of capitalism and of the particular situation of women in it, and the best strategy for a liberating revolution. Nevertheless, during the past decade the most penetrating new analyses of women's situation have not come from Marxists but from independent feminists who, in the United States, adhere to tendencies sometimes identified as "radical-feminist," concerned with patriarchy as an alternative to class. These ideological tendencies have called our attention to questions of reproduction; to the centrality of mothering in determining the female gender; to social networks, family and community, sex and friendship. These are the subjects the development of which has contributed most to women's history and has allowed women's history to contribute so much to history in general.

There are several reasons for this lack of Marxist leadership in feminist theory and scholarship. One is the persecution of Marxist intellectuals—the driving of radical scholarship and thought out of those institutions which allow intellectuals to live, teach, and write. Another is the suppression of creative Marxist thought for many decades by the Stalinist domination of the Communist movement. Had we had a different Marxism thriving into the 1930s, 1940s, and 1950s, we might have avoided the near total suppression of the feminist movement during those decades. And we might have had a more lively and creative social history from which to learn. A third reason has been a Marxist tendency to overemphasize industrial production; ironically, the capitalist class rather than the working class; and formal organization. These emphases are inadequate for a good history of men and almost eliminate women from view.

More deeply, however, it may also be that the situation of women cannot be fully explained in terms of the capitalist mode of production—the subject central to Marxist thought. Our sex/gender system has roots in the organization of reproduction, which appears to have predated all forms of class society. Capitalism has not itself completely individualized people, and production relations are often mediated by other social relations created by reproductive forms of organization—by friendship, kinship, informal work groups.

We need to construct materialist analyses of patriarchal and reproduction forms, which should not be understood as patriarchal "survivals." The relationships that are not directly dictated by capital accumulation are as vital—as "modern"—as capital itself, though not usually as powerful.

In some cases such social patterns, including the sex/gender system, may even prove strong enough to react back upon the process of capital accumulation—for example, through conditioning the kind of labor force available, the forms of worker resistance, even the kinds of demands directed against the State.

As an example of the practicability of such a project, take some recent work on the impact of industrialization on women, which has proven particularly fruitful by trying to encompass both reproductive and productive forms of social organization.[8] The complex patterns that emerge might be viewed as the continuation of a patriarchal economy of reproduction with a capitalist economy of production. This rather old-fashioned use of the word "economy" to include child-raising, kinship, and social cooperation, has the advantage of suggesting that the "old values" were not merely a cultural overlay but also a kind of worker consciousness, different from capitalist-industrial class consciousness but formed in the same way: materially, by the social relations of labor.

This line of research and analysis means an enormous collective labor but need not lead to "jumbo history." Small-scale studies may even prove more beneficial since more amenable to the sketching of women's lives in total context. Women's history has a special need to maintain the sense of totality. If the focus on women is to be understood as merely another specialization within a profession, the legitimacy of our enterprise might indeed be challenged. The most radical assertion we have to make may be the (apparently) simplest: As Joan Kelly pointed out a few years ago,[9] sex must be taken as a fundamental social category, not reducible to any other category, not even "ultimately." In practice, all kinds of topics in social history—family, trade unions, riots, entertainment, housing, nutrition—will have to be analyzed so as to include two sexes, and then put back together with the experience of both sexes included. Sex and gender are not merely analytic categories that one can choose to apply, but basic parts of the human experience that one may neglect only at the risk of great historical distortion.

Politics in the United States today is demonstrating that the sex/gender struggle has the potential to become, once again, a vital historical force. This is the context in which I hope we can place our discoveries about women in the past.

Notes

1. Linda Gordon and Allen Hunter, "Sex, Family and the New Right: Anti-Feminism as a Political Force," *Radical America*, XI (1977) and XII (1978).

2. Kathryn Sklar, "American Female Historians in Context, 1770-1930," *Feminist Studies*, II (1975), 171-184.

3. C. Wright Mills, "The Professional Ideology of the Social Pathologists," *American Journal of Sociology*, XLIX (1943), 165-180.

4. Barbara and John Ehrenreich, "The Professional-Managerial Class," *Radical America*, XI (1977).

5. Natalie Zemon Davis, *Society and Culture in Early Modern France: Eight Essays* (Stanford, 1975).

6. Sklar, *Catharine Beecher: A Study in American Domesticity* (New Haven, 1973).

7. Elizabeth Fox-Genovese and Eugene D. Genovese, "The Political Crisis of Social History," *Journal of Social History*, X (1976), 205-220.

8. For example, Joan W. Scott and Louise A. Tilly, "Women's Work and the Family in Nineteenth-Century Europe," *Comparative Studies in Society and History*, XVII (1975); Leonore Davidoff, "Mastered for Life: Servant and Wife in Victorian and Edwardian England," *Journal of Social History*, VII (1974), 406-428; Batya Weinbaum and Amy Bridges, "The Other Side of the Paycheck: Monopoly Capital and the Structure of Consumption," in *Capitalist Patriarchy and the Case for Socialist Feminism*, ed., Zillah R. Eisenstein (N.Y., 1978); Judith Walkowitz, "The Making of an Outcast Group: Prostitutes and Working Women in Nineteenth-Century Plymouth and Southampton," in *A Widening Sphere*, ed., Martha Vicinus (Bloomington, Ind., 1977); Peter N. Stearns, "Working-class Women in Britain, 1890-1914," in *Suffer and Be Still*, ed., Martha Vicinus (Bloomington, Ind., 1972). This is, no doubt, a most idiosyncratic list of personal preferences. Nevertheless, that such a high proportion of these articles are about European history indicates, I think, the weak theoretical tradition in American historiography.

9. Joan Kelly-Gadol, "The Social Relation of the Sexes: Methodological Implications of Women's History," *Signs*, I (1976), 809-823.

THE DOUBLED VISION OF FEMINIST THEORY: A POSTSCRIPT TO THE "WOMEN AND POWER" CONFERENCE

JOAN KELLY

Feminist theory is today bringing about a major advance in social vision. If we take as an index of the reemergence of feminist theory Juliet Mitchell's 1966 essay on the four structures by which to assess "woman's estate,"[1] we can appreciate how our understanding of women and society has developed. For more than a decade, the women's movement has been confronting sex oppression in the domains she helped name for us–production, reproduction, sexuality, and socialization. Since 1966 we have struggled personally, intellectually, and politically against the socializing of girls/women into the servicing, mother role, and against the socializing of boys/men into requiring it. We have moved in thought, feeling, and action against the restriction of female sexuality to phallus and family. We have struggled to understand how and why male-dominant institutions control biological and social reproduction, and we have been fighting that control. And we have moved in several ways against an organization of work that fosters and profits from the sexual division of labor and the unequal relation of the sexes that flows from it. In practice and consciousness, this phase of the women's movement is no longer where it was when Juliet Mitchell marked out the paths along which we did indeed move; and our theoretical understanding has developed accordingly.

Responding to women's changed, and rapidly changing social situation and consciousness, feminist theory is now at a point where a significant transformation in social vision is both called for and being accomplished. What I propose to do here is characterize an aspect of this advance in theoretical outlook that I see emerging out of the several schools and strands of feminist thought and scholarship. It consists of what I call a unified, "doubled" view of the social order, and it promises to overcome certain conflicts in theory and practice that stem from earlier notions of sex oppression and social change.

Feminist Studies 5, no. 1 (Spring 1979).

TWO SOCIOSEXUAL SPHERES

In examining the sex order (or sex/gender system) of our society, recent feminist theory has shown how the industrial world of the nineteenth and early twentieth centuries construed society as divided into two sociosexual spheres. The bourgeois conception of a private and a public domain, a domain of work and one of leisure, also separated the sexes. Settling women and men into their respective spheres of home and work, it defined the place and roles of the sexes as separate and "complementary."

Our understanding of this view, and its implications for women, has been clarified by virtually all feminist scholarship. Feminist thinkers in the Marxist tradition[2] have traced the divided sociosexual order to the organization of capitalist production outside the home. They have shown how the separation of work (production) from leisure (consumption) really exists for men only. As a conception of society, the notion of home as a refuge from the world of work masks a sexual division of labor. It mystifies women's work in the home, obscuring the fact that this domestic labor helps "reproduce" capitalist and patriarchal society. I.e., procreation and the daily work that goes into consumption (housework) and socialization (childrearing) in the private family sustains the working population; trains people to know and keep their place; and provides for their replacement. At the same time, this unwaged and unacknowledged work of women in the home keeps women dependent on men and bound to a subordinate, servicing role.

Radical feminists,[3] concerned more with sexuality and socialization than with labor, have supplemented this analysis. Focusing upon consciousness and culture on the one hand, as well as the obscure levels of the unconscious, they have analyzed the psychic, sexual, and ideological structures that differentiate the sexes, setting up an antagonistic relation of dominance and subjection between them. We owe to this tradition our understanding of gender, of the lived inequalities of the "complementary"sex order, and how those inequalities are perpetuated by casting all women into the role of Mother.

With different emphases, one on societal structures, the other on psychic-sexual ones, both the radical and socialist currents of feminist thought thus point to the centrality of *reproduction* in women's lives. The defining of women as reproductive beings—as housewives and mothers—is seen as shaping women's self-image and sense of worth; sexual preference and expression; and women's relations with other women, with children, and men. In the Marxist inspired analysis, women's work of biological and social reproduction in the home (procreation and domestic labor) is seen as supporting an economic, social, and political order dominated by men, while at the same time preventing women from participating directly in that order. Industrial society made women marginal to the realm of production as it developed. It excluded women from the modern state. And "official" thought and culture, shaped by the male-dominant institutions of Church and Academy, sought to legitimate this sociosexual division by justifying the confinement of women to their separate sphere.[4]

To define the present state of feminist theory, it is important to note that in the nineteenth and early twentieth centuries, even opponents of the prevailing social order accepted in certain ways its establishment of two sexual social domains. This limited feminist and socialist theories of sex oppression, putting them in conflict with each other at certain points, and in internal conflict as well. To be sure, the different experience of middle-class and working women is reflected in the emphasis one theory put on gender and the other placed on class. But that feminists in the liberal/radical line of thought (as set forth by Harriet Taylor, for example) should generally ascribe the subjection of women to the "personal" satisfactions of male privilege,[5] while socialists saw it rooted in the property arrangements of class society, also points to conceptual difficulties in arriving at a view that would encompass the situation of all women.

This difficulty is especially evident in nineteenth-century socialist theory, which sought to be genuinely comprehensive on the Woman Question. It attempted an analysis of sex and class, and of the public and private domains. But it was never able to "see" sex/class operating simultaneously in both realms. Marxist thought on women, as developed by Engels and Bebel, found in the propertyless condition of the modern wage-earning family *the* material basis (and not just a basis) for the liberation of women. Once the productive property that was now held privately by the families of the bourgeoisie was publicly owned, there would be no patrimony to bind middle-class women to reproduction of the patrilineage. Nor would there be poverty that was forcing working women into sexual service to men. Although this view covered the different situation of both groups of women, it was not adequate to explain either the nature of sex oppression or its causes. Sex oppression was taken to be "private," as having to do only with sexuality and procreation, while causes were all in the "public" domain of capitalism's productive relations. Many socialist feminists developed more complex views. Crystal Eastman, for example, was sharply aware of sex hierarchy in the work force and of male domination in the socialist movement.[6] But the mainstream of Marxist views on the "Woman Question" did not become responsive to the issue of sex hierarchy in social production and social organization, and it continued to regard male interest in the subordination of women (independent of property) as vestigial only.[7]

In addition to differences between socialists and feminists, and between the claims of sex and class, other currents of feminist thought expressed other versions of the divided sociosexual world. Many feminists came in different ways to defend and prize the so-called female realm and its values. In the voluntary motherhood circles, e.g., and even among suffragists and free lovers, as Linda Gordon has shown, traditional sex roles were generally accepted.[8] While resisting male control over sexuality and reproduction, over what they themselves took to be their "natural" domain, many of these women sought to deepen appreciation of family, motherhood, and/or the particular virtues of Woman. Even some socialist women held similar notions, maintaining that socialism would simply make it possible for all women to lead domestic, mothering lives.[9]

In somewhat different form, these conflicting tendencies still divide the contemporary women's movement and feminist theory. In the United States, we oscillate between participating in, and separating from, organizations and institutions that remain alienating and stubbornly male dominant. We are pulled in one direction by a Marxist-feminist analysis of the socioeconomic bases of women's oppression, and in another direction by a radical feminist focus on male control of women's bodies as the key to patriarchy. Our differences have not hampered the ad hoc coalitions formed around struggles for abortion and protection against sterilization abuse; for affirmative action, maternity leave, and daycare; for the Equal Rights Rights Amendment and the right of sexual preference. But differences in theoretical position do affect our broader social commitments and political alliances. They affect our conception of the scope of the women's movement; its relation to issues of race and class; and specifically, whether or how to join with what are still male-dominant movements of resistance to inequities stemming from an imperialist organization of the world economy and society.

Women will not forget how this phase of the women's movement was forced to repeat the first wave in its inception. Women's groups developed out of the radical movements of the 1960s much as they did in the 1840s and 50s when women from the abolition and peace movements came to form their own organizations because men, in those very movements against oppression, retained sex-oppressive structures and behavior. It is when we remember this that we feel the strongest temptation to stay within the supportive network of our women's groups, to restructure our own relationships along nonhierarchical lines, to live our own women's culture. The tension between the need for separation and the will to create social change runs deep in the women's movement and in each of our lives, as do the related tensions between the claims of class, race, and sex.[10] It is my belief that we will live with these tensions for a long time. We will live with them perhaps as long as there is race, class, and sex oppression. For the truth is that the women's movement encompasses all these positions. We need both separation and full social participation to liberate ourselves from our several forms of sex oppression; and sex oppression will not itself be overcome without liberation from all forms of domination and hierarchy.

To say this does not resolve these oppositions. But it may urge us toward other ways of conceiving them. It helps us feel in practical terms the course that feminist theory needs to take and, I believe, is taking. Indeed, the argument I want to make here is that these oppositions stem in part from a social order, and a conception of society, that we have already moved somewhat beyond. Conceived as antagonistic ways of explaining and dealing with sex hierarchy, the conflicts between separation and social participation, and between the claims of sex on the one hand, and race and class on the other, are themselves expressions of the nineteenth-century conception of two sociosexual spheres. It is this conception that feminist social theory is at the point of overcoming—not by suppressing such oppositions, but by understanding the systematic connections between them.

SUPERIMPOSING THE SPHERES

One of the new and striking features of contemporary feminist thought, and of the objectives of the women's movement, is how, despite such tensions, certain differences are being superseded. In thought and practice, neat distinctions we once made between sex and class, family and society, reproduction and production, even between women and men seem not to fit the social reality with which we are coping.[11]

Studies such as Adrienne Rich's on the institutionalizing of motherhood, and those of Dorothy Dinnerstein and Nancy Chodorow on the psychic and social effects of female care of infants, demonstrate how sexual/reproductive arrangements, for example, shape men as well as women—as fathers and husbands, and also as policymakers, as the male gender in whatever role. Those arrangements, societal as well as affective in origin, shape public life and policy in the very attitudes toward nature, life, and power borne by the gender that must overcome the Mother. Similar to this appreciation of the public import of personal relations, is our recognition of the role of social agencies in the childrearing once ascribed to women and private families. In addition to families—and even assuming many of their former functions—nurseries, daycare centers, schools, and the media all participate in the so-called domestic work of social reproduction.[12] And finally, just as the entire economy and society works to reproduce itself, so we have come to realize that women produce, and always have produced, goods and services for society at large as well as for their families. Woman the gatherer may have sustained hunting-gathering societies even more than man the hunter did, and in every age women as well as men have engaged in the basic production of their societies.[13]

These new perceptions are emerging out of a newly complex social experience. With more of the work originally done at home becoming socially organized, and women following their work into the domain of socially organized production, women in increasing numbers are living in both the woman's and the man's world. We are living in the sphere of the family and of social production, and as we do so, we become increasingly aware of how the social relations arising from each sphere structure experience in the other. To be a mother in one domain deeply affects one's position, tasks, and rewards in the other domain. Mothering determines where and at what hours women work, and thus the jobs for which they are available. Conversely, the inferior pay and benefits of women's work in a sex-segregated labor market perpetuate women's economic dependence upon men. They pressure women to form sexual and/or familial attachments to men; and in the family ensure that the man's position will determine the place of residence and the unbalanced allotment of responsibility for domestic work and childcare to women.

Experiences such as these increasingly make us aware that *woman's place is not a separate sphere or domain of existence but a position within social existence generally.* It is a subordinate position, and it supports our social institutions at the same time that it serves and services men. Woman's place is to do women's work—at home and in the labor force. And it is to experience sex hierarchy—in work relations and personal ones, in our public and our private lives. Hence our analyses, regardless of the tradition they originate in, increasingly treat the family in relation to society; treat sexual and reproductive experience in terms of political economy; and treat productive relations of class in connection with sex hierarchy.[14]

In establishing these connections, feminist thought is moving beyond the split vision of social reality it inherited from the recent past. Our actual vantage point has shifted, giving rise to a new consciousness of women's "place" in family and society. From today's more advanced social situation, what we see are not two spheres of social reality, but two (or three) sets of social relations. For now, I would call them relations of work and sex (or class and race, and sex/gender). In a Marxist analysis, they would be termed relations of production, reproduction, and consumption. In either case, they are seen as socially formed relations. They are seen to obtain for women and men, and to do so *at the same time* in any particular experience—be that work or leisure, familial or social, personal or public. Relations of work and sex (or production, reproduction, and consumption) affect women and men differently, making "women" and "men" social categories, just as worker and bourgeois are, and black and white. Relations of work and sex combine so as to give women and men different relative positions in society and the family, different powers, hence different sexual, affective, and social experience. And such relations also affect women differently by race and class. Thus female sexuality is subject to male control by the welfare relation as well as by the marital one. Class and race determine access to contraception and abortion on the one hand, and sterilization on the other.[15] And similarly, with regard to work and class position, women's subordinate position in the sex/gender system is expressed in super-exploited sex-typed jobs for the majority, but also in the discriminatory pay and advancement of more privileged women who do find equal work.

From this perspective, our personal, social, and historical experience is seen to be shaped by *the simultaneous operation* of relations of work and sex, relations that are systematically bound to each other—and always have been so bound. That is, we are moving beyond a nineteenth-century conception of society because our actual vantage point has shifted. But just as the earth and planets revolved around the sun long before Copernicus "saw" that those were the relations of the solar system, so this dialectical (or relational) unifying of our vision of the social order gives us a sounder basis for understanding society—even society of the nineteenth and early twentieth centuries. The conception of two social spheres existing side by side simply masked this more complex social reality. It did not describe the society in which it arose so much as reflect it ideologically. Wittingly or unwittingly, it served to legitimate certain of the bourgeois patriarchal practices of that society. At worst, by separating women out of production and making them "the Sex," it drew a veil of Motherhood over the forms of women's oppression that bourgeois society intensified: the economic super-exploitation of working women; gross abuse of the sexual advantage this gave middle-class men; subordination of bourgeois women to the property and personal interests of men of their class; and subjection of women to the demand for ever-increasing population to meet the needs of war and production.

Even in feminist and socialist thought, formed in opposition to capitalism and patriarchy, the theoretical outlook of two sociosexual spheres led to partial theories of social change, and to partial theories of women's oppression and liberation. From today's position, we have already begun to see how earlier feminist and socialist thought itself partakes of the bourgeois and patriarchal outlook insofar as it subscribes to the dualities that society established.[16] We can no longer focus upon productive relations of class, suppressing those of consumption (sexuality/family) as Marx did, or focus on sex and familial arrangements (Freud, and Juliet Mitchell in *Psychoanalysis and Feminism*) without those of class, any more than we can place one sex in the category of sexuality/family and the other in that of society. To do so violates our social experience and the new consciousness that is emerging out of it. A more complex pattern of sociosexual arrangements is called for—and is appearing in feminist social thought. Feminist thought regards the sexual/familial organization of society as integral to any conception of social structure or social change. And conversely, it sees the relation of the sexes as formed by both socioeconomic and sexual-familial structures *in their systematic connectedness.*

The current political goals of the women's movement also indicate how the earlier, split vision of bourgeois patriarchal society is fading. These goals are neither to participate as equals in man's world, nor to restore to woman's realm and values their dignity and worth. Conceptions such as these are superseded in the present will to extirpate gender and sex hierarchy altogether, and with them all forms of domination.[17] To aim at this, as almost all parties (at least within the women's movement in the United States) now seem to do, is to make a program out of the essential feminist perception, that the personal is political. It is a program that penetrates both to the core of self and to the heart, or heartless center, of the male domain, for it will require a restructuring of all social institutions to change our subjective experience in this way. To restructure how we come to know self and others in our birthing, growing up, loving and working, feminist politics must reach the institutions that fatefully bear upon sexuality, family, and community. Schools and all socializing agencies will have to be rid of sex and sexual bias. Work and welfare will have to be transformed, placed in the humane context of the basic right of all to live, work, and love in dignity. And there will have to be genuine participation by all in shaping the modes and purposes of our labor and distributing its returns. A feminist politics that aims at abolishing all forms of hierarchy so as to restructure personal relations as relations among peers has to reach and transform the social organization of work, property, and power.

The theoretical outlook is just forming in which these several relations between sex and society will be examined. Feminist social thought is just beginning to overcome the dualisms it inherited; to account satisfactorily for sex, class, and race oppositions within a unified social theory. It is difficult, therefore, to describe this project clearly, because we are not yet in a position to look back and reflect upon a development that is not yet completed. Yet there is no doubt that most contemporary feminist thought adopts such a unified social outlook; and even at this early stage, certain consequences can be seen to flow from the redirection of thought it entails. I should like to conclude by mentioning three of them.

(1) Understanding women in such systematically unified terms should resolve those conflicts in feminist theory and practice that result from attempts to reduce sex oppression to class interests, or to see the relation of the sexes as always and ever the same, regardless of race, class, or society. Oppositions of this kind are no longer possible in a view that acknowledges the combined power of sexual-familial and productive relations in our lives, and the fact that these relations serve male and socioeconomic interests at one and the same time.

That is, a sharpened sense of particularity results from this vantage point; but the perspective itself unifies what is at once an economically and a sexually based social reality. Just as we see women and men in this perspective experiencing work and personal situations differently because of their respective sex (or gender) position, so women, because of our different class and race positions, experience sex oppression differently. The relation of the sexes operates in accordance with, and through, socioeconomic structures, as well as sex/gender ones. Hence, it operates differently in every society, and in the class and racial groupings of each.

(2) This unified view should enable us to understand better the persistence of patriarchy. In any of the historical forms that patriarchal society takes (feudal, capitalist, socialist, etc.), a sex/gender system and a system of productive relations operate simultaneously. They operate simultaneously to reproduce the socioeconomic and male-dominant structures of that particular social order. The labors of women that support societal life and foster its values are

thereby perennially harnessed to sustain and reproduce male dominance. And to men oppressed by the organization of labor and maldistribution of social wealth and power in society after society, the dual order of patriarchal society provides in many (but not all) instances the satisfaction of dominion over women.

(3) While our social understanding becomes more complex as the earlier, split vision of society merges into this unified, "doubled" view, the fact that we have such a view indicates that we are in a new social and political position with regard to patriarchy. It has been a strength of patriarchy in all its historic forms to assimilate itself so perfectly to socioeconomic, political, and cultural structures as to be virtually invisible. It could even couch demands for female subordination in terms of the prevailing social and cultural values: Athenian civilization, bourgeois equality (separate but equal), socialist priority of class struggle. If we are now in a position to see—as I believe we are now seeing—how the sexual/reproductive and the economic productive/reproductive orders operate together, our historical moment must be such that there is no longer that perfect mesh between the two that allowed us to see only one order or the other, but never the combined operation of the two. We must be at some distance from a social order that made one sphere, and one set of relations, fade from view as we looked at the other, so that at best we could establish only a few of the social connections between them. Now, conscious of women's subordinate place in the "private" (sexual/reproductive) and "public" (socioeconomic) domain; conscious of how relations of production, reproduction, and consumption operate to make women, as well as men, support a patriarchal social order; ours may be an historical moment when those relations are in sufficient conflict for us not only to "see" how the patriarchal system works, but also to act with that vision—so as to put an end to it.

NOTES

[1]Juliet Mitchell's article, "Women: The Longest Revolution," first appeared in 1966 in *The New Left Review*, no. 40. She revised it somewhat and incorporated it in her first book, *Woman's Estate* (New York: Vintage, 1973).

[2]What follows is not a comprehensive list, but rather examples of contemporary Marxist-Feminist analyses of women's work, in the home and in the work force: Charnie Guettel, *Marxism and Feminism* (Toronto: Canadian Women's Educational Press, 1974), and Dorothy E. Smith, *Feminism & Marxism—A Place to Begin, A Way to Go* (Vancouver: New Star Books, 1977) for general statements of position. For the special analyses of domestic labor and women's work, Margaret Benston, "The Political Economy of Women's Liberation," *Monthly Review* 24, no. 1 (September

1969); Mariarosa dalla Costa, *The Power of Women and the Subversion of the Community* (Bristol: Falling Wall Press, 1972); the English studies in *The New Left Review* (particularly Jean Gardiner in no. 89 [January-February 1975], "The Role of Domestic Labour"); the United States studies by Lise Vogel, "The Earthly Family," *Radical America* 7 (July-October 1973); and the issues of *Radical America* on women's work (7, nos. 4 and 5 [July-October 1973], 8, no. 4 [July-August 1974]; as well as the three issues or URPE's *Review of Radical Political Economics* on women (July 1972, Spring 1976, Fall 1977). The finest synthesis of much of this thinking is Sheila Rowbotham's *Woman's Consciousness, Man's World* (Middlesex, England: Pelican, 1973). All these studies are contemporary but find their forerunner in Mary Inman, *The Two Forms of Production Under Capitalism* (Long Beach, Calif.: Mary Inman, P.O. Box 507, Long Beach, Calif. 90801, 1964), originally in the *Daily People's World*, 1939.

[3]Outstanding examples are Adrienne Rich, *Of Woman Born* (New York: W. W. Norton & Company, 1976), Mary Daly, *Beyond God the Father* (Boston: Beacon Press, 1973), Shulamith Firestone, *The Dialectic of Sex*, rev. ed. (New York: Bantam, 1971), Dorothy Dinnerstein, *The Mermaid and the Minotaur* (New York: Harper & Row, 1977).

[4]There are several historical studies of this development. See, e.g., Nancy Cott, *The Bonds of Womanhood: "Woman's Sphere" in New England, 1780-1835* (New Haven: Yale University Press, 1977).

[5]"When . . . we ask why the existence of one-half the species should be merely ancillary to that of the other . . . the only reason which can be given is, that men like it." Harriet Taylor Mill, "Enfranchisement of Women" (1851) in John Stuart Mill and Harriet Taylor Mill, *Essays on Sex Equality*, ed. Alice Rossi (Chicago: University of Chicago Press, 1970), p. 107.

[6]Because of her sensitivity to sex discrimination in the work force, she was one of the few women committed to the labor movement and socialism who was an active advocate of the Equal Rights Amendment; and, although a socialist and probably a communist in the 1920s, she saw "the woman's battle as distinct in its objects and different in its methods from the workers' battle for industrial freedom." "Now We Can Begin," in *Crystal Eastman on Woman & Revolution*, ed. Blanche Wiesen Cook (Oxford: Oxford University Press, 1978), p. 53 *et passim.*

[7]E.g., ". . . the economic dominance of man over woman which long ago led to her dependency and subjection, does not exist any longer for the modern proletarian. The consequences in other spheres which also flowed from that dependency are now obviated." Henriette Roland-Holst, "Feminism, Working Women, and Social Democracy" (1903), reprinted in *Green Mountain Quarterly*, no. 2 (February 1976): 24. Sometimes called the Dutch Rosa Luxemburg, Roland-Holst was a leading Marxist at roughly the same time Crystal Eastman was active, although she lived until 1952.

[8]Linda Gordon, *Woman's Body, Woman's Right: A Social History of Birth Control in America* (New York: Viking, 1976), p. 114 *et passim.*

[9]Ibid., pp. 240-44.

[10]For the ways race, class, and sex (including heterosexist) oppression are experienced in their combination, and the need for a theoretical position that will respect each and encompass all, see Audre Lorde, "Scratching the Surface: Some Notes on Barriers to Woman and Loving," *The Black Scholar* 9, no. 7 (April 1978): 31-35; Barbara Smith, "Toward a Black Feminist Criticism," *Radical Teacher*, no. 7 (March 1978): 20-27; and and "The Combahee River Collective: A Black Feminist Statement," in *Capitalist Patriarchy and the Case for Socialist Feminism*, ed. Zillah Eisenstein (New York: Monthly Review Press, 1978), pp. 362-72.

[11] For new work systematically connecting sex and class analysis, see Zillah Eisenstein, "Developing a Theory of Capitalist Patriarchy and Socialist Feminism" and "Some Notes on the Relations of Capitalist Patriarchy," in *Capitalist Patriarchy*, ed. Eisenstein. For connections between family, sex, and society, Eli Zaretsky, *Capitalism, the Family, and*

Personal Life (San Francisco: Agenda Publishing Co., 1973); Gayle Rubin, "The Traffic in Women: Notes on the 'Political Economy' of Sex," in *Toward an Anthropology of Women*, ed. Rayna Rapp Reiter (New York: Monthly Review Press, 1975), pp. 157-210; and Rayna Rapp, "Family and Class in Contemporary America: Notes Toward an Understanding of Ideology," *Science and Society* 42, no. 3 (Fall 1978): 278-300. For systematic and historical connections between production and reproduction, Linda Gordon, *Woman's Body, Woman's Right*, and for the social/psychic formation of gender, male and female, the works by Dinnerstein and Rich in n. 3 above, and Nancy Chodorow's several studies which have now led to *The Reproduction of Mothering: Psychoanalysis and the Sociology of Gender* (Berkeley: University of California Press, 1978).

[12] Renate Bridenthal, "The Dialectics of Production and Reproduction," in *Conceptual Frameworks for Studying Women's History* (Bronxville, N.Y.: Sarah Lawrence Publications, 1975). Rosalind Petchesky and Kate Ellis, "Children of the Corporate Dream. An Analysis of Daycare as a Political Issue under Capitalism," *Socialist Revolution* 2, no. 6 (November-December 1972): 8-28.

[13] Traditional Marxist thought regards the relations of production, reproduction, and consumption as forming one systematic social totality. Reproduction is not a separate "mode" of activity; it *is* the social process of production viewed "as a connected whole, and as flowing on with incessant renewal," (*Capital* I, chap. 23). Hence for Marxists, the idea of reproduction includes the notion of procreation and socialization, but applies to the reproducing of the productive system as well. It was chiefly the Frankfurt School and Wilhelm Reich in the twenties who began to work out the distinctive role of the family and sexuality in this reproductive work. Contemporary Marxist-Feminist analysis (in n. 2 above) distinguished women's work within the family. The role of "women's work" in the productive system as a whole has been worked out in the studies by Jean Gardiner, Batya Weinbaum and Amy Bridges, and Heidi Hartmann in *Capitalist Patriarchy*, ed., Eisenstein, and for hunter/gatherer societies by Sally Slocum, "Woman the Gatherer" in *Toward an Anthropology of Women*, ed., R. Rapp Reiter, pp. 36-50; Jane Lancaster, "Carrying and Sharing in Human Evolution," *Human Nature* 1, no. 2 (February 1978): 82-89; Adrienne Zihlmann, "Women in Evolution, part 2: Subsistence and Social Organization Among Early Hominids," *Signs* 3, no. 4 (Fall 1978): 4-20.

[14] On the old model of separate spheres, and the new one see Rosalind Petchesky, "Dissolving the Hyphen: A Report on Marxist-Feminist Groups, 1-5" in *Capitalist Patriarchy*, ed., Eisenstein, pp. 373-90. All the contemporary works cited in notes 10-13 above–and many others not cited here–are establishing these connections.

[15] *Workbook on Sterilization and Sterilization Abuse* (Bronxville, N.Y.: Sarah Lawrence Publications, 1978); Helen Rodriguez-Trias, M.D., "Sterilization Abuse," *Reid Lectures* (New York: Barnard College, 1976).

[16] It was in critiquing Juliet Mitchell that this became especially evident. See Eli Zaretsky, "Male Supremacy and the Unconscious," *Socialist Revolution*, nos. 21-22 (January 1975).

[17] Two major exponents of this view (and there are many, many others) are Mary Daly and Sheila Rowbotham, nn. 1 and 2 above.

Politics and Culture in Women's History: A Symposium

ELLEN DUBOIS

This essay concerns the relationship between the history of feminism and the history of women. It rests on two propositions that I believe are closely related: A feminist perspective is necessary to make women's history a vital intellectual endeavor, and women's history should give special attention to the history of the feminist movement. My approach is basically historiographical: What have contemporary women's historians had to say about the history of feminism and how has this affected their interpretations of other matters?

The revival of women's history in the 1960s began with a criticism of the past traditions of feminism, both as an approach to the liberation of women and as a basis for researching women's history. I am thinking here of everything from William O'Neill's *Everyond Was Brave: The Rise and Fall of Feminism in America* and Aileen Kraditor's *Ideas of the Woman Suffrage Movement, 1890-1920*, to Gerda Lerner's "The Lady and the Mill Girl: Changes in the Status of Women in the Age of Jackson," Carroll Smith-Rosenberg's "Beauty, the Beast, and the Militant Woman: A Case Study in Sex Roles and Social Stress in Jacksonian America," and Mari Jo Buhle, Ann Gordon, and Nancy Schrom's "Women in American Society: An Historical Contribution."[1] The perspective common to all these works was the belief that the feminist movement that had preceded women's liberation did not have a sufficiently broad understanding of women's oppression and therefore achieved its goals, the most important of which was the vote, without contributing much to the emancipation of women. Similarly, previous work in the history of women, much of it influenced directly by the woman's rights movement, was also criticized for its narrowness and its inability to capture the breadth and complexity of women's historical experiences. Mary Beard's criticism of women's history, that it had misconstrued women's past as the history of unchanging oppression and had seriously underestimated women's active historical involvement, was frequently cited and applauded.[2] The women's history revival criticized its predecessors for limiting themselves to the history of a few individuals and organizations, for ignoring the varieties of oppression experienced by women other than the white middle-class constituents of woman's rights, and for mistaking men's images of women for the historical realities of their lives.

Although the women's history revival began with a criticism of traditional feminism and women's history written under its influence, it did so on the basis of a broader feminist perspective. The goal of this revival was a more comprehensive and analytic history of women's oppression that reached beyond questions of political and economic inequality to the total social relations of the sexes. Women's historians of the 1960s and 1970s asked: How did the masses of women experience their lives? What grievances did they articulate? In what ways did they act on their dissatisfactions? What traditions of protest and resistance did they leave us above and beyond the women's rights movement? The answers to these questions have produced a much enriched women's history and a greatly enlarged sense of the relevance of feminism to it. Women's historians have found feminist politics, not just in the woman's rights movement, but in the labor movement, the birth control movement, the Socialist party, temperance and abolitionism.[3] Even more broadly, they have found evidences of protest against male domination and affirmation of sisterhood in domestic novels, benevolent organizations, female friendships, which suggest a very widespread, largely inchoate feminist consciousness among nineteenth-century women. These discoveries greatly strengthen the feminist conception of women's history, which is that the oppression of women and their efforts to understand and overcome it, are central themes of women's experience.

The most significant theoretical formulation coming from these discoveries has been the concept of women's culture. The term "women's culture" has been used by historians to refer to the broad-based commonality of values, institutions, relationships, and methods of communication, focused on domesticity and morality and particular to late eighteenth- and nineteenth-century women.[4] The concept of women's culture shares a great deal with the concept of slave culture and probably derives in part from it. Reacting to a historical theory of slavery that saw black people only as their masters' ideas of them, historians of slavery have analyzed the social structures and belief systems that slaves formed for themselves and discovered the existence of a semiautonomous slave culture.[5] Although this slave culture did not directly challenge the slave system, it did encourage blacks to resist the masters' power and established limits to their exploitation. It is this "resistance" aspect of slave culture on which historians have focused.

The analogy to women's culture is obvious. Like slaves, nineteenth-century women have been ignored in favor of their images—passive, dependent, content, dedicated to home and family. The investigation of women's culture is a reaction to this, a way to see women creating themselves and not just being created. Here too the emphasis has been on resistance. In woman's culture, women developed group solidarity and some degree of psychic autonomy from men. Women's culture itself did not constitute an open and radical break with dominant sexual ideology any more than slave culture openly challenged slavery. Indeed, it was part of the dominant system, sharing most of its assumptions about women and men—separate spheres, women's domesticity, male dominance.

The pressing historical questions about the concept of women's culture center on its relation to feminism. At what point can we say that feminism surfaced out of women's culture? How was feminism in conflict with, as well as a development of, women's culture? What was the impact of feminism, and particularly of the emergence of a women's politics, on the course of women's culture? Women's historians are just beginning to address these questions. In *The Bonds of Womanhood: "Women's Sphere" in New England, 1780-1835*, Cott stresses that "woman's sphere [was] the basis for a subculture among women" in the 1830s, and that it led to the development of women's consciousness of themselves as a group, which was a necessary prerequisite for the emergence of a feminist movement. Yet, as Cott herself suggests, it is important not to confuse women's culture and feminism, or to assume a simple and direct development out of one into the other.[6] From my own work on the political ideas of Elizabeth Cady Stanton, I am beginning to see how woman's rights feminism grew out of a critique of what we are calling women's culture. Stanton was deeply critical of many of women's traditional values. She thought religion stifled women's minds and wanted to replace it with a political outlook, a viewpoint foreign to women's sphere. She criticized the female ideology of self-sacrifice and sought to replace it with one of self-development. Above all, she disagreed with the idea that woman had a special mission in society, and she thought that woman's place should be determined by the same general principles of individual rights and abstract equality as man's was.

From the point at which the woman's rights movement began

to develop, it is impossible to understand the history of women's culture without setting it in dialectical relation to feminism. On the one hand, some defenders of women's culture saw in feminism a serious threat to their conception of women's place. In her biography of Catherine Beecher, Kathryn Sklar writes that Beecher "began the task that was to occupy her for the rest of her career–that of interpreting and shaping the collective consciousness of American women" in direct reaction to the feminism of Sarah and Angelina Grimke, to counter any influence they might have had on women's thinking. The culmination of this was that Beecher published one of the first antisuffrage tracts.[7] On the other hand, the mammoth and powerful Woman's Christian Temperance Union of the 1870s and 1880s developed out of Frances Willard's very creative efforts to synthesize the militance and political outlook of woman's rights with the traditional values and intense loyalties of women's culture.[8]

However, the dominant tendency in the study of women's culture has not been to relate it to feminism, but to look at it in isolation and to romanticize what it meant for women. Another way to put it is that the concept of women's culture, the discovery of the humanity and historical activity of all those whom we once dismissed as "true women," threatens to satisfy the impulse that led us into women's history; it may forestall further inquiry into the system that structured women's historical activity and shaped their oppression.

These tendencies can be seen in the pioneering study of women's culture, Carroll Smith-Rosenberg's "The Female World of Love and Ritual: Relations Between Women in Nineteenth-Century America." Smith-Rosenberg vividly portrays the quality of women's culture and the nature of women's attachment to it and to each other. However, she never really gets outside the female world, to see the larger social and historical developments of which it was a part. She is not concerned with how women's culture arose in history, or how it was transformed. Above all, she takes the separateness of the women's world at face value and does not investigate its relation to the dominant male culture. Conflict between the two worlds is underplayed, so much so that the concept of women's oppression begins to seem irrelevant; and Smith-Rosenberg says explicitly that, despite the discrimination, inequality, and misogyny rife in the ninteenth century, women's historical experiences were too rich, the evidence of their power and autonomy too impressive, to call them an "isolated and oppressed subcategory in male society."[9] Nor does she address the limitations of the values of women's culture, the ways that they restrained and confined women, for instance, by being hostile to both politics and sexuality. Such a picture of women's history has little to do with classical woman's rights feminism, with its focus on political equality, and elsewhere, Smith-Rosenberg has dismissed the woman's rights and woman suffrage movement as "of little importance either to American politics or to American women."[10]

The consequences of interpreting women's social history without reference to feminist politics can be seen very clearly by comparing two recent histories of birth control and women: Daniel Scott Smith's "Family Limitations, Sexual Control, and Domestic Feminism in Victorian America," which ignores the role of political feminism, and Linda Gordon's *Woman's Body, Woman's Right: A Social History of Birth Control in America*, which stresess it. Daniel Scott Smith argues that mid-nineteenth-century American women gained increasing control over marital intercourse, and this enabled them to reduce the number of children they had. He attributes this to the spread of "domestic feminism," by which he means an ideology that encouraged women to win greater freedom and control within their families and through their individual efforts. In addition to helping women to "seize power within the family," domestic feminism functioned among women as a critique of "male, materialistic market society." Clearly Smith's domestic feminism is very close to the concept of women's culture, and indeed some subsequent historians have used it that way.[11] Smith explictly contrasts domestic feminism with the woman's rights movement, which he describes as having a "narrow social base among women," and dismisses because he considers its focus on equality and individuality in public life "limiting as a political ideology" for most nineteenth-century women.[12]

Linda Gordon's approach to the history of birth control and women is very different. Her focus is on the history of political struggles over birth control, and particularly on the rise and fall of a feminist political movement committed to winning reproductive freedom for women. She makes a distinction between the desire and struggle for birth control, which she believes characterizes women's history in all periods, and the rise of a birth control movement at a particular historical moment. She begins her history of birth control where Smith leaves off his, at that point in the nineteenth century when substantial numbers of women began to embrace a birth control ideology. Unlike Smith, Gordon believes that "public" feminism in the woman's rights movement had a great deal to do with the spread of these beliefs among average nonpolitical women. Furthermore, she recognizes that the widespread existence of a pro-birth control attitude among women was not sufficient to win them birth control freedom. What was necessary was a feminist political movement, committed to that goal and capable of struggling with other forces in the political arena over who would control reproduction and to what ends. She traces the rise of that movement in the 1870s, its transformation into a socialist movement in the early twentieth century, and its ultimate collapse in the 1920s.[13]

Gordon's political focus has subjected her book to much more intense criticism than just about anything else written in women's history. In addition to attacking Gordon because of her explicitly feminist and Marxist point of view, the critics all challenge the prominent role that she gives the political history of birth control. They charge that she has taken the ideas of a few irrelevant birth control ideologues and political activists and offered them as a substitute for what the reviewers believe is the real history of birth control use and ideology among "average" women. Here the critical attacks on Gordon come very close to Daniel Scott Smith's approach, in that they all categorically dismiss any impact that woman's rights feminist politics had on the birth control history of the average woman. The critics prefer to concentrate either on the changing character of family and marriage, or technological breakthroughs in contraception to explain why and how women's use of birth control changes.[14]

There is a very sneaky kind of antifeminism here, that criticizes feminism in the name of the common woman, and political history in the name of social history. Underlying all the criticisms of Gordon's book is a challenge to the feminist perspective on contemporary society on which it is based. The question Gordon asks is the one posed by the contemporary feminist movement: Why do women today lack real reproductive freedom, especially in light of the modern technological capacity for contraception? Gordon's critics do not accept the validity of this question. For them, the birth control "revolution" is over, because they see it as a matter of "sexual liberation" or "population control," and not as a question over which people have and will struggle politically: women's freedom.

As we have seen, the interest that women's historians have shown in questions of culture parallel similar concerns in black and labor history, So too do my criticisms, that questions of culture may have come to replace questions of politics, and that it may be time to return to the study of politics from the more sophisticated perspective which the study of culture has afforded us. In a recent review of the work of Herbert Gutman, David Montgomery has made this observation about tendencies in working-class history and furthermore identifies a lurking inclination to rely on modernization theory, rather than political factors, to explain historical change.[15] Like labor history and black history, women's history was deeply "political" in its origins, arising in connection with contemporary political movements and holding certain political perspectives without any need for apology. As these developments have coalesced into the new field of "social history," many of us have felt some anxiety that these intellectual projects will become "depoliticized" and academic in the worst sense of the word. One way to work against this tendency is to insist that in our own writing, we give adequate attention to political questions, and thereby insure that the women's history—or black history or working-class history—which we produce retains its focus on social change.

NOTES

Several people read earlier versions of this paper and gave me excellent criticisms on them: Phillida Bunkle, Barbara Epstein, Gayle Rubin, Mary Ryan, and Judith Stacey. I particularly want to thank Eli Zaretsky who contributed a great deal to the conceptualization of the paper.

[1] William O'Ne''', *Everyone Was Brave: The Rise and Fall of Feminism in America* (New York: Quad.angle, 1976); Aileen Kraditor, *Ideas of the Woman Suffrage Movement, 1890-1920* (New York: Columbia University Press, 1965); Gerda Lerner, "The Lady and the Mill Girl: Changes in the Status of Women in the Age of Jackson," *Mid-Continent American Studies Journal* 10 (Spring 1969): 5-15; Carroll Smith-Rosenberg, "Beauty, the Beast, and the Militant Woman: A Case Study in Sex Roles and Social Stress in Jacksonian America," *American Quarterly* 23 (October 1971): 562-84; Mari Jo Buhle, Ann D. Gordon, and Nancy Schrom, "Women in American Society: An Historical Contribution," *Radical America* (July-August 1971): 3-66.

[2] See Buhle, Gordon, and Schrom, "Women in American Society," p. 4; and Gerda Lerner, "New Approaches to the Study of Women in American History," originally published in 1969 and reprinted in *Liberating Women's History*, ed. Berenice Carroll (Urbana: University of Illinois Press, 1976), p. 350. Also see new research on Beard: Berenice Carroll, "On Mary Beard's *Woman as Force in History*," originally published in 1972 and reprinted in *Liberating Women's History*; also, Ann Lane, ed., *Mary Ritter Beard: A Sourcebook* (New York: Schocken Books, 1977).

[3] On feminism in e labor movement, see Nancy Schrom Dye, "Feminism or Unionism? The New York Women's Trade Union League and the Labor Movement," and Robin Miller Jacoby, "The Women's Trade Union League and American Feminism," both in *Feminist Studies* 3, no. 1-2 (Fall 1975): 111-40. On the birth control movement, see Linda Gordon, *Woman's Body, Woman's Right: A Social History of Birth*

Control in America (New York: Viking-Grossman, 1976). On feminism in the Socialist party, see Mari Jo Buhle, "Women and the Socialist Party, 1901-1914," originally published in 1970 and reprinted in *From Feminism to Liberation*, ed. Edith Hoshino Altbach (Cambridge, Mass.: Schenkman Publishing Co., 1971), pp. 65-86. On temperance, see Anne Firor Scott, *The Southern Lady: From Pedestal to Politics, 1830-1930* (Chicago: University of Chicago Press, 1970); much of the work on feminism and temperance has not yet been published, for instance, Barbara Epstein's forthcoming book on the topic, to be published by Wesleyan University Press. Feminism in the abolitionist movement, on the other hand, is very well documented. For two of the most recent studies, see Ellen DuBois, *Feminism and Suffrage: The Emergence of an Independent Women's Movement in America, 1848-1869* (Ithaca, N.Y.: Cornell University Press, 1978); and Blanche Glassman Hersch, *The Slavery of Sex: Feminist Abolitionists in America* (Urbana: University of Illinois Press, 1978). Here and elsewhere, I am using the term "politics," which contemporary feminism has expanded to mean anything that has social (as opposed to individual) origins, in its more limited and classical sense, to mean anything that has to do with the government of community life and institutions, especially the state.

[4]The first use of the term I am able to find is in the introduction to Nancy Cott's *Roots of Bitterness* (New York: E. P. Dutton & Co., 1972). Also important is Johnny Faragher and Christine Stansell, "Women and their Families on the Overland Trail to California and Oregon, 1842-1867," *Feminist Studies* 2, no. 2-3 (1975); 150-66. Both Faragher and Stansell, and Cott use the term "subculture" rather than "culture." Faragher and Stansell cite: Kathryn Sklar, *Catherine Beecher: A Study in American Domesticity* (New Haven: Yale University Press, 1973); Smith-Rosenberg, "Beauty, the Beast, and the Militant Woman"; Gail Parker,ed., *The Oven Birds* (Garden City: Anchor Books, 1972); and Ann Douglas Wood, "The 'Scribbling Women' and Fanny Fern: Why Women Wrote," *American Quarterly* 23 (Spring 1971): 3-24. Wood, who was one of the earliest contributors to the concept of women's culture, has since reversed her position and written a snide attack on nineteenth-century female sentimentalists, *The Feminization of American Culture* (New York: Alfred A. Knopf, 1977). Other works using the concept of women's culture include: Susan Porter Benson, "Business Heads and Sympathetic Hearts: Women of the Providence Employment Society," *Journal of Society History* 78 (Winter 1978): 302-12; Anne M. Boylan, "Evangelical Womanhood in the Nineteenth Century: The Role of Women in Sunday Schools," *Feminist Studies* 4, no. 3 (October 1978): 62-80; Mary P. Ryan, "The Power of Women's Networks: A Case Study of Female Moral Reform in Antebellum America," *Feminist Studies* 5, no. 1 (Spring 1979): 66-85.

[5]Important recent works on slave culture include: John B. Blassingame, *The Slave Community: Plantation Life in the Antebellum South* (New York: Oxford University Press, 1972); Herbert Gutman, *The Black Family in Slavery and Freedom, 1750-1925* (New York: Pantheon, 1976); Lawrence Levine, *Black Culture and Black Consciousness* (New York: Oxford University Press, 1977); and Eugene Genovese, *Roll, Jordan, Roll: The World the Slaves Made* (New York: Pantheon, 1974). Stanley Elkins, *Slavery* (Chicago: Chicago University Press, 1959) is the classical study of slavery that sees slavery only from the viewpoint of the slaveowners, and against which many of these later historians reacted.

[6]Nancy Cott, *The Bonds of Womanhood: "Woman's Sphere" in New England, 1780-1835* (New Haven: Yale University Press, 1977), pp. 197-206, and especially p. 205.

[7]Sklar, *Catherine Beecher*, p. 132. The anti-suffrage tract was *Woman's Profession as Mother and Educator with Views in Opposition to Woman Suffrage*, published in 1872.

[8]On the WCTU, see Eleanor Flexner, *A Century of Struggle: The Woman's Rights Movement in the United States* (New York: Atheneum, 1968); and Mary Earhart (Dillon), *Frances Willard: From Prayers to Politics* (Chicago: University of Chicago Press, 1944).

[9]Carroll Smith-Rosenberg, "The Female World of Love and Ritual: Relations Between Women in Nineteenth-Century America," *Signs* 1, no. 1 (Autumn 1975): 9.

[10]Carroll Smith-Rosenberg, "The New Woman and the New History," *Feminist Studies* 3, no. 1-2 (Fall 1975): 186.

[11]Mary Beth Norton, "The Paradox of Women's Sphere," in *Women of America: A History*, ed. Berkin and Norton (Boston: Houghton Mifflin Company, 1979), p. 145.

[12]Daniel Scott Smith, "Family Limitation, Sexual Control and Domestic Feminism in Victorian America," in *Clio's Consciousness Raised*, ed. Mary Hartman and Lois Banner (New York: Harper and Row, 1974), especially pp. 119-20, 123-24, 130-32. This article was reprinted from *Feminist Studies* 1, no. 3-4 (Winter-Spring 1973): 40-57.

[13]Gordon, *Woman's Body, Woman's Right*, especially pp. 70-71.

[14]Hostile reviews include: Edward Shorter, *Journal of Social History* 11 (Winter 1977) 1977: 269-74; David Kennedy, *Journal of American History* 64 (December 1977): 23-24; Stanley Lemons, *American Historical Review* 82 (October 1977): 1095; and the bibliographic essay in James Reed, *From Private Vice to Public Virtue* (New York: Basic Books, 1978), p. 439.

[15]David Montgomery, "Gutman's Nineteenth Century America," *Labor History* 19 (Summer 1978): 416-29. Genovese, *Roll, Jordan, Roll*, criticizes the tendency to overestimate the potential for resistance carried in slave culture, but his argument is weakened because it is so often implicit and obscured. Both he and Montgomery are criticized for insufficient attention to political history in articles by British Marxists: Jean Monds, "Workers' Control and the New Economism," *New Left Review*, no. 97 (May 1976): 81-108; and Richard Johnson, "Thompson, Genovese and Socialist Humanist History," *History Workshop Journal*, no. 6 (1978): 79-100.

Politics and Culture in Women's History: A Symposium

MARI JO BUHLE

The relationship of women's culture and feminism is a major issue in contemporary scholarship. Ellen DuBois has made a strong case against historians who limit their studies to women's culture alone.[1] I would like to suggest, in turn, how historians might utilize the knowledge provided by these students of women's culture to recast the history of late nineteenth-century feminism.

The promise is great for that relatively uncharted period, the seeming hiatus between the valiant woman's rights campaigns of the antebellum era and the well-organized and skillful woman suffrage movement of the early twentieth century. Whereas the early and late waves of the women's movement have attracted scholars, the middle period between 1870 and 1890 has, in contrast, drawn relatively few. Two historians have touched upon this era, both to offer dismal assessments of its significance. Aileen Kraditor, in *The Ideas of the Woman Suffrage Movement, 1890-1920*, traced the devolution of political ideology over the course of the nineteenth century by comparing the philosophical integrity of the natural rights basis of antebellum feminism with the expedient, hence pragmatic, arguments employed by latter-day suffragists. William O'Neill, in *Everyone Was Brave: The Rise and Fall of Feminism in America*, invented the term "social feminists" to describe a generation of activists at the close of the century who sacrificed the struggle for women's equality to the "unfeminist" aspiration to reform society.[2] Although O'Neill and Kraditor offered necessary counterpoints to the heroic emphasis, common to most histories of the women's movement written prior to the 1960s and usually by former activists, their revisionist message motivated few scholars to pursue the subject further.

By virtue of sheer magnitude and measurable political influence, the Gilded Age women's movement nevertheless remained a troubling detail. Above all, there was the persistent legacy of Frances Willard, acclaimed by her contemporaries as the century's greatest woman. Willard had aroused masses of women presumed indifferent to woman's rights, had created a national organization of women unprecedented in scale and coordination, and had managed to challenge the concept of male hegemony in all sectors of society.

The suffrage movement itself had flagged until the Woman's Christian Temperance Union (WCTU) touched a responsive chord in hundreds of thousands of Protestant women, white and black, small town and urban, from coast to coast. Although historians could not fail to note Willard's remarkable achievement, its significance evaded them. Mary Earhart Dillon's biography, *Frances Willard: From Prayers to Politics*, offered important clues, but its focus on Willard's political machinations obscured the importance of the movement's social base.[3] Recent scholars unwittingly compounded the difficulty. Most viewed the ninteenth-century experience as the movement of women from the household to market economy, beginning with the appearance of the famed Lowell mill girls and quickening as industrial capitalism grew to maturity; they thus designated the home as the primary locus of women's oppression. What, then, was Willard's Home Protection campaign if not reactionary? For historians writing in the early 1970s, the story of the WCTU was destined to remain outside the parameters of feminist history.

Only recently has the study of the WCTU at last come into its own. Ruth Bordin, who examined the origins of the movement in the 1870s, concluded that women participating in the temperance crusade experienced a "baptism of power and liberty."[4] Barbara Easton, in a forthcoming book on women's experiences in religious revivalism and in temperance, documents fully the process by which women moved into political activism via the WCTU, how they emerged as prime agitators for political rights, economic equality, and sundry causes to elevate women's status in civil society. My own research has led me to believe that training in the WCTU prepared a sector of native-born Protestant women for leading positions in the American Socialist movement at the turn of the century.

This new wave of sympathetic analysis flows directly from the interpretive advances of the mid-1970s. The concept of women's culture, as DuBois rightly points out, is undoubtedly one of the most significant theoretical formulations of recent years. Nancy Cott's *The Bonds of Womanhood: "Women's Sphere" in New England, 1780-1835* has been especially instrumental in establishing the relationship between women's emerging awareness of themselves as a distinct group and the formation of a women's movement.[5] Historians must resist, as Cott advises, assuming simple causal relationships between culture and politics. Yet it is clear that the heuristic scholarship of Cott and others already allows us to look past the abstractions of previous historians and to view the nineteenth-century woman reformers and their demands within the context of their own constituency's sensibilities.

Willard's genius is no longer such a mystery, the success of the Home Protection campaign less than completely puzzling. The WCTU obviously spoke to the inheritors of a tenacious women's culture, defended that culture outside the home, and thereby pushed thousands of women into political activity. Willard was able to tap the sensibility of her sex by addressing women according to the ideals they knew best. This insight does not answer the unsolved question of whether Willard herself was a feminist, but it takes us at least to the point where that question becomes relevant.

Other avenues of women's activity in the postbellum period also need further exploration. Urban reform endeavors, from the women's clubs, charity organizations, settlement houses, to the Young Women's Christian Association, and the women's sector of the great agrarian reform movements, together provide an apt illustration of the magnitude of women's public involvement in the last decades of the nineteenth century. As yet we have few means to understand the mentality or political world view of this expansive movement. As O'Neill has noted, the leadership of this period often reneged on the struggle for equality to concern itself primarily with the fate of the social order. And in so doing, women reformers typically drew on values distasteful or disturbing to our generation: motherhood, the home, sentimental sisterhood, and purity. With political and cultural strikes against them, these women have stood in past interpretations as villains in the history of feminism.

Like the WCTU, these endeavors now demand a reassessment. We will not find feminist role models in the Gilded Age, but we may find something ultimately more valuable. By situating the reform crusades amidst the real experiences of mid-nineteenth-century women, we begin to understand the mediation between the presence of distinct cultural values and their transformation into a political arsenal for the self-advancement of a sex. The significance of leaders' ability to tap latent resources and to foster thereby an unprecedented women's mobilization, becomes a compelling scholarly goal.

Nevertheless, no simple solution can be provided to the problems of how and where to begin this task. Let me suggest briefly two avenues of investigation, useful because they illustrate the themes. They are a collective biography of the movement's leaders, focused on the concept of women's culture; and a concommitant examination of the ideology of the Woman Question, 1870-1890, relative to the ideology of woman's sphere.

Out of the mass of biographical details one can gather on the

Gilded Age's most prominent political women, a single characteristic stands out: their age. Movement ideologues, Mary Livermore and Julia Ward Howe, the WCTU' first president, Annie Wittenmyer, founders of the premier women's clubs, Jane Cunningham Croly and Caroline Severence, chief female litterateur, Louisa May Alcott—these among other outstanding figures of the late nineteenth century had been born between 1819 and 1832 and became leading agitators for women's advancement only in middle age after the Civil War. Many had been involved in benevolent reforms since the 1850s, but a surprisingly large portion had *self-consciously* abstained from the woman's rights campaigns of that era. Many of the emerging leaders of the 1870s and 1880s were thus of the same generation as their peers who constituted the prewar woman's rights movement, but had come to political consciousness at a much later point in their lives. This fact is a little astonishing, almost inexplicable for the sheep-and-goats method of separating our feminist precursors from the presumably more compromised and conservative women of the time. One of the weighty problems that historians might explore is the significance of this lag: Why it happened, how it influenced the ideology of the postbellum movements, and finally the reasons for the later movement's vast appeal beyond the limited circles of woman suffrage and women's rights supporters.

The political ideology of the Gilded Age women's movement provides one clue. Leaders spoke with reverence about womanhood, motherhood, and the home. At the same time, they displayed an acute awareness that these institutions were in the process of alteration. Perhaps the most consistent theme running through the writings, speeches, and memoirs of women leaders of this period is an understanding that the vaunted woman's sphere of their youth had been blown to the winds. Nostalgia was a minor element, displaced by a heartfelt optimism for future, new vistas. Indeed, the advancement of women from private to public life became the premise of the entire Woman Question. To believe in progress, of course, was a mere sign of the times, but these women unequivocally named its agent: industrialism. They believed that industrialism had substantially changed American society and necessarily created a new conception of womanhood. Women leaders in this fashion came to grips with the shifting prospects for the emancipation of their sex.

By recognizing the historicist kernel of Gilded Age ideology, we can begin to reexamine the movement's goals and demands. It is true that suffrage came to be viewed not as symbol of woman's equality with man, but rather as means for woman to obtain other, more pressing objectives. In a strategic shift, parallel to the displacement of utopian by "scientific" or proletarian socialism, the reformers turned to economics as the true key to woman's future. Their principal demand reconciled contemporary women's predispositions with the need for a sweeping change in society: woman's absolute right to labor and thereby her right to secure the autonomy to act with force upon the public sphere. While recognizing the political system under capitalist rule afforded little opportunity for women's immediate and direct participation, the reformers gave to the familiar demand for equality a decisive economic interpretation. The first tenet of the National Council of Women—called into existence by Stanton and Anthony on the fortieth anniversary of the Seneca Falls convention— was not women's enfranchisement, but the demand of equal wages for equal work.

DuBois says rightly that we cannot stop at studying women's culture alone without endangering larger purposes. I would like to add a corollary, that only through a study of women's culture can we assess nineteenth-century feminist consciousness and activity within its social context. The new scholarship on women's culture is therefore crucial if we wish to gain a new perspective on the postbellum women's movement, for its leaders spoke directly to the values that historians have only recently described. We may now see beyond the unfamiliar rhetoric and take seriously the activists' desire to forge, as they said, a political sisterhood to advance women's "entry" into public life. We cannot judge this political expression unless we understand the culture from which it sprang.

The lavish, tenth anniversary meeting of the women's club Sorosis, which was convened in 1878 to celebrate women's accomplishments since the Civil War, affords a unique glimpse into the reformers' *mentalité*. Amidst toasts to "The 'Superfluous' Woman," "The Working Woman," "Principles, not Men," the guests' eyes undoubtedly strayed to the table's centerpiece of violets which read, "Give her the fruits of her own hands, and let her own works praise her."

NOTES

[1] Ellen DuBois, "Politics and Culture in Women's History," *Feminist Studies*, this issue.

[2] Aileen S. Kraditor, *The Ideas of the Woman Suffrage Movement, 1890-1920* (New York: Columbia University Press, 1965). William L. O'Neill, *Everyone Was Brave: The Rise and Fall of Feminism in America* (New York: Quadrangle, 1969).

[3]Mary Earhart Dillon, *Frances Willard: From Prayers to Politics* (Chicago: University of Chicago Press, 1944).

[4]Ruth Bordin, " 'A Baptism of Power and Liberty' The Women's Crusade of 1873-1874," *Ohio History* 87 (Autumn 1978): 393-404.

[5]Nancy F. Cott, *The Bonds of Womanhood: "Women's Sphere" in New England, 1780-1835* (New Haven: Yale University Press, 1977). See DuBois, "Politics and Culture," for the historigraphical development of this concept.

Politics and Culture in Women's History: A Symposium

TEMMA KAPLAN

Specificity about class relations is relevant in all discussions of feminism or women's culture in Europe and the Third World, as it ought to be in any examination of the history of women in the United States. Feminism appears to have two different strains. The more familiar strain includes feminist organizations or ideologies designed to win gains for women. The other tendency emerges as female collective action in pursuit of generalized human goals, which we would do well to examine for implicit feminist overtones.

Women have organized to win equality with men of their class, and this has been the source of feminism among the aristocracy and bourgeoisie in Europe. Female-centered networks and institutions take on political organizational form to assure the survival of groups to which peasant and working-class women belong. Under extreme conditions, in which the ability of women to provide food for their families is impaired, females often mobilize to preserve their community rather than to win gender equality. Until quite recently, this may have been the prevalent form of female political action among working-class and peasant women throughout the world.

Feminism as a political ideology recognizes inequalities between women and men in a given class and attempts to equalize those relationships among propertied groups. By demanding for themselves rights equal to those held by male kin, women, such as the Renaissance aristocrat Christine de Pizan, generated feminist theory about the rights of all women. In the same way, Mary Wollstonecraft elaborated the Rights of Man and Citizen of the French Revolution to include all women and men, regardless of class.[1] With this development, the political theory of feminism assumed the universalist claims that have implicitly characterized it up to the modern period. The failure thus far to achieve the goals of absolute equality—beyond gender and class anywhere on earth—only indicates the magnitude of the liberation struggle feminists, often unconsciously, have undertaken.

Working-class and peasant women from Russia to West Africa have attempted to provide food for their children and to defend their productive rights. Social weapons by which the collectivity of women could chastise a man who battered his wife or who failed to provide for her sometimes became transformed into loosely organized female collective activities against state authorities who violated their obligations to women. Insofar as females have responsibilities that grow from their productive and reproductive activities to protect human life, women periodically violate positive law in favor of their customary rights. This sort of struggle represents a rather different, and rarely discussed, strain within female political life.

Just as socialists, apart from Rosa Luxemburg, have generally ignored the relationship betwen socialist ideology and "spontaneous" eruptions such as occurred in Paris in May 1968, feminists have seldom viewed mass struggles, such as the attempts of women to control food prices or to protect their productive capacities, in light of feminist theory.[2] Working-class and peasant women throughout the world have often fought to maintain their traditional right to feed their families. Under certain conditions, their attempts to defend a traditional division of labor by sex, by which they provide food, clothing and shelter for their households, has brought them into conflict with male political authorities and has turned them into revolutionaries.

Failure even among leftist feminists to confront class issues has benefitted conservative historians who wish to cleanse women's history of the political implications of feminism. The political ideology of feminism carries bourgeois democratic theory to its logical conclusion, namely, it demands absolute equality of all people in every sphere of human life. This invariably raises the issue of class, which often divides women. The extent to which feminism can overcome class differences is still a question, but the class issue itself cannot be wished away.

It is impossible to speak of "women's culture" without understanding its variation by class and ethnic group. Women's culture, like popular or working-class culture, must appear in the context of dominant cultures. Sometimes it is a variation upon the ruling culture. Sometimes it is created from the shards of broken tribal or peasant cultures. Sometimes the alternative culture grows in opposition to the dominant culture. Female aristocrats in seventeenth-century France and nineteenth-century Germany formed salons with men of their class or sometimes apart from the men to develop and assert their class culture against that of a growing bourgeoisie to whom they felt socially, if no longer economically or politically, superior. Under such circumstances, class issues prevailed over feminism.[3]

Women's rituals may provide the context for enormous social solidarity within ethnic groups. The proletarian, female Jewish community of Frankfurt, Germany, had principal responsibilities for preserving Jewish life and for financially supporting their talmudic scholar husbands and sons in the seventeenth century. The ancient female ritual, "measuring the ground," invoked the power of ancestors to aid women during difficult labors and to protect the community against plagues and pogroms. Women used this ritual to mobilize the female population of the community when anti-Semitic female, as well as male, artisans invaded their ghetto in 1614.[4] They failed to ward off their Christian enemies, and ultimately, they were driven from their homes, which were sacked. But their cultural form, here applied defensively, permitted them to mobilize *as women* and implicitly to proclaim women's right to preserve human life.

Female cultural practices sometimes take on a direct political form. West African women, for example, have a variety of ways to make their wills known to husbands, and they adapted these tactics in struggles against imperialism. Traditionally Bakweri women use escalating shame rituals in dealing with men of their village. When a woman has been insulted by a man, she uses other women as witnesses and calls forth the offender. If he fails to satisfy her claims, the women demand that the village head hear their case. If the judge rules in favor of the women, the culprit must pay a fine and submit to female shaming rituals. The women then surround him and sing songs accompanied by obscene gestures. Such a ritual sends other men into hasty retreat rather than stay to watch as their wives, sisters, and other kinswomen join the victory dance.[5]

Igbo women had such a ritual, too. When women wanted to punish a man who had stinted in his provisions to a wife, or had taken concubines, they called the other wives of the village together and humiliated him by singing outside his hut. If the man refused their demands, no woman would cook for him. If he continued to hold out, the women burnt down his hut.

Judith Van Allen has written extensively about the Aba Women's War of 1929 during which Igbo women of Eastern Nigeria adapted such shaming rituals to their struggle against the British.[6] Several years before, British rulers of the Igbo district had taxed men's production and livestock just after they took a census. When the British attempted to assess women's possessions, the women became alarmed, and word traveled along the female market networks that women would be taxed. Black officials, who represented the British, could not convince the women that their fears were groundless.

In mid-December 1929, ten thousand peasant/market women converged on the administrative center of Aba, sang humiliating songs in front of Barclays Bank, attacked British shops, and burnt down administrative centers. When the movement escalated, the police panicked and shot eighteen women. The attempt by peasant/market women to signal the British about the collective rights of women through rituals demonstrated female efforts to speak a cultural vocabulary that the British not only misunderstood, but also reacted against with force.

Ellen DuBois argues that in the United States, domestic and political feminism sometimes represented alternatives to one another. But she does not specify the class of the women for whom this was true. European examples indicate that domestic feminism was not so much an alternative as a stage from which some bourgeois women emerged to participate in moral reform movements or socialist struggle. The vast majority of bourgeois women appear to have led lives of "quiet desperation," as Emily Dickenson described it. "Dora," a bourgeois woman of eighteen whom Freud treated for three months at the end of 1900, never escaped the domestic ties to female relatives, servants, and family friends that enchained her. In real life Dora was Ida Bauer, whose brother Otto Bauer became the leading theoretician and orator of the Second International. Despite common class and parental background, he was able to subordinate his neurosis to an active public life. She, on the other hand, could not escape the domination of her family, to which she was closely tied through female networks. Unable to transcend the sexual hypocrisy she constantly denounced, and despite her identification with female servants, she turned her anger inward to become a life-long invalid. Bertha Pappenheim, whom Freud called Anna O, when he described her case of hysteria, came out of some kind of mental breakdown to become an ardent feminist and social reformer in Frankfurt, but only after her mother's death and her escape from the domination of her mother's wealthy relatives.[7]

During the First World War, working-class women in Russia struggled with problems of economic survival that led them to confront the state and indirectly helped them bring down the Czar. On February 3, 1917, poor women in St. Petersburg demanded bread, stole food from the bakeries, and then joined female textile workers in a general strike the Bolsheviks opposed. When ordered by the Czar to restore order, the generals called in the cossacks. The women pitted their bodies against the soldiers who retreated. By March 12, Czar Nicholas II had fallen.[8]

The extent to which feminism is limited to organizations exclusively dedicated to improving the lot of women and the implicit feminism of mass mobilizations of women to preserve or win human rights remain to be explored. Ellen DuBois stresses that in the United States, theories of women's culture and domestic feminism underestimate the way in which some women, notably suffragists and birth control reformers, attempted to undermine the systematic oppression of all women and the exploitation of working-class women. Although it is obvious, it never hurts to reiterate that suffragists wanted the vote because they hoped to influence legislation, particularly as it could improve the social conditions of women. Birth control reformers attempted to assist poor women whose life expectancy was severely limited by over-exploitation of their bodies through excessive childbearing. Emphasis upon the goals for which suffragists and birth control reformers fought should counteract what Ellen DuBois calls a "sneaky kind of antifeminism . . . that criticizes feminism in the name of the common woman. . . ."

Nineteenth-century working-class women needed all the help they could get, although they allied with bourgeois women for common goals only under certain conditions. What emerges from studies of organizations such as the Women's Trade Union Leagues in Britain and the United States, the Ladies' National Association for Repeal of the Contagious Diseases Acts in Britain, and the Catholic feminist organizations in Spain and Belgium is that working-class women might accept public assistance from middle-class women, but they would not mobilize around strictly middle-class issues such as equal property rights for women. However, when middle-class women used their political skills to aid working-class women to protect themselves from economic and sexual exploitation, they won the solidarity of working-class women.[9]

Class analysis of organizations, movements, and cultures in which women are principal participants illuminates female lives in ways that focusing solely upon women's culture or feminism does not. The original task of women's history—to explore the totality of female experience—requires some investigation into how class in the United States, as well as elsewhere in the world, structured differences in women's experiences and thus in women's culture and in the fortunes of feminism.

NOTES

[1] For the best bibliographical overview of early modern women's history, see Natalie Zemon Davis, " 'Women's History' in Transition: The European Case," *Feminist Studies* 3, no. 3-4 (Spring-Summer 1976): 83-103.

[2] See my forthcoming article, "Community and Class Consciousness in Nineteenth Century Andalusia," *Political Power and Social Theory* 1, no. 2 (May 1980).

[3] Carolyn Lougee, *Le Paradis des Femmes: Women, Salons and Social Stratification in Seventeenth Century France* (Princeton, N.J.: Princeton University Press, 1976) presents quite a different theory from mine, but I am nevertheless indebted to her work.

[4] A. Freimann and F. Kracauer, *Frankfort*, trans. Bertha Szold Levin (Philadelphia, Penn.: The Jewish Publication Society of America, 1929), pp. 73-107; and Mark Zborowski and Elizabeth Herzog, *Life Is With People: The Culture of the Shtetl* (New York: Schocken Books, 1976), p. 314.

[5] Shirley Ardener, "Sexual Insult and Female Militancy," in *Perceiving Women*, ed. Shirley Ardener (New York: John Wiley and Sons, 1977), pp. 29-53, 30.

[6] Judith Van Allen, " 'Sitting on a Man': Colonialism and the Lost Political Institutions of Igbo Women," *Canadian Journal of African Studies* 6, no. 2 (1972): 165-181; 181; " 'Aba Riots' or Igbo 'Women's War'? Ideology, Stratification, and the Invisibility of Women," in *Women in Africa: Studies in Social and Economic Change*, ed. Nancy J. Hafkin and Edna G. Bay (Stanford, Calif.: Stanford University Press, 1976), pp. 59-85.

[7] Temma Kaplan, "Female Nature and Nurturance: Freud and the Dora Case," *From Feudalism to Feminism: Women in Social Movements* (forthcoming).

[8] Dale Ross, "The Role of the Women of Petrograd in War, Revolution and Counter-Revolution, 1914-1921" (Ph.D. dissertation, Rutgers University, 1973), pp. 30-32; Bernice Glatzer Rosenthal, "Love on the Tractor: Women in the Russian Revolution and After," in *Becoming Visible: Women in European History*, ed. Renate Bridenthal and Claudia Koonz (Boston: Houghton Mifflin Co., 1977), pp. 370-99.

[9] For discussions of the Women's Trade Union League, see Nancy Schrom Dye, "Creating a Feminist Alliance: Sisterhood and Class Conflict in the New York Women's Trade Union League, 1903-1914," *Feminist Studies* 3, no. 2-3 (1975): 24-38; and Nancy Schrom Dye, "Feminism or Unionism? The New York Women's Trade Union League and the Labor Movement," and, Robin Miller Jacoby, "The Women's Trade Union League and American Feminism," both articles in *Feminist Studies* 3, no. 1-2 (Fall 1975): 111-40. For an outstanding exploration of feminist cross-class alliances in the Ladies' National Association for Repeal of the Contagious Diseases Acts, see Judith R. Walkowitz and Daniel J. Walkowitz, " 'We Are Not Beasts of the Field': Prostitution and the Poor in Plymouth and Southampton Under the Contagious Diseases Act," *Feminist Studies* 1, no. 3-4 (Winter-Spring 1973): 73-106.

[10] For a preliminary discussion of Catholic feminism in Spain, see Mary Nash, "La problemática de la mujer y el movimiento obrero en España," in *Teoría y práctica del movimiento obrero en España*, ed. Albert Balcells (Valencia, Spain: Fernando Torres, 1977), pp. 241-80.

Politics and Culture in Women's History: A Symposium

GERDA LERNER

Ellen DuBois raised a number of interesting and valuable questions, yet I find it impossible to address her questions in the terms in which they were posed. For example, regarding her proposition that "women's history should give special attention to the history of the feminist movement," and her question, "How was feminism in conflict with, as well as a development of, women's culture?" the answers really depend on how we define the terms. All the words we use derive from a language based on androcentric thought and from academic scholarship that tends to subsume, trivialize, or marginalize women and their activities. Therefore, the problem of redefinition is a basic problem of feminist scholars in our search for an appropriate conceptual framework. The terms we use define the questions we can ask: The terms we use either sharpen or blur the distinctions we make between various concepts. Unless we sharply and distinctly redefine, we always retain the traditional meaning.

The traditional meaning of the word "feminism" is so generalized that its use defies precise analysis and tends to obliterate distinctions and stages of development. Here are a few current definitions:

Feminism means a) a doctrine advocating social and political rights of women equal to those of men; b) an organized movement for the attainment of these rights; c) the assertion of the claims of women as a group and d) belief in the necessity of large-scale social change to increase the power of women. Definition a) which, describes a belief system, is frequently combined with definition b). Definition c) implies the concept of the oppression of women, which makes of them a distinct group seeking redress. Most persons using the term subsume under it definitions a-c, but d), the necessity for basic social change in the system to which women demand equal access, is not necessarily accepted by feminists. To add to the vagueness and complexity of the term, there is unclarity about what is meant under b), since the organized movement for women's rights encompasses in fact a number of distinct historical movements, i.e. the nineteenth century suffrage movement, the nineteenth century woman's rights movement, the twentieth century women's liberation movement. The imprecision and looseness of the term demands clarification and more disciplined definitions.

Just what do we mean, then, when we say feminist? I have some time ago called attention to the utility of more precise definitions in an effort to distinguish between the nineteenth- and twentieth-century woman's movements.[1] I then suggested that, as a first step, we distinguish between "woman's rights" and "woman's emancipation" [liberation].[2]

The *woman's rights* movement means a movement concerned with winning for women equality with men in all aspects of society and giving them access to all rights and opportunities enjoyed by men in the institutions of that society. Thus, the woman's rights movement is akin to the civil rights movement in wanting equal participation for women in the status quo, essentially a reformist goal.

Woman's emancipation means: freedom from oppressive restrictions imposed by sex; self-determination; autonomy.

Freedom from oppressive restrictions imposed by sex means freedom from biological and societal restrictions. Self-determination means being free to decide one's own destiny; being free to define one's own social role; having the freedom to make decisions concerning one's own body. Autonomy means earning one's own status, not being born into it nor marrying it; it means financial and cultural independence; freedom to chose one's own lifestyle and sexual preference, all of which implies a radical transformation of existing institutions, values, and theories.

The striving for women's emancipation predates the women's rights movement. It is not always a *movement*, for it can be a level of consciousness, a stance, an attitude, as well as the basis for organized effort. Where woman's rights advocates ask for equality with with men, emancipationists seek women-defined goals and process. Many women, who do not consider themselves feminists or part of any woman's movement, are emancipationists. The term also includes the "cultural feminists", such as Frances Wright and Emma Goldman, and sexual reformers of such different types as Margaret Sanger and Isadora Duncan. While some of the early suffragists embraced both levels of consciousness, the majority did not. Most emancipationists also advocated woman's rights. Thus, I would argue, that "woman's emancipation" is a more advanced stage of consciousness than "woman's rights."

Returning to Ellen DuBois's "the feminist movement," the term is inadequate, for it can mean the suffrage movement or the woman's emancipation movement of the nineteenth century. Both were "feminist," but each represented feminism of a different kind. I would suggest, as a useful beginning, that we separate "woman's rights feminism" and "woman's emancipation feminism." The latter would, in the nineteenth century, embrace the social and cultural transformations sought by utopians, advocates of free love, reproductive freedom, and self-determination for women, and revolutionary feminist thinkers such as Charlotte Perkins Gilman. Was Catharine Beecher a feminist? Yes, and so were Mary Lyon and Dorothea Dix, all three opponents of the organized woman's rights movement. They were feminist in working for the emancipation of women from educational and institutional restrictions; as such their impact on the development of feminist consciousness was perhaps more decisive than was the impact of the early suffrage movement. Yet their feminist consciousness remained on the first level, that of "rights." In the post-Civil war period, the true distinction between Stanton and Anthony and the American Woman Suffrage Association (AWSA) was not so much their embracing different political strategies, but the fact that Stanton and Anthony worked for woman's emancipation, defining their feminism more radically and thus embracing sexual and cultural transformation, whereas the AWSA worked for woman's rights. Later, Anthony would retreat from that position, while Stanton advanced in it, leading to her isolation from the suffrage movement leadership.

Applying the terms to twentieth-century feminism, the distinctions are more complex, since the modern women's movement, even in its broadest alliance (the Houston platform) embraces both woman's rights and woman's emancipation demands. Still, the terms help us to distinguish between those individuals and groups who define their goal as wanting into the system on an equal basis (or better, who want into the system in male-defined terms) and those emancipationists who want that and more—the transformation of patriarchy into a different system. It is a system for which we have, as yet, neither a name nor a definition on which we can agree. Yet, whatever our disagreement on means and ends, emancipationists will agree that women must be not on the margin, but at the center of definition and in control of the transformation of any new system. Thus, emancipationists are woman-centered in their thinking.

Keeping these complexities in mind, I believe it is desirable to be as specific as possible, when discussing a particular historical situation or movement. To come back to Ellen DuBois's initial question, I would recast it to read: "Was the feminist ideology of the nineteenth-century woman's rights movement in conflict with the concept of woman's culture?" This brings us to yet another troublesome term.

Ellen DuBois uses the term "woman's culture" as though it were meant to define "woman's sphere." The important distinction here, as elsewhere, is whether we use the term within a male-defined context or within a female-defined context. Historically, "woman's sphere" is a nineteenth-century term, denoting those aspects of activity and function men determined appropriate to women. The fact that many women, through social conditioning, also accepted that definition as "natural," does not make it a woman's definition. Despite the rhetorical claims of its advocates, that the domestic sphere women were to occupy was a "higher sphere," the essence of the doctrine of "separate spheres" is that it consigns women to activities which are subordinate in importance and power to those of men.

If one speaks of women's activities and goals from a woman-centered point of view, one calls that which women do and the way in which they do it, woman's culture. Confining the term to the nineteenth century, which I think is appropriate and useful, "woman's culture" is women's redefinition in their own terms. The term implies an assertion of equality and an awareness of sisterhood, the communality of women.[3] Carroll Smith-Rosenberg has shown particularly well how this process worked in the case of the women in the moral reform societies in the 1830s.[4] Similarly, women in the antislavery movement stepped outside their male-defined auxiliary role, challenged the limitations of this role openly, and found their own mode of work and organizing in petitioning, educational work, and fundraising.

The term "woman's culture" has also been used in its anthropological sense, to encompass the familial and friendship networks of women, their affective ties, their rituals. It is important to understand that "woman's culture" is not and should not be seen as a subculture. It is hardly possible for the majority to live in a subculture. As Joan Kelly has so aptly put it, "woman's place is not a separate sphere or domain of existence but a position within social existence generally."[5] Women live their social existence within the general culture and, whenever they are confined by patriarchal restraint or segregation into separateness (which always has subordination as its purpose), they transform this restraint into complimentarity (asserting the importance of woman's function, even its "superiority") and redefine it. Thus, women live a duality—as members of the general culture and as partakers of women's culture. What happens to women's culture in periods of relative egalitarianism and the opening to women of access to most institutions of the society, remains to be studied. It is, at all events, a most useful and specific term applied to the nineteenth-century United States.

To state, as DuBois does, that (Daniel Scott) Smith's "domestic feminism is very close to the concept of women's culture" is confusing and misleading. The term "domestic feminism" is based on Smith's assertion that nineteenth century women in making birth control decisions (a factual assertion which is in itself open to question), exercised some kind of real power. He observes slight shifts in status and decision making of a powerless group and interprets these as power. "Domestic feminism" is not close to "women's culture," it is simply good old "woman's sphere," updated. It is an objectional term, like the media-engendered shift from "housewife" to "homemaker." Most labor historians would not describe a union contract as proof of workers' decision-making power over their employers, although many recalcitrant employers might so describe it. The historian would accurately describe a union contract as an instrument by which a relatively powerless group seeks to exert some countervailing pressure within the context of employer or corporate power. When it comes to familial and sexual relations, the issue becomes more easily blurred.

If we call what women do in a patriarchal world and the way they do it "woman's culture," then there is no point in counterposing this concept to "feminism." Woman's culture is the ground upon which women stand in their resistance to patriarchal dominance and their assertion of their own creativity in shaping society. Out of this ground rise different levels of feminist consciousness: first, the recognition of a collective wrong suffered; then, efforts to remedy these wrongs in political, economic, and social life. These efforts, when institutionalized, become "movements." Movements in turn give rise to new forms of woman's culture, for example, sex-segregated or separatist institutions or modes of livin; Finally, feminist consciousness gives rise to autonomously defined demands and theory. At a certain level of thought and activity, women make the shift from the andro-centricity, in which they have been schooled, to "woman-centeredness." In the field of scholarship, woman-centered scholarship seeks to find a new framework of interpretation from within women's historical culture, leading to their emancipation.

As Ellen DuBois observed, as long as historians stay within the confines of andro-centric thought while viewing women in history, they are not generally subject to attack and distortion. They may even receive a pat on the back for "scholarly impartiality." But when we begin to practice woman-centered scholarship, stepping outside of androcentric question-setting and value judgments, then we are likely to be, as Linda Gordon was, attacked for injecting "political judgments" into supposedly value-free scholarship. Nevertheless this must be done, not by all historians of women's history, but by those whose consciousness works at that level. The terms of our discourse and our definitions are our tools in the struggle for our intellectual emancipation. Let's keep them clean; let's keep them sharp.

NOTES

[1]Gerda Lerner, "Women's Rights and American Feminism," *American Scholar* 40, no. 2 (Spring 1972): 235-48.

[2]I prefer the term "emancipation" to "liberation", because it avoids the meaning which resonates in "liberation" that women are like other groups (colonials, slaves). While there are likenesses, the *distinctions* between women and other oppressed groups are crucial and should be stressed, rather than blurred.

[3]To use the otherwise *not* analogous slave comparison: to speak of slave culture implies the humanity and implicit equality of the slave, if not in actuality, so in right. No member of the master class would refer to or accept the concept of a slave culture.

[4]Carroll Smith-Rosenberg, "Beauty, The Beast and the Militant Woman: A Case Study in Sex Roles and Social Stress in Jacksonian America," *American Quarterly* 23 (October 1971): 562-84.

[5]Joan Kelly, "The Doubled Vision of Feminist Theory: A Postscript to the 'Woman and Power' Conference," *Feminist Studies* 5, no. 1 (Spring 1979): 216-27.

Politics and Culture in Women's History: A Symposium

CARROLL SMITH-ROSENBERG

Ellen DuBois's article attempts a new feminist critique of women's history. Questioning the close ties that have linked women's history and contemporary social history, it espouses a revisionist women's history that would focus upon political issues and elite cadres of activists. Central to this critique is an evaluation of the relation of women's history to feminism and to "women's culture." Although many of us have found these three phenomena mutually reinforcing, the author argues that "women's culture" is extrinsic to feminism and, indeed, frequently opposed to it. Within the author's revisionist framework, "women's culture" thus becomes an aberrant factor within the canon of women's history. Rather than studying women's interaction with each other, the author admonishes, we should focus our attention on feminists' resistance to male oppression.

I take issue with this article on three grounds. First, I cannot accept a revisionist women's history that views with suspicion an analysis of the experiences of the average woman. Second, as a historian, I disagree with an analytic framework which insists on the causal centrality of the political and ignores the economic, demographic, and institutional factors that helped shape the political. Third, I reject both the author's argument that women's culture is dialectically opposed to feminism and her warning of the dangers inherent in the continued exploration of women's culture. We cannot understand the public acts of a few women without understanding the private world that produced them. Women's interaction with each other formed an intrinsic component of the female experience and of feminism. It constitutes, consequently, a legitimate and fruitful category within women's history.

While ostensibly advocating a women's history that does not overemphasize women's "unchanging oppression," ignore the "breadth and complexity of women's historical experience," or confuse "men's image of women" with women's "historical reality," the article ends by proposing just such an analytic framework.[1] The author urges historians of women to focus primarily upon men's oppression of women and women's efforts to understand and overcome it [that oppression]." Historians of women, we are told, ought to answer the question "How did . . . women experience their lives?" by examining women's "traditions of protest and and resistance."[2] But just as the reality of our world is not limited to men's image of us, so the parameters of our experience are not set by male exploitation, either direct or indirect. To insist, as Ellen DuBois does, on the centrality of the male-female oppressive dyad, ironically maintains men as the central actors in women's past and thus transforms women's history into a subcateogry of the history of male values and behavior.

This insistence upon a political focus causes additional problems. The author refers approvingly to a second major criticism of earlier histories of women—that they focused primarily upon the exploitation experienced by white middle-class women and upon bourgeois definitions of oppression. Yet, at the same time, by urging us to direct our attention primarily at political issues such as birth control, temperance, abolition, socialism, which had little appeal to the Catholic and black women who comprised a majority of the nineteenth-century working classes, she ends by advocating the bourgeois analysis she commenced by condemning. Emma Goldman's advocacy of birth control is crucial to us as bourgeois feminists in the 1970s. It tells us very little, however, about the values and economic realities of working-class French Canadian and Italian women in northern factory towns, or of either black or white women in the rural South during the late nineteenth or early twentieth centuries.[3] A sophisticated understanding of these women's lives, on the other hand, might help us fathom some of the appeal that the antiabortion movement of the 1970s holds for their daughters and granddaughters.

This insistence on the centrality of political issues distorts not simply our understanding of women's experiences, but also our analysis of the origins of their oppression. While paying lip service to an exploration of the roots of women's oppression in social structural factors, the article proceeds to warn women historians against "a lurking inclination to rely on modernization theory, rather than political factors, to explain historical change." Insisting on the preeminence of political and ideological factors as causal diminishes the importance of demographic, technological, and economic developments. It ends by pitting political history against social history which it condemns as "academic in the worst sense of the word."[4]

To define women's history as the study of male oppression and of women's organized resistance challenges the basic direction that women's history has taken over the past decade. One of the principal goals of women's history has been to so redefine the canons of traditional history that the events and processes central to women's experience assume historical centrality, and women are recognized as active agents of social change. Indeed, a historical analysis that fails to do so distorts our understanding of past societies. A second goal of women's history has been to explore the complexity of the female experience. The purpose of women's history, thus, is not to create a pantheon of ideologically correct heroines, but to analyze the evolution of women's roles, in thecontext of the effect of economic change upon a society's allocation of economic resources and power, institutional developments, and ideological conceptualizations.

The stated goal of this article is to evaluate current historical scholarship from the perspective of contemporary feminism. Yet at no time does the author clarify her usage of "feminism." She comes closest when discussing Linda Gordon's *Woman's Body, Woman's Right: A Social History of Birth Control in America.*[5] A "feminist" orientation seems there to involve first a stress upon "the role of political feminism" (later referred to as " 'public' feminism") and second, a primary concern with issues of women's reproductive freedom. In contrast, the investigation of women's relations with other women is categorized as counterproductive. None can question the centrality of reproductive freedom to the contemporary women's movement. But physiological and sexual autonomy cannot be defined in such limited and simplistic terms. It is wedded to female economic autonomy and involves issues and options of behavior far broader and more fundamental in their challenge to power relations and social structure than the simple prevention of conception. This focus on birth control not only reinforces traditional views of female sexuality, it again posits men as the active agents in women's lives. It says, in effect, that the key feminist sexual issue is how to control the effect of sperm. Even more fundamentally, to fail to include the concept of female solidarity in a definition of feminism ignores what is probably the most central component of both nineteenth-century and contemporary feminism. This omission compounds the article's male orientation and its emphasis on women's victimization.

How can we understand this adherence to men and politics? The answer may be discerned in the author's fear of and condemnation of "women's culture." She envelops the phrase in innuendo and foreboding. DuBois tells us that "The concept of women's culture threatens to satisfy the impulse that led us into women's history. . . ." "Questions of culture," she says later "may have come to replace questions of politics. . . ." No trend could be more dangerous, we are warned, because "women's culture," far from forming the keystone of feminism, constitutes its dialectical opposite. The crux of this argument, as I understand it, is as follows. Historians and feminists have recently turned their attention away from an analysis of men's political exploitation of women to an exploration of the "female world." To study the sources of our strength and solidarity, however, the article implies, will lead us to withdraw from the struggle with and against men. We are in danger of becoming modern Narcissae and, like the unicorn, entrapped by the impassioned contemplation of ourselves.

Although a discussion of "women's culture" lies at the center of the author's argument, her definition is unclear and contradictory. The article begins by defining "women's culture" as "the broad-based commonality of values, institutions, relationships, and methods of communication, focused on domesticity and morality particular to late eighteenth- and nineteenth-century women." The article later defines the study of "women's culture" as "a way to see women creating themselves and not just being created." But the author proceeds to undercut her own definition of "culture" by arguing that "women's culture" shares most of the dominant values of male culture—especially men's view of women's proper place. "Indeed," the author states, "it was part of the dominant system, sharing most of its assumptions about women and men . . . and reinforcing them in the process." These definitions are contradictory and confusing. DuBois, while choosing to use the term "culture," ignores the very attributes that define that term. A culture must have its own autonomous values, identities, symbolic systems, and modes of communication. If this putative "women's culture" accepted and reinforced the values of the dominant, male culture to such an extent, it cannot be classified as a "culture" at all—or even as a subculture.[6]

But the author does not proceed to address the complex and controversial relation of female and male cultural forms within the same society. Rather, she hastily drops all ethnographic components from her definition of culture. Although originally defining "women's culture" as a composite of female values, institutions, relationships, and modes of communication, the author proceeds to redefine it as an ideological statement of women's subservience to men. No longer, that is, does she use "women's culture" to conjure up a world women created for themselves. It has become "the Cult of True Womanhood," an idea men created about women. DuBois ends her discussion of "women's culture" by describing it as a system of ideas defended by Catherine Beecher and assailed by Stanton and the Grimké sisters.

The one constant in this shifting definition of "Women's culture" is the author's juxtaposition of "women's culture" and feminism. Indeed, this tenacity provides the key to understanding the implications of her argument. Although the author asks us to examine how political feminism emerged out of the female world, DuBois preempts such an analysis by insisting on their dialectical opposition. "From the point at which the women's rights movement began to develop, it is impossible to understand the history of women's culture without seeing it in dialectical relation to feminism." One's first response is simply to dismiss the author's statement as a confused use of the term culture. But far more is implied in the author's argument than is overtly stated. By not clarifying her definition of women's culture, the author is able to imply a causal relation between two unrelated meanings. If women's culture is equated both with the Cult of True Womanhood and with female-identified institutions, relationships, and methods of communication, then the argument is implicitly made that women's networks and communities, separate from men, will generate neither a sense of female solidarity and strength nor a radical critique of society. Rather, such female interaction will encourage conservative collaboration with the dominant male power system. This is DuBois's real message.

Both the nature of a female world, separate from men, and its political implications for women and men are, of course, far more complex than the article suggests. Certain aspects of the interaction of bourgeois, nineteenth-century women with each other, for instance, did encourage conformity and resistance to change. This is especially evident in the relationship that developed between mothers and daughters, beginning in the 1870s and 1880s, as role options expanded for daughters. Jane Addams has written eloquently on the role of the unmarried woman within her family of origin. Mothers and other older women frequenty acted to thwart their daughters' new role aspirations. Daughters ceased to find spaces of safety within their mothers' homes. Feminism, on the other hand, is intricately rooted in women's experience of their separateness from men and in their primary identification as women. Only by studying women's interaction with each other can we begin to untangle the intricate relation between the female world and the economic and institutional power structure of the "external world."

Woven into the article's criticism of "women's culture" is an analysis of my work. Yet it is difficult to recognize my own analyses in this critique. On the most fundamental level, my words are quoted out of context and terms are attributed to me that do not appear in any of my writings. I never stated explicitly or implicitly that "despite the discrimination, inequality, and misogyny rife in the nineteenth century, women's historical experiences were too rich, the evidence of their power and autonomy too impressive, to call them an 'isolated and oppressed subcategory of male society' ". The part of that statement that is attributed directly to me is quite brief: "an isolated and oppressed subcategory. . . ." I did not write these words as part of an argument for the autonomy of female culture, but rather as part of a methodological discussion in which I argued that advice books written by men about women did not encompass the totality of the female experience. "Women, however," I wrote, "did not form an isolated and oppressed subcategory of male society. Their letters and diaries indicate that women's sphere had an essential integrity and dignity that grew out of women's shared experiences and mutual affection." "To interpret such friendships more fully," I continued, "they must be related to the structure of the American family and to the nature of sex-role divisions and of male-female relations both both within the family and in society generally. The female friendship must not be seen in isolation. . . ."[7]

At no time did I refer to "women's power" or "autonomy" or dismiss "the discrimination, inequality, and misogyny rife in the nineteenth century. . . ." My reference to the study of women suffrage was also taken out of context. It appeared as part of a plea that we define feminism in terms broader than suffrage and that we redefine the traditional male canons of history in such a way so that the events that were important to women became central to our social and political anlyasis. At no time did I criticize the study of feminism or of the feminist movement. Nor have have I ever used the term "women's culture". I have never asserted that women's sphere was free from male oppression or that it existed separately from the economic and ideological forces that shaped its society. In my article to which the author so prominently refers, "The Female World of Love and Ritual: Relations Between Women in Nineteenth-Century America," I analyzed not women's culture but female sexuality. I began with a question. How can we understand the nature of the emotionally intense and erotic friendships between eighteenth- and nineteenth-century married women and society's benign approval of such relationships. To answer this question, I explored the nature of women's emotional, physical, and social interaction across the life cycle. I made no claim for this world being a separate culture of being free from male control. Indeed, in my work over the past ten years, I have frequently explored male ideology concerning women and male modes of female oppression.[8] Gradually, however, I had come to realize that such an exclusive emphasis on male oppression of women had transformed me into a historian of men. Indeed, my research convinced me that the most complex and suggestive questions we can ask about the female experience or women's location in the power structure do not necessarily revolve around an analysis of overt exploitation.

The debate over this article does raise fascinating and complex questions. What terms can we use to describe the type of world women form when forcibly segregated along gender lines? What relation exists between the values, rituals, and symbols women expressed among themselves and those of the larger society to which they also gave allegiance? How is power distributed within a segregated female world and how does this distribution reflect power relations between women and men?

In hundreds of cultures around the world and across time, women have lived in highly sex-segregated communities; spending their time with other women; developing female rituals and networks; forming primary emotional, perhaps physical and sexual, ties with other women. Such women develop visions of the world, values, and, indeed, I would argue, even symbolic and cosmological systems different in highly significant ways from those of the men with whom they shared sex, food, and children. This is true among Tiwi aborigines, Victorian ladies, Nazi women, and working-class women of London in the 1960s. What do these patterns of differentiation and separation tell us about cultural evolution and the relation of cultural forms to modes of production, women's economic productivity, institutional organization, and the distribution of economic power? If one can assume that cosmological and symbolic systems develop in relation to social structure, then women, with less power, will frequently develop their own *weltanschauungen*. Indeed, even in response to the same instances of economic and institutional change, women and men of the same class, ethnicity, and religion develop quite distinctive symbolic and metaphoric systems.

An analysis of the sex-segregated world of bourgeois women in nineteenth-century American society provides an ideal historical laboratory for the exploration of these issues. American society changed radically during the middle period of the nineteenth century. Rural communities were disrupted, the function and structure of the family was fundamentally altered, and daughters were pulled into roles their mothers had no knowledge of (factories, the world of the urban bourgeoise, academies, and the frontier). Immigrant ghettoes and destitution marked not only the major seaports, but also interior towns and cities. Tens of thousands of women used prostitution—the imposition of a cash nexus upon relations between the sexes and the division of sex from family—to symbolize these disruptive changes. (Significantly, the symbolic and metaphoric language in which these women clothed their response to economic and institutional change differed radically from that language adopted by men from the same geographic, economic, ethnic, and religious communities.) Interestingly, these women did not suggest that the immigrant, the black, or the poor woman brought prostitution and social disruption to American society. At these times, these bourgeois and socially conservative women identified with the prostitute and vilified their same class males. It was male exploitation of women, they argued, and male acceptance of new capitalist and commercial values that threatened women, their families, and communities. But this identification with women across class and the denigration of same class males did not carry with it either a sustained radical critique of society or an insistence on nonhierarchical relations between women. These women sought escape from the power of male-controlled capitalism in a retreat to a mercantile patriarchal world which women knew to contain spaces of safety for women, but not places of power. Symbolically, they insisted on mothers' rights to control their daughters and, implicitly, on bourgeois women's rights to dominate working-class women. This was a world in which identification as a woman was complex indeed.[9]

The world of women does not automatically produce feminism But can feminism develop outside a female world? "The pressing historical questions about women's culture," I would argue do not "center on its relation to feminism," but rather the pressing questions about feminism center on its relation to the existence of a female world. The planning meeting for the Seneca Falls convention, as others have so aptly pointed out, was, in reality, a Quaker women's meeting, with the addition of one non-Quaker woman. The early women's movement, as Blanche Glassman Hersh so cogently argues in her study of the feminist movement, flourished because of the experiences women had gained from decades of work in single-sex voluntary associations and schools, fighting for issues they defined as women's issues.[10] The greatest strength they gained from this experience, I would argue, was to define themselves first as women and second as reformers. This identification as women—what I would call the defining characteristic of a female community—continued to characterize female reform movements through the Progressive Era and the winning of suffrage. Settlement houses were not only creative female social innovations, they were also fictive female families, created by autonomous women who no longer felt that they had spaces of safety within their female kin networks. These women experienced the need, however, to transpose the support systems and modes of communication of the more traditional female world into new institutional forms. The women of Hull House, Henry Street, and the other settlements created both new forms of the female family and successful reform coalitions. As Blanche Wiesen Cook has so persuasively argued, they felt the one necessary to produce the other. On the other hand, Cook argues, politically active women divorced from such support systems—Emma Goldman, for instance—sadly complained of their need for female nurturance and support.[11]

The period 1890 to 1920 saw a concerted male attack upon the legitimacy of this world of female identification and solidarity, an attack abetted by economic and demographic changes which undermined female institutional structures. By the 1920s and 1930s, the community of self-defined, autonomous women had become the subject of derision and ridicule, denigrated alternatively as lesbian, sexually repressive, and old-fashioned. Decreasingly did middle-class women define themselves principally as women. Alice Paul maintained a struggle that younger women viewed as anachronistic. Radical women during the 1930s failed to maintain Crystal Eastman's integration of feminism and Marxism.[12] No understanding of feminism as a contemporary political force or of the history of feminism can be complete until we explore the relation between the demise of this rich and vital world of women-identified women and the death of feminism in the 1920s and 1930s.

NOTES

[1]The author cites my article, "Beauty, the Beast and the Militant Woman: A Case Study in Sex Roles and Social Stress in Jacksonian America," *American Quarterly* 23 (October 1971): 562-84, as one "critical . . . of the past traditions of feminism. . . ." I do not criticize either nineteenth-century feminists or earlier historians of women in this article; the designation is therefore inaccurate.

[2]Ellen DuBois, "Politics and Culture in Women's History," this issue.

[3]See, for example, Elizabeth Pleck, "A Mother's Wages: Income Earning Among Italian and Black Women, 1896-1911," *The American Family in Social Historical Perspective*, 2nd ed., ed. Michael Gordon (New York: St. Martin's Press, 1978). pp. 490-510; and Tamara Haraven, "Family Time and Industrial Time," *Journal of Urban History* 1 (May 1975): 365-89.

[4]DuBois, "Politics and Culture in Women's History," this issue.

[5] Linda Gordon, *Woman's Body, Woman's Right: A Social History of Birth Control in America* (New York: Viking-Grossman, 1976). I wish to state very clearly that my criticisms of DuBois's use of Gordon's book are not intended to be applied to Gordon's own analysis. Her and DuBois's are, I feel, quite separate.

[6] I wish to thank Judith Friedlander, Esther Newton, and Rayna Rapp for their suggestive discussions concerning the nature of culture and the interaction between female and male cultural forms within a single society. My citations to Ellen DuBois's article are to the version I had been asked to respond to. I understand editorial revisions have changed the text somewhat since I submitted my response.

[7] Carroll Smith-Rosenberg, "The Female World of Love and Ritual: Relations Between Women in Nineteenth-Century America," *Signs* 1, no. 1 (Autumn 1975): 9-10, 3.

[8] See, for example; Carroll Smith-Rosenberg, "The New Woman and the New History," *Feminist Studies* 3, no. 1-2 (Fall 1975): 185-98; Carroll Smith-Rosenberg and Charles Rosenberg, "The Female Animal: Medical and Biological Views of Women's Role in Nineteenth-Century America," *Journal of American History* 60 (September 1973); Carroll Smith-Rosenberg, "Puberty to Menopause: The Cycle of Femininity in Nineteenth-Century America," *Feminist Studies* 1, no. 3-4 (Winter-Spring, 1973): 58-72; Carroll-Smith-Rosenberg, "The Hysterical Woman: Some Reflections of Sex Roles and Role Conflict in Nineteenth-Century America," *Social Research* (Winter 1972); and Smith-Rosenberg, "Beauty, the Beast and the Militant Woman."

[9] Carroll Smith-Rosenberg, "Bodies, Boundaries and Invasion: Some Observations on Prostitution and the Family in Jacksonian America," lecture given at Stanford University, May 1979. See also, Carroll Smith-Rosenberg, "Sex as Symbol in Victorian America," *American Journal of Sociology* (Summer Supplement 1978) for a discussion of male symbolic systems. My thinking on these issues has been strongly influenced by Judith Walkowitz's and Ruth Rosen's fine studies of British and American prostitution and by Mary Ryan's excellent study of Utica, New York.

[10] Blanche Glassman Hersh, *The Slavery of Sex: Feminist-Abolitionists in America* (Urbana: University of Illinois Press, 1978).

[11] Blanche Wiesen Cook, *Women and Support Networks* (New York: Out and Out Books, 1979).

[12] Blanche Wiesen Cook, "Introduction," in *Crystal Eastman On Women and Revolution*, ed. Blanche Wiesen Cook (New York: Oxford University Press, 1978). I have benefited greatly from Cook's comments on this article.

Bei Fragen zur Produktsicherheit wenden Sie sich bitte an:
If you have any questions regarding product safety,
please contact:

Walter de Gruyter GmbH
Genthiner Straße 13
10785 Berlin
productsafety@degruyterbrill.com